The War on Labor and the Left

The War on Labor and the Left

Understanding America's Unique Conservatism

Patricia Cayo Sexton

Westview Press
BOULDER • SAN FRANCISCO • OXFORD

Copyright © 1991 by Westview Press, Inc.

Published in 1991 in the United States of America by Westview Press, Inc., 5500 Central Avenue, Boulder, Colorado 80301, and in the United Kingdom by Westview Press, 36 Lonsdale Road, Summertown, Oxford OX2 7EW

Library of Congress Cataloging-in-Publication Data
Sexton, Patricia Cayo.
  The war on labor and the left : understanding America's unique conservatism / Patricia Cayo Sexton.
    p. cm.
  Includes bibliographical references and index.
  ISBN 0-8133-1062-8.—ISBN 0-8133-1063-6 (pbk.).
  1. Labor movement—United States—History. 2. Trade-unions—United States—History. 3. Union busting—United States—History. 4. Conservatism—United States—History. 5. Trade-unions and communism—United States—History. 6. Capitalism—United States—History. I. Title.
HD8066.S44 1991
322'.2'0973—dc20   91-22028
                                                                                CIP

Printed and bound in the United States of America

⊗ The paper used in this publication meets the requirements of the American National Standard for Permanence of Paper for Printed Library Materials Z39.48-1984.

10   9   8   7   6   5   4   3   2   1

FOR BRENDAN SEXTON

AND MICHAEL HARRINGTON

IN ABSENTIA

In rereading Michael Harrington's seminal book *Socialism*, I came upon this inscription in the copy on my shelf: "For Brendan. Not just because you're a fine guy or because of your magnificent record as a trade unionist, but also because us Irishmen on the left have to stick together. With affection, thanks and three cheers for James Connolly.

Mike. Chicago, April 1972."

Contents

Acknowledgments

I am happy to thank, and unable to thank enough, the various colleagues, scholars, friends, and relatives who have read, with wildly varying degrees of agreement, all or part of this book during its prolonged gestation period—Brendan Sexton (father and son) and, in alphabetical order, Paul Bamberger, David Bensman, Jon Bloom, David Brody, Tom Brooks, Jacqueline Brophy, Jack Clark, Jack Conway, Bogdan Denitch, Elizabeth Durbin, Harry Fleischman, Douglas Fraser, Manny Geltman, Bill Goode, Victor Gottbaum, Lois Gray, Michael Harrington, Fred Hoehler, Irving Howe, James Jasper, Bill Kemsley, Bill Kornblum, Ira Katznelson, Mark Levinson, Seymour M. Lipset, Harry Maurer, S. M. Miller, Oscar and Dolores Paskal, Paul Schrade, Carl Shier, Charles Tilly, Gus Tyler, Daniel Walkowitz, and Dennis Wrong. Special thanks to Rita LaBonne and Tita Cooley for just being there. I am indebted and grateful to Dean Birkenkamp, a special person and a wise and congenial editor, and to the Westview staff, whose performance has surpassed anything I have found in New York.

Patricia Cayo Sexton

Introduction

AMERICAN LABOR IS UNIQUE among developed democracies in two major and related respects: Its union movement is weak and declining (as measured by membership), and it lacks the kind of labor party that flourishes in almost all other democracies. A vast amount of literature, in fact, is devoted to the political uniqueness of America—its conservatism and its singular lack of a mass labor, or social democratic, or democratic socialist party. This phenomenon has been noted even in the *Wall Street Journal*, where it was said that a European conservative "would be comfortable somewhere in the middle of the American Democratic party," that European leftists are "genuine socialists" with no mainstream equal in the United States, and that only 1.5 real capitalist countries exist in the world—the United States and, after a fashion, Great Britain under Margaret Thatcher.[1]

Countless explanations of American conservatism have been offered, most of them having to do with the presumed conservatism of American labor or that group's internal weaknesses. I will argue here, however, that although those popular views have some validity, the source of conservatism lies much less in labor than in its adversaries, in their unique corporate power and wealth and the use of those resources in waging what has been in many ways a uniquely repressive war on the "labor-left" (unions and left of center politics).

The casualties of that war mount ever higher in the current era, as do the complexity and potency of the strategies used. Historically, those strategies have included the use of private and public armed force against unionism, dominance of the mass media, the stigmatizing of much labor-left activity as "un-American," manipulation of the legal system and labor relations, control of economic policy and the globalization of the U.S. economy, and especially the heavy influence brought to bear on government policy and on a political system that is uniquely inhospitable to challenges from the labor-left. All strategies are subjects of discussion in this book.

In the past, the war has been hot, coercive, violent, and, as at present, always political. In recent decades, the violence has somewhat receded,

1

and the war has assumed new global dimensions. Economic elites have pioneered new ways of moving capital and industry around and out of the country, and what was once a simple domestic war has been transformed into a star-wars version of the same, the casualties of which include millions of American jobs lost, usually the best jobs, union jobs, and often the unions themselves. Ousted from these "exported" jobs has been a vast army of American workers, many of them skilled and experienced people whom employers have brought in as a reserve army of permanent replacements for striking workers, thus robbing labor of its major defensive weapon, the strike. The results of these trends are broken strikes, broken unions, victories for conservatism, and further losses of labor's political influence.

The war has had few intermissions, but it has generally escalated during business recessions when employers try to drive down wages and drive out unions. Indeed, labor's adversaries become most warlike when recessions weaken their economic powers. This weakness might be expected to give labor an advantage, except that at such times, labor's bargaining powers are even weaker than those of employers and its political influence—unlike its equivalents in other democracies—is similarly weak.

Comparisons

Although it is generally believed that there has been *less* repression of the labor-left in the United States than in other developed democracies, the records do not bear this assumption out. In fact, they strongly suggest that the ferocity of the war in the United States has been in many ways unparalleled in the experience of comparable democracies. Cross-national comparisons, however, are both the "most valuable and most dubious way of writing history," W. D. Rubinstein writes, valuable because they illuminate events and dubious because all nations have a unique history.[2]

Yet the riddle of America's unique conservatism conceals many secrets about the country's experience and future and invites whatever facts or speculations, comparative or otherwise, that might be brought to bear on its solution. With that invitation in mind, an inquiry into the relatively unexplored subject of repression as a feature of American conservatism is initiated in this book. The subject is one about which many volumes, perhaps libraries, could be written, and it is hoped that other people will join the search in order to confirm, deny, denounce, or supplement what is said here.

Comparisons with other societies, however, are not really needed to make many major points, for it can be demonstrated from the American experience alone that repression of various sorts has played a key role in sustaining American conservatism. Yet comparisons with other societies can add support to domestic references and are included when data are available. Since democracies vary so much in their histories, the comparisons are made almost exclusively with other English-speaking countries, as their cultures and histories most closely resemble the American situation.

Comparisons are made only with regard to experiences in developed democracies under duly elected governments. It certainly is not argued that U.S. repression of the labor-left has exceeded that of dictatorships, present or past. Clearly, the Nazi record on this score was infinitely worse, being one of total repression of unions and leftist political groups. After World War II, however, the German labor-left resumed its pre-Nazi political status and even greatly increased its power. The Nazi terror did not permanently destroy the German labor-left. In the United States, on the other hand, repression of the labor-left has had a cumulative debilitating effect, interrupted for any sustained period only by the New Deal era.

Nor is it suggested that the uprisings of U.S. labor have matched the scope of revolutionary uprisings against dictatorships. Mass uprisings against governments rarely occur in developed democracies, mainly because people seeking relief have an electoral option, the ballot box. The fact that true options—significantly different approaches to government—may not be available to voters is likely to result, not in revolution, but in abstention from the electoral process, social alienation in its many forms, social unrest and personalized discontent, and militant unionism in the workplace.

Framework of the Book

The ultimate concern of this book is with labor's contemporary position, but the emphasis is on the historical prelude to it, the worn path that has led to America's unusual conservatism and labor's present predicament. The history is analytic and narrative, as histories are, but it is not the typical historical chronology of dates and events, an orderly progression through the pages of history. Instead, I seek to identify and explore some of the critical variables in the life of the American labor-left that may help in understanding its present crisis.

My aim is to speak to a general audience of interested readers rather than to a specialized one of historians or related professionals. The facts about labor conflicts that are used to illustrate major points about repression are well known to labor historians, but they are given a new frame here: a new way of looking at the forces at work in these major conflicts, the power and repression involved in them, and the respective roles played by workers, unions, employers, the media, and government. It is hoped that a new view of labor history might reduce some of the factional disputes about that history, but repression, as it turns out, is a highly charged and controversial subject that stirs up some impassioned and unexpected responses, so the debates may not recede, only turn in a new direction.

Social researchers generally seek their subjects among subordinate rather than dominant groups, in losing rather than winning contestants, and in the usual victims of labor disputes rather than the usual victors. This inquiry will seek to add more balance to such an approach. The case studies of labor struggles described herein end with the 1940s and the final organization of the Congress of Industrial Organizations (CIO)—the main point the case studies build toward—and discussions of the manipulative strategies employed mainly since the 1940s then follow. Again, other people are invited to update the case studies and refine the broad brush strokes of this inquiry. The literature on America's uniqueness is already voluminous, but much more can be said. Similarly, the notes herein, though culled only from the most relevant writing, are plentiful but only a preamble to what might yet be cited on the subject.

Most popular explanations of America's uniqueness draw many sweeping and emphatic conclusions about the sources of American conservatism without much evidence to sustain them. My intent here is to challenge these views, not with other generalities, but with references to records of critical events in American history and to the repressive and often unique strategies used with such telling results in the war on labor.

The book is not prescriptive, but it does deal in various places with some prospects for change. The labor-left is not caught in the iron grip of history. The fact that it advanced as far as it did during the 1930s and 1940s, and the successes of the labor-left in other democracies, indicate that change is possible and that, given the current crisis of both capitalism and communism, the long-term revival of the American labor-left is altogether likely. In labor circles it is said that employers, not unions, organize workers. Perhaps in the political arena, employers will also stimulate the success of a new politics.

The book expanded far beyond what was originally intended, a historical review of the violent and more coercive repression of labor. This review made it clear, however, that much more was involved than physical coercion. Law and government had to be included, perhaps especially when they touched on the "radical" politics that are presumed to be marginal to labor history. But far from being marginal, the absence of a labor party or a serious politics on the left accounts for much of labor's woes, so the subject could hardly be omitted. Nor could economics be left out, for how can labor's present decline be explained without reference to business cycles, deindustrialization, and the globalized economy? Comparative materials had to be included, incomplete as they may be, since they tell us so much about the meaning of the American experience. Control of the media, the messengers of conservatism, is also a crucial part of the whole and could not be overlooked, and labor relations, an inventive source of antiunionism and the concern of most professionals involved with labor, could hardly be omitted since the broadened scope of this inquiry is especially relevant to that topic.

Finally, foreign policy and the related subject of domestic un-Americanism could not be slighted. Although seemingly tangential to the whole, they may instead be the core of it, for how can the U.S. economic decline—and the decline of labor—be explained without reference to imperial overreach, military costs (in money and talent), neglect of domestic production, and global politics? And how can the virtual "death of dissent" be explained without reference to the excesses of the cold war and the domestic crusade against un-Americanism?

Americans obviously love their country, and for many good reasons, but it does not follow that they also love the raw brand of capitalism that dominates its economy and politics. Yet crusades against un-Americanism have tried to equate the two and to make criticism of the latter a sin against the former.

Definitions

The word "repression" is used broadly herein. To repress is to check, restrain, or hold down; these words clearly apply to the history of the labor-left. Less coercive means of repression, however, are usually referred to as "manipulative," yet they sometimes produce greater repression than the coercive varieties. Objections to the phrase "blaming the victim" have become popular. Victims usually bring on their own problems, it is said, and therefore need to be blamed, but this assumption is overgeneralized and also a sad sign of the times. Surely if people are indeed victimized by others, as so many dissenters who have struggled to combine and organize have been, it is clearly unfair to blame them when they fall.

Like "repression," the word "power" is one that goes in and out of fashion with the times, rising in popularity during periods of insurgency and declining during conservative eras. But the word has an objective reality that is unrelated to its popularity, and its use is indispensable in discussing politics and collective bargaining. Debates over what power is and who has how much of it are numerous; in this book, "power" refers to control over critical resources (financial, institutional, coercive, political, ideological, and communicative resources), to decisions controlling the use of those resources, and to the ability to produce intended effects.

Max Weber regarded the concept of power as an amorphous subject because even the least of us can in some situations produce intended effects on others. Certainly power is diffused, so that everyone has some of it, but the point is that some people have far more of it than others. This book deals with four forms of power: the force of arms and the law, the manipulation of economic policy and subtler forms of subjection, the persuasion conducted most conspicuously by the mass media, and the institutional authority exercised by economic elites.

The terms "elites," "capitalists," "business," and "employers," though obviously not synonymous, are close enough to be used somewhat interchangeably, recognizing however that "business" and "employers" are more restrictive terms than "capitalists" or "elites" and that there is some range of social perspective in each of these groups.

As for political parties, the terms "labor," "social democratic," and "democratic socialist" are often used interchangeably, not because they are exact synonyms, but because the parties of the democratic Socialist International with which they are affiliated often use these various terms without respect to party program. In other, stricter usages, labor parties have closer ties to unions, and based on post-1945 understandings, the policies of democratic socialist parties are to the left of social democratic parties.

"Labor" as used herein refers to workers, the working class, and unions, though "organized labor" is the preferred term for the last. The working class, it should be noted, includes not only blue-collar and industrial workers but also those who are neither top executives nor self-employed—that is, the vast majority of employed people. Many American workers in all these job categories now belong to unions; in Sweden, where upward of 95 percent of the work force is organized, virtually all working people are union members.

The term "left" refers to a broad spectrum of politics on the left of center, and "labor-left" refers to the twin organized endeavors of labor: unionism and politics. Of special concern are the political paths taken by organized labor, paths that intersect, parallel, and sometimes join those of most groups on the political left. Labor and the left have been more or less part of the same general social movement, and their histories, concerns, and destinies are intertwined, though not always in happy or wholesome embrace. My task in this book, among others, is to shed more light on where these paths have converged and why they have so often diverged.

For Europeans but not for Americans, the distinction between "socialist" and "communist" is very clear. Despite gross misunderstandings in the United States about the meaning of these terms, it may be time at last to resurrect the words and their profound distinctions for use in standard discourse. In all cases in this book, the word "socialism" refers to "democratic socialism," as socialism, according to an informed and commonly accepted definition, is not possible without democratic sociopolitical institutions. It may seem strange, in light of events in Eastern Europe, to flaunt the words "democratic socialism," but it was not socialism that fell in the East but communism—socialism's opposite number. Indeed, democratic socialism is alive everywhere, and usually thriving, among the developed democracies of the world. Only in America has the average citizen been trained to automatically recoil at what is for so many people in the world a friendly term, "democratic socialism."

"Free markets," "economic competition," and "profits" are not at all incompatible with democratic socialism, at least for most of its advocates. But many aspects of raw capitalism *are* incompatible, including private monopolies that replace free markets and competition, socially irresponsible capital investment policies, economic instability and depression, the growing polarization of income and wealth, and oligarchic control of political, economic, and social institutions.

The phrase "the war on labor" was chosen with some reflective attention to the unacademic sound of it, but it is my conviction that academics are as entitled as others to call a spade a spade. The phrase is not a war *with* labor but a war *on* labor; the preposition matters for it conveys the reality of American labor relations, past and present, and of a struggle that is hardly a contest between equals. This book has a point of view, but no more so than other discourses on American uniqueness, the main difference being that no effort has been made here to soften or obscure that viewpoint.

Social Welfare and the Balance of Power

The conservative assault on the labor-supported social welfare state—social security and other loosely woven safety nets—has paralleled the war on labor in the workplace, and although this assault is not singled out for elaboration, it is a vital part of the whole and references to it recur in the book. This assault on what is a generally accepted part of the quality of community life in most democracies has in the United States added to the social and private burdens of deprivation, anomie, and pathology. It also deprives the labor-left of a natural constituency among both consumers and producers of public services and drives it to hard bargaining with employers when services such as public health insurance are lacking.

The decline of organized labor, in the workplace and politics, poses grave dangers to American democracy for it is the primary countervailing influence on a society whose leadership grows ever more monolithic, ever more apathetic about distress among the nonrich, and ever more unable to balance its own books or ours.

As Harvard economist Robert B. Reich has put it, this leadership has in effect "seceded" from the union, withdrawing into insulated communities or "cocoons" that shelter them from public concerns; engaging in occupations that manipulate symbols (words, numbers, visual images) and that touch others only as services are needed, calling for better schools but insisting that school funding be shifted from the federal level to the financially strapped cities; and extending their private charity not to public schools or health clinics, but to their own insular use— private universities, museums, opera houses, ballet companies.[3] It is a leadership that has abandoned its followers.

The Economic Ledger

The facts from the economic ledger are no secret. The U.S. standard of living between 1972 and 1988 increased only 8 percent, or a fourth of the average gain in West Germany, France, Italy, Britain, and Canada and a seventh as much as in Japan; in 1988, the U.S. standard of living was below West Germany's and scarcely ahead of that of other major countries in Western Europe. The United States is now ninth in per capita gross national product (GNP), behind Austria, Switzerland, the Netherlands, West Germany, Denmark, Sweden, Norway, and Japan. Total U.S. national assets rose from $31 trillion to $36 trillion between 1985 and 1987, but Japan's rose from $20 trillion to $44 trillion.

By 1988, 30–50 percent of the downtown office buildings in such cities as New York, Los Angeles, Chicago, and Boston were under foreign ownership, and by 1989, the Japanese had funded a third of the corporate buyout boom.[4] In 1990, foreign banks controlled 23 percent of U.S. banking assets and held 29 percent of U.S. business loans.[5] The underlying source in the shift of world wealth, as Kevin Phillips points out, was the Reagan administration's need to borrow large sums at high interest rates to pay for defense buildups, the maintenance of a global military role, the 1981 tax cuts, and the recession spending of the early 1980s.[6]

Largely because of a conservative aversion to public spending on civilian sector growth, U.S. public investments in the nonmilitary domestic economy were skimpy during a recent twenty-year period: 0.3 percent of national output, compared with 1.8 percent in the United Kingdom, 2 percent in France, 2.5 percent in West Germany, and 5.1 percent in Japan.[7] The absence of a strong labor movement, not its presence, has coincided with this serious erosion of the nation's economy, its world position, and the domestic quality of life.

More important than dollars alone, the United States is lagging in "human development," according to a 1991 UN study, which ranked Japan first, Canada second, and the United States seventh. The United States ranked thirteenth on a UN list of "human freedom" and tenth on a women's equality list. The U.S. murder and rape rates and the proportion of the population in prison were the highest in the world, and the United States was singled out as a major laggard in foreign aid (0.15 percent of gross national product, compared to 1 percent in Scandinavia), with most of the U.S. spending being military aid to Israel, Egypt, Turkey, Pakistan, and the Philippines.[8]

Political Ecology

It appears that the "political ecology" of our society, and of some similar ones, is seriously out of balance, that predators have grown too big and their appetites too omnivorous, and that their weight threatens to tip the balance of nature in our political life. Although this book is critical of such disturbances of the ecology, it is not antibusiness; it is very much pro–enlightened business and very much in favor of controls over predator behavior that can permit enlightened business of various shapes and sizes to prosper along with everyone else. By and large, the business community is more the victim than the beneficiary of the policies of predators and of unbending conservatism, as the deep recessions of modern times have shown, and the real interests of business are far more congruent with those of labor than tradition permits them to recognize.

PART ONE

Conservatism and Union Decline

1

Conservatism
and the War on Labor

THE WAR ON THE LABOR-LEFT has been waged with relentless vigor for
well over a century. The New Deal era did transform and empower
labor for a time, but starting in the mid-1950s and accelerating rapidly
in the 1970s and 1980s, the war drove labor into retreat and even turned
its sights on the most conservative trade unions and their moderate
politics. The calculated result of this effort has been a steady decline
in union "density" (the unionized share of the work force) and a parallel
loss of labor's political influence and bargaining power.

In the mid-1950s, union members were some 36 percent of the labor
force; by 1989, that figure had dropped to about 16 percent, the lowest
density of any developed democracy with the possible exception of
France. But even at its peak in the 1950s, union density was lower in
the United States than in almost all comparable countries. By the 1990s,
it was much lower, about 16 percent compared with over 95 percent in
Sweden and Denmark, 85 percent in Finland, over 60 percent in Norway
and Austria, over 50 percent in Australia, Ireland, and the United
Kingdom, and over 40 percent in West Germany and Italy. Unions almost
everywhere were on the defensive, but only U.S. union density had
declined sharply in the 1970s and 1980s. In 1987, U.S. union density
was 37 points below the average of seventeen countries surveyed, down
from 17 points below average in 1970, and it was less than half the
Canadian density, down from rough equality in 1970.[1] During the same
period, density declined in only three other countries: in Austria by 3
percent, Japan 7 percent, and the Netherlands 4 percent. In the United
States, it declined by 14 percent.

Density losses have been greatest in the most unionized sectors of
the economy—in manufacturing, down from 42 percent in 1953 to 25
percent in the late 1980s; in transportation, from 80 percent to 37 percent;
in mining, from 65 percent to 15 percent; and in construction, from 84
percent to 22 percent.[2] Losses in the private sector (42 percent) greatly

13

exceeded those in the public sector (10 percent) from 1971 to 1985.[3] The
U.S. private sector loss of 42 percent was significantly greater than in
other developed democracies: 2 percent in Canada, 3 percent in Norway,
6 percent in West Germany, 7 percent in Switzerland, 9 percent in
Austria, 14 percent in the United Kingdom, 15 percent in Italy—and
zero in Sweden. U.S. unions were disadvantaged by the relatively small
size of U.S. public sector employment—only 16 percent of total employment (public and private), compared with 33 percent in Sweden,
30 percent in Canada, 27 percent in the United Kingdom and Germany—
and by the lower degree of U.S. union penetration of the public sector.

The war's escalation contrasts with the experiences of other developed
democracies, where labor has also been subjected to considerable repression but nowhere on so massive a scale as in the United States. Aside
from Britain, in other developed democracies neither employers nor the
state has joined in equivalent hostilities to labor, despite more serious
economic problems in some cases. Even British employers have generally
abstained from heightened hostilities to unions, despite antiunion campaigns and legislation sponsored by the Thatcher government.[4]

Causes of Union Decline

Explaining contemporary union decline (historical declines are dealt with
later) is complicated by the need to consider not only why U.S. unionism
has declined but also, for our purposes here, why it has declined so
much more than unionism in other countries—or its "relative decline."
Among the most popular explanations of the decline are public disapproval
of unions and the behavior of the unions themselves.

Public approval of unions, however, explains nothing about the U.S.
union decline, since approval has actually improved over the period of
the decline. Between 1981 and 1988, for instance, public approval of
U.S. unions climbed 6 percentage points, with 61 percent of Americans
approving of unions in 1988, 25 percent disapproving, and 14 percent
having no opinion—approval being lowest among those aged thirty-five
to forty-four.[5] Moreover, polls show little difference in public "confidence"
in unions between nations with declining density and those with stable
or rising density: 33 percent confidence in the United States, 26 percent
in Britain, 32 percent in Italy, 36 percent in Germany and France, and
a less favorable attitude in Canada, where unions have grown.[6]

As for union behavior, some critics claim that "sellouts" by union
leaders have been the major cause of union decline. They blame contract
concessions on union bureaucrats and "business unionism" and urge
strikes against the give-backs demanded by employers. Yet almost all

concession strikes in the 1980s ended in defeat, and in some cases the unions themselves were broken. In a context of weakened unions, reduced political influence, the use of replacement workers, and employer threats to close plants, the success rates of strikes and other union tactics have plunged.

Other observers claim that U.S. unions excite employer hostility by their bargaining tactics and by making too many wage demands. Although the allure of cheaper labor may be greatly responsible for U.S. employer responses and union decline, high wages do not explain the *relative* decline of U.S. unions. In 1987, average hourly labor costs as measured in U.S. dollars were, in fact, higher in eight Western European countries than in the United States: the United States $13.44, Norway $17.39, Switzerland $17.14, West Germany $16.87, Netherlands $15.46, Sweden $15.12, Belgium $15.02, Denmark $14.56, Finland $13.52.[7] Private sector unions in almost all those countries had declined somewhat between 1971 and 1985, but none so sharply as in the United States.[8]

Employers, Government, Repression

Almost all theories of the contemporary U.S. union decline fall finally under the rubric "repression," typically originated by employers and sustained by government. I deal briefly with only four of the theories: those based on (1) the "wage gap"; (2) public sector penetration; (3) closings and cutbacks; and (4) labor relations and labor law.

The Wage Gap. The decline of U.S. union density is explained by economists David Blanchflower and Richard Freeman largely in terms of the gap between union and nonunion wages, which is greater in the United States than in comparable countries. This gap, they say, stimulates employers to oppose unions in order to hire cheaper nonunion labor.

Yet in Canada, despite a union/nonunion wage gap second only to that in the United States, and an equal stress by unions on wage demands, union density has nonetheless risen. This deviation is attributed to the fact that labor law in Canada seriously limits the antiunion activity of employers.[9] In the end, then, union decline is caused, not by excessive wage demands, but by employer efforts to repress unionism and employer-inspired labor laws that allow them to do so.

Public Sector Penetration. According to comparisons of U.S. and Canadian unionism made by economist Leo Troy, the size and union penetration of the public sector, rather than employer opposition, account for the stronger position of Canadian unions. The Canadian public sector is proportionately much larger than the U.S. sector, and Canadian unions grew rapidly in that sector, to a density of 66 percent by 1985, when

U.S. unions had a density in a smaller public sector of only 36 percent.[10] In the final analysis, however, the U.S. public sector and union penetration of it are small compared to Canada because the growth of both have been far more vigorously opposed by American than by Canadian economic elites and more vigorously supported by Canada's labor party.

Closings and Cutbacks. Deindustrialization and the closings and cutbacks of unionized plants account for much of contemporary U.S. union decline, some economists say more than 70 percent. According to an International Labor Office (ILO) study of seven countries, laws sharply restricted such closings during the 1980s in Japan. West Germany, France, the United Kingdom, and Italy, but in the United States and Canada, employers could generally cut back the work force without notice, in the absence of contrary agreements.[11] Again, employer opposition to laws restricting closings and the political power to enforce such opposition account for much of U.S. job and union density loss.

In Japan, for example, workers through their union sued their American employer, Proctor and Gamble, when it closed the plant where they worked, even though all workers were offered job transfers to a nearby Proctor and Gamble plant and jobs elsewhere were in plentiful supply. Other U.S. employers, because of habits permitted by U.S. law, have run into similar problems in Japan with layoffs and closings. Japanese law permits such suits, and tradition encourages them. Japanese plants rarely close or even lay off workers permanently; deeply troubled companies are usually taken over by affiliates, or workers are transferred to other companies.[12]

Labor Relations and Labor Law. Richard Freeman's study shows that management opposition to unions in the workplace best explains the relative decline of U.S. unions.[13] U.S. labor relations, he says, exemplify what aggressive management can do to unionism. In the 1970s and 1980s, U.S. management "turned against unions and collective bargaining to a degree not seen anywhere else in the free world." Almost all U.S. firms facing union elections conducted "expensive aggressive campaigns to persuade/pressure workers to reject unions," unfair labor practices rose to five and six times the rates of earlier decades and included the firing of more than 1,000 union activists in a year, and some 45 percent of the relatively moderate members of the Conference Board's Personnel Forum (a prestigious business group) claimed in 1983 that their main labor goal was to be union free. Even when workers voted to unionize, management refused a first contract in a third of the cases.[14]

 Freeman says that a militant, market-oriented ideology has developed that excuses almost all antiunion activities on the grounds that they give management more flexibility. Because Canadian laws prohibit most such activities, many of the same employers who have fought U.S. unions have accepted them in Canada. If present trends continue, Freeman concludes, nations will be divided between those with strong unions functioning in a neocorporatist setting, such as in Scandinavia, and those with ghetto unions restricted to a small segment of the work force, as is happening in the United States.[15]

Political Contexts

Canadian and U.S. Law

Comparisons of American and Canadian unions are instructive. The union structures are similar, and in some cases unions in both countries can even be part of the same "international" union, but one twin, the Canadian, has grown to a density almost twice that of the American. The difference is not in the unions but in the nature of the "class forces" they confront, the laws and their enforcement, and the general political context of unionism.[16]

The main source of divergence between the twins has been that Canadian laws (federal and provincial) encourage public sector unionism and seriously limit the antiunion practices of employers. In 1967, the Canadian Parliament passed a law that gave almost all federal employees the right to organize, bargain, and strike, and most provinces promptly passed similar laws. Moreover, the Canadian government, especially in the major provinces of Ontario and Quebec, prohibits the kind of warfare waged on labor by U.S. employers.[17] Ontario provides for first-contract arbitration; U.S. employers are free to refuse a contract even when employees vote for a union. In British Columbia, when a first contract cannot be agreed on, one is imposed by law. In Quebec, where union density has risen most, the provincial Ministry of Labor extends contracts negotiated by unions in a given industry to the whole of the industry. Other provincial laws regulate strikebreaking, union membership for some professions, and other matters.

Most important, under Canadian law, unions usually only need to submit membership cards signed by a majority of employees in order to be considered a certified bargaining agent. Such a provision is a far cry from the costly and prolonged election procedures to which American unions seeking National Labor Relations Board (NLRB) certification are subjected. Because of such laws, the union certification rate in highly industrialized Ontario was 76 percent in 1982, for example, compared with less than 50 percent in the United States. Canadian law is more hospitable to unions because the political system has facilitated the rise of a potent labor party, the New Democratic Party, which in 1991 came to power in Canada's most populated and industrialized province, Ontario.

Neocorporatism and Tripartitism

Even before the enactment of prolabor laws, union growth and influence were stronger in Canada than in the United States. This fact can be attributed to Canada's history of having tripartite boards (labor, employers, government) to deal with labor disputes, greater government involvement in economic life, a parliamentary rather than a congressional system of government, and the participation of democratic socialist parties in both provincial and state elections.

In most developed democracies, unions function in neocorporatist settings characterized by strong labor parties and strong unions, in which bargaining tends to be more centralized and more attention is paid to reducing wage inequalities for comparable work and adjusting wages in keeping with national income policies. Richard Freeman concludes that unions fare best in these neocorporatist settings.[18]

After World War II, tripartite boards in many developed democracies formulated policy on a broad range of issues, including economic policy, the framework for collective bargaining, minimum wages, occupational health and safety, and equal opportunity. In some cases, unions became disenchanted when the boards ignored their views, but the union position generally remained strong because the unions themselves and their parties remained strong. As a result, public policy was likely to support favorable labor laws, include unions in the delivery of social services, and provide a climate for union stability or growth. In many countries, unions also won seats on governing boards of corporations and pension funds, though in some cases the resistance of conservative governments and employers during the 1980s slowed this trend.[19]

In West Germany, a neocorporatist state and the leading European economy of the postwar era, union density has risen in recent decades. Work hours in the metal industry have declined, shift work has disappeared, union codetermination has grown, manipulative labor relations programs have declined, and unions have made few wage or other concessions. Few plant closings or takeovers have occurred, and laws limit worker layoffs and restrain deregulation of industry. Such improvements are largely attributable to the fact that West Germany has had relatively strong unions, a strong Social Democratic Party, codetermination in industry, and an economic elite that is not all that hostile to labor.

U.S. labor, on the other hand, has lacked the essential political influence to enter as a full partner into such arrangements, so tripartitism has not fared well in the United States. Even joint labor-management efforts to define policy have often failed. In 1978, as an example, Douglas Fraser, then president of the United Automobile Workers (UAW), resigned from the high-level Labor-Management Group formed to reduce workplace conflict, charging that business leaders, with few exceptions, had discarded the unwritten contract of coexistence and had chosen to "wage a one-sided class war in this country—a war against working people, the unemployed, the poor, the minorities, the very young and the very old, and even many in the middle class of our society." Moreover, he said, the two major parties have no "clear-cut ideological differences" and, because of business domination, are ineffective in protecting the victims of this class war.[20]   *But why now?*

The Unique Absence of Labor Parties

Labor's strength obviously depends on the success of its politics and on government policy; at the same time, its politics depend on its success in collective bargaining. The two are mutually dependent, and both are the object of repression.

Most of what is said about America's unique conservatism deals with politics rather than unionism, especially with the singular absence in the United States of a mass labor or democratic socialist party. Usually the conservatism of U.S. politics is attributed to the attitudes of labor itself, and when militant union struggles are referred to, they are usually considered as a puzzling aberration from these assumptions about labor conservatism. The failure to connect the history of unionism and politics is indeed a major deficit in these assumptions, for one cannot be understood except in the context of the other, and in the larger social and comparative context.

Although the United States has no labor (or social democratic or democratic socialist) party, in almost all other democracies—including those in Western Europe, Japan, Israel, Australia, New Zealand, Canada, India, and many third world nations—parties of the democratic left have flourished and often exercised dominant power. By the 1990s, these parties included almost fifty full-member affiliates of the democratic Socialist International (SI) based in some forty-five countries around the world. Even in Japan, the seat of corporate giants, a self-identified democratic socialist party has won enough votes to challenge the undefeated conservative party. These various parties of the democratic left are usually associated with organized labor and with the International Confederation of Free Trade Unions (ICFTU) and its secretariats, and all identify with the label "democratic socialist."

Americans may be the only people in developed democracies who are generally unaware of the successes and profoundly democratic nature of these labor, social democratic, and democratic socialist parties. This unawareness and the general disrepute in the United States of the word "socialism," even in association with the word "democratic," would suggest that a euphemism should be used in this book, but that would only defeat a major purpose of any inquiry into America's unique conservatism: explaining how the word came to be so unfairly stigmatized in the first place.

It is said that socialism itself gave "socialism" a bad name, as Westerners legitimately came to fear what the communist world called "socialism." But that does not explain why so many Western Europeans and others who are politically aware obviously regard "democratic socialism" as good, clearly distinguish it from Stalinist brands of communism and Soviet command economies, and vote heavily for democratic socialist parties at election time. Nor does it explain why the communist world's adoption of the word "democratic" (as in "democratic peoples' republics") did not also vilify *it* in the American lexicon.

It is popularly assumed that "socialism," even the democratic sort, is dead in word and deed, but in fact, its afflictions are far from fatal. Communism of the Leninist-Stalinist sort may be dead or dying, but democratic socialism survives almost everywhere in the democratic world and may yet prosper in Eastern Europe as an alternative to communism or raw capitalism.

As Michael Prowse wrote in the *Financial Times*, the great majority of Eastern Europeans want freedom, "but free-market capitalism is not the only environment in which freedom can flourish. There is also such a thing as democratic socialism. My guess is that if the residents of East Germany, Czechoslovakia, and Hungary were asked to rank the socio-economic systems of western countries, they would put Sweden and Austria far ahead of the US and the UK." Although they want to improve their economies, they "do not want rampant crime, poor schools, squalid public transport, bag ladies, a growing underclass and soaring social and economic inequality of the kind promoted in Britain and the US."[21] Confirming this view, AFL-CIO President Lane Kirkland spoke of

the myth that the collapse of communism is the victory of capitalism and the final vindication of raw market theory. . . . Millions upon millions have found out, in the hardest way and in grueling detail, exactly what is wrong with the jungle of the unregulated marketplace. Both [communism and capitalism] have something elemental in common. Both can atomize society by reducing humans to the level of isolated survivors. Both can be lethal to the institutions of civil society that make life tolerable to ordinary people. They are not so much opposites as mirror images.[22]

What capitalism claims to offer Eastern Europe is a "free-market" economy, but that term does not properly describe American capitalism, as its markets are largely controlled by private monopolies. Nor is political freedom a necessary companion of capitalist markets, because almost all dictators are in partnership with what are essentially capitalistic, privately owned markets.

The policies of labor-left parties are not wholly unfamiliar in the United States. Most have sought, but far more avidly and fruitfully than American parties, to support decent levels of social welfare, distribute opportunity and wealth more equitably, extend democracy into economic policy making, and through public interventions stimulate and direct economic growth. Pragmatic rather than doctrinaire, labor-left parties hold sacred neither public nor private ownership of industry and are inclined to favor whatever competitive mixture of the two leads to best results. They support regulation of the private sector as required by the public interest, cooperative or public ownership when the need is indicated, social planning to stabilize and stimulate the economy, full employment, and public action to control the disastrous business cycles that figure so prominently in world depressions and wars.

Above all, these parties insist that a government belongs to its citizens, not to an oligarchy of wealth and institutional power, and that it is possible, as Bogdan Denitch writes, "for ordinary men and women to make effective changes in their societies" and for those "traditionally excluded from power, the so-called objects of history, to become its subjects."[23] This belief, rather than advocacy of social ownership of industry, or high growth rates, or a centrally planned economy, is now central to democratic socialist belief.

German unions, for example, have won key legislative gains, including codetermination, through their support of the German Social Democratic Party (SPD), which alternates between first and second place in German politics and is a leading party of the Socialist International. The SPD is far from "communistic." It is essentially a labor party opposed to a command or a nationalized economy or one controlled by a wealthy elite. Like other labor and social democratic parties, it favors a mixed economy guided by an elected government, equitably shared, and democratized at all levels. The SPD has not won all it wants, but it has won a major role in German politics.

One indication of the economic stability promoted by the policies of these parties is the fact that three of the five countries least affected by the economic recession starting in the 1970s were Sweden, Norway, and Austria, all of which have strong social democratic governments; the other two countries, Japan and Switzerland, are conservative with respect to the welfare state but have also been committed to full employment sustained by government initiatives. Because of the influence of labor-left parties, some Western nations have rivaled or exceeded the American standard of living, and many have achieved degrees of social justice, stability, tranquillity, cultural maturity, and economic democracy that reach well beyond the American standard.

Most labor parties and governments have had their own problems in recent years, but from 1945 to the 1990s their voter support has been extremely stable. Some European parties have gained (mainly in southern Europe) while others have declined somewhat;[24] some have formed majority governments while many others have played a dominant role in coalition governments. All have favored market economies over command economies and, where indicated, a competitive mixture of private, public, and cooperative enterprises.

The recessions of the 1970s and early 1980s put the social democratic agenda on hold for a time in many places, and governments cut back on social welfare programs, sold state-owned properties in order to reduce national debts, and made regulatory, tax, and other concessions to attract investment capital. But the expedient "move to the right" first slowed, then largely halted in the mid-1980s, and is likely to be reversed in the 1990s. Even with those cutbacks, however, the social democracies have remained well to the left of American politics—though S. M. Lipset and others see them as having joined the true path of conservatism and as proof that no "third way" is possible.[25]

Many third world countries have also "moved to the right" and made free-market concessions to investors and lenders, but here the pattern is clearer. In Latin America, for example, many of the changes have been required by the policies of the World Bank and other foreign lending institutions or enforced by military and economic intervention. In the developed democracies, the pressures for change have been more subtle.

Some people are convinced, perhaps too optimistically, that the Europe of 1992 and beyond is likely to be more self-contained, more independent, and freer of pressures to attract investment capital—domestic or foreign— and is likely to be dominated by labor and social democratic parties, as their plurality in the European Parliament suggests. Most likely, then, the cold war will have been lost, not to capitalism, but to social democracy and to policies that humanize, moderate, and discipline the raw forces of capitalism. Although it is believed that democratic left parties in Europe need a clearer sense of identity, a stronger vision of their future, and longer-term goals, they have "done more for humanity in the past century," as Michael Harrington puts it, than any other social movement, both morally and materially, and these "bewildered half-exhausted democratic-socialist parties continue to be the major hope for freedom and justice."[26]

Relations between democratic left parties and labor unions have not always been as supportive as they might be, and once in power, the parties have not always dealt fairly with labor. The parties of southern Europe that came to power in the 1970s and 1980s, sometimes unsupported by strong democratic unions, have often been heavily influenced by middle-class technocrats. In some cases, they have adopted more conservative programs than those promised, and sometimes they have even broken legitimate strikes. Even in those cases, however, the contrast with the American conservative agenda has been conspicuous. The parties of northern Europe have been more closely tied to established union movements and therefore have been less susceptible to technocratic influence. As for the priority of party versus union, European unionist Dan Gallin writes that it is difficult but not impossible "to imagine social-democratic objectives achieved without the help of a party; it is impossible to imagine such objectives achieved without workers organized into unions, whose class interests require the achievement of a human, just and sustainable society for all."[27]

Of major importance, European social democrats worked closely with progressive Catholics in the 1970s and 1980s, and they came to agree on the principles of an extended welfare state (which reduces class conflict), the defense of workers and unions, government intervention in critical economic decisions, and aid to the third world. Progressives in the Catholic church, sociologist Bogdan Denitch notes, have become important in the European left, entering into coalitions with social democrats (as in Germany), often voting for democratic socialist parties, and rejecting the "cult of the market as the supreme regulator of what is socially desirable."[28] Similarly, many Catholic unions moved toward the left and secularism in the 1970s, and their programs are indistinct from those of democratic socialists.

Consequences of U.S. Union Decline

Is the United States better off without unions and striking workers? Not at all. By almost any measure, it is worse off. For instance, labor has played a key role in enacting and defending legislation of general public benefit, including social security, medicare and medicaid, education funding, unemployment compensation, occupational safety and health laws, mine safety and health laws, black lung disability funds, the National Labor Relations Act, minimum wage laws, civil rights legislation, and all progressive tax law.[29] In effect, labor in the United States, as elsewhere, has led in developing the nation's entire social welfare system and in pursuing a stable full-employment economy. In countries with weak unions, unemployment rates have generally been higher than in countries with strong unions, social welfare spending has been meager, and income inequality has been greater.[30]

Economists Richard Freeman and James Medoff have found that productivity is generally higher in unionized firms than in comparable nonunion firms, that American unionism reduces inequality, that union wage gains are not a major factor in inflation, and that unions provide members with both material benefits and a voice in decisions affecting their lives. In a study of 1,000 metal-working companies, all of which had employee involvement committees, Bennett Harrison and others found that the labor relations arrangement that made the biggest productivity difference was "an organizational form that many people believe has outlived its usefulness and only stands in the way of progress: the trade unions" and that at corporate branch plants, the average production time per unit of output was 35 percent greater in nonunion than in union plants.[31]

Based on an extensive study of electoral politics, journalist Thomas Edsall claims that there is no broad-based institution in American society other than unions that can "represent the interests of those in the working and lower-middle classes in the formulation of economic policy" and that in no Western democracy is any other organization able to cut across racial and ethnic lines in defending a more equitable distribution of taxes and spending.[32] Economist Robert Kuttner claims that unions have served as a "prime constituency for a social democratic conception of society" and embodied a broad "moral authority as the advocate of society's nonrich, as the constituency for universalistic social insurance, full employment policies, and distributive justice." They have given the most loyal backing to liberal-left politics and served as an "ideological counterweight to both the claims of the market and the influence of capital in a political democracy whose economic institutions remained fiercely capitalist." It is only when unions are weakened and defensive, he notes, that they take on the appearance of narrow interest groups.[33]

Unions, then, seek equality of opportunity, a fair sharing of income and wealth, strong safety nets, economic democracy, full employment, and a robust economy. They provide members (potentially some 90 percent of the labor force) a voice and a vote in setting the terms of employment and, increasingly, the governing policies of the workplace. More important, they help people to organize for political action and to press toward such goals as national health insurance, a goal long ago achieved by almost all other developed democracies.

Almost alone, unions have denounced the massive flight of industry, capital, and industrial jobs; the damage to society of corporate raids and junk bonds; the excessive deregulation of industry; the environmental and work hazards of corporate pollution; and the privatization of key government functions. They have also protested the massive sale of U.S. resources, land, and industry to foreigners, but they have lacked the bargaining power to prevent these transactions.

If unions are good riddance, as some say, and if they cripple business, why is it that West Germany, the leading economy in Europe, also has one of the strongest labor movements in the world? In fact, unions, fallible as they are, provide an essential check on the runaway powers of economic elites—whether capitalist, communist, or monarchical—and in many cases, such as in the Scandinavian countries, they dominate humane, responsible, thriving economies.

It is predicted that union density in the private sector will fall to below 5 percent by the turn of the century. This prediction resembles the observations of George E. Barnett, president of the American Economic Association, who noted in 1932, on the eve of the organization of the CIO, that the past decade had seen a change of "amazing magnitude"— "the lessening of trade unionism in American economic organization."[34]

American conservatism and union decline have had serious consequences for the society, including the decline in real wages of American workers since the 1970s, the displacement of millions of workers from jobs and communities, and the growing gap between the rich and others. Union decline has even been associated with losses by the Democratic Party and other liberal forces. As just one example, in the nine states where union decline has been greatest—California, Colorado, Idaho, Nevada, Oregon, South Carolina, Texas, Utah, and Virginia—the number of Democratic senators dropped from ten out of eighteen in 1970 to only one in the mid-1980s.[35]

The average weekly earnings of nonsupervisory workers in the private sector, adjusted for inflation, fell 15.3 percent from 1972 to 1988.[36] And largely because of this real wage decline, the U.S. standard of living in that period rose only 8 percent, or a fourth of the average gain in West Germany, France, Italy, Britain, and Canada and a seventh as much as in Japan.[37]

In the 1980s, the U.S. jobless rate was two and three times higher than the Japanese, and although U.S. job creation rates were often high, 85 percent of the new jobs added were in low wage industries, mainly in service and retail trade.[38]

Between 1979 and 1984 alone, some 11.5 million U.S. workers were displaced from their jobs because of plant shutdowns or the abolition of jobs—or about 10 percent of the total labor force. For blue-collar

[handwritten in margin: Promote full employment!]

workers who found other jobs, the average income loss was 16 percent, but the loss was more than 25 percent for more than a third of the displaced,[39] and in the late 1980s, some 5 million workers who wanted full-time work had to accept part-time jobs.[40] The eligible jobless receiving unemployment benefits declined to 31 percent in 1987 from 72 percent in 1975.[41]

In 1979, income *in*equality was greater in the United States than in West Germany, Japan, and many other countries.[42] In the 1980s, the after-tax income of the top 5 percent of U.S. households rose 51 percent, and for the top 1 percent it rose 87 percent, while that of the poorest fifth declined 5 percent.[43] As for the wealth gap, in 1983 the richest 10 percent of families controlled 86 percent of all financial assets, and more than half of all families had zero or negative assets.[44]

Taxes on the rich have fallen, and those on people of modest income have risen. Consumer debt has escalated, the national debt has climbed to the highest in the world, and the ability and willingness of citizens to pay higher taxes for needed public services have fallen. Meanwhile, conservative policies have increased the need for public spending.

The American welfare system, as Fred Block and his coauthors point out, is "a flawed and fragmented creation" that is "notorious among Western democracies for the narrow and niggardly protections it provides."[45] The flaws appear even in the health of the nation's citizens. In 1985, infant mortality rates were higher in the United States than in seventeen other countries, and by 1988, it was higher than in twenty other countries—despite being second among all nations in per capita income. In 1988, Japan had the lowest infant mortality rate, Taiwan was sixth, Hong Kong seventh, Singapore seventeenth, and the United States twenty-first.[46] Life expectancy, even removing the effects of infant mortality, was lower in the United States than in almost every other developed democracy, and for males it was only a fraction above that in mainland China (70.5 and 70.1, respectively). In 1991, an infant born in Shanghai, China, had a better chance of surviving than an infant born in New York City, and life expectancy at birth was at least three years longer in the former than in the latter.[47]

In 1989, some 37 million Americans lacked health insurance, and South Africa was the only other industrialized nation without some form of national health insurance, a situation that has tended in the United States to shift such costs to the workplace and put both employers and labor at a competitive disadvantage. The Ford Motor Company in 1989, for instance, spent $49.80 per vehicle on employee health care in Canada (which has a highly successful, quality, low-cost health plan), but a half-hour away in its Michigan headquarters, the cost per vehicle was $311—more than six times greater.

Of seven major countries (the United States, Japan, Canada, Italy, France, the United Kingdom, and West Germany), the United States had the lowest adult literacy rate in 1985 (96 percent), the lowest proportion of scientists and technicians (55 per 1,000 in 1970–1986, compared to Japan's high of 317), the lowest gross domestic savings as a percentage of the gross domestic product (GDP) in 1987 (13 percent compared with Japan's high of 34 percent), and the highest military expenditure as a percentage of GNP in 1986 (6.7 percent compared to Japan's low of 1.0 percent).[48]

Policies and Parties

The topics explored in this book, however, do not deal with the merits or prospects of labor-left parties but with the reasons for their absence on the American scene or, of greater concern, the absence of equivalent social policies. What matters most is not the lack of a mass labor party in the United States but the lack of decent, progressive public policies. The parties and the unions also matter, of course, since elsewhere they have been the major vehicles of progressive, democratic change.

Few disagree that America *is* indeed unique in its conservatism. Eric Foner, one of those few, says that although there is no socialism—a "revolutionary transformation of society"—in the United States, there are none in the other Western democracies either.[49] Yet he acknowledges that the United States lacks an influential labor party and that those in Europe have "gone far in improving living conditions." Hence, he too agrees that in this significant respect, America is unique. European labor parties do not claim to pursue a "revolutionary transformation of society," preferring steady work to dramatic breakthroughs. The reforms they sponsor, however, are reshaping their societies and are a legitimate part of the debate about American uniqueness.

Although Foner argues that the Western democracies are all essentially alike, Aristide Zolberg claims that all are unique, as all follow different paths in forming their working classes and all end up in different places.[50] Again, the argument does not deny that the United States differs from the other democracies in not having a mass presence on the labor-left, that it is in that critical respect unique, and that exploring the "path" the United States has followed can shed light on its uniqueness.

Although no major left party survives in the United States, some labor-left policies have obviously infiltrated the American two-party system, turning the Democratic Party in some places into a quasi-labor party. Yet the Democrats, on the whole significantly more liberal than the Republicans, remain a constantly changing coalition of highly diverse elements, some of which are often hostile to labor and increasingly business dominated, and the party's policies usually fall far short of those sponsored by labor-left parties elsewhere. Despite assertions that the Democratic Party moved to the left in the 1970s and 1980s, mainly on cultural issues, on economic issues it clearly moved toward the right or lapsed into apathy.[51]

The two major U.S. parties have different agendas, but in Thomas Ferguson's words, "investors," not voters, now control American politics, Democratic and Republican, and they overwhelmingly support candidates and legislation favoring economic elites.[52] Some corporate interests have supported liberal Democrats (as finance, oil, large real-estate interests, and various multinationals supported Franklin D. Roosevelt), but even that support has shifted largely to conservatives in both parties, or to those from whom votes and favors are sought in exchange for campaign contributions.

The dominance of capital in both political parties comes close to disfranchising labor in social policy making, and the virtual absence of labor in U.S. public policy making is unique among developed democracies.[53] Almost no working-class people or active unionists fill policy positions, whereas in Sweden, half the Social Democratic Party deputies have come from unions during the more than four decades that the party has governed, and similar proportions of unionists can be found in many other European parliaments.

The repression of the labor-left in the United States has been far more visible in the workplace than in politics, simply because more blood has been shed at the worksite and there are bodies to count (though no careful body count has ever been made). Yet political repression has been as real as union repression. In explaining labor's political setbacks, however, historians and others have tended to dwell on the political attitudes and behavior of labor and to slight those of labor's adversaries. Their repressive activities, discussed at length in later chapters, have seriously inhibited the expression of labor-left political sentiment through the use of arms, legislation and the legal system, an inhospitable political system, the vastly superior wealth and institutional power of elites, and the stigmatization of almost all leftist dissent as "un-American."

2

Consensus, Constraints, Conflict

EUGENE DEBS, labor and democratic socialist leader, speaking about a century ago, said:

We have got a number, and a limited number, of poorly paid men in our organization, and when their income ceases they are starving. We have no power of the Government behind us. We have no recognized influence in society on our side. . . . On the other side the corporations are in perfect alliance; they have all of the things that money can command, and that means a subsidized press, the control of newspapers, and a false or vitiated public opinion. The clergy almost steadily united in thundering their denunciations; then the courts, then the State militia, then the Federal troops; everything and all things on the side of the corporations.[1]

Debs's words have resonated down through the years to the present time. Manipulation and economic violence have become more common, and often more lethal, than armed force; labor has won some meager legal protection; and the vast energies of industrial unionism finally broke loose in the 1930s. But the powers of capital and labor have remained dangerously imbalanced, conservative interests dominate one major party and come close to it in the other, and the war on the labor-left continues much as in Debs's day.

Yet over the years, the various explanations offered for labor's losses have virtually ignored the uniquely hostile forces faced by the American labor-left. Indeed, most of the explanations call upon generalized inferences from history that bear no demonstrable relation to specific, critical defeats in the war on labor, or they look at the defeats but pay only negligible attention to the role of repression.

Consensus

American conservatism is most often explained by the "consensus" claims that, in effect, American workers—and the general public, for that matter—have been basically conservative, admiring, and unques-

29

tioning fans of capitalism. Such popularized views, however, fail to explain the uniquely bitter and enduring labor struggles that have occurred in both the workplace and politics.

These struggles, of course, have been interwoven with conciliatory and "cooperative" behavior and with the pursuit of joint interests—much as in collective bargaining itself. In many democracies, but not in the United States, such conciliation occurs even at the highest public policy levels in agreements involving labor, capital, and government. In the United States, the balance of power in this bargaining process has usually been heavily weighted in favor of the economic elites and their proxies in government. Indeed, the contest could be compared to a boxing match in which the winner controls the rules and the referees. In such matches, an assessment of the outcome would need to look beyond the loser's performance to questions about the fairness of the contest.

In 1906, Werner Sombart, an early advocate of consensus ideas, argued in *Why Is There No Socialism in the United States?* that favorable American conditions (political, economic, and social) had driven out serious socialist sentiment and that from the "business standpoint," there was "no question of the worker having first to engage in long conflict with the employer for the equality between them to be formally recognized."[2] His claims about favorable conditions, as he finally acknowledged, were highly questionable. In the period he referred to, gains in real wages were slight, living costs were as high as in Britain, the work was often hard and hazardous, and the hours were long. As a steelworker warned a prospective immigrant, "in America there are neither Sundays nor holidays; he must go and work." One in every 10 operating railroad workers was injured on the job in 1893, and 1 in 115 was killed. Knowing about the hard labor awaiting them, only the hardier men immigrated.[3]

Sombart in the end even deplored political conditions and the American political system. The latter was so complex that only money (big money) could deal with it, and there was no real difference between the two parties, both of which were like "giant trusts that control such vast capital . . . that any competition against them by third parties is out of the question."[4]

"Objectively," the American worker was "more exploited by capitalism than in any other country in the world," and nowhere else was he required to "work himself so quickly to death as in America."[5] But only "subjective" responses mattered, and through "brilliant feats of diplomatic artifice," the American employer had kept the worker happy and prevented awareness of exploitation, making him "the sober, calculating businessman without ideals whom we know today." The worker sees some truth in "all the nonsense spoken by the Carnegies . . . who want to lull the 'boorish rabble' to sleep by telling them miraculous stories about themselves or others who began as newsboys and finished as multimillionaires." Emotionally, "the American worker has a share in capitalism; I believe that he loves it."[6]

Love or Hostility?

What the proletarian psyche saw neither Sombart nor others can know for sure, hidden away as it is in a long departed and little noted memory. Beyond the absence of a mass American socialist party, Sombart offered nothing but impressionistic evidence about labor's love of capitalism. Only once did he mention workers' struggles with capitalism, and that was in connection with the great Colorado mine strikes of 1902. He noted briefly that battles raged in the mines, bombs were thrown, and buildings set afire; Colorado's governor called up the militia, deported strike leaders, and broke the strike; and the newspapers headlined the conflict as a "civil war in Colorado." These events suggest something more than a lovers' quarrel between workers and employers and say much about the level of repression in such conflicts.

Sombart dismissed unions as being only engaged in "political action" rather than concerned with socialist politics. Yet he noted that although the American Federation of Labor (AFL) defeated resolutions supporting socialist parties, its program called for similar policies: an eight-hour day; municipal ownership of streetcars, waterworks, and gas and electric plants; public ownership of telegraphs, telephones, railroads, and mines; and better land distribution. Such a program, he said, "does indeed mean a serious shaking of the foundations of our existing social order," yet he portrayed American unionism as a captive of capitalism and collective bargaining as only a "business matter."[7]

Walter Galenson concurs with Sombart, writing that the American labor movement is not socialist because American workers, exposed to persuasive prophets such as Daniel DeLeon, Morris Hillquit, Eugene Debs, William Z. Foster, William Haywood, and Norman Thomas, chose the business unionism of Samuel Gompers instead.[8] Their choice flowed from conditions of American life, he concludes, including a high living standard, the absence of class consciousness, and the AFL preference for the two-party system and for collective bargaining over political action.

Galenson's assumption that workers had a free choice in the matter does not fit well with the facts, and at no point does he mention in this context the repression of radical unionism, employer hostility to even pure-and-simple unionism, or the remarkable struggles engaged in by American labor. Nor does his reference to high living standards agree with such observations as Robert V. Bruce's about Chicago in that period: "half of the children . . . died before they were five, and it is not clear which half were the luckier."[9] As for beckoning opportunity, the data show that upward mobility rates in the United States during and since that period have only slightly exceeded the European rates.[10]

Marc Karson also favors consensus arguments: the vitality of American capitalism, the middle-class psychology of workers, the faith of Americans in individual rights, and the impact on politics of the antisocialist sentiments of Gompers and the Catholic church.[11] Thus, Karson joins others in making dubious claims about consensus and in pointing only to the attitudes of labor in explaining American conservatism while ignoring the uniquely potent opposition faced by the American labor-left and the resources controlled by that opposition in shaping popular sentiments.

The psychology of workers, Karson says, is very much shaped by business values, but he does not elaborate on how those values are shaped. Similarly, S. M. Lipset, in contrasting U.S. and Canadian labor, stresses "the role of national values in affecting behavior and institutions," that is, the American ideology of individualism, achievement, antistatism, meritocracy, and populism; the revolution against colonial rule; and a truly revolutionary tradition, which, he claims, has somehow moderated political radicalism.[12]

Missing from such commentaries is proof that significant and intractable differences in national values pertaining to the labor-left have shaped national development. Undoubtedly some differences do in fact exist, especially in response to the word "socialism," but the historical record shows that they have not inhibited the emergence of massive labor-left sentiment and that only the combination of repression and the mobilization of nationalistic, jingoistic responses by an elite-controlled mass media submerge such sentiments with any success.

These commentaries also fail to note the extent to which the powers and resources of ruling classes (rather than their virtues or achievements) shape national values with respect to the labor-left. It is said that the ideas of the ruling class are everywhere the ideas that rule, an observation easily born out by the historical tendency of rulers to switch from one religion, and its associated values and beliefs, to another, as Henry VIII shifted the English from Catholicism to Protestantism. Fortunately for U.S. citizens, the predatory and asocial values that often pervade ruling elites seem not to have replaced the relatively cooperative, altruistic, open, and antiauthoritarian values of the general population. Only with respect to certain political and nationalistic values have lessons sometimes been driven home.

Individualism may or may not be a key part of the American psyche, but, given a chance, it is routinely combined in the United States and elsewhere with solidarity and intense communal relations. In Australia, for example, the extreme individualism that reputedly typifies the national temperament has in no way inhibited the growth of the labor-left in that country. It may even nourish it, cultivating as it does the desire to "be one's own boss" and a disdain for the rankings and arbitrary authority of employers and elites.

Frontiers, Feudalism, Votes

Frederick Jackson Turner and other people saw the western frontier as an avenue of social mobility and as a place of escape for the discontented who might otherwise have turned to radical politics. In fact, however, rather few people profited from cheap frontier land, and many migrants were radicalized by the frontier, as the appeal of the radical Western Federation of Miners and the Industrial Workers of the World (IWW) in the West indicates. Nor was America alone in having a frontier escape route. All new countries had a frontier, and in all other Anglo ones, unions and democratic socialist movements have prospered.

The Old World also had a frontier to which the discontented escaped—the New World—and some 40 million people left the one for the other between 1850 and 1915, among whom young males were significantly overrepresented. Thus, Europe lost many of its most militant and vigorous people, those most open to radicalism, and the United States and other new countries were on the receiving end. Moreover, the losses for Europe were permanent, but the American migration to the frontier meant only a geographic reshuffling of young, restless males. Thus, the American frontier should have produced a more, rather than a less, radical politics, and in fact it did, but it was a politics that could not survive the repression and manipulation it encountered.

America was "born free," Louis Hartz claimed, and is unique because it lacks a feudal past and therefore a genuinely revolutionary tradition. The danger of this deficit, he said, lies in the very consensus and unanimity it inspired in Americans.[13] But other new nations (Canada, Australia, and New Zealand) were also born relatively free of feudalism, yet all developed influential labor-left movements. Moreover, class sentiments based on feudal relations were brought by immigrants to America no less than to the rest of the new countries. If some feudal relations were present in Australia—between large farmers and farm laborers—they were not in New Zealand, a land of small family farms, yet labor parties grew in both places. Such relations were also present, by the same token, on the American plantation among owners, slaves, and sharecroppers, yet labor has not prospered in the South.

If the lesser influence of an aristocratic class affected American conservatism, it was more likely because it permitted the swift rise to unchallenged power of a capitalist class that largely rejected the benign Tory social values that lingered in many places, including the British Commonwealth nations. Thus, American labor lacked the shield against the worst depredations of capitalism that was sometimes provided by the landed gentry in England, France, and elsewhere. In many cases, these aristocracies even formed alliances with labor against the rising bourgeoisie, helping thereby to reduce the repression visited on labor. At the very least, the relationship between feudalism and American conservatism is a murky one.

Adding to Hartz's "civic integration" thesis, S. M. Lipset refers also to the early voting rights of white American males and the "way in which the economic and political elites responded to the demands of workers for the right to participate in the polity and the economy."[14] American elites, he says, also gave favored treatment to labor unions, whereas in Europe "repression fostered socialist or anarchist ideologies that emphasized the common interests of all workers" and forced trade unions to act in politics.[15] This view, however, mistakes the levels of repression in Europe and the United States and understates the high levels of mobilization actually achieved by U.S. labor—a subject of much further discussion.

The contention that early voting rights (and their pacifying effect on political dissent) explain much about American conservatism conflicts with data that show very little relation between conservatism and the timing of universal enfranchisement.[16] In 1870, a date roughly marking the rise of industrialism, France had the highest rate of enfranchisement as a percentage of the total population, with 26 percent, followed by 24 percent in Spain, 23 percent in Greece, 20 percent in Serbia, 15 percent in Rumania, and 15 percent in Denmark. Because 20–25 percent of a total population amounts to universal manhood suffrage, the figures indicate very high rates of enfranchisement in those countries at a time when many U.S. males were, in fact, disfranchised. But countries such as France, Rumania, and Denmark pursued very different courses of political development, none greatly resembling the American one. If enfranchisement produces civic integration and conservatism, how did it happen that raw capitalism did not prevail in those countries as well as in the United States?

These portraits of born-free workers and benign elites are attractive ones and a conservative's dream, but they do not fit many of the less pleasant realities of American life, and the contention that the ballot box has been the "coffin of class consciousness" seems as unwarranted as "no feudalism, no socialism." In 1917, Australia and America were at a roughly similar point: Both had been more or less "born free," both had similar records on the extension of voting rights, and both had socialist parties that vigorously opposed World War I. Yet in one, a labor government was elected in 1917, and in the other, labor was soon to be dealt a nearly fatal blow. What apparently distinguished the two was that Australian labor, confronting a relatively weak capitalist class and operating under a parliamentary system of government, had forged a mass labor party out of a strong labor union base while American labor, confronting an enormously more powerful adversary, was not strong enough to prevent its crushing defeats after the war.

Consciousness

The point most of the consensus theorists make is that favorable conditions diminished class consciousness and made conservatives out of American workers. Their theories, however, rest heavily on questionable assertions about favorable conditions and impressionistic assumptions about consciousness. Indeed, the behavior of the American working class belies what is assumed about consciousness.

Perhaps the level of American class consciousness has stirred so much debate because consciousness is not a tangible thing and indeed is so elusive that even psychoanalysis often cannot retrieve it. American workers in the nineteenth century, David Montgomery writes, engaged in fierce conflicts with their employers yet failed to exhibit a class consciousness in their political behavior.[17] If Montgomery means that the revolutionary impulse to abolish capitalism was generally lacking, his point is well taken, but if he means that no significant efforts have been made to create a left movement in politics, history tells another story, one in which the expression of class consciousness has been inhibited by coercion, manipulation, and the superior resources of economic elites over the course of labor history.

A 1948 UNESCO (United Nations Educational, Scientific, and Cultural Organization) study of nine countries ranked the United States third in the level of working-class consciousness, behind only Britain and the Netherlands and ahead of such reputedly class-conscious nations as France, Germany, Italy, and Norway,[18] and a more recent, comprehensive review of class consciousness found little current or historical difference in American and British working-class perceptions of class divisions.[19] At least as measured by opinion polls, the American working class appears to be far more class conscious and less conservative than is commonly assumed.

Polls consistently show public attitudes to be sharply left of those held (or acted upon) by elected officials, deeply suspicious of big business, supportive of many specific public programs even when increased spending is required, and moving toward even greater liberalism.[20] In 1983, only 5 percent of Americans thought government regulation of business was "too strict," and 42 percent thought it was not strict enough; 74 percent favored a public jobs program even if it increased the federal deficit. In the 1970s, those who thought government should limit business profits almost doubled, from 33 percent to 60 percent, and those thinking there was "too much power concentrated in the hands of a few large companies for the good of the nation" grew from 61 percent to 79 percent. Pollsters continue to find sharp increases in alienation, distrust, and loss of faith in all social institutions and their leaders. S. M. Lipset and William Schneider conclude in reviewing the "confidence gap" that "if the prolonged loss of confidence in American institutions since 1965 has in fact produced a significant loss of legitimacy, the chances that the country can withstand a future crisis of effectiveness may be much reduced."[21]

Consensus views have been distorted by focusing too much on the presumed advantages of American conditions over those of the Old World and on the consciousness and culture these advantages are assumed to have produced. Looking at the actual behavior of people, the picture changes to one of conflict and struggle, in both political and economic arenas. There is a sense in which ruling elites attain, in Antonio Gramsci's term, "hegemonic" influence—a control of social institutions so general that it pervades what people think as well as what they do. Such an influence on U.S. culture has not been measured, but the dissonance it causes and the defection from it, the extent to which expressed opinion has escaped "hegemonic brainwashing," have been far greater than most histories reveal.

Strikes and Conflict

Strike patterns offer quantitative indicators of labor's behavior, its dissatisfactions, and its lack of affection for either raw capitalism or the conditions of work and life. American (and Canadian) strike patterns have been unique in several respects, as U.S. strikes have tended to last longer, involve more lost time, and occur more consistently over the years than European strikes.

Starting in the 1930s, European strike patterns began to change and become shorter, larger, and more frequent than before; starting in 1945, they began to "wither away" in most countries. By contrast, neither the duration nor the volume of American strikes changed much over that period, and there has been no "withering" tendency. Indeed the "shape" of U.S. strikes has been uniquely consistent since 1881, and in the 1980s, the volume of strikes was still higher in the United States than elsewhere.[22]

The withering tendency of European strikes is often explained in terms of the growing successes of European labor-left parties and the consequent declining need for strike action in the workplace.[23] After 1930, as the influence of European social democratic parties rose, strikes tended to shift from the workplace to the "political center" and thus assume new and distinctive patterns.

Based on the most comprehensive study of American strikes to date, P. K. Edwards locates the explanation for the unique U.S. pattern in the unusual resistance of American employers to the loss of "job control" as well as in the fierce resistance to the labor-left in the political arena.[24] Despite notable changes in the context of bargaining, he says, two factors still affect strike patterns; the "intensity of struggles for job control" and the hostility of employers.

What distinguishes strike patterns in the United States and the United Kingdom, according to Edwards, is the exceptional intensity of the struggle for control in the United States, a struggle that has assumed a particularly extreme form because crucial interests of the parties have been at stake, interests going beyond economic issues to include the basic rights of the parties. Thus, "America has had a history of intense opposition to trade unions from employers," and employers have seen "any attempt to extend bargaining as a challenge to the 'right to manage.' " Especially before the New Deal, "the hostility of most employers to unions was intense and unwavering," and strikes became lengthy struggles involving "crucial and fundamental battles over the control of the work place."

Strikes over control, he says, have also characterized the post–New Deal period, less violently than in other periods but no less intensely— as, for example, the 1946 strike in the auto industry over company profits and access to information about them. Strikes over union recognition and first contract—about a sixth of all strikes—are also control struggles in Edwards's view. But "the well-known hostility of American employers toward unions has not been restricted to strikes specifically over recognition or bargaining structure"; employers are likely to find in all contested issues some measure of challenge to their control.

American employers, far more than the British, "have not only been hostile to unions in general terms, but also prepared to put this hostility into practice when faced with a strike." Moreover, they have devised strong systems of labor control in order to do so. The long strikes in the U.S. auto industry, Edwards claims, can be attributed to "the existence of effective managerial control systems," which have "prevented a more general struggle for control." Thus, the strike patterns of the long-established U.S.-owned auto firms in Britain—Ford and Vauxhall—have been larger and more protracted than those in the rest of the British auto industry. In Britain, Ford "has always made a point of defending managerial prerogative," and "its strikes have been long and often bitter battles. As in America, even wage disputes have taken on the character of intense battles." Unfortunately, detailed studies have not yet been conducted of the control systems used by U.S.-owned firms abroad, nor has the apparent tendency of Japanese firms to resist unions in the United States and recognize them in the United Kingdom and elsewhere been much examined.

Most explanations of the unique U.S. strike pattern ultimately refer to the same force in U.S. labor history, the intense preoccupation of American employers with having an entirely "free hand" to control their operations backed up by their unusual economic and political resources. At the same time, strike records point to a unique militancy among American workers. In early peak strike years (1881–1886), more than 3,000 strikes were conducted, and more than 1 million strikers were involved. In peak post–World War II years (1948–1953, for instance), American strikes accounted for over half of all days lost in strikes around the world and almost a quarter of all workers involved in strikes. The average annual days lost per worker during 1954–1963 in mining, manufacturing, and transport were United States 1.05, Italy 0.82, Canada 0.61, Japan 0.41, Australia 0.39, France 0.33, United Kingdom 0.30, Norway 0.29, West Germany 0.07, and Sweden 0.01.[25] Data for other periods show a roughly similar pattern, with the United States most often leading the list.

Many strikes by American unions have involved struggles for union recognition. A review of comparative unionism by George Bain and Farouk Elsheikh concludes that "employer hostility to unionism has generally been far more vigorous and virulent in the United States than in Sweden and the United Kingdom, and this has made it much more difficult for American unions to obtain recognition from employers."[26] As a result, union density has been low in the United States, but it has not been low because labor has shunned conflict with employers, for such conflict has been more persistent and often more violent than in other democracies.

Internal Constraints

Internal constraint theories, like consensus ones, focus on the working class in explaining American conservatism. In this case, labor is seen as a "crippled" combatant rather than as the "sweetheart" of capital.

The working class, it is said, has been too misled, divided, or otherwise crippled to defend itself effectively against its adversaries. The role of class conflict and elite behavior is recognized, but overriding that role is the emphasis on internal labor conflict based on race, ethnicity, religion, ideology, skill level, and other divisions.

Most labor historians, for example, recognize that conflict rather than consensus has dominated American labor relations, yet many attribute labor's defeats in such conflicts to internal problems or to the peculiarities of American labor. What they say or imply is that with better leaders and policies, and a more cohesive working class, the United States might not be so conservative. Usually overlooked in such assessments, as in the consensus view, are the unusual *external* impediments to labor-left success.

Immigrants and Ethnicity

Immigrants figure prominently in such views. Especially constraining in an earlier period, it is claimed, was the conflict between the "old immigrants" from northern Europe and the "new immigrants" from eastern and southern Europe, the latter largely non–English speaking, rural, and unskilled. The claims have some validity, for the size and diversity of the immigration did handicap American labor, but it was neither a crippling nor a unique handicap, and its manipulation was to a large extent a deliberate maneuver in the continuing war on labor.

Certainly the non–English speaking immigrants were harder to reach and organize than the old immigrants, and as a consequence, they were underrepresented in early labor-left organizations and in the skilled work force, as they still tend to be. In the early twentieth century, they composed only about 11 percent of Socialist Party members and unionized workers, but in that period, and every period since 1850, the foreign born have never exceeded 15 percent of the total population, so the underrepresentation may be less severe than is assumed.

In the early nineteenth century, socialist opinion divided over immigration policy. Morris Hillquit favored legislation against the importation of strikebreakers and contract laborers, brought in to weaken unionism and lower wages, but most socialists favored a "more open" immigration policy. Debs led and won the fight within the party against immigration restrictions, and the party majority tried to include immigrants in the movement. Immigration policy in the United States (and elsewhere), of course, has never been wholly unrestricted, so what has always been the issue is not whether limits should be set but what the proper limits should be.

Many new immigrants, it is said, preferred their traditional ethnic organizations to the class politics of the labor-left, yet the record shows that new immigrants repeatedly engaged in mass actions carried out by the AFL and other unions and by World War I, the Socialists had done a fairly creditable job of organizing them. Many new immigrants also found political expression in the labor-oriented Democratic Party. As one study of immigrants concludes, the solidarities that are internal to ethnic groups are not necessarily in conflict with solidarity among groups and often aid their political mobilization.[27]

No doubt the mixing of immigrant languages and cultures retarded working-class mobilization to some extent, but it is doubtful that this constraint was as decisively handicapping to labor-left growth as is often contended. AFL unions, for example, were slow to organize the new immigrants, but their major industrial strikes, called during peak immigration periods, were lost, not for lack of immigrant support (old or new) or contention among ethnic groups, but because the strikes were fiercely opposed by employers and government. Similarly, the IWW organized new immigrants successfully into one big industrial union, but it was finally routed by an even more crushing opposition.

To a large extent employers, guided by the "divide and conquer" maxim, manipulated immigration law and hiring practices in order to mix incompatible groups, obtain cheap labor and strikebreakers, and break unions. Such immigration policies unfortunately overlapped with the unrestricted replacement of skilled workers by machinery operated by the unskilled. As a result, skilled workers often attributed the loss of their jobs to the new immigrants rather than to the mechanization of jobs by employers.

Divisions in labor may be less uniquely American than has been assumed. Skilled workers everywhere have typically been organized long before the unskilled, and tensions between these "aristocrats of labor" and the unskilled can be found everywhere. In Germany, for instance, skilled workers were unusually hostile to the unskilled, and industrial unionism therefore was slow to develop; yet Germany produced a strong democratic socialist movement before other European countries.[28] Similarly, cultural and religious conflict in Britain between English and Irish workers may have been more bitter and divisive than ethnic conflict in America, yet a vigorous labor-left movement finally emerged in Britain too.

British workers also sought to exclude immigrants, especially those imported as strikebreakers. Indeed, the starting point for the organization of the first Socialist International was the effort of British union leaders to organize workers on the Continent in order to prevent their importation during strikes or as labor market competitors. The immigrant problem is hardly unique to America. Even in recent decades, the foreign-worker immigration into almost all advanced democracies—Turks and southern Europeans in Germany and Sweden, Arabs in France, blacks in the United Kingdom, etc.—has caused considerable division in the working classes, but not demonstrably at any significant cost to labor-left growth.

Race

The numerous writings on the role of race in shaping America's uniqueness leave little more to say on the subject. Obviously, race has been a major source of contention for well over a century and has no doubt retarded the growth of the labor-left, especially in the South. But given a favorable political climate, race did not prevent the organization of the CIO in the 1930s and 1940s, nor has it retarded union growth in the large mixed-racial public sector since then.

Race conflict has also had a major impact on U.S. politics but largely because of its manipulation by conservatives in both parties. Thomas B. Edsall points to the role of race in "sustaining economic elites and economic privilege" and to studies by such historians as V. O. Key and W. J. Cash that show "how the powerful would raise the black threat to white supremacy to choke off populist stirrings among small farmers, sharecroppers, and textile workers." As Key wrote in *Southern Politics* in 1949, "Preoccupation with the Negro stifles political conflict. . . . When the going gets rough, when a glimmer of informed political self-interest begins to well up from the masses, the issue of white supremacy may be raised to whip them back into line."[29]

In Edsall's appraisal, the New Deal coalition split over race, because busing, housing integration, and affirmative action placed the black and white poor and the working and middle classes in competition for jobs, schools, and neighborhoods.[30] But others point to the facts that racial attitudes have improved in recent decades and that public opinion about race, even during the Reagan years, has not become more conservative.[31]

Racial divisions have indeed hurt the labor-left, but less than supposed and largely because conservative policies have opposed civil rights laws, used minorities as strikebreakers and replacement workers, forged political coalitions between northern and southern elites in exploiting the race issue, and used race as a wedge issue in winning elections.

Political Conflict and Sectarianism

Catholics and Socialists

In 1900, by one count, more than half of U.S. labor leaders (52 percent) were Catholic; in 1946, more than a third (35 percent). Catholics have also been numerous among the most militant and progressive labor leaders: for example, Peter McGuire, an AFL founder and its first secretary, and the remarkable John Fitzpatrick, leader of the 1919 steel strike. Catholics were also the largest group in the militant and radicalized CIO, led for some twenty years by Irish Catholics Philip Murray, president, and James Carey, secretary-treasurer.

Historian Philip Foner contends that the Catholic church was an important force in offsetting socialist influence in American unionism, and he estimates that about half of all AFL convention delegates and executive council members during the period of conflict over socialist politics were Catholics.[32] Marc Karson claims that the Catholic church largely accounted for the moderate politics of the AFL.[33] Making socialism the official "ism" could drive the Catholics out of the unions, so "consciousness" for American labor became a matter of "job consciousness," he says, limited to job control and bread-and-butter issues.

Karson's thesis, however, exaggerates the influence of the Association of Catholic Trade Unionists (ACTU) and of the Militia of Christ on both Catholic opinion and union policies, as the militia never had more than 700 members or more than a few chapters and ACTU's reach was similarly limited. Moreover, ACTU was strongly prolabor (though antisocialist) and undoubtedly stimulated union and liberal sentiment among the people it reached.

Some Catholic unionists supported (others opposed) socialist ideas and an AFL endorsement of socialist policies,[34] and many AFL unions led by Catholics went far beyond "job consciousness" and deep into terrain that was socialist in all but name. Catholicism undoubtedly muted the influence of Marxism on American labor, but the active role played by Catholics, especially Irish Catholics, in building labor unions and supporting socialist goals (often under other labels) suggests that their contribution to American conservatism has been overstated—especially with respect to program achievement rather than to explicitly socialist parties.

Socialist Sectarianism

According to Philip Foner, a decisive reason for socialism's weak influence on the American labor movement was "sectarian dual unionism" such as that pursued by Daniel DeLeon and the Socialist Labor Party (SLP).[35] Although DeLeon's aloofness from mainstream unionism, his opposition to the AFL, and his extreme sectarianism did not help the SLP, it is problematic that a different course would have made much difference in light of the persecution of the left that was to follow.

James Weinstein claims that the failure of American socialism has been internal, the result of left sectarianism, the mistaken politics of the Communist Party (including its assaults on the Socialist Party), the failure of the labor-left to unite behind the several attempts to create a farmer-labor party resembling the British Labour Party, and the Socialist Party split in 1919, largely over the Russian revolution.[36] Sectarianism, of course, was debilitating but not uniquely American. Moreover, it is doubtful that a mass labor party could have flourished and survived to the present day even with the full support of conciliatory left parties.

Irving Howe explains American conservatism largely in terms of American acceptance of the Emersonian cult of individualism and the conservative structure and costs of American politics. Beyond these factors, he sees an important margin of failure in sectarian socialist strategies that helped make American socialism an isolated sect rather than a measurable force.[37] The strategies were mistaken, he concludes, so the American socialist movement must "take upon itself a considerable portion of the responsibility for its failures."[38] At the zenith of its powers in 1912, Howe says, the Debsian Socialist Party, more than a sect but not yet a mass party, suffered from various internal disorders: streaks of racism; extreme denunciations of the AFL and Gompers; endorsement of the IWW, which further alienated the AFL; Debsian evangelicism, which "carried within itself a dybbuk of sectarianism"; failure to understand progressivism; and, most destructive of all, the Socialist Party's opposition to World War I.[39]

This censure of Debs and the Socialist Party is a refreshing change from the relentless criticism heaped on Gompers and the AFL, yet it slights AFL complicity in the sectarian dispute and ignores the real source of despair on both sides—the repression visited on both the AFL and the Socialist Party. Moreover, it credits Emersonian individualism with too great a hold over the American working class.

Debs and Gompers, the two main sectarian protagonists, quarreled about the new mass industries, especially railroad and steel. Gompers thought workers (skilled and unskilled) should be organized into existing, separate "trade" unions; Debs wanted to organize them into one big industrial union. Gompers tried it his way in steel, and two years later, Debs tried it his way in the railroad industry. Both were crushed, not by one another, but by the combined hostility of employers and government.

Debs, because of his trade union experience, saw the idiocy of fragmented craft unions in railway and other industries and the urgent need to organize the unskilled and build industrial unions. This position led to his early support of the IWW (quickly withdrawn), the creation of the American Railway Union, and his leadership of the Pullman strike. Gompers from his experience saw that industrial unionism and endorsement of socialism invited repression of established unions. Playing it safe, the AFL hung on by its fingertips after World War I; Debs took chances, and his organizations—but not his vision—all but perished.

Gompers and Debs also clashed over politics, but the Debsian Socialist Party, like Debs's railway union, was virtually destroyed, not by Gompers, but by government repression. The AFL supported Woodrow Wilson's Democratic Party in 1912 rather than Debs's candidacy, but its support for Debs would not have elected him. Even in supporting Wilson the AFL lost ground, as the Democrats retreated from support of labor in the 1920s because of ascendant business conservatism. A parliamentary system, with proportional representation, might have united Socialists and the labor Democrats in a strong coalition, but the political system permitted only conflict.

Debs might have supported the war and salvaged more of the party, but the Social Democratic Federation, which supported intervention in the war, was an even heavier loser in the war's aftermath than the Socialist Party.[40] Debs's opposition to the war stemmed more from legitimate pacifism than sectarian purity. In retrospect, he seems very right about the war. Certainly the repression of American Socialists during and after World War I could hardly have been fully anticipated beforehand, unparalleled as it was by the treatment of dissenters in other belligerent nations. In Australia, for example, the largely Irish Catholic opponents of this "Anglo capitalist" war rose in rebellion, defeated the prowar government, and installed their own antiwar leaders in power.

Most socialist parties finally supported the war. The American Socialist Party opposed it, as did vast numbers of Americans, perhaps a vast majority, but the harsh repression of American war and draft dissenters was even more exceptional than the dissent itself. Multitudes of antiwar and anticonscription activists in other countries carried on in normal ways. In England, for example, many laborites opposed conscription yet continued to be recognized and function as members of the government. Debs's party would clearly have been better off supporting the war, but even had it done so, its survival, given the ascendancy of a punitive postwar conservatism, would have been questionable.

Some damaging doses of sectarianism were undoubtedly present in American socialism, yet they were not demonstrably greater than in similar movements elsewhere. Sectarianism was not made in America, but in its most disruptive form it was a by-product of the frustration felt by political groups that lacked any real political power.

3

Unions and Leaders

A MAJOR VARIANT of the "working class as a crippled combatant" thesis is the "sell-out" thesis, popularized by some "new" labor historians and other academics, which contends that union bureaucrats and business unionism, sponsored mainly by Gompers and the AFL, rather than rank-and-file workers, have "sold out" labor and joined the business establishment. None of these critics minimize the forces of capital arrayed against labor, but few have much to say about them. Since they are people of some influence, and reflect the opinions of a much larger group of academics and intellectuals, what they say requires some attention.

The "old" labor history, born and raised at the University of Wisconsin in the 1910s and 1920s and fathered by John R. Commons, was devoted to a generally sympathetic study of trade unionism and its leadership. Many new labor historians have turned away from studying the unions, often disdainfully, to exploring the ethnic, community, and job lives of the working class itself. In doing so, they have found abundant evidence of class consciousness, militancy, and latent radicalism among working people, the presence of which is persistently denied by consensus theorists. E. P. Thompson's *The Making of the English Working Class*, for example, describes how industrialization ripped away the traditional culture of working people and stimulated a new consciousness of class. Similarly, on the American scene, Herbert Gutman describes how a new consciousness developed among working people as the preindustrial traditions of work, community, and culture were transformed by the factory system.[1]

David Montgomery, recalling his life as a factory worker, union organizer, and Communist Party militant in the 1950s, contends that the U.S. working class has always devised alternatives to bourgeois society, on the job and in the political struggles coming out of their everyday lives.[2] Montgomery and others have uncovered convincing evidence of a continuing struggle to gain more control over work and the system in which it is embedded—a struggle that goes far beyond

45

the mere job consciousness that is said by some older historians to have gripped American workers.

Such findings persuasively rebut claims that a unique conservatism and love of capitalism have kept American workers relatively happy and politically passive. Interpretations of the findings, however, often merely shift the "blame" for American conservatism from workers to union leaders who, it is said, have tamed much of this native working-class racialism. Views of old and new historians overlap, of course. Some old historians (Philip Foner and others) have been as critical of the AFL and much union leadership as have the new ones, and many new ones have moved to a more neutral political position. Montgomery, for instance, examines the AFL's "cooperation" with employers in the National Civil Association, for which the AFL has been much censured, and concludes that not much cooperation occurred and that its significance in any event has been greatly overrated.[3]

Failure of Union Leaders

Alan Dawley refers to the failure of both AFL and CIO leaders to propose programs in response to the "demonstrated radicalism of American workers," programs that would "abolish the wage system, take control of investment out of the hands of private capital, and equalize the distribution of income."[4] He refers briefly to an external condition that diverted radical sentiment, the Civil War, the "pivotal political event" of the nineteenth century, which distracted a whole generation from struggles with capitalism.[5] But his argument drifts from this valid stress on external factors to criticism of even the CIO for failing to support radical goals, which he finally concludes, in a puzzling reversal, were not really working-class goals after all.

Among histories that cover several industries over time is James R. Green's *The World of the Worker*, in which he asks why worker militancy has been "invariably repressed, deflected, or channeled into bureaucratic organizations."[6] Green promises to look at a wide context of union growth, but he ignores employer repression, and his scanty coverage of employer "relations" with workers is submerged in descriptions of the misdeeds of union leaders. Only a brief passage, reversing all else he says, deals with the employer role: Organized labor's collapse in the 1920s, he says, should be viewed in the "larger context of Fordism, consumerism, and the emergence of a powerful 'new capitalism.' "[7] Union leadership is blamed at length for labor defeats, and only in final asides is the context of the conflict mentioned. Expressing a contrasting and increasingly popular view, historian Eric Foner claims that the portrait of class-conscious workers betrayed by corrupt or moderate leaders is incorrect; "one might, in fact, argue that at a number of points in American history, the image is false and that often the view of moderate leaders curbing militant workers should be reversed."[8]

Some bitter and puzzling charges against union leaders are made by Jeremy Brecher in *Strike!*, charges that unions, even radical unions, *break* strikes—rank-and-file strikes![9] The union contract is the culprit, he feels. After a union recognition contract is signed, unions turn around and use employer tactics to break strikes—including red baiting, physical attack, importation of strikebreakers, loss of employment, and blacklisting.

Remarkably, however, in *not one* of the mass strikes he describes at length was the relevant union or its officials responsible for breaking the strike. In almost all cases, in fact, local or national unions either supported or ran the strikes, and most of the strikes he cites as being "models" of rank-and-file action (1877, Homestead, Pullman, and others) ended in disastrous defeats for labor at the hands of very hostile adversaries. Only in an aside does Brecher say that the mass strike has stopped short of revolution largely because "the state, its army and police forces, have remained solvent and intact."[10]

False Promises or False Charges

In the volume *False Promises*, Stanley Aronowitz echoes Brecher's charges, updates them, and mixes together various and conflicting ideas about the sources of America's uniqueness, including a conservative consensus, internal labor constraints, and only to a very limited extent, the imbalance of power resources between capital and labor.[11] Long-term contracts, he says, have robbed workers of so much power that they now know that "the union has become an inadequate tool to conduct struggles, even where they have not yet perceived the union as an outright opponent to their interests," but he acknowledges that "despite the despicable performance of labor movement leadership" in the past thirty years, members still regard the leaders as their "only defensive weapons."[12]

When the union leadership fails to thwart member initiatives, it "supports a strike publicly while sabotaging it behind the scenes"; in the main, national union "bureaucracies" have helped employers "impose labor peace upon a rebellious membership."[13] Further, unions are "an appendage of the corporations" and "a vital institution in the corporate capitalist complex," many of them retaining "the forms but not the content of democracy." The culprit is not the union leader, he then claims, but unionism itself. Leaders can be replaced, but it is "not possible to transcend the institutional constraints of trade unionism itself."[14] The constraint that he stresses most is the union contract, which reads "like a corporate contract or a mortgage agreement" but is, in fact, "a bill of sale."[15] No explanation is offered as to why union contracts in Canada and elsewhere, which closely resemble the American ones, have not also weakened unionism in those countries.

In another book ten years later, Aronowitz reverses field. He was wrong, he says, in failing to see that "the trade union remained the only institution capable of defending and extending workers' interests" and for not recognizing how even the modest gains of labor in the 1960s "would be challenged by an alliance of employers and conservative politicians in the 1970's and 1980's." He also recants his former view that participation in the Democratic Party is "an instance of corporativism for one of the major capitalist parties" and acknowledges that the rise of the CIO owed more to AFL supporters of industrial unionism than to the IWW or the Knights of Labor.[16] And reversing his former critical view, he writes that "contrary to accepted wisdom, Gompers was the first advocate of social unionism"; there never was "an articulated alternative to Gompers with a chance of success after the collapse of radical labor perspectives shortly before the First World War."[17]

Sociologist Michael Goldfield locates the source of labor decline in rising employer and government opposition but ends on the same note as many new historians.[18] Although he writes that most U.S. capitalists, in contrast to employers elsewhere, "never fully accepted the legitimacy of unions" and that the sharp rise in union busting during the 1970s resulted in an unparalleled weakness of U.S. unionism,[19] he concludes by reverting to "internal constraint" explanations of union decline including internal union changes, bureaucracy, suppression of union democracy, expulsion of communists, support for the New Deal, sweetheart agreements with employers, and failure of will in southern organizing drives. He fails, however, to prove that growing unions have avoided these pitfalls better than declining unions or to show that in early labor history, when unions were younger and presumably purer (unions such as the American Railway Union, the IWW, and the Knights of Labor, all now extinct), they were better defended against the assaults of employers.

Leftist criticisms of unions, often amounting to condemnation, also come from outside academe. Community organizer Saul Alinsky, for example, spoke of the selfishness, lethargy, and conservatism of organized labor, its capture by employers and capitalism, and the need for communities to organize since unions no longer sought to mobilize the people.[20] Although he believed unionism was dead or moribund, unionism has had far more staying power and a far greater social impact than the community organizations he and others sponsored, remarkable as those achievements have been.

New Critics

For both sound and unsound reasons, the pioneer figure in the old labor history, John R. Commons, has become a prime target of criticism, mainly because of his sympathetic focus on unionism and his support during the troubled 1920s for some forms of labor-management cooperation. Dawley raises questions about Commons's interpretations of history, Montgomery claims that Commons supported Frederick Taylor's antiunionism, and Gutman criticizes Commons for focusing only on union members. Maurice Isserman writes that the Wisconsin school, led by Commons, has been criticized for its "preoccupation with mainstream labor organizations and purely economic disputes" and for its tendency to focus only on national union leadership.[21] The criticisms are sometimes fair, but as Robert Ozanne points out, most of them fail to credit Commons for his founding contributions to labor history, conducted with very limited resources, and in some cases the criticisms merely reflect a popular antipathy to union leadership.[22]

New labor historians do not speak with one voice, and in most cases their views have evolved over time. Their accounts of worker struggles have generally enriched, even ennobled, their subjects and greatly enlivened the study of labor history, but in some cases their relentless censure of elected union leaders has denied working people their most notable achievement—the creation of their unions and the election of their own leaders. Moreover, these critics provide no persuasive evidence that more radical union leaders could have succeeded where others failed, or even survived at all in their hostile setting. Indeed, the pages of labor history are strewn with the graves of radical unions and their leaders, against whom repressive forces have been particularly savage.

Critics who blame union leaders and the AFL for America's unique conservatism too often assume that unions make up a monolithic entity in which highly centralized power resides in its federation (the AFL and more recently the AFL-CIO) and in the federation heads. In fact, the federation has served mainly as a coordinating agency for affiliated unions, operating with a relatively small budget and staff and playing almost no role in collective bargaining, the key function of unions, and only a minor role in organizing, community and public relations, education, research, and other union functions. Even its role in political action has been secondary to that of its affiliated unions. In recent decades, the central focus of the federation has been on foreign policy, about which serious dissent has grown among affiliates.

Almost all major functions, then, have been largely retained by the national unions, many of whose treasuries, staffs, and jurisdictions dwarf those of AFL-CIO headquarters. Yet despite the virtual autonomy, reserved powers, and varied policies of the affiliates, many studies of labor concentrate on the federation. Critics, for example, often blame the federation's heads for failing to conduct more sweeping organizing drives when, in fact, such organizing has been a function far more of the affiliates than of AFL-CIO headquarters.

Samuel Gompers has also been a favorite target of rebuke. Former radical Ronald Radosh, for example, claimed that Gompers gladly collaborated with domestic conservatism and that labor leadership from Gompers to at least the time of Sidney Hillman espoused corporate ideology.[23] Jerome Karabel says that conservative union leaders, assisted by government and some shrewder capitalists, have dominated the modern labor movement.[24]

Gompers, AFL head for some half a century, was certainly no champion of labor uprisings, earned no medals for daring or heroics, and deserves no postmortem purple hearts. But he was undeniably a militant trade unionist who, right or wrong, was intent on saving the federation from political-ideological splits and from what he feared would be suicide missions. Moreover, he supported, with the AFL's scarce resources, a few mass strikes conducted by affiliates, most of which ended disastrously. He played a key role in the eight-hour-day struggle, but his sixth sense about danger apparently kept him at a safe distance from the Haymarket calamity that helped crush the Knights of Labor.

Gompers opposed an AFL endorsement of a socialist platform, but largely to protect the vulnerable federation from red hunts and to reduce the serious internal conflict generated by ideological debates. At the same time, he consistently claimed he wanted just what democratic socialists wanted—what was best for labor and the society—and that only his methods differed from theirs.

Charges concerning the damage done to unions by "labor bureaucrats" have been popularized. What remains unproved is that the problems of bureaucracy are unique to American labor and explain its weakness, or that nonbureaucratic leaders could have done a better job. Since Robert Michel's and Max Weber's classic treatises on bureaucracy were both written with European, not American, politics and movements in mind, it cannot be assumed that union bureaucracy was either born in the United States or raised exclusively within its borders. Nor is there any evidence that U.S. unions are currently more bureaucratized than thriving unions abroad. In classical bureaucratic terms (specialization of function, governing rules and procedures, assignment of roles by achievement rather than kinship, efficiency, etc.), Swedish unions may be the most bureaucratized in the democratic world, yet they are the most successful, among the most highly regarded, and among the most admired by many social historians and radical activists.

Another common charge said to weaken labor is "economism," or a concern with material benefits to the exclusion of longer-range "assaults" on the core of the political system or calls for social "transformation." Economism is usually seen as advancing the selfish pecuniary interests of labor, as opposed to political transformations that might benefit everyone. Although such constant reminders about class relationships and broader, longer-term goals can benefit labor, the critics offer few guidelines, aside from enduring calls for a third party, as to how such assaults and transformations are to be carried out successfully.

It is easy enough to identify the weaknesses of American labor, but they have not kept it from carrying on a vigorous struggle over the years to establish itself in the workplace and in politics. Labor retreats in this struggle have been many, but that is hardly remarkable considering the opposition it has faced. Charges against leaders obviously have some basis in fact, as insurgency movements in some unions have shown, yet what leaps out of the pages of American history is the story of exceptional repression, not sell-outs or exceptional conservatism or materialism on the part of union leaders.

Analysis of the Debate

Although much labor history more than measures up to the rich materials available for research, the debates among labor historians sometimes resemble nagging tribal feuds over who did what, who was right, and who gets credit or blame for what happened. Often the debate consists simply of sectarian recriminations among various labor-left factions. The debate is not simply an internal one but is as widely publicized as labor's critics can make it. Some of it stimulates useful discussion and goads organizational change, but its obsessive quality blinds the debaters to the role of labor's class adversaries, allows them to escape scrutiny, and may even serve adversary interests to the extent that they fuel antiunionism among opinion leaders and the public generally.

Whoever has been right or wrong, it seems highly unlikely that different actors or policies on the labor-left would have made America much less conservative than it is. My purpose, therefore, is to try to get the debate back on track by focusing on the behavior of labor's adversaries rather than on labor's internal problems. It would seem that the labor-left everywhere (not just in America) is beset by sectarian and often fratricidal conflict, usually aimed more at internal organizational politics than at maximizing labor's gains. This situation is not the labor-left's "basic problem," nor is it at all unique to America, but it certainly has not helped much either.

PART TWO

Unionism: Strategies of Repression

4

Employers, Mercenaries, and Armed Force

VIOLENCE AND THE USE OF ARMED FORCE have characterized the hot war on labor—violence conducted by employer-inspired vigilantes, mercenaries, and various public armed forces. Labor everywhere has "war stories" to tell, but nowhere has the record been as violent as in the United States. For somewhat mysterious reasons, casualty figures from these wars have not been among the voluminous official statistics kept on labor disputes. One review of some major U.S. strikes puts the figure at 700 dead and untold thousands seriously injured in labor disputes,[1] but these figures, though impressive, include only strike casualties reported in newspapers between 1877 and 1968; and may therefore grossly understate the total casualties. (During the 1877–1968 period, state and federal troops intervened in labor disputes more than 160 times, almost invariably on behalf of employers.[2])

In the seven years from 1890 to 1897, an estimated 92 people were killed in some major strikes,[3] and from January 1, 1902, to September 1904, an estimated 198 people were killed and 1,966 injured. These casualties were overwhelmingly strikers killed or injured in some major strikes and lockouts.[4] In the absence of protective labor legislation, Philip Taft and Philip Ross write, "many employers fought unionism with every weapon at their command in the certainty that their hostility was both lawful and proper."[5] After the adoption of some protective legislation, between 1947 and 1962, violence and militia intervention declined, but an estimated 29 people were killed in major strikes during the period, 20 of them in the South. By contrast, only 1 person in Britain has been killed in a strike since 1911.[6]

Mercenaries and Spies

Until the organization of the CIO (and even to some extent beyond, especially in the South), many employers hired their own "armies" of mercenaries and spies to crush labor organizations, but most large employers also contracted out these services to a thriving labor espionage industry. In more recent decades, labor "consultants" have performed much the same work.

These lucrative agencies used various approaches, including subversion, mass violence, and deliberate lawbreaking, in conducting the war on labor. They penetrated union organizations, identified union activists, gathered information about union plans, created factional and ethnic conflict among employees, obtained positions of leadership within the organizations, undermined the existing leadership, engaged in sabotage, and provoked labor violence in order to discredit unionism and excuse employer violence. Sometimes deputized by employers as public law officers, the agencies and hired mercenaries broke strikes and unions, killed strikers, and carried on such penetrating espionage and sabotage as to make many unions virtual company unions.

The agencies were—and are—big business, and in the 1920s, they employed thousands of people and cost U.S. employers millions of dollars a year. Their size and scope are unique to American labor relations. Their history dates back at least to the Civil War and continues in various incarnations to the present day.

In 1912, the Congressional Commission on Industrial Relations conducted an inquiry into the work of the labor espionage agencies, and in the mid-1930s, the LaFollette Civil Liberties Committee of the U.S. Senate conducted a second investigation. Conducted in two different time periods, the inquiries found much the same record of corporate spying and private police action, and the reports provided much of the information used by subsequent writers.

The Espionage Business

Spies placed in factory jobs sent to their agencies daily detailed reports about their activities and the conversations they held or overheard; on Sundays and other nonwork days, they met and associated with employees outside the shop. They became union activists and even ran for high union offices in pursuit of information, influence on union policy, and a better chance to disrupt union activities. Spies often sought the position of union treasurer so they could discredit union leaders by absconding with union funds. In positions of leadership, they opposed effective union policy, approved poor contracts, and pressed militantly for unattainable demands. Many became provocateurs and caused labor to lose public and membership support by inciting workers to extreme actions.

The spies who took union funds, Leo Huberman writes, knew that it only took a few raids on the union treasury before thousands of union members were reduced to a handful, that an inadvisable or poorly timed strike could break a union, and that a union official who sold out to an employer destroyed union morale.[7] The espionage agency, on behalf of employers, trafficked in munitions and tear gas, supplied employers with strikebreakers and armed men to disperse strikers, and often set up company unions to head off the organizing of legitimate ones.

According to the commission report, the labor spy "breaks the morale of the striker by propaganda and betrays it by guile. He cows the morale of the striker by brutality and contaminates it by provocation. The striker knows he is there and his presence is a perilous and vicious goad. And he comes at the employer's command to take the situation if not the law into his own hands. His presence has made the crises of American labor history peculiarly cruel and bitter."[8]

The labor spy agency traces back at least to the detective work Allan Pinkerton conducted before and during the Civil War. Pinkerton, a Scottish immigrant and founder of a whole dynasty of Pinkertons, wrote twenty books before he died in 1884, among them a description of the great railroad strikes of 1877, *Strikers, Communists, Tramps, and Detectives*.[9] Pinkerton placed the blame for the strikes on the Communist Internationale and more specifically on the Paris Commune of 1871, but his book makes no mention of the possible source of the strikes in what he himself referred to as a deep depression in 1873, one that virtually crushed existing labor organizations.

In 1871, during the Paris Commune, according to Pinkerton, that "city fell an easy prey to a horde of bad men . . . the class, the world over, who are at the bottom of all troubles of a communistic nature. They were the real cause of the great strikes of '77, and their prompt and utter extermination, in this and all other countries, is the only method of removing a constant menace and peril to government and society." Communists may not have caused the strikes of 1877, Pinkerton wrote, but the strikes were nevertheless "the direct result of the communistic spirit spread through the ranks of railroad employees by communistic leaders and their teachings . . . and when the strikes were well under way, every act of lawlessness that was done was committed by them. . . . They are a class of human hyenas worth of all notice and attention."[10]

Pinkerton acknowledged that, compared to England, communists in America had a tardy and unnoteworthy influence on unions, but it was growing, he claimed: "Indeed, it has been several years since communism first blossomed out and began to flourish in the United States." Pinkerton described even the Catholic-led Knights of Labor, a moderate but lively union, as "probably an amalgamation of the Mollie Maguires and the Commune."[11]

Pearl Bergoff, another prominent name in the spy business, began his career by breaking the Philadelphia Rapid Transit strike in 1909. To this end, according to Edward Levinson, he hired "prison-pedigreed" strikebreakers who started riots, gassed civilians, and fought with strikers. "Swindler and slugger, fence and fugitive, briber and usurer, . . . have all placed their left hands on their hearts, raised their right hands in oath and been sent forth to uphold law and order" for employers.[12]

Given carte blanche by a large manufacturer whose workers struck in 1917, the Sherman Service (publisher of the magazine *Harmony in Industry*) assigned fourteen secret agents to gain influence with the strikers in order to identify their leaders, strike plans, and moral and financial support. The agency assigned recruiters to hire strikebreakers and supply them with bed and board during the strike—*and* it assigned spies to report on the strikebreakers. When the agents (two of whom had become union officers) reported that the union was seriously weakened, the company stopped meeting with the union, discharged many activists, created dissension among union leaders, and broke the strike. The manufacturer, dominant in its industry, remained "union free."[13]

In another case, "harmony in industry" was achieved by cultivating Italian workers and inciting them to start a general fight at a union meeting. The agency then deputized guards, served ejectment papers on the union committee, ordered its members to leave town, and "exterminated the trouble-making organization."[14] In yet another instance, the agency's stated goal was to circulate false rumors and cause conflict and "racial hatred" between Italians and Serbians, all to the employer's advantage. Officials of the Sherman Service were later indicted in Chicago for such activities but never brought to trial.

Over the years, labor espionage has been a large and profitable business. In April 1936, for example, some 230 agencies were in the business, the largest of them being William J. Burns's International Detective Agency, Inc. (operating in forty-three cities) and Pinkerton's National Detective Agency (operating in thirty-four cities). In just three top agencies, an estimated 135,000 men were employed at one point, operating in over 100 offices and more than 10,000 local branches, and earning some $65 million annually for the agencies.[15] The gross income of the Pinkerton agency in 1935 was $2,318,039.18,[16] and during the 1930s the agencies charged employers an estimated $80 million a year. General Motors testified before the LaFollette committee that it paid about a million dollars to such agencies from January 1934 through July 1936; among their other tasks, the spies hired by GM spied on the spies hired by Chrysler.[17]

In the 1930s, espionage agencies worked for the railroads and such large employers as Western Union Telegraph Company, the United States Steel Corporation, and such patriot and employer groups as the National Manufacturers' Association, the National Founders' Association, and the National Erectors' Association.[18] In more recent decades, the agencies have been overshadowed by a booming industry of gentrified union-busting "consulting firms" (discussed in a later chapter) whose operations are modernized, computerized, and more legalistic but similarly profitable, repressive, and apparently wholly unique to the American corporate scene.

Results

The agencies promised and often got results, and the labor spy claimed he could corrupt any union out of existence. In 1910, the Foster Service wrote a prospective client that if it was employed before a union was formed, there would be no strike or disturbance. If a union was already formed and no strike was expected within thirty to sixty days, the agency would carry on an intrigue that would result in factions, conflict, officer resignations, and membership decline. If given a free hand, the agency could control the union's activities and policies.[19]

R. J. Coach, who ran an espionage agency in Cleveland, Ohio, and who claimed to "own" every union in the city, never admitted to defeat in crushing a union and claimed that at least once he had put 10,000 strikebreakers into a single strike.[20]

One manager of an espionage agency working for U.S. Steel gave as a hypothetical operation: forty to fifty men working as spies, ten or fifteen of them influential in the local, five or more being union officials, and some even being placed as international officers and members of the state labor federation. Boasting of his work in Akron, Ohio, he claimed that no labor trouble existed there, as his agency controlled all the unions.

One labor spy named "R-O" worked in Wheeling, West Virginia, at the turn of the century and after some years became the business agent of his local and president of Wheeling's Central Labor union. He was always "the most eager for radical reform," Howard writes. "He was the loudest, too, at denouncing the injustice of press and police, and the most loyal for a delicate or a confidential mission." When he died, the union buried him ceremoniously. His true identity was revealed only after a public stenographer, working for another spy in Wheeling, saw reports implicating R-O as the author of many steel company blacklists in West Virginia.

Early in the century, when "undesirable aliens" were being massively deported, one agency printed 500 copies of the *Communist Manifesto*, took them to New York City and distributed them among various workers' organizations, thus giving the Department of Justice an excuse for seizing and deporting union activists.

Violence

Violence was a specialty of the labor spy agency. "Espionage is closely related to violence," the 1912 commission concluded, sometimes a direct cause and often an indirect cause. If the secret agents of employers, working as union members, "do not always instigate acts of violence, they frequently encourage them. If they did not, they would not be performing the duties for which they are paid, for they are hired on the theory that labor organizations are criminal in character. The union spy is not in the business to protect the community. He has little respect for law, civil or moral."[21]

The extralegal (or illegal) labor spy "as thug, gunman, agent provocateur and armed guard," in Howard's opinion, has always been the heart, if not the cause, of labor violence. American businesspeople have been prepared to "chastise where the law holds back, to defy law where law impedes, to assume to themselves the prestige of law and to justify themselves afterwards. Questioned in their right to administer even death penalties and banishments, they have stood before courts indignantly unabashed." Similarly, the *New York World* concluded that "espionage is properly a war measure, and war, open or underground, follows it immediately. It wipes out all common ground between employer and employed and ends mutual sympathy and understanding."

Time did not gentle employers' violence; it only gave them new weapons of war. Where agents once used only blackjacks, clubs, and bullets to break strikes, the weapons of 1937 included tear gas and a gas that caused violent nausea and vomiting, a sense of suffocation, and intense pain in the chest and head.[22]

Nonphysical forms of violence were also used. After hearing a case concerning employees who had been discharged because of labor spy reports, National Labor Relations Board member Edwin S. Smith claimed he had

never listened to anything more tragically un-American. Man after man in the prime of life, of obvious character and courage, came before us to tell of the blows that had fallen on him for his crime of having joined a union. Here they were—family men with wives and children—on public relief, blacklisted from employment, so they claimed, in the city of Detroit, citizens whose only offense was that they had ventured in the land of the free to organize as employees to improve their working conditions. Their reward, as workers who had given their best to their employer, was to be hunted down by a hired spy like the lowest of criminals and thereafter tossed like useless metal on the scrap heap.[23]

Senator LaFollette concluded from his committee's work in the 1930s that "in the light of the testimony this committee has taken, the evidence is overwhelming . . . that the use of this labor espionage is demonstrated and proved to be one of the most effective weapons in destroying genuine labor collective bargaining activities on the part of workers."[24]

Public Armed Force

While private armed forces have included mercenaries, espionage ("protective") agencies, and vigilantes, public armed forces have included local and state police, sheriffs, deputies, state militia, national guard units, and all of the U.S. armed forces with the possible exception of the air corps. Often private and public armed forces have been indistinguishable. For employers, the use of public forces has had obvious advantages over mercenaries: They are more legitimate in the public mind; they are empowered to arrest, jail, and punish strikers; and they are also much less costly to employers and better equipped for violence. Usually they have taken longer to call up, however, and in the case of the state militia, they have not always been totally loyal to employers.

Local and State Police Forces

Police have engaged in strikebreaking more often than other forces, simply because they are on the spot and often under employer control. Consequently, they have been the source of much of the violence inflicted on strikers. Sometimes they have run amok, as they did during the Lawrence, Massachusetts, textile strike of 1912 and the Chicago Memorial Day Massacre of 1937, when they "wantonly assaulted strikers and their sympathizers without provocation or justification."[25]

Often armed forces, hired and paid by employers (as the Pennsylvanian Coal and Iron Police) were the official public police force. In company towns, the police were usually on the company payroll, and they were actually a privatized armed force commissioned to enforce public law. In many other places, employers supplied arms and equipment to police, supplemented the official force with their own sworn deputies, or provided extra pay to police who performed special company services. In one case reported by John Fitch, a factory superintendent paid $35.00 a week to each police officer who performed services for him while on duty.[26]

Employers have often given significant sums to individual police and police benefit funds. As reported in Pittsburgh papers, one steel company paid each policeman on duty $150 during the great steel strike of 1919; after the strike, a high Pittsburgh police officer retired at half pay and took a job as head of police in a large Pittsburgh steel company. Beholden to employers for election support, jobs, favors, and subsidies, many public officials have responded with alacrity to employer requests for the deputizing of mercenaries or for the intervention of police and other public armed forces on the employer's behalf.

Among the cases of such intervention was the 1910 Pennsylvania coal mining strike, in which state police and deputy sheriffs openly opposed the strike—the deputies because they were on the company payroll. During a 1912 textile strike in Little Falls, New York, over a 10 percent wage cut, police broke up the meetings of strikers and arrested and jailed the speakers, including Schenectady's mayor. Strikers were assaulted at night, organizers were arrested and sometimes jailed without counsel, and police even tried to close a soup kitchen that had been opened to strikers.

In the 1912 Lawrence textile strike, police refused strikers the right to hold outdoor meetings and conducted what observers described as wanton attacks on strikers. When a group came from Boston to inquire about the strike's causes, police on horseback met them at the railway station, dispersed and threatened them, beating some with clubs and forcing others to leave town.

In only a few strikes have public forces taken the employer's side so fully as did local and state police in Pittsburgh during the great steel strike of 1919, mainly because of U.S. Steel's dominating political influence. Testimony before a Senate committee indicated that police harassed and interfered with strikers constantly, often arresting them without cause and in many cases confining them to company buildings before transferring them to jail or police headquarters, and beating them on the streets, in public buildings, and even in their own homes.

Police hostility to strikers has been intensified when the public officials have also been company officials or their friends and relatives. In the 1919 steel strike, for instance, the mayor of Bethlehem, Pennsylvania, was a vice-president of the Bethlehem Steel Corporation, the mayor of Duquesne was a brother of a steel company president, the sheriff of Allegheny County was a brother of a mill manager, the burgess of the steel town of Clairton was chief clerk of Carnegie Steel, and the burgess of the steel town of Munhill was a mill superintendent. These were the men issuing orders to police during the strike.

State Militia

When local police forces could not cope with labor disputes (even when supplemented by deputies, vigilantes, and mercenaries), state governors have responded to employer requests to call up state troops (militia or national guards) to protect property and strikebreakers—and when that has not been enough to crush strikes, the president has often responded to similar requests for the intervention of U.S. military power. The use of these forces has usually turned labor relations into a kind of public war on labor, one side fully armed and sanctioned by law and the other not.

Although troops in some states intervened in strikes as early as 1806, when they broke a textile strike, the state militia (renamed the national guard in 1903) was created in the 1870s to intervene as an industrial police force in strikes and demonstrations. Thirteen mining strikes occurred in Colorado from 1880 to 1904, and ten of them were broken by the state militia. In one case, a 1903 strike of metal miners, the militia deported several hundred strikers, sending some to other parts of the state, some to Kansas, and some to New Mexico. In Colorado mining towns and other western areas during this period, relations between employers and public armed forces were so symbiotic that the state militia even integrated mercenaries into its ranks as public law enforcement during strikes. Often when state troops intervened in strikes, employers put cars at their disposal and offered them free housing, sometimes even turning their factories into barracks.

Yet public officials and armed forces have sometimes sided with labor. In a strike of copper miners after the turn of the century, for instance, the Arizona governor ordered the militia to prevent strikebreaker importations. Also, when prolabor officials have been in control, state troops have maintained order without significant violence to strikers.

The unpopularity of strikebreaking among working-class youths has, of course, often impeded recruitment to the state militia. Earlier, the militia was more of an irregular armed force with strong family and community connections, as contrasted with the full-time, professional police and national military forces. But the partial takeover of the state militia and the assumption of its major costs by the federal government, then its incorporation by the armed forces reserve, has made the national guard a more "professional" force, detached it more from its community roots, and made it more effective in suppressing strikes and demonstrations.

Between 1877 and 1892, about a third of the militia's work involved strike duties, and its use in strikes was most common from 1875 to 1925.[27] In 1877, for instance, 45,000 state militiamen in eleven states were called up to break the great railroad strike of that year. Before 1960, the guard was used in public worker strikes only once—in 1919 when Massachusetts Governor Calvin Coolidge called up 4,500 state guardsmen to break the Boston police strike—but in the 1970s, when public workers were organizing, the guard replaced public workers in some forty-seven strikes.[28]

Federal Forces

Regular federal troops have also been used extensively in strikes, beginning with their critical intervention in the 1877 railroad strike. In the Pullman strike of 1894, President Cleveland sent federal troops into Chicago, even over the opposition of Illinois Governor John Altgeld. In some cases, federal troops have been ordered to actually replace striking workers in the private sector.

The first case of "presidential seizure" in labor disputes occurred in 1863 when federal troops replaced striking longshoremen on the New York docks.[29] In 1917–1918, they replaced striking loggers in firms supplying wood to the military, and in 1919, they twice replaced longshoremen in loading military ships. In 1941, the navy used civilians to replace striking machinists in the San Francisco shipyards, and in 1944, soldiers and sailors replaced striking Bethlehem steelworkers in New York and New Jersey ship-repair yards.

At a later date, in connection with a "national emergency" unrelated to military operations, President Nixon declared an emergency and called up 30,000 federal troops and national guardsmen to replace postal workers during a 1970 strike, breaking the strike in just two days. In 1981, President Reagan used federal troops and military air controllers to break an air traffic controllers' strike.

The use of federal troops in strikes is said to violate the legal prohibition imposed by the Posse Comitatus Act of 1878, a congressional reaction to President Grant's frequent use of troops in labor and other civil disputes. Amended in 1956, the act provided that use of the army or air force as a posse comitatus or to execute laws unless authorized by the court or Congress was punishable by fines and imprisonment. Yet the repeated use of federal troops to quell strikes has not been challenged by the courts, nor has the even more frequent use of state troops received the attention that the presumed national commitment to settling disputes only through collective bargaining would seem to warrant.

The war on labor has been conducted not only by the military but also by other administrative, legislative, and judicial "arms" of government. Such agencies have repeatedly defended employer claims in labor disputes, refused legal protection to labor, and treated unions as illegal trusts and criminal conspiracies. These unarmed "violations" of labor have caused much conflict and armed violence, sanctioning as they have employer violations of labor rights.

Certainly labor has also engaged in violence, but no major American labor union, Taft and Ross claim, "ever advocated violence as a policy," and violence has almost always injured labor, as the roll call of lost strikes involving violence reveals.[30] Worker violence that has occurred has usually resulted from worker frustration at having their strikes broken by employers.[31] Workers have seldom committed acts of violence against employers themselves.

Although CIO sit-downs of the 1930s met with violent repression, strike violence began to decline sharply in 1933, as the National Industrial Recovery Act gave workers some guaranteed rights to organize, and again after the passage of the National Labor Relations Act in 1935, which indicated that strike violence can be reduced by increased government protection of labor against employer hostilities.

Comparisons

Employers' use of red and radical scares to excuse violence, even against traditional unionism, has been exceptionally virulent and effective in the United States, even though real "reds" have been much scarcer and less influential than in Europe. Other aspects of armed violence in labor disputes are also unique to the United States: the extensive use of strikebreakers by employers, the extent of the violence, the heavy casualties, the pro-employer bias of government, and the privatization of armed force.

Much violence has been sparked by the penchant of American employers to actively break strikes rather than simply wait for their collapse, as British and many other European employers have tended to do. The use of strikebreakers is not uniquely American. British and other employers have also hired "scabs" or "blacklegs" (both bovine diseases) to break strikes, and in some cases specialized firms have supplied them upon request, as in the United States, but European strikebreaking has been much less common and much less likely to be supported by armed force and violence. The British employer has generally refrained from such activities, believing them to be degrading and destructive.

The use of espionage agencies and *professional* strikebreakers has been almost unknown in European and other developed democracies. In most of Canada's history, the use of professional strikebreakers, labor spies, and vigilantes in labor disputes has been virtually absent. The labor espionage agency did appear finally in Canada, but at a later date, in a more modest and benign form, and often in U.S.-owned industry.

In the United States, employers were often not merely above the law, they were the law. Nowhere else in the available history of Western democracies have employers, with impunity, organized vigilante mobs or used mercenary armies with such frequency to protect their property interests. European democracies have operated from different ground rules, and nothing remotely similar to U.S. vigilante activity or the armed repression of labor disputes has occurred there.[32] On the relatively rare occasions when armed forces, under democratic governments, have intervened in European disputes, the forces have almost always been army regulars or national police—disciplined forces acting under orders that have seldom included strikebreaking or the use of violence. Only in the United States, at employer request, have army regulars been called out so repeatedly by heads of state to break mass strikes, and nowhere else, it appears, has the national guard, state militia, state police, sheriff, or local police responded so swiftly to employer demands in labor disputes.

In 1935, *Fortune* magazine wrote about Pearl Bergoff's labor espionage agency, one of the largest in the field: "Bergoff is in a business that is permitted to exist nowhere except in the U.S. . . . The U.S. remains the one industrial nation of any account that permits any private citizen to influence the balance of power between capital and labor."[33] Sidney Howard agrees that such espionage is unique to American employers and "a dangerous weapon at best and not one which ought, under any circumstances, to be used for private advantage."[34]

In the United States, the employer use of private and public armed forces has been facilitated by employer influence on various public institutions, the mass media, religious groups, schools, various public and private institutions, and the multiple coercive powers of government. All combined to produce a climate that has been extremely inhospitable to the mobilization of the American labor-left. As H. A. Clegg concluded from a study of six countries, in no other major democracy have government and public institutions been so influenced by business as in the United States.[35]

5

The Legal System:
"We Are the Law"

IN MOST OTHER WESTERN DEMOCRACIES, the legal system has been somewhat sympathetic, or at least relatively impartial, in its relations with organized labor, often resisting employer demands, protecting labor at critical moments, and sometimes even embracing it. American labor has been less fortunate. Rarely has the legal system been its advocate, protector, or even a neutral party, and more typically it has been an adversary. As Jay Lovestone writes, when strikes threaten, war is declared. Employers "abrogate the civil law," and martial law and a state of siege begin. The judge "throws off his mask of impartiality and poses as an open representative of the employer" and, on the employer's behalf, crushes the strike.[1]

In the United States, Klaus von Beyme concluded from a comparative study of unions, U.S. employer associations have not cooperated, as in Europe, in legalizing institutional relations.[2] More often, American employers have made and enforced their own laws, acquired the services of public officials and law enforcement agents, resisted labor's claims to legal legitimacy, and assumed an imperial posture: "We are the law."

Britain, in contrast, enacted laws that defined the rights of labor early in the nineteenth century and has repeatedly extended those rights, with some slippage such as the Taff-Vale decision, which imposed heavy strike penalties on unions. In the United States, it took until the 1930s for federal law—the Norris-LaGuardia Act of 1932, which outlawed the yellow-dog contract; the National Industrial Recovery Act of 1933; and the National Labor Relations Act (NLRA) of 1935—to affirm and define some of labor's collective rights and to place some limits on employer antiunion practices. The NLRA, important for the detailed protection of labor it sought to offer, was a response to the unique disadvantages of U.S. labor. Since its enactment, however, the NLRA has been effectively "deradicalized" by conservative administrative boards.

The general absence of protective law has made courts the chief guardian of labor's legal destiny, and unluckily for labor, the courts have been punitive guardians. The U.S. Supreme Court has played the dominant role in the denial of labor rights. As the highest judicial body in the land, appointed and tenured—supposedly to make it independent of special interests—the Court has been far more responsive to status-quo views than to the popular will or forces seeking progressive change. Assigned the unique power of constitutional review, it can reject laws enacted by Congress, the highest lawmaking body in the land. Thus it often passes a legal hurdle, absent in most democracies, to the enactment of favorable labor law at federal and state levels.

American unions began with the law against them. Individualism is sanctified by the U.S. Constitution, British historian Henry Phelps Brown writes, and legal sentiment against worker combinations is even stronger than under British common law.[3] Before the New Deal era, the common-law criminal conspiracy doctrine effectively prevented much worker combination. The major substantive federal laws that applied to labor were the Sherman Antitrust Act of 1890 and the Clayton Antitrust Act of 1914, and the major procedural or enforcement laws were labor injunctions and restraining orders, and to a lesser extent, criminal actions and damage suits against labor. Since the 1930s, labor law has been largely governed by the National Labor Relations Act and the Taft-Hartley Act.

Criminal Conspiracies

In early U.S. history, the legal system treated unions as criminal conspiracies; later it recognized them as legitimate but treated strikes as criminal conspiracies; still later, it accepted some strikes as legal in principle but often treated the activities connected with them (picketing, boycotts, meetings, publications) as criminal conspiracies.

As early as 1806, the courts found Philadelphia cordwainers (shoemakers) guilty of a combination to raise their wages (a criminal conspiracy) and fined each member for the offense. Britain repealed all criminal conspiracy laws in 1824, but the first brief break for American labor did not come until 1842, when the Massachusetts Supreme Court in *Commonwealth v. Hunt* declared unions exempt from criminal conspiracy prosecution—yet allowed little room for them to do anything. Other courts disagreed with the ruling, and after the Civil War, especially during the turbulent 1880s and 1890s, conspiracy prosecutions against labor surged. These combined with a torrent of labor injunctions to seriously impede the rising movement of labor.

As late as 1894, a New Jersey court ruled in *Barr v. Essex Trades Council* that a strike, picketing, or boycott by employees constituted an unlawful conspiracy. In the early twentieth century, many courts agreed about labor's "general right" to strike but still declared many strikes illegal because of "the increase of power which a combination of citizens has over the individual citizen," as the Massachusetts Supreme Court held in 1906.[4] Thus, in many cases a combination of workers was still forbidden to do what one worker alone could legally do. And when courts disapproved of a strike's purpose, they still treated the strike as a violation of the conspiracy doctrine. When the use of conspiracy laws did decline, workers found it easier to form unions; what unions could legally *do* was another matter. In fact, most union activities were still forbidden by many courts well into the twentieth century, with such decisions often being based on presumably discarded criminal conspiracy doctrines and the newer antitrust laws.

Antitrust Actions

In 1890, Congress enacted the Sherman Antitrust Act and thus outlawed combinations in restraint of interstate trade and commerce. The act was aimed at giant corporate trusts, but the courts soon included labor in its coverage and thereby added the force of statutory law to the old conspiracy doctrine.[5] The Sherman Act gave courts a concrete statute to sink their teeth into, and labor had to wait more than forty years for relief from its grip.

The act was the first major federal statute affecting labor. Within three years of its passage, unions were prosecuted under interpretations of its coverage, and within seven years, it had been invoked against labor twelve times. Its first national use was in connection with the bitter American Railway Union strike of 1894, when the courts held that the union's strike on behalf of Pullman workers was a violation of the act and issued injunctions that broke the strike and led to the imprisonment of Eugene Debs and others.

After this devastating union defeat—by the combined forces of employers, the courts, and the U.S. Army—labor apparently "lost heart" for mass strikes, and the Sherman Act was little heard of until 1908 when the fateful Danbury Hatters decision was handed down by the U.S. Supreme Court and the union was fined $240,000 in damages for violating the act. This severe blow to labor and its slim treasury is said to have alarmed labor more than any previous court decision.

Between 1908 and 1914, the Sherman Act was invoked some twenty times against labor in lower courts, but the AFL's long and hitherto fruitless efforts to exempt labor from the Sherman Act had been gathering force, and in 1914, on the eve of war, the Clayton Antitrust Act was passed by a Democratic Congress. In a much quoted and abused passage, Section 6 of the act asserts that "the labor of a human being is not a commodity or article of commerce." This language, though abstruse and legalistic, appeared to free unions at last from antitrust prosecutions.

But the act was strewn with legal booby traps. Gompers proclaimed it the Magna Carta of the working people, but William Howard Taft, future Chief Justice of the U.S. Supreme Court and, as such, the chief interpreter of the act, disagreed. He said the labor sections of the act had no new meaning for labor.

In court interpretations, the act proved something worse than an empty promise. In the first twenty-four years after its passage, many more cases of antitrust violations (injunctions and criminal cases) were brought against labor than in the twenty-four preceding years. More than half of the injunctions requested were granted, and more than half of the criminal cases tried resulted in convictions, heavy fines, and/or long prison terms.[6] Moreover, the Clayton Act allowed *private* parties to obtain antitrust injunctions, whereas previously only the federal government could obtain them.

The trust-busting against unions peaked in the 1920s. In that decade, unions and unionists were charged in some seventy-two cases with violations of antitrust law, far more than in the three preceding decades. Most of the injunctions requested under the law were granted, and more than half of the criminal cases resulted in convictions and often long prison terms. The courts were on such a roll that even as late as 1937, despite the 1932 LaGuardia Act's rescue of labor from antitrust law, a U.S. district judge fined a union $712,100 in the Apex Hosiery case for violations of the Sherman Act.

Also in the 1920s, the Supreme Court issued eight major antitrust decisions affecting labor, compared to some three in the prior thirty years. In 1921, the Taft Supreme Court, reversing a lower court, held in the Duplex case that the machinist union's secondary boycott was in violation of the Clayton Act and that union actions were still subject to antitrust law. Several weeks later in the Tri-City case, the same court held that picketing was not exempted by the Clayton Act. The way was now paved for a rush of antitrust action.

In 1925, the Supreme Court ruled in the Coronado case that strikes designed to organize the unorganized parts of an industry were not exempt under the Clayton Act—a decision that stymied union organizing. In 1927, the Court ruled in the case of the *United Mine Workers v. Red Jacket* that the miners' union had violated the act in organizing West Virginia mines. Also in the 1920s, the attorney general enjoined the railway shopmen's union from conducting a national strike on the grounds that it violated antitrust law and constituted a communist threat to the nation.

Criminal syndicalist laws also did significant damage to labor's organizing efforts. Enacted in some twenty (mainly western) states between 1917 and 1920, they gave a major assist to the assault on the IWW in the 1920s. In those states, the mere advocacy of syndicalist ideas (interpreted by authorities as pro-union or class struggle ideas), either orally or in writing, was treated as a felony. The language of the laws was ambiguous, but they were upheld by all the state courts and finally by the Supreme Court. And though the IWW's "syndicalist" interests in worker-owned industry (or producer cooperatives), and its advocacy of them, seem hardly felonious, the IWW was effectively outlawed by these statutes.

Injunctions

The labor injunction (a court order prohibiting various union activities) came into prominent use during the uprisings of 1877, and the unrest of the following years offered many more opportunities for its use. By 1886, the AFL had been reorganized, and the Knights of Labor had reached a peak of more than 700,000 members. This gathering of labor forces caused a general alarm, and the courts responded with labor injunctions that almost overwhelmed both mainstream and left-wing unionism. State courts responded most eagerly to employer requests for injunctions, as appointments to those courts were largely local affairs, especially in the early days, and a judge's job and livelihood depended on the goodwill of local employers.[7] In 1896, Democrats raised the slogan "Government by injunction" to inveigh against the practice, and in virtually every state and federal legislative session, anti-injunction bills were consistently introduced and as consistently rejected.

Injunctions were a major deterrent to the rise of national unionism after the 1880s. During the half-century 1880–1930, 1,845 labor injunctions were issued by federal and state courts—half of them (921) during the 1920s.[8] These proceedings included a 1919 federal injunction in the miners' strike, the injunction issued in the huge railway shopmen's strike of 1922, and those issued during the United Mine Workers' efforts to organize West Virginia and Kentucky mines.

Neither statutes nor precedents could impede the injunctive power of the courts. With this potent writ, a judge had imperial powers—lawmaker, prosecutor, judge, and jury—and could create his own criminal code, making criminal such lawful and moral acts as walking on a public highway or talking and preaching.[9]

The Clayton Act had promised relief from the injunction, but that promise was thwarted by court interpretation. Among other decisions, the Supreme Court authorized injunctions against strikes over grievances, holding that "employees may not ordinarily use collective action to prosecute their grievances, no matter how deeply they are injured by management's actions," and declared that injunctions may be issued even "against strikes provoked by potentially life-threatening coal mine safety hazards."[10]

The injunction became the employer's favorite legal weapon because of its speed of delivery and immediate restraint of the often irrepressible forward motion of a strike. Injunctions could be obtained by employers appearing alone in court, without union representatives being present, and preliminary restraining orders could be issued that delayed strikes long enough to break them. The injunction's real purpose, some people claim, was to circumvent the right of unionists to jury trials, as juries could not be counted on to convict. "Individual" injunctions against union leaders were also issued, but after a time these were replaced by "blanket" injunctions.

The purview of the injunction was extended beyond equity claims to the restraint of "crimes," but its use denied the accused such criminal court protections as a jury trial, the right to confront witnesses, right of appeal, and release on bail. Such "criminal" injunctions were used against Debs in the Pullman strike of 1894, against people accused of violating California's "criminal syndicalist" laws, and in numerous other cases. Injunctions were used to *make* law rather than simply enforce it, to outlaw what legislatures had declared legal as well as what they had not declared illegal. Even where picketing was perfectly legal, for example, courts repeatedly enjoined unions from engaging in it.

Anti-injunction laws were passed in many places, but the courts nullified them. In 1903, for instance, the California legislature voted to abolish the labor injunction, but in 1906 and 1909, the state supreme court ruled that the law did not apply to "wrongful acts" of labor, which to the courts could mean any kind of union activity.[11] In 1913, an Arizona law forbade the use of injunctions against striking, picketing, and boycotting, and the law was upheld by the state supreme court, but the U.S. Supreme Court declared the law unconstitutional. The next year the Massachusetts Supreme Court declared unconstitutional a law that limited use of the injunction to cases of irreparable damage to property in labor disputes.

The U.S. Supreme Court also consistently upheld injunctions issued by lower courts. In 1914, an Illinois court enjoined striking steelworkers from "picketing in every form" and termed the pickets outsiders and "wanton intermeddlers." The decision was upheld by the Supreme Court, which declared that since picketing is not peaceful, by its very nature, it is therefore unlawful.

Criminal Prosecutions

Criminal prosecutions were not a part of labor law, yet they, too, have had a serious impact on organizing and union growth, one that has yet to be assessed. The arrest records in just a few strikes of the 1920s tell the story. In a 1926 New York garment strike, police arrested 7,500 in the first fifteen weeks on criminal charges; in the same year, they arrested 884 New York fur strikers, of whom 477 were convicted; in a 1928 textile strike, police arrested 2,000; in another textile strike in 1929, they arrested 300 in a single day.[12] Charges ranged from felonies (murder, riot, assault, criminal libel, unlawful assembly, malicious mischief, sedition) to misdemeanors (trespass, loitering, disorderly conduct, assembling without a permit, disturbing the peace). In Idaho, Montana, Colorado, West Virginia, and other states where the national guard actively policed strikes, people were arrested without any charge except "military necessity" and jailed for long periods.[13]

One criminal case illustrates how such prosecutions were conducted. John Lawson, a leader of the Colorado coal strike of 1913–1914, was indicted for murder by a grand jury. Much of the jury had been handpicked by the local sheriff, half of the members were closely identified with the coal employers, and one was the private secretary of a coal mining president. Lawson was convicted of murder and sentenced to life in prison. Later affidavits showed that jurors who might have voted for acquittal had been intimidated and threatened by the bailiff until they reached a guilty verdict. It was also found that before his appointment, the judge had worked for coal companies involved in the strike. The conviction was reversed, but only after Lawson had spent many months in prison.[14]

Legal and Illegal Employer Practices

The law upheld hostile employer acts but punished those of labor; according to historian Irving Bernstein, no other advanced nation in the world has conducted industrial relations with "such defiance of the criminal law."[15] No laws protected unionists against labor spies or strikebreakers. Some states had "Pinkerton laws" preventing the importation of armed guards from other states, but those laws were easily evaded. The use of private police was legal everywhere, and in Pennsylvania, Maryland, and South Carolina, private police could, by statute, be deputized as officers of the law. Company towns and their control of public officials and all aspects of the lives of the townspeople were perfectly legal.

Discharging an employee for union activities, a crippling tactic that discouraged activism and deprived unions of their leaders, was legal and used unstintingly by employers. Some jurisdictions did make such discharges illegal, but the courts routinely invalidated those laws. In the early 1900s, a federal law prohibiting such discharges by interstate carriers was passed, but in 1908, the U.S. Supreme Court declared even that law unconstitutional.

The law permitted an employer to coerce or threaten employees who wanted a union, discharge them if they joined, refuse to deal with a union, organize a company union and force employees to join it, and hire detectives to join, spy on, disrupt, and report on union activities. Under such circumstances, legal scholar William M. Leiserson has concluded: "To speak of labor's right to organize was clearly a misuse of terms." Employees could try to organize, but whether or not they succeeded depended on the relative economic strength of the organizations of employer and employee.[16]

The "yellow-dog contract," a written contract forbidding workers to join unions, was legal, fully enforced by the courts, and a potent weapon in repressing unionism. The penalty for workers who violated such a contract was dismissal, and as the contract was legally binding, unions could be enjoined from organizing workers who had signed such contracts. Unions pressed with some success for anti–yellow-dog laws, but the Supreme Court struck down these laws until passage of the Norris-LaGuardia Act in 1932.

By the end of the 1920s, some 1,250,000 workers had signed yellow-dog contracts, more than sixty injunctions had been issued to enforce them, and in West Virginia such contracts covered almost the whole mining industry.[17] Unions found it almost impossible to organize, and injunctions made them virtually helpless. In Britain and other places, no counterpart of the yellow-dog contract impeded union growth.

Judicial Attitudes

Judges tend to be very conservative about unions, John Fitch wrote in *The Causes of Industrial Unrest*, published in 1924. Most of them come from the employing class and are outside the ranks of wage earners. In law school and after, most have no personal contact with the harsher realities of working-class life, and many leave law school with only a vague concept about unionism and much doubt about its legality. They may enter politics to further their law practice, or they may enter corporate law and become imbued with the employer's point of view before becoming judges.

Their background and training make them slow to recognize the social changes that require changes in the law, and they are likely "to view with suspicion the attempt of men to do in concert what they may legally do as individuals." Their attitudes are also shaped by individualistic concepts and the idea, deeply imbedded in the law, that both parties in a labor dispute are individuals of equal power, even though the employer may be a billion-dollar corporation and the worker an illiterate, immigrant laborer.[18]

Fitch had numerous examples on which to base his portrait. For example, Justice Van Siclen of the New York Supreme Court declared in 1921 that the courts must always stand as the representatives of capital and captains of industry, devoted to the idea of individual initiative, protective of property and person, and strongly opposed to the nationalization of industry.[19] Also, another New York Supreme Court justice, again in 1921, noted that the defendants in a picketing case had alleged that they were peacefully picketing, but "Why picket at all? Why not leave plaintiff alone as it desires and thereby permit the pickets to employ themselves at some useful and commendable occupation where they may do a real man's work and earn a laborer's honest wage?"[20]

In yet another 1921 case, the Massachusetts Supreme Court said that if peaceful measures fail to settle a labor dispute, the employer may reasonably expect that the union will damage his property; that it will try to injure him in his business, even to his ruin, if it can; and that it will use "vile and opprobrious epithets" and actual or threatened violence to keep people from entering his employ.[21] The union in this case, as the court itself stated, had engaged in no personal violence or injury to property.

The United Kingdom Contrast

In Britain, the Combination Acts of 1799 and 1800 declared unions to be criminal conspiracies, but these laws had little serious impact, and Parliament—far more benign than the American courts—repealed them in 1824, at which time the right of workers to form unions was conceded by law.[22] The legal status of unions remained circumscribed, but most "remained untroubled by the law" and serious legal abuse was more occasional than normal.[23]

By 1865, British unions were generally accepted as legitimate despite continuing employer complaints. In 1871, the law exempted unions from prosecution for "restraint of trade" and made collective bargaining agreements legally enforceable; laws of 1875, 1906, 1913, and 1945 further extended labor's rights. In the United States, the rights of unions were not legalized in the British or general European sense until the National Labor Relations Act of 1935.

A major slippage occurred in Britain when the Taff-Vale court decision of 1901 held unions financially liable for all employer losses occasioned by union activities. Because Taff-Vale's threat to meager union treasuries endangered union survival, labor prevailed upon Parliament to nullify the decision in the Trade Disputes Act of 1906. British labor experienced other legal setbacks, but its basic rights were recognized by law and practice long before they were recognized in the United States.

In the United States, exemption from antitrust prosecution did not come until the 1932 Norris-LaGuardia Act; by contrast, similar British laws were passed in 1871. British labor strenuously objected to the Industrial Relations Act of 1971, and it was repealed three years after enactment; American labor still objects strenuously to the Taft-Hartley Act of 1947 but has been unable to change it.

Court injunctions have proved especially disabling to American unionism, but in Britain, only two restraining orders against unions have been issued during the long history of the British counterparts of the U.S. courts of equity, which issue injunctions, and both were overturned within a few years. By contrast, U.S. courts have issued thousands of injunctions and restraining orders against unions and are still issuing them despite protests against the practice.[24]

*   *   *

In summary, the unique challenges to American labor have included the tendency of American employers to make their own laws, the virtual absence of federal protection of unionism until well into the twentieth century, the consequent power of the courts in determining labor's rights, the extensive use of court injunctions to circumscribe most union activity, the authority assumed by the U.S. Supreme Court to interpret the Constitution, the Court's use of that authority to strike down prolabor laws, and the abiding hostility of most courts, especially the Supreme Court, to the very idea of unionism. Indeed, the heavy-handed conservatism of the legal system led many unions to agree with Gompers's words, "We are not in an ideal world, we are in the bitter struggles of an unjust society."[25]

6

Steel: 1892 and 1919

WITHOUT STEEL, industrialism as we know it would not have been possible, as steel shaped the machine tools needed for industrial production and provided the basic materials for the modern age. Steel is more versatile than iron—hard enough to support skyscrapers and soft enough to be bent by hand or even spun into thread—and over time, almost every industrial item has come to be made of steel, machined by steel, or transported by steel.

Steel production, profitable and large-scale, also became an early target of mass industrial unionism, and the most memorable early effort to organize steel occurred at the Homestead, Pennsylvania, plant of the Carnegie Steel Company. The lockout and strike at Homestead in 1892 is of special interest because it points up how imbalanced the forces involved in labor struggles have been, how readily employers have used the armed forces of mercenaries and government troops, and yet how determined and unified labor responses have been.

In Britain, unions took root in the steel industry in the 1880s, grew steadily, and by the time of World War I had successfully organized much of the industry. In 1890, the density of American steel unionism rivaled the British, much as the country's steel production at least equaled that of the British. But in 1892, at Homestead, American steel unionism took an almost fatal turn for the worse, declined thereafter, and reemerged only in the 1930s.

A second major effort to unionize steel was made in 1919, when the most ambitious industrywide strike ever conducted by an AFL union was attempted, this time directed at Carnegie's successor, the United States Steel Corporation. But steel unionism had been so weakened by Homestead, and then by the determination of U.S. Steel to keep unionism out, that once again the strike ended in a bitter defeat.

DEFEAT OF INDUSTRIAL UNIONISM AT HOMESTEAD

At the time of Homestead, British unions and workers were at least as fractured by ethnic splits and disputed union jurisdictions as the Amer-

ican, and the British were no more organized along either unskilled or
vertical (industrial) lines. Nor was British labor much more directed
toward independent political action at that point; nor does much evidence
exist to support claims that the British working class leaned more toward
the political left. In general, AFL unionism was only an ocean removed
from British unionism, just as the American steel industry was a kind
of New World extension of the British. Samuel Gompers and Andrew
Carnegie were both British immigrants—and ironically now lie in nearly
adjoining graves in Sleepy Hollow, New York—and the pragmatism that
characterized the AFL was based essentially on the British model. Thus,
the internal union factors—the actors, ideologies, strategies—were similar;
it was the external factors—the roles played by employers and government—that differed.[1]

Labor could hardly have done much better at Homestead. Skilled
workers were locked out, but their demands were fully supported by a
strike of semi- and unskilled workers. The strike lasted more than four
months without any serious defection in union ranks. It was finally
broken because first a small army of Pinkertons and then a large
contingent of national guardsmen intervened on Carnegie's side. The
outcome was largely the result of the Carnegie Steel Company's dominance of the industry, its political connections, and its bitter hostility
to unionism. Despite having written kind and statesmanlike words about
unions, Carnegie and his deputy Henry Frick decided early on to break
the Homestead union and they did so, operating an "open shop" in
their mills thereafter.

Carnegie and Steel

Carnegie built his fortune on railroads and steel. As a youth, he worked
for the Pennsylvania Railroad, and in an early venture into labor relations
informed his mentor, Thomas Scott, about a threatened strike of railroad
men; as a result, Scott dismissed the union activists and the strike was
aborted.[2] Before the Civil War, though a professed pacifist, Carnegie
"vociferously argued for force to bring the seceding states back into the
union," and his voice was even stronger than that of most northern
businessmen.[3] When drafted at the age of twenty-eight to serve in the
war, Carnegie bought his way out by paying a new Irish immigrant
$850 to replace him. He invested in booming war industries and, as
his biographer writes, became so absorbed in making money that he
lost interest in the war itself.

After the war, he resigned from the railroad with a small fortune
and turned to iron and steel. His first steel mill, the Edgar Thomson,

built rails for the railroads, and by 1880 it was producing more than twice as much steel as its largest British competitor. Its manager, Captain William Jones, had sharp differences with Carnegie over labor relations but convinced him for a time that good wages, fair treatment, and a three-turn, eight-hour shift was better for the workers and for company profits than the twelve-hour shift. After Jones's death and replacement by Charles Schwab, later the first head of U.S. Steel, the twelve-hour shift was reinstated on Carnegie's orders, and enlightened labor policies were abandoned.

Carnegie's quest for coke for his blast furnaces led him to acquire a controlling share in Henry Frick's coke works and Frick's services as his chief executive. He finally completed the integration of his steel works in 1896, and at that time, he was a leader of both industry and industrial relations and probably the most powerful man of his era.

At its birth in mid-1892, only months before the Homestead lockout, Carnegie Steel was the largest steel company in the world, able to produce quantities equal to over half the total amount of steel produced in Britain. Company mills clustered around the vast bituminous coal beds and limestone deposits that ran from downtown Pittsburgh along two navigable rivers, the Allegheny and the Monongahela, which meet to form the Ohio River. This area was close to the Great Lakes ports from which Lake Superior iron ore was shipped and transported by rail to the Carnegie mills to be converted by coke and limestone into steel. The mills that stretched along the Monongahela Valley, including Homestead, were the cradle of the American steel industry.

At the time of Carnegie's purchase of the Homestead plant—built on a farm ironically named Amity Homestead—it was the largest and most modern steel mill in the country. At the time of the purchase, six lodges of the Amalgamated Association of Iron, Steel, and Tin Workers (the Amalgamated), an AFL affiliate, existed in the plant, and Homestead had a record of labor unrest. Its former owner had required all workers to sign yellow-dog contracts, but when nobody signed, he had ordered a lockout and wage reduction. Aided by a thriving steel market, the Amalgamated had won the dispute, but a recession followed, labor unrest grew, and the company sold out to Carnegie.

In 1876, three craft unions, with a total membership of 3,000, had merged to form the Amalgamated; by 1892, membership had grown eightfold. At its inception it was a union of craftsmen, but each convention included new classes of workers, and two years before the Homestead strike, the list of eligible members simply included all people working in and around the mills, except laborers, who could join at the discretion of the subordinate lodges.[4] As in one of the major British steel unions,

British Steel Smelters, large numbers of lesser-skilled workers were now eligible for union membership.

Strike

Although the mills were still highly profitable, despite the recession of 1892, Carnegie and Frick agreed to rid the mills of unionism, but they disagreed on tactics. Carnegie's initial approach was more direct and assaultive than Frick's. He proposed that a notice be posted in the mills saying: "As the vast majority of our employees are Non-Union, the Firm has decided that the minority must give place to the majority. These works therefore will be necessarily Non-Union after the expiration of the present contract agreement."[5] This blunt proposal contrasted with the gentle words he had written some six years before, "The right of working men to combine and to form trade-unions is no less sacred than the right of the manufacturer to enter into associations and conferences with his fellows,"[6] but they were in keeping with what he wrote only a few months later, "Rioters assembling in numbers and marching to pillage will be remorselessly shot down."[7]

Frick felt that Carnegie's notice would be too provocative at Homestead and decided instead to offer the union terms it could not possibly accept, thereby putting it on the offensive and softening public opinion in the company's favor. Wage rates based on steel *prices*, which were declining, would be substituted for wage rates based on *tonnage* production, and wages would be effectively cut 20–60 percent for both the skilled and the less skilled. Carnegie approved the plan and left for a remote corner of Scotland where only messages from Frick and top staff could reach him.

Anticipating a strike, Frick's first act was to build a ten-foot-high, three-mile-long wooden fence around the entire mill, running down to the river approaches. The fence was pierced with holes every twenty-five feet for gun emplacements and topped with barbed wire. Behind the fence were guard towers with searchlights beamed in all directions. Two days before the union contract expired, Frick suddenly shut down the open hearths and the armor plate mill and locked out 800 skilled men from their jobs. The next month, 3,000 mechanics and laborers in the plant, who were not Amalgamated members, voted to strike in support of the locked-out workers. A few days after this walkout, Frick issued discharge slips to all employees and released a public statement that the mill would henceforth operate as a nonunion shop. The union selected a committee to lead the strike, guarded the mill and its approaches to prevent strikebreakers from entering, and devised signals to enable a thousand strike supporters to gather at a trouble spot in five minutes' time.

Frick tried to mobilize a hundred sheriff's deputies to protect both plant and strikebreakers, but when volunteers could not be found in the community, the sheriff sent along what he had—twelve men from his office force, who were intercepted by strikers and sent back to Pittsburgh by boat. Frick had already won a few strikes with the help of hired Pinkerton agents and the state militia and planned to do so again, even though enlisting such strikebreakers was an unpardonable act according to Carnegie. Frick had negotiated with the Pinkerton agency before the strike began and had agreed to pay for 300 of its agents, whom he directed to arm themselves and move by boat up the Monongahela to Homestead.

The agents were sighted by strikers at 4:00 A.M. about a mile below Homestead; the alarm sounded, and men, women, and children ran to warn them against landing. When the boat's gangplank was lowered and the agents started down it, a shot came from an undetermined source, and the Pinkerton men fired into the crowd, hitting several people. Strikers returned the fire, and the agents tried to retreat but their boat had steamed away leaving only their barge. A thirteen-hour battle ensued, during which three Pinkerton agents and seven workers were killed and many more people were wounded. The day after the battle, strikers repaired all damage to the fence. The plant itself was never touched, nor was any attempt made to damage or seize it. The union had volunteered to guard the plant, in place of mercenaries, but its offer had been refused.

At this point, the union appeared to have won a clear victory. The strike had held, and the Pinkerton agents had been routed. But as a result of pressure from Frick and other powerful sources, the governor of Pennsylvania reluctantly sent 8,000 national guardsmen to Homestead, and martial law was declared. Guardsmen entered in early morning, while the people of Homestead still slept, and took up positions on every block in the town and on surrounding hills.

Protected by guardsmen with fixed bayonets, the company prepared to bring in strikebreakers, taking cots and food into the mill and erecting a hundred houses inside the fence. Frick notified the locked-out workers that those who had not interfered with company management of the plant could return to work. None did. Frick moved in boatloads of strikebreakers under guard protection, and within a week the plant reopened with 700 men eating and sleeping inside the plant. Sympathy strikes were called by the Amalgamated at two other union mills, but the company shut those plants and said they would henceforth be nonunion shops. In a much quoted pre-Homestead statement, Carnegie had written that "the employer of labor will find it much more to his interest, wherever possible, to allow his works to remain idle and await the result of a dispute than to employ a class of men that can be induced to take the place of other men who have stopped work. Neither the best men as men, nor the best men as workers, are thus to be obtained."[8] At Homestead, those words were not heeded.

The company pressed charges, and a grand jury returned 167 charges against unionists for murder, conspiracy, and aggravated riot. It returned no charges against the company agents, who had conducted most of the violence. Union activists, leaders, and funds were tied up in defense of the charges, and the press eagerly labeled unionists "murderers." The chief justice of the state supreme court had twenty-seven strike committee members arrested on charges of "treason against the state," crippling the strike's leadership. Also damaging to the Amalgamated's public standing, an anarchist, Alexander Berkman, who was in no way connected to the strike or the union, shot and wounded Frick.

The union's leader, Hugh O'Donnell, was charged with murder, but he fled to New York and spoke to Whitelaw Reid, publisher of the *New York Tribune* and a Republican leader. Reid was troubled, as were most Republicans, about the adverse publicity the strike gave big business in a presidential election year. At Reid's request, O'Donnell composed a letter to Carnegie saying that the Amalgamated wanted only a chance to negotiate with the company, nothing more, but Carnegie's position was clear. He had wired Frick the day after the Pinkerton battle: "All anxiety gone since you stand firm. Never employ one of these rioters. Let grass grow over the works. Must not fail now. You will win easily next trial."[9] He now wired Frick that Reid's proposal was probably not worth considering but that it was useful in showing the Amalgamated's distress. "Use your own discretion about terms and starting," he wired, "Andrew Carnegie solid. H. C. Frick forever!"[10] Reid then sent someone to talk with Frick, and the emissary reported back that Frick had emphatically declined to settle with the union, even if President Harrison and the whole Republican leadership were to ask him to do so. He would "fight this thing to the bitter end" and would "never recognize the Union, never, never!"[11]

In the end efforts to jail unionists were frustrated because juries failed to convict those brought to trial, but the union was crushed anyhow, by court costs, the time consumed in defending itself, and the movement of strikebreakers into the mill. After more than four months, the mechanics and laborers voted to return to work, and three days later, when the Amalgamated voted to lift the ban on returning to work, only 200 of the 800 original members were present for the vote. Frick wired Carnegie: "Our victory is complete. I do not think we will ever have any labor trouble again. . . . We have taught our employees a lesson that they will never forget."[12] Skilled men who returned to work after the strike found their rates cut by more than half, and the twelve-hour day, seven-day week still prevailed in the industry.

Carnegie and Frick blamed each other for Homestead. Carnegie claimed that his striking Homestead workers had sent him a wire saying, "Kind master, tell us what you wish us to do and we will do it for you." The fantasy was perhaps inspired by the belief that American workers "loved" their masters, but visiting Homestead after the strike one European observed, "The managers represented 'Triumphant Democracy,' but nearly all that I saw while with the men might be described under the title of 'Feudalism Restored,' "[13] The public protest over Homestead is credited with defeating Carnegie's candidate in the presidential election, Benjamin Harrison. The victor, Democrat Grover Cleveland, was destined to play his own notorious role in the great strike at Pullman (in which Carnegie was a major stockholder) several years later.

British Response

The U.S. press overwhelmingly sided with Carnegie; the British press did not. The arch-Tory journal *St. James's Gazette* editorialized: "A strike is one thing, and we know what a strike is; but armed private mercenaries are another, and they are a thing which in this effete old country we emphatically would not tolerate." The lesson of liberty England can still teach is that "freedom can only exist where all rights are safely secured. Mr. Andrew Carnegie has preached to us upon 'Triumphant Democracy,' he has lectured us upon the rights and duties of wealth. . . . It is indeed a wholesome piece of satire."[14] The London *Times* also condemned the company's actions and insisted that the use of a private police force should be neither "permitted nor required in a civilized community. Such a force, at the disposal of any capitalist . . . is a standing provocation to the labouring class."[15]

The *Journal* in Dunfermline, Scotland, Carnegie's own birthplace, sided with the union on the critical issue of the terms of contract, claiming that it had a perfect right to refuse wage reductions,[16] and the *Edinburgh Dispatch* said, "We on this side of the Atlantic, . . . may well feel thankful that neither our capitalists nor our labourers have any inclination to imitate the methods which prevail in the land of 'Triumphant Democracy.' "[17] The Glasgow Trades Council, which had once cheered Carnegie for his noble words about labor, now declared him a new Judas Iscariot, and the Labour Representation League and the London

Trade Council urged all British workers to refuse any more of Carnegie's philanthropic gifts.

Aftermath

With its defeat at Homestead, the Amalgamated lost control of the three giant Carnegie plants in the Pittsburgh area, without which a national steel agreement could not be reached. Carnegie had conducted total war on the union and had won a total victory: The union never reappeared in his mills.

Carnegie's fortunes contrasted with those of two Irishmen who were most associated with the Homestead union: Hugh O'Donnell, a skilled roller in the mill and chairman of the strike advisory committee, and John McLuckie, mayor of Homestead. Carnegie became one of the world's richest men and an internationally celebrated philanthropist and advocate of peace and freedom. McLuckie—mayor, skilled worker, union activist— was found a few years after the strike working as an unskilled laborer in a Mexican mine. Carnegie offered him charity, but he refused. O'Donnell was finally cleared of murder charges that had been levied against him, but he was blacklisted in the steel industry and unable to find a job in his trade. Other union leaders at Homestead lost their homes and were also blacklisted from jobs in steel.

Hamlin Garland visited Homestead in 1894 and saw a mean and squalid town, masses of worker sheds dotted with blackened smokestacks and covered with clouds of smoke, and above them dingy rows of tenements fronting on sunken, broken sidewalks and streets paved with yellow mud. Through them slouched pale, lean men in garments grimy with mill grease, discouraged and sullen, as were the men he saw in towns throughout the Pennsylvania hills.[18]

Carnegie and Frick finally locked horns, in a scandalous and symbolic conflict over power and money—what price Frick would charge Carnegie for coke, and who was the real boss of the Carnegie works—and Carnegie won. As majority stockholder in both the Frick and Carnegie companies, he pushed Frick out of the chairmanship of both, then forced him to sell his shares in both companies for book rather than actual value. Although Frick and Carnegie had easily disposed of some fifteen other partners in the same way, Frick now sued and forced a settlement. The two exchanged few words thereafter. "For the first time," one biographer writes, "Carnegie's authority had been openly challenged, and his response had been ruthless in its totality."[19] Even the conservative *New York Times* expressed shock at the revelation during the trial of the enormous profits made by Carnegie's tariff-protected, and hence publicly subsidized, operations.[20]

When J. P. Morgan purchased the Carnegie works to create U.S. Steel—which made Carnegie the major shareholder of that company, the largest capitalized company in the history of American manufacturing at the time—Morgan reportedly congratulated Carnegie on being the richest man in the world. But Keir Hardie, a leading Scottish socialist, wrote that Carnegie appeared to think he could square his account with humanity "by agreeing that eight percent of the swindler's grab shall be returned to the community from whom it has been taken by force and fraud, as a kind of hush money after the robber is dead,"[21] and in reviewing Carnegie's essay on the gospel of wealth, theologian William Jewett Tucker, later president of Dartmouth College, wrote that he could "conceive of no greater mistake . . . than that of trying to make charity do the work of justice."[22]

Carnegie's view of economic justice was revealed in his message to youth during the great depression of 1896. It was because he knew "how sweet and happy and pure the home of honest poverty is" that he sympathized with the rich boy. To abolish "honest, industrious, self-denying poverty" was to destroy the virtues that "enable our race to reach a still higher civilization."[23] Carnegie himself lived lavishly, and his philanthropies immortalized his name. But his gifts to workers were penurious, and his legacy to labor was the abject defeat of industrial unionism in steel. Yet Carnegie was probably among the best, not the worst, of the industrialists with whom labor has contended.

THE GREAT STEEL STRIKE OF 1919

The second major bid to organize steel resulted in what came to be known as "the great steel strike of 1919." This major convulsion in American labor history involved more than 365,000 workers, or some two-thirds of the steel industry's work force, and resulted in twenty-two deaths, numerous injuries, and another major loss for industrial unionism.

Unlike Homestead, the 1919 strike was industry-wide and included almost every nonunion iron and steel mill in the country, but its principal adversary was the largest industrial power yet assembled, the United States Steel Corporation, or "the Corporation." Organized along semi-industrial rather than simple craft lines, the striking unions included not only craftsmen but also multitudes of unskilled workers. At Homestead, the unskilled had fully supported the locked-out skilled workers; in 1919, they engaged in the strike as union members.

The strike also featured a new employer strategy, or a more vigorous variation of an old one—radical baiting of the union. Backed by the press, legal sanctions, and public and private armed forces, the combination again crushed steel unionism. Some historians dwell on the union's own complicity in its defeat, but the strike was, in its execution, a remarkable success story. Financed on a shoestring budget, it halted or slowed production in almost the entire iron and steel industry, and a wild mixture of immigrants stood solidly behind it—without initiating the predicted violence—for almost fourteen weeks.

On the initiative of J. P. Morgan and Charles Schwab, U.S. Steel, the "combination of combinations," was formed in 1901, as the world's largest steel industry, controlling at its birth some 65 percent of the nation's steel capacity. Because the Corporation's share of the market was vast and growing, its price-fixing practices became a matter of public concern. During the 1907–1911 recession, for instance, Judge Gary, Corporation head, held dinners for leaders of the entire steel industry for the purpose of preventing price competition. Such conduct became so gross that the federal courts finally charged U.S. Steel with price fixing and demanded its dissolution. The war intervened, however, and the case was not decided until 1920. By that time, the trusts had more influence than the trustbusters, and the Supreme Court decided by a four-to-three vote against dissolution.

Thus, when the great steel strike began, U.S. Steel was a virtual monopoly, under threat of dissolution, and bulging with war profits. In 1913, its profits had been $81 million; in 1916, $272 million; in 1917, $493 million.[24] In just two years, 1916 and 1917, the Corporation's net profits had exceeded its total capital stock by $20 million.

Wages, Hours, Conditions

Despite the Corporation's phenomenal success, most steelworkers in the Monongahela Valley still worked twelve hours a day, many of them worked seven days a week, and most earned from forty-two to forty-eight cents an hour. Despite an unprecedented ability to pay (or perhaps because of it), the Corporation adamantly opposed postwar improvements in wages or conditions. The war had given labor a brief leg up, and the Corporation seemed determined to put it down again.

Basic union recognition was the chief strike issue, but demands included better wages, hours, and conditions, all of which had worsened since Homestead. The twelve-hour day was standard; most men got only rare Sundays off, some only one every six months. Housing was squalid and overcrowded, usually only two rooms to a family, with four or five sleeping in a single room. William Z. Foster, an ill-fated strike leader, wrote that steelworkers "found themselves, for the most part, crowded like cattle into the filthy hovels that ordinarily constitute the greater part of the steel towns. Tuberculosis ran riot among them; infant mortality was far above normal. Though several increases in wages were granted after the war began, these have been offset by the terrific rise in the cost of living. If the war has brought any betterment in the living conditions of the steel workers, it cannot be seen with the naked eye."[25]

Foster's book and reports by the distinguished Commission of Inquiry of the Interchurch World Movement (a group of religious leaders) are among the best documentary sources about the strike and its causes— along with the record of Senate Education and Labor Committee hearings and a review by Colston Warne.[26] The commission reported that most unskilled steel workers earned less than enough for the average family's minimum subsistence and that "extreme congestion and unsanitary living conditions, prevalent in most Pennsylvania steel communities, were largely due to underpayment of semi-skilled and common labor."[27] The long hours of work made the steelworkers' lives "one constant round of toil," said Foster. "They have no family life, no opportunity for education or even for recreation; for their few hours of liberty are spoiled by the ever-present fatigue."[28] The twelve-hour day, the commission said, "made any attempt at 'Americanization' or other civic or individual development for one-half of all immigrant steel workers arithmetically impossible."[29]

The twelve-hour day was required by production needs, employers claimed, but the adoption of the eight-hour day in various places (England, the Pacific Coast, several other American steel companies, etc.), plus expert claims that production actually improved with the eight-hour day, convinced the commission that the twelve-hour day was "not a metallurgical necessity" and that "steel masters are not caught in the grip of their gigantic machinery."[30] In 1919, the average compulsory work week in American steel mills was twenty hours longer than in British ones, and American hours were longer than they had been in 1914 or even 1910.[31]

In the steel mills, Foster wrote, "the men are speeded up to such a degree that only the youngest and strongest can stand it. At forty the average steel worker is played out. The work, in itself extremely dangerous, is made still more so by the employers' failure to adopt the necessary safety devices. Many a man has gone to his death through the wanton neglect of the companies to provide safeguarding appliances that they would have been compelled to install were the unions still in the plants."[32] Steel is a man killer, the commission concluded, and steelworkers are chiefly "attendants of gigantic machines. The steel business tends to become, in the owners' eyes, mainly the machines. . . . These masters are attended by sweating servants whose job is to get close enough to work but to keep clear enough to save limb and life. It is concededly not an ideal industry for men fatigued by long hours."[33]

The Organizing Drive, Strike Prelude

The central strike issue, on which all others hung, was union recognition. The Corporation's arbitrary controls extended to all job conditions and resulted in daily grievances that could not be resolved; "lacking were any above-board means of learning how the decreed conditions affected the workers."[34] The trigger for the strike was Judge Gary's repeated refusal to even talk with worker representatives about their grievances.

After the defeat of a 1909 steel strike, the AFL had marked steel for unionization, but employer opposition "was unrelenting and formidable."[35] When the War Labor Board finally eased the way for steel unionism by pressing employers to negotiate, the 1918 AFL convention endorsed an organizing drive. Sam Gompers and later John Fitzpatrick (Chicago AFL head and mainspring of the drive) served as chairmen, William Z. Foster was secretary-treasurer, and twenty-four AFL unions, representing some 2 million workers, pledged support for the drive.

Fitzpatrick and Foster were fresh from a Chicago victory in which combined craft unions had organized the packinghouse industry and won an eight-hour day with ten hours' pay; they were thus the natural choices to lead the steel drive. John Fitzpatrick, an "honest, unassuming Irishman represented the best in American organized labor," David Brody writes; "schooled in the craft-oriented, pragmatic tradition of American labor, Fitzpatrick nevertheless harbored a deep sympathy for the immigrant workingmen of Chicago."[36] Foster was regarded by Fitzpatrick and Gompers as a man of some oratorical and organizing skill, but he was plagued during the strike by a pamphlet on syndicalism written in his youth. Long after the Socialist Party split that produced the American Communist Party, Foster became the latter party's general secretary. In 1919, however, as Gompers believed, Foster was clearly a labor radical, not a communist.

Organizing the Drive

The steel drive began in 1918 under the supervision of the AFL's National Committee for Organizing Iron and Steel Workers, made up of one representative from each cooperating AFL union. Scarce union resources limited the drive at first to the Chicago area, but the drive soon became national and its offices were moved to Pittsburgh, the heart of the steel industry.

Pittsburgh could not be won in a frontal attack, so the plan was to flank it with unionized posts. Much of the drive's success could be attributed, according to Foster, to a "thoroughly systematic" strategy that included two types of organizers among the over 125 assigned to the drive: the stationary organizers, who were recruited from the AFL, the United Mine Workers (UMW), and from among newly hired workers—who were the backbone of the drive, working wholly for the National Committee—and the floating organizers of the cooperating unions, who mainly attended to their newly formed locals. Those new locals formed central labor councils that were invaluable in the drive, according to Foster, because they "knit the movement together and strengthened the weaker unions. They also inculcated the indispensable conception of solidarity along industrial lines and prevented irresponsible strike action by over-zealous single trades."[37]

The drive was semi-industrial in that it was led by an organizing committee that resembled the later CIO. It differed from the CIO in that new union members were assigned, by trade or job, to new locals of the appropriate cooperating unions rather than to a single steelworkers' union. The appropriate AFL union, the Amalgamated Association, had been ravaged at Homestead and elsewhere and was too weak to dominate the drive, so other strong AFL unions had to be included. There was no "one big industrial union," but there was the next thing to it: a central strike committee, local secretaries and organizers who were in full charge, and locally organized central labor bodies of the cooperating unions. The structure was not as integrated as the CIO's, but neither was it the affliction that some people claim.

Stumbling Blocks

In early steel organizing, a few AFL organizers had been sent out in response to steelworker requests, but these organizers had been arrested and driven out of town. Almost everywhere, locals told organizers it was impossible to organize in their towns, thus illustrating, said Foster, "the villainous reputation the steel companies had built up as union smashers." But the organizers persevered: "Side-stepping these pessimistic croakers, the organizers would go on to their task with undiminished self-confidence and energy. The result was success everywhere."[38]

Civil liberties, free speech, and free assembly were nonexistent in the Monongahela steel towns: "Company men ran the local government and its police force. The one-party system was entrenched. The Republican

Party was owned body and soul by the steel corporation."³⁹ The union's first job, therefore, was to try to establish the basic constitutional rights of workers. To that end, on April 1, 1919, a rally was called in the town square of Monessen. The town's mayor threatened to jail anyone attending, but when 10,000 coal miners marched into town to hear Mother Jones, William Z. Foster, and Philip Murray of the UMW speak, he backed down, and thousands of union cards were publicly signed. Other mass meetings were held despite bans, even in the valley's major town, McKeesport, where the mayor had also threatened mass jailings.

In Duquesne, the mayor was also president of the First National Bank, director of public safety, and town magistrate; his brother was president of the McKeesport Tin Plate Company. When the union held meetings in Duquesne, the mayor called in city and company police, deputized businesspeople and American legionnaires, and with this force smashed the meetings; arrested, jailed, and fined scores of union men; and had many activists fired from their jobs. Still, workers joined the union.

Permits for union meetings were refused. No halls could be rented, and when a landlord agreed to rent, the board of health closed the building. The distribution of literature was prohibited, company spies penetrated the union and reported on activities, mass dismissals of union activists began, and in some towns Pinkerton agents stopped union men at railroad stations and forced them to leave town.

In Pennsylvania and elsewhere, Foster wrote, "the workers enjoy few or no more rights than prevailed under the czars. They cannot hold meetings at all. So far are they below the status of pre-war Germans in this respect that the comparative freedom of the latter seems almost like an unattainable idea. And this deprival of rights is done in the name of law and patriotism."⁴⁰ According to Foster, employers first stationed people in front of union offices and meetings to take down the names of the men attending; then they called active unionists to their offices and threatened dismissal; then they applied their "most dreaded weapon," discharge. Such policies, meant to frighten other workers, often backfired and fed a determination to fight back.⁴¹

Gompers testified at Senate hearings that for years the right of association had been denied workers, both through lawful power and "through denial by illegal and unwarrantable and brutal means." The whole system, Gompers said, "was a greater espionage upon the workmen than was ever employed upon a man suspected of a great crime against the laws of our country." Men going to meetings "had to pass through two lines of detectives and thugs, run the gamut of a hundred or more on each side of them. Men who met in public meetings in lofts, privately owned, who had obtained permission to hold the meetings, have been run down, charged upon, and dispersed; some of them assaulted and some of them beaten."[42]

Judge Gary told the Senate hearings, "We stand firmly on the proposition, that industry must be allowed to proceed untrammeled by the dictates of labor unions or anyone else except the employer and the employees and the Government. That is where we stand."[43] When John D. Rockefeller, Jr., called on Henry Frick, still a leading figure in the Corporation, he "found him utterly opposed to collective bargaining and representation and ready to close up every mill if a strike occurred. He believes that this is the only course and is prepared to follow it at any cost."[44]

Strike!

By early spring 1919, so many men had been fired for union activity that the situation had become desperate. In trying to accomplish the impossible, the organization of steel, Foster wrote, the unions "found themselves in grips with the employers long before they were strong enough to sustain such a contest." Most serious was the growing mass of discharged men. "So bad was the situation by early spring that, lacking other means of relief, local strikes were threatening all over the country."[45]

A letter was sent to Judge Gary informing him that more than 100,000 of his employees had joined the union and now wanted "by American methods, and American understandings, not by revolutionary methods or the inauguration of a cataclysm," to sit down and discuss labor conditions with him.[46] When no response to the letter came after weeks of waiting, the cooperating unions voted overwhelmingly to strike. The committee went to Gary's offices to request a meeting but was turned away. A second letter was sent, to which Gary responded in part, "In view of the well-known attitude as above expressed, the officers of the Corporation respectfully decline to discuss with you, as representatives of a labor union, any matter relating to employees."[47] When a third letter went unanswered, Gompers and the committee went to President Wilson, who agreed to arrange a meeting with Gary. But even the president was unable to get Gary to meet with the unionists, and the cooperating unions set a strike date, September 22, 1919.

Wilson and Gompers requested a delay until October 6 so that Wilson could call a conference to discuss the matter with labor, management, and public participation. But the National Committee held to the planned strike date, and Fitzpatrick wrote to Wilson, "You may not be aware that seven of our organizers and members have been brutally murdered in cold blood during the past few days and the campaign of terrorism on the part of the steel companies is beyond description . . . recalling the reign of despotism in Russia."[48] Because unionists were being discharged by the thousands, Foster wrote, "it would have been folly to have the steel workers abandon their strike preparations," even if it could have been done. "It was like asking one belligerent to ground arms in the face of its onrushing antagonists."[49]

U.S. Steel's preparations for the strike were a repeat of Homestead. It fortified its mill, erected stockades, and topped them with charged wires and machine gun installations. The Allegheny County sheriff, responding to employer requests, deputized as law officers some 5,000 men—handpicked, paid, and armed by employers—to surround the mills. Some fifty state troopers, known to the strikers as "cossacks," took up commanding points in the district, dragged people from their homes, clubbed them in the streets, and jailed them without cause. "It is as though preparations were made for actual war," *New York World* commented.[50]

On Sunday before the strike, a few thousand steelworkers gathered in a field outside Pittsburgh, despite bans on meetings, and were listening to a speaker when a half-dozen helmeted state troopers on horseback galloped toward the speaker's platform. According to an eyewitness, "they rode right in where the meeting was, it was packed with men, women and children. These constables were using their big long clubs, striking the people on both sides of their horses, cursing and swearing." In the chaos of "plunging horses and the screams of women and children," Brody says, "the crowd scattered." Some picked up stones but were told to go home before they were shot. Many were jailed overnight, then taken to Pittsburgh and charged with disorderly conduct. "It was the beginning of the terror in the Pittsburgh district."[51]

Despite all management tactics, 23,213 workers in the Monongahela towns had joined the union; nationally, some 250,000 had signed cards; and on September 22, 1919, some 365,000 workers struck iron and steel plants in fifty cities in ten different states. The strike, Foster claimed, was 90 percent effective, an estimate that is virtually undisputed. Local, state, and federal officials—who, with few exceptions, sided with the company—declared martial law in many towns and called in armed forces to occupy towns and enforce company policy.

"Violations of personal rights and personal liberty were wholesale," the commission reported; "men were arrested without warrants, imprisoned without charges, their homes invaded without legal process, magistrates' verdicts were rendered frankly on the basis of whether the striker would go back to work or not."[52] Many of the charges against strikers, for which they were imprisoned or fined, were unrecorded, but recorded charges included "cursing," "refusing to obey orders," "going out of his house before daylight," "laughing at the police," and "smiling at the state police." Jail terms ran into months, and often men were taken, not to jail, but to the steel mill where, according to doctors and eyewitnesses, they were often clubbed and beaten.[53]

Labor's wartime friends in Washington had vanished. Instead, there was the U.S. Army, which intervened for employers where called upon. There was also U.S. Attorney General A. Mitchell Palmer who intervened everywhere to hunt down radicals among the strikers. Two large detective agencies provided strikebreakers to employers; one agency manager said he used over 500 agents during the strike.[54]

Although the strike's main target was the Corporation, most steel mills were affected. U.S. Steel's largest plants, at Gary and Youngstown, were closed by the strike, but those near Pittsburgh were less affected. In Gary, the mayor had a division of army regulars called up, declared martial law, prohibited outdoor meetings, arrested pickets and union activists, and broke the strike there; in a neighboring town, the state militia was called in, used the same tactics, and got the same results. "The collapse of these strongpoints," Brody writes, "was a critical defeat for the unions."[55]

Against heavy odds, the strikers struggled on for some three months, but on January 8, 1920, the union announced that the strike of U.S. Steel had been defeated by the "arbitrary and ruthless misuse of power" by steel employers. Almost the entire steel industry became nonunion.

Reds and Radicals

Catholic Bishop Francis J. McConnell and other members of the Commission of Inquiry met with Judge Gary during the strike to mediate a settlement. "It was a remarkable meeting," Brody comments. Gary produced a report accusing the commission of being infiltrated by "red radicals," expounded on welfare capitalism, insisted that his men were contented and that the strike had a radical intent, and gave the distinguished group no chance to mediate. The group reported back that "Mr. Gary insisted that the point of issue was not now unionism as such, but whether the American Government should be supported and American institutions be upheld." Gary had claimed that "the whole movement of the steel strike was a movement of red radicals. . . . The only outcome of the victory for unionism would be Sovietism in the United States and the forcible distribution of property."[56]

Just before the strike, an industry publication, *Iron Age,* had commented editorially on "The Real Question at Pittsburgh," claiming it had "discovered evidence connecting at least the leading spirit of the strike agitation with extreme Syndicalism and other forms of revolutionary propaganda."[57] During the strike, the politics of William Z. Foster became a major public issue. Foster's views had never been secret, nor his involvement with the IWW and syndicalism. Now the *Pittsburgh Labor World* wrote that "the syndicalist is as 'unscrupulous' in his choice of weapons to fight his every-day battles as for his final struggle with capitalism. He allows no considerations of legality, religion, patriotism, honor, duty, etc., to stand in the way of his adoption of effective tactics."[58]

Such charges, printed in the *Congressional Record* and in papers across the country, became featured news. The AFL's politics were not questioned, but Foster and other "radicals" were charged with using the strike to foment revolution. "Some radical men not in harmony with the conservative elements of the AFL are attempting to use the strike as a means of elevating themselves to power within the ranks of organized labor," one Senate committee concluded.[59] The *New York Tribune* contended that the strike's motive was political and that the issue was Americanism versus alienism.[60] The Slavic steelworkers were "penetrated with the Bolshevik idea," said the *Philadelphia Inquirer*, and the *New York Times* added that they were "steeped in the doctrines of the class struggle and social overthrow, ignorant and easily misled."[61]

Raids on known radicals in Gary found radical literature, proving something to the *Boston Evening Transcript* about "the extraordinary hold which 'Red' principles have upon the foreign born populations in the steel districts."[62] No connection between these radicals (or their literature) and the steel strike was ever shown, yet the message was driven home to the nation that a revolution, not a strike, was happening in steel.

Early in the strike, employers launched a massive advertising campaign aimed at public opinion and at persuading strikers to return to work. In eleven days, over thirty full-page ads appeared in Pittsburgh papers, printed in English and various foreign languages. The ads said it was un-American to strike, denounced the strike's leaders, and tried to undermine striker morale. Many ads featured a half-page drawing of Uncle Sam, clothed in the stars and stripes and saying to strikers, "Go Back to Work."[63] Full-page ads in several papers said in bold type: "The steel strike can't win. It is uncalled for and unAmerican. It is led by men who apparently are trying to establish the 'red' rule of anarchy and bolshevism in this land of opportunity and liberty."[64] One ad, typical of others, read:

Here are ten reasons why the strike will fail, ten reasons why you and every other man who is loyal to America will go back to work: There is no good American reason for the strike. A very large majority of the workers did not want to strike. The strike is not between workers and employers, but between revolutionists and America. It is becoming more and more apparent that the strike is merely the diabolical attempt of a few Radicals to seize industry and plant Bolshevism in this country. The strike is doomed to fail, just as all unpopular and unpatriotic movements have failed in this country. Public sentiment is against the strike; Americans have great sympathy for genuine wrongs but they have neither sympathy nor tolerance for Radicals who seek to use organized labor as a tool in their nefarious campaigns against industry and American liberty. The strike is an economic failure and the loss will be felt by everyone including you. America will never stand for the "red" rule of Bolshevism, IWWism or any other "ism" that seeks to tear down the Constitution. Radicalism must be put down. There is a strong possibility that the Huns had a hand in fomenting the strike, hoping to retard industrial progress in America. Keep America busy and prosperity will continue.[65]

According to Brody, the press campaign excluded the possibility of government intervention on labor's side, if such a possibility ever existed. "Leading figures of the administration, in fact, openly supported the employers, and the activities of the Justice Department materially damaged the strikers' cause," giving the steel companies complete freedom of action in the strike.[66]

The union's National Committee lacked any resources for ads aimed at a broad public audience. Internally, it issued bulletins to strikers, scheduled numerous meetings, and warned the strikers that the press was against them. For external communications, a professional public relations man was hired, but this attempt was hardly a match for the costly Corporation broadsides against the union.

Commission's Conclusions

The Commission of Inquiry concluded that "no interpretation of the movement as a plot or conspiracy fits the facts; that is, it was a mass movement, in which leadership became of secondary importance. Charges of Bolshevism or of industrial radicalism in the conduct of the strike were without foundation."[67] The allegations were traced to two main sources: first, the newspapers, which led to the second and main source, the steel companies.

Gary insisted that the workers following Fitzpatrick and Foster were Bolshevists and that the strikers were demanding "the closed shop, soviets and the forcible distribution of property." Gary was asked if he really meant that labor was getting too strong, and he generally assented. The commission asked Gary to supply some proof that the strikers were Bolshevists. Gary offered none, either to the commission or at the Senate hearings on the strike, nor did any other steel official.

The commission wondered how it happened that so many newspapers around the country had printed on their front pages the first week of the strike the same long extracts from Foster's pamphlet on syndicalism. The work had been out of print for a few years, and no copy of it was found on any striker or union leader, though a reprint was widely circulated by steel officials to newspapers, preachers, and investigators.

The commission concluded that the drive was controlled by the twenty-four sponsoring AFL unions, that Foster's acts, therefore, had to coincide with those of "old line unionism," and that a movement involving so many workers and unions "cannot be controlled to secret, opposite ends."

Strike leaflets had been confined to strike topics and although some communists had passed out leaflets, these had been confiscated by strike leaders who had also thrown the distributors out of the hall. Foster had refused to include in strike bulletins even mild statements about the need for a labor party until Fitzpatrick, whose political credentials were unquestioned, had ordered that the idea be included. The plans and leaders of the steel strike were the same as those in the stockyard drive, the commission pointed out, yet that earlier campaign was won without anyone calling it Bolshevist and without any attempt to organize the "one big union" that employers found so threatening.

No strike leaders were convicted of "radicalism." Hundreds of strikers were arrested in "radical raids," but none were tried and convicted. The commission asked whether these men were radicals or simply rebelling against their present way of life. The steel industry, it said, was full of people who wanted big changes, "but the changes were all related definitely to the right to organize, the twelve-hour day, the seven-day week, the foremen's ways, the company's methods, or some other definite thing which they were sick of. It is possible that the workers throughout the whole steel industry might much more easily have been organized on a radical appeal. But the Strike Committee were opposed in principle to any such appeal."[68]

Opposition Tactics

Part of the steelmakers' strikebreaking strategy, Foster wrote, "was to alienate public sympathy from the strike by denouncing it as an incipient revolution which had to be put down at all costs. Public opinion was already violently inflamed against everything savoring no matter how slightly of radicalism, and it was not difficult for the reactionary newspapers to make the steel strike unpopular."[69] Foster insisted that the steel drive had been carried on according to the "strictest trade-union principles," overseen as it was by the National Committee and the AFL unions, under whose close scrutiny he had served. "Yet none of these trade unionists, keen though they be to detect and condemn unusual practices and heresy in the ranks, had found fault with the character of my work. Nor could the crew of detectives and stool pigeons of the steel companies and Department of Justice, who had dogged my footsteps for a year past, cite a single word said, a thing done, or a line written by me in the entire campaign which could not measure up to most rigid trade-union standards."

To cover up an "inveterate opposition to Organized Labor in all its forms and activities," said Foster, "and to blind the workers to the real cause of the defeat, namely lack of sufficient power on the employees' side," the companies claimed that the strike failed because "dangerous" people were connected with it. If Corporation opposition had not taken this form, "it would have manifested itself in some other way as bad or worse. It was to be depended upon that some means would have been found to thoroughly discredit the movement."

Each important move made by labor during the drive was opposed, Foster said, with "unexampled fury" by both employers and government officials. Throughout the war years, they "watched with undisguised alarm and hatred the rapid advance of the unions, but they were powerless to stop it. Now, however, they are getting their revenge. The usual method of defeating such movements . . . is to attach some stigma to them; to question the legitimacy of their aims, and then . . . to crush them by the most unscrupulous means."

Fitzpatrick, asked in Senate hearings if he thought democracy was safe in western Pennsylvania, responded: "There is absolutely no democracy there. It is a tyranny and an autocracy, and I do not think that the equal of it ever existed in Russia. . . . When I go into western Pennsylvania, I kiss my wife and babies good-bye, absolutely, because I do not ever expect to see them again. . . . The only Bolshevists I saw over there are the mill town officials and the men who deliberately defy the Constitution of the United States."

Immigrant Workers

Because "foreigners" were almost as suspect as "reds," employers tried during the strike to link the two and to create a common front against foreigners and un-Americanism. A victorious war had just been fought for democracy and the "American way of life," so the ground had been laid for a full-scale campaign against internal enemies.

Father Adelbert Kazincy, a Catholic priest who was familiar with Slovak and other immigrant steelworkers, told the Senate that the men of Braddock "have been branded as anarchists and Bolshevists, and they resent it. . . . they are Catholics, you know, and Catholics can not afford to do that unless they give up their religion."[70] The general manager of Homestead (now a U.S. Steel plant) testified that many Russians worked in the plant. Asked if they had a tendency toward bolshevism, he responded, "Yes, sir." Fitzpatrick, pressed about the "foreign element" in the strike, answered that the unions organized only workers the employers hired, and mainly they hired immigrants.

During the 1892 Homestead strike, non-Anglo participation had been relatively small. Of the 143,000 workers in the iron and steel industry in 1890, 79,000 were native born, 5,800 "colored," and 58,000 foreign-born whites, most of them (44,000) from Britain and Germany.[71] In the years following, waves of southern and eastern European immigrants, especially Slavs, moved into the industry. In the steel mills of Allegheny County in 1907, for instance, some 60 percent of the workers were foreign born, the largest group being Slovak (6,477), followed by Polish (1,644), Magyar (1,192), Italian (896), Croatian (848), German (716), Irish (608), English (602)—and some 331 "colored." The eastern and southern Europeans were overwhelmingly unskilled and unnaturalized, and about half of them could not speak English.

In the coal mines, the new immigrants became solid members of the UMW, and in the steel mills, as their strong ethnic communities turned to unionism, the immigrant workers did too. Most had fraternal organizations attached to their churches, and when a priest talked unionism to them, a whole industry could go union. Cleavages existed, of course, but any one group was a force to be reckoned with, and together they were an impressive movement.

Aftermath

Foster and Gompers exchanged recriminations about the strike's defeat. Gompers claimed that labor had not been ready for a contest of that dimension and that he had feared (without much grounds as it turned out) that the inexperience and volatility of the new members might damage the union. He at first had opposed the organizing drive but supported it once the decision was made to go ahead. He had also supported Foster's appointment and stood behind him when he came under attack, but he felt that Foster's youthful indiscretions were a great liability.

When the strike date was set, Gompers wanted it postponed so President Wilson could bring the sides together. "Though I knew that the strike would fail, the best I could do was to suggest and advise."[72] When Wilson's conference was finally held, it turned out, in Gompers's view, to be a bust. It was to have included employers, labor, and the public, but the public members, he said, were 90 percent employers, and after the conference totally rejected any compromise with labor, union representatives walked out in protest. It was a mistake, Gompers said, to expect such a conference to "serve as a working basis" for a strike settlement.

Foster focused on liabilities other than his own. He claimed that Gompers and the AFL had given too little, too late to the strike, that the drive should have begun nationally rather than in Chicago, and that the AFL had delayed acting on the Chicago call for the drive. The early postwar period provided "an opportunity to organize the industry such as might never occur again," Foster claimed. That the unions "did not embrace it sooner was a calamity."[73]

In fact, the AFL's convention endorsed the steel drive unanimously only two months after the Chicago federation called for it, and certainly the cooperating unions needed at least that amount of time to win membership support. As for the support from the AFL unions and the Federation, few leaders of defeated strikes claim to have gotten enough support for the strike from others. Gompers felt that the union was not ready for a strike, and he was undoubtedly right, but there had been a mass firing of Union activists and, as Foster knew, the strike was irrepressible.

The flood of steelworkers into the union suggests that they virtually organized themselves and that organizing them and getting their active support for the strike did not figure in the strike's defeat. Moreover Foster felt that the semi-industrial structure of the drive went far in solving the problems that arose and that "the organizers and secretaries entered whole heartedly" into strike activities.[74]

Brody refocuses discussion of the strike's defeat from internal to external constraints: "The steel strikers, for their part, could not hope to exert sufficient pressure to break down such determination to preserve the open shop and the prerogatives of management. Strengthened by five years of abnormally high incomes, the powerful steel industry could have withstood even a total shutdown, and unionists never expected the strike to be total."[75]

After his fussing with Gompers, Foster also considered external factors. The industry, he wrote, was "hard and fast in the grip of absentee capitalists who take no part in production and whose sole function is to seize by hook or crook the product of the industry and consume it,"[76] and he saw the strike's enemies as an alignment of steel companies, the state, the courts, the local churches, and the press.

The London *Times* commented on the strike: "The steel workers' strike . . . turns on the question of recognizing unions, an issue which has gone into the limbo of almost forgotten things here. . . . The employers in America have evidently something to learn in these matters." The *Times* went on to say that management's comparative immunity from labor troubles in the United States resulted, not from superior management, but from the exceptional belligerence of American employers.[77]

The sharp decline of the U.S. steel industry in the last decades has been attributed to mismanagement, starting in the 1950s when Bethlehem Steel built the world's largest steel plant but installed in it an outdated technology—the open-hearth rather than the basic-oxygen process, a mistake followed by other steel companies—and thus precipitated what has been called one of the major disasters in U.S. industrial history. In 1983, the steelworkers' union began to spark the industry's revival by hiring consultants to deal with the industry's finances and by involving the union and steelworkers in managerial policy and shop-floor decision making.[78]

7

Critical Conflicts:
Railway, Craft,
and Industrial Unionism

OTHER CRITICAL CONFLICTS, besides the two in steel already discussed, relate to American labor's central historic problem: its inability until the 1930s to sustain mass industrial unionism. Only four of these conflicts will be looked at here: two early railroad strikes (1877 and 1894) and two clusters of conflicts involving craft and finally industrial unions. These notes of necessity touch only on the broadest outline and most relevant aspects of twentieth century conflicts. Others are invited to fill out this brief outline.

Similarly, labor struggles after the formation of the CIO will be left for other people to examine.[1] These countless struggles—southern textile workers, J. P. Stevens strikers, the Farm Workers' movement, airline controllers, Eastern and other airline workers, Pittston miners, newspaper employees everywhere, national telephone and Greyhound strikers, and others—are all relevant to this book's general thesis but less so to its specific emphasis, which concerns repression of industrial unionism before the 1930s. Here the more contemporary emphasis, described in later chapters, will be on newer strategies of repression, the legalistic and manipulative ones, the subtler technologies, and the disastrous results of macroeconomic policies. The hot war of armed repression has continued and intensified, but a newer, colder, and in some ways more deadly one has been launched.

The Great Railroad Uprising of 1877

In a real sense, capitalism rode the rails to power, and it was on the railroads that it had its first major encounters with industrial unionism, all of which it won hands down. A prelude to the most massive of

101

these encounters, the great railroad uprising of 1877, occurred on the Philadelphia and Reading line (P&R). In mid-1864, the new Brotherhood of the Footboard, fresh from midwestern victories, struck the P&R over wages and closed it down completely. The company persuaded the War Department to supply men from military railroads to operate the line, and within a week the strike was broken, and half the strikers had been fired.

The defeat, John Blackman says, "adversely affected for many years the rise of the great railroad brotherhoods."[2] Reeling from this crushing, unprecedented defeat by the federal government, the union changed its name to the Brotherhood of Locomotive Engineers (BLE) and elected as a new president one who opposed strikes and militant unionism. In 1877, railroad conditions having worsened, the BLE deposed its president, elected another, and entered a strike against the Boston & Maine Railroad. In the first known case of peacetime presidential intervention to break a strike, President Hayes directed the arrest of strike leaders for conspiring to obstruct the mails. The leaders were convicted and punished, and the precedent for federal intervention had been established.

The great railroad uprising that began later the same year was the first national strike of industrial workers, skilled and unskilled, against major employers. Federal troops deployed by Republican President Hayes broke the strike by operating the struck trains, firing on strikers who tried to prevent train movement, killing a hundred strikers, and injuring hundreds more.

Causes and Beginnings

In 1873, the worst depression to that date had begun, a depression that brought with it the halving of railroad wages and, as Robert V. Bruce writes, "a vale of tears that grew wider and deeper until by 1876 it seemed like the valley of death itself."[3] On the Baltimore and Ohio (B&O) line, where the strikes started, railwaymen rebelled against further wage cuts, workdays as long as eighteen hours, continuous on-call duty, the "layover" at the end of one-way trips (at workers' own expense), and employer refusal to deal with grievances or talk to union committees.

Unionism had fallen on such hard times that only nine tattered national unions remained in 1876. Most serious railway unionism had perished, and in 1877, only three mild brotherhoods (conductors, firemen, and enginemen) and the more aggressive BLE remained.

In mid-1877, an "industrial union," the Trainmen's Union, which included all railway workers, was formed in the Pittsburgh area to defend against wage cuts, and this union soon spread to the B&O, the Pennsylvania, Erie, and Atlantic and Great Western railroads. A date was set for a simultaneous strike on all lines, but when disagreements arose and the strike was postponed, localized strikes broke out and spread to most of the nation. Although not simultaneously initiated, as had been planned, the strikes were not without organized preparation or coordination by the Trainmen's Union. In an opening act, some forty B&O firemen and brakemen walked off the job in Baltimore, but they were soon dispersed by police.

The strike began in earnest in Martinsburg, West Virginia, when some thirty firemen on the B&O walked out. The mayor tried to arrest the leaders and run trains with strikebreakers, but the crowds prevented such actions, and when brakemen also struck, all freight trains in the area were halted. At the B&O's request, West Virginia's governor called up two companies of Martinsburg militia, but these men fraternized with the strikers, many of whom they knew, and refused to fire on them. The angered governor tried to lead two other militia companies into the fray but was driven back by the crowds. Finally, at the governor's request, President Hayes sent in 400 federal troopers from out of state. Strike leaders were arrested, strikers were driven off with bayonets and guns, some were killed, and troopers moved the trains, thus ending the strike in Martinsburg. But the uprising was irrepressible and spread across much of the country—only New England and the South were largely untouched.

Pennsylvania Strikes

Pennsylvania became a major battlefield, and in Pittsburgh, the strike against the Pennsylvania Railroad was probably bloodier than any conflict since the New York Civil War draft riots. The railroad had cut wages, doubled the work load, and laid off almost half the flagmen and brakemen. In response, 500 trainmen walked out. The governor called out the local Pittsburgh militia, but when they fraternized with the strikers, as in West Virginia, he sent in 1,000 Philadelphia militiamen who fired into a gathering crowd, killing twenty people and wounding twenty-nine seriously, including a woman and three children. A crowd of some 20,000 people soon surrounded the troops' roundhouse, ran a burning railway car against it, and shot three militiamen as they tried to escape. The militia in turn shot and killed some twenty strikers.

Labor spy Allan Pinkerton wrote about the Pittsburgh strike: With "vulture-like prescience of coming opportunities for prey and pillage, these straggling bodies of human vultures came down upon Pittsburgh. River pirates of the lowest and most savage order came creeping up the Ohio, or floating down both the Allegheny and Monongahela, to be in at the death for their share of the picking. . . . Every little community along the railroads lost its roughs and desperadoes . . . ready to give vent in any way that might quickest offer an excuse to their murderous antagonism against capital and authority." The situation "had begun to take on a communistic air. This curse of the two continents . . . which calls for as prompt an extermination as we would give a deadly reptile, began shaking its beastly head and raising its red hand, that its power might be known and felt."[4]

The Philadelphia troops shot repeated volleys at the strikers. Pinkerton says, "The mob retreated aghast, rallied, retreated, rallied again, and through their numbers the deadly bullets mowed wrinkled and crumpled swaths, until upon the hill and along the tracks the wild and frenzied rioters precipitately withdrew, carrying their dead and wounded, whose number God alone may know. But they left only to return in the blackness of the night with fury and forces increased, to bring with them arson and flame, destruction and ruin."[5]

The strikers became "such a fierce assemblage" that one brigade was ordered to retire to the roundhouse grounds. Strikers seized a cannon, set it on the hill, and tried to load it with spikes and car links. The troops opened fire. "As every soldier aimed to kill, the first volley brought down several of the rioters. . . . The only result of repeated attack was repeated defeat, and the dead bodies piled about the frowning gun."[6]

The strike spread throughout Pennsylvania, and the alarmed governor sent in the Pennsylvanian Coal and Iron Police and the entire state militia to control it. Directing operations from a struck train, the governor commanded the troops to fire into all crowds until they dispersed. As a grand finale, on the governor's request, President Hayes deployed 3,000 U.S. Army regulars, and they arrived on the scene in a train supplied by the Pennsylvania Railroad. Marines landed in Philadelphia; in Reading, soldiers killed ten and wounded forty strikers; in every town on the line, strike leaders were arrested and held without bail. More than 10,000 troops were finally assembled, and this overwhelming force finally broke the Pennsylvania strike.

Strikes in New York and the Midwest

In New York, trainmen struck the Erie Railroad. In just one issue of the *New York Times*, strikers were referred to as disaffected elements, roughs, hoodlums, rioters, mob, suspicious-looking individuals, bad characters, thieves, blacklegs, looters, communists, rabble, labor-reform agitators, dangerous class of people, gangs, tramps, drunken sectionmen, lawbreakers, threatening crowd, bummers, ruffians, loafers, bullies, vagabonds, cowardly mob, bands of worthless fellows, incendiaries, enemies of society, reckless crowd, malcontents, wretched people, loud-mouthed orators, rapscallions, brigands, robber mob, riffraff, terrible fellows, felons, and idiots.[7] The Brooklyn militia was called in, and strike leaders were arrested, but the Erie finally settled with the strikers.

In Buffalo, strikes of the New York Central and the Lake Shore railroads were broken by armed force. In the Midwest—Michigan, Ohio, Indiana, St. Louis, Chicago—and Canada, some strikes were settled by rescinding wage cuts, but most were broken by force. As the strikes moved west, strikes in other industries were triggered, and the railway uprising began to take on the proportions of a massive general strike. Everywhere trainmen met overwhelming citizen support, especially from farmers and even businesspeople who had their own grievances with the railroads. So alarmed did President Hayes become that, fearing an assault on the capital, he ordered troops and warships to Washington to protect public buildings and threatened to declare martial law throughout the entire nation if the strikes continued.

The *New York Times* reported that Chicago was "the City in Possession of Communists,"[8] and the secretary of war commanded General Philip H. Sheridan, who was fighting Indians in Sioux country, to move his forces immediately to that city. The Workingmen's Party, which was strong in Chicago, called support meetings and urged a general strike of all workers. Some 10,000 people assembled on Halsted Street and threw stones at police who tried to disperse them. Mounted police and foot soldiers arrived, shot into the crowd, and killed at least twelve people.

In the final count, the Chicago strike was patrolled by six companies of the regular army, two regiments of state militia, several companies of cavalry, a battery of artillery, 500 veteran soldiers, 5,000 special deputies, volunteers from various patriotic organizations, and the entire Chicago police force. More federal troops, returning from the Indian wars, arrived each day. Some thirty to fifty Chicago strikers were killed in street fighting, and about a hundred were wounded.

In St. Louis, a more general strike, said to be almost revolutionary in character, was conducted under Workingmen's Party direction. Strikers stopped Mississippi steamers until wage raises were granted and visited factories throughout the area, calling on all workers to join the strike. Finally, U.S. Army regulars were sent in, the mayor closed all places of business, the governor threatened martial law, strike leaders were arrested and held in prison, and after five days, the St. Louis general strike collapsed.

End of the Uprising

After some two weeks, the trainmen's strikes were largely over. The *Nation* wrote: "The kindest thing which can be done for the great multitudes of untaught men who have been received on these shores, and are daily arriving . . . is to show them promptly that society as here organized . . . is impregnable, and can be no more shaken than the order of nature." It would threaten security "to allow a state of things to subsist in which 8,000 or 9,000 day-laborers of the lowest class can suspend, even for a whole day, the traffic and industry of a great nation, merely as a means of extorting ten or twenty cents a day more wages from their employers."[9]

Employers opened an attack on all labor groups—union, fraternal, and political—and even the Railway Conductors, some of whose members had been strike*breakers*, came under attack. Unionists were blacklisted, and conspiracy laws were enacted in many states and applied by the courts to unions. "Labor confronted a powerful and well-organized movement to suppress all its attempts to unite, " Samuel Yellen writes, "either for reform of, or bargaining about, conditions of work."[10]

The Reverend Henry Ward Beecher preached at Plymouth Church, New York, during the strikes: "We look upon the importation of the communistic and like European notions as abominations. Their notions and theories that the Government should be paternal and take care of the welfare of its subjects and provide them with labor, is un-American. . . . God has intended the great to be great, and the little to be little."[11] Railroad employers and most business leaders of the period, Bruce writes, "held fiercely to the doctrines of Social Darwinism." They had survived and were therefore the fittest or at least "the most heavily endowed with energy, shrewdness and ruthless will."[12]

The Trainmen's Union (an early semi-industrial union) was broken along with the strikes. Employers had hired Pinkerton agents to penetrate that union, disrupt its work, and conduct espionage within it. The union had been so riddled with agents that Allan Pinkerton later suggested that anyone (presumably including his own agents) could get into the Trainmen's Union "no matter how low and vile."[13] Indeed, 1877 was a bad year for labor but a good one for Pinkerton. Since the great strikes of 1877, Pinkerton wrote, "my agencies have been busily employed by great railway, manufacturing and other corporations, for the purpose of bringing the leaders and instigators of the dark deeds of those days to the punishment they so richly deserve. Hundreds have been punished. Hundreds more will be punished."[14]

Employers had used the U.S. Army almost as their own, courtesy of President Hayes. In the disputed election outcome of 1876, Hayes had won the presidency with Thomas Scott's help, and Scott, Carnegie's mentor, was head of the Pennsylvania Railroad in 1877. Hayes was informed of his election while traveling in Scott's private railroad car, and the car had also been put at the Pennsylvania governor's disposal for a six-week family trip across country. The governor returned the favor to Scott: Through him, both the state militia and the U.S. Army intervened in the Pennsylvania strike on behalf of the railroad.

Not all people supported the railroads wholeheartedly, however. A surprising *Daily News* editorial said during the strike: "For years the railroads of this country have been wholly run outside the United States Constitution. Their managers have been plundering the roads and speculating on their securities to their own enrichment. Finally, having found nothing more to get out of stockholders . . . they have commenced raiding not only upon the general public but their own employees."[15]

Also, some people felt the grievances underlying labor unrest needed to be addressed. The government, the Honorable J. A. Dacus wrote during the strike, "has just been subjected to a strain greater than any which our system has been before required to sustain," for the uprising is "far more threatening to social organization and political stability than was the terrible contest waged between sections from 1861 to 1865."[16] The causes of the uprising must be addressed, he insisted: "Somewhere great wrongs have been committed, and society must pay the penalty for crimes. . . . Capitalists cannot afford to oppress laborers, because such oppression endangers their own security."[17]

Pullman, 1894

The second major bid to organize a mass railway union, the Pullman strike and its supporting boycott, came on the heels of the AFL's disaster at Homestead in 1892 and occurred in the same year as three other major strikes: one at the Coeur d'Alene, Idaho, silver mines (broken by federal troops), one in coal mines around Tracy City, Tennessee (broken by the militia), and one of railroad switchmen in Buffalo (also broken by the militia). The 1894 Pullman strike/boycott was in some ways a replica of the 1877 uprising: It involved railroads and resulted from depression, layoffs, and deep wage cuts. Again it was national, affecting some twenty-seven states, and again general strikes threatened, especially in Chicago. As in 1877, the U.S. Army and various other armed forces broke the strike, smashed the union, and left many strikers dead or wounded. Unlike 1877, a lethal blow was struck by a federal court injunction, unprecedented in its scope, which led to the wholesale arrest of strike leaders and provided a cover for armed force.

The Pullman strike has a special place in labor history for two main reasons. First, the union involved, the American Railway Union (ARU), was one of the earliest industrial unions, led by Eugene Debs who was to become the nation's leading democratic socialist, and second, though nearly successful, the strike/boycott resulted in a major setback for mass unionism and the labor-left. The ARU included all crafts and skill levels in its membership. In that respect it differed from craft unions and the railway brotherhoods (including the Firemen's Brotherhood, of which Debs had been an official) and resembled the National Labor Union, the Knights of Labor, some AFL unions, the IWW, and eventually the CIO.

Causes and Beginning

The strike began when the Pullman Company cut wages some 25–40 percent, despite a sound financial status and the high dividends paid stockholders.[18] Workers voted to strike when Pullman not only rejected an appeal to restore wage rates but laid off the three union committee members who made the appeal. The Pullman workers turned to their union, the ARU, for strike support, and after much internal debate, the ARU finally voted to boycott Pullman and refuse to handle its sleeping cars on any railroad line.

The ARU thus took on not only Pullman but the entire railway industry. The General Managers' Association, representing twenty-four railroads, took over the strike on the Pullman side and hired strike-breakers, set up a publicity office, and fired anyone interfering with the switching of Pullman cars. Still Pullman's cars did not move. "The country had never before seen a strike so well organized on so large a scale," Yellen writes, but with few exceptions, the press backed the association. *Harper's Weekly* editorialized: "The brigand who demands ransom for his prisoner, with mutilation or death as the alternative . . . these are the types of blackmailers whom all the world loathes. The boycott ordered by the railway union is morally no better than any of these acts. It is an attempt at blackmail on the largest scale."[19]

To provide an excuse for federal intervention, the railroads hooked U.S. mail cars behind the sleeping cars so that detaching the Pullman cars from the trains, as strikers were doing, also meant detaching the U.S. mail. U.S. Attorney General Richard Olney, formerly a railway attorney and director, agreed to appoint as many deputies as were needed to protect the mails, and all of his 3,600 deputized strikebreakers were selected by the association and paid for by the railroads.

Violence and Federal Intervention

In Chicago, a main railroad switching center, where labor had both the mayor and the governor on its side, the superintendent of police described the deputies as "thugs, thieves, and ex-convicts."[20] Freight trains were burned in Chicago, and strikers claimed that company agents had done it. Governor John Altgeld agreed with the strikers, as did Chicago's mayor, who secured forty affidavits showing the cars had been burned by company agents. "Even papers that had never been friendly to labor," Gompers wrote in his biography, "conceded that no effort was spared to precipitate violence and then to give the impression it was due to strikers. Thus an opportunity was created for sending in troops."[21]

President Cleveland, inspired by Olney, sent 2,000 U.S. Army regulars to Chicago to move the trains and protect both mails and railroad property. The remarkable Altgeld wired Cleveland: "Surely the facts have not been correctly presented to you in this case or you would not have taken this step, for it is entirely unnecessary, and, as it seems to me, unjustifiable. . . . The newspapers' accounts have in many cases been pure fabrications, and others wild exaggerations."[22] The *Nation* wrote, "Altgeld is probably as unconscious of his own bad manners as he is of the bad odor of his own principles; but boorish, impudent, and ignorant as he is, he can scarcely fail to wince under the treatment which he receives from the President."[23]

With some 14,000 men under arms in Chicago, street fighting broke out everywhere. Deputies fired into a crowd and killed two; another crowd, trying to prevent strikebreakers from moving a train, was fired on, and some thirty people were killed. The federal government had made another decisive entry into the conflict: At the association's request, Attorney General Olney had issued an unprecedented, broad-ranging federal injunction restraining Debs and the ARU from interfering with the mails, commerce, or the business of twenty-three named railroads. Issued first in Chicago, then elsewhere, the injunctions prohibited almost all ARU activity, including picketing and any attempt to persuade people to leave their work. No jury trials were available to anyone charged with violating the injunction.

Debs called for a general strike in Chicago, but three days before it was scheduled to begin, federal agents broke into ARU offices to seize records and legal documents, and Debs and other ARU officers were indicted for insurrection. The general strike, plagued by injunctions, indictments, and armed suppression, did not materialize. Debs tried again for a settlement of the strike, but the association again refused to talk. By this time, all strike leaders were under indictment, 190 were under arrest on federal charges, and 515 were charged with murder, arson, riot, assault, etc.

Reasons for Failure

The Chicago strike/boycott was broken, and federal troops were moved elsewhere. Finally, even the western holdouts were subdued. Debs was tried and sentenced to six months in prison, along with many others, and union activists were fired from their jobs and blacklisted. The ARU itself was smashed and with it the mass union base that could have supported Debs's later effort to build a mass labor-left political party.

Some accounts dwell on the ARU's "unreadiness" for the strike, as they do on union "unreadiness" for the 1919 steel strike—in effect faulting the unions for striking before they were fully prepared. The Pullman strike's momentum, however, was irresistible, and the forces fielded against the ARU boycott were overwhelming and unpredictable. How could any union be "ready" for a conflict in which powerful antiunion employers, the nation's president, the U.S. attorney general, the federal courts, and the U.S. Army (among other forces) were thrown against it? Even so, the strike might have been settled had not a sweeping and an unprecedented federal injunction put all the major leaders under arrest and out of commission for the duration of the strike and beyond.

Later, the CIO was ready because it had the support of the federal government. Its government allies were the ARU's adversaries, and even the remarkable solidarity of ARU locals with Pullman workers was no match for such adversaries. The railway brotherhoods, as Debs knew, could not deal separately with the railroads, but uniting them in one union, as the ARU did, was not enough either.

Gompers had called Pullman "the most consummate type of avaricious wealth absorber, tyrant, and hypocrite," but neither the AFL nor the railway brotherhoods had supported the strike, which they said could not be won[24] (in 1877, Debs as a brotherhood official had also abstained from support of the railway uprising, believing it to be a lost cause). Gompers hardly covered himself with glory in the Pullman strike, and largely for that reason, he suffered his one-term defeat as AFL president. Yet AFL participation could not have prevented the massive intervention of the federal government on the side of employers, any more than its support had prevented the defeat of a steel strike two years earlier.

As in 1877, an economic depression had squeezed the railroad industry, and despite continuing profits, the industry had squeezed its workers, who finally fought back. The railroads did not cause the depression, but as a major industrial power, they inevitably influenced the public economic policy that caused the depression. Over the years, depressions have led predictably to worker rebellion, sometimes with good results for labor but often not. In the wake of the 1930s' depression, the New Deal adopted policies that put people to work, stimulated the economy, and allowed unions to grow and have more influence on federal policy. The ARU and its predecessors were less fortunate.

American and British Railway Unions

The ultimate blame for the violence of 1894, Philip Taft and Philip Ross write, rests largely on the behavior of owners like George Pullman, a Carnegie associate who, like many industrialists, "was unwilling to allow his workers the slightest influence" on decisions affecting their welfare. Railway owners, "arrogant, intransigent, unwilling to meet with their employees," depended on power—their own and the government's—to suppress unionism. Behind this "powerful shield they could ignore the periodic outbreaks by their labor force; they knew that these seldom were strong enough to gain victory."[25]

The grievances of Pullman workers were not necessarily winnable, they were simply intolerable and uncontainable, as were those of the railroaders in 1877. "Never did men have a cause more just," wrote the Reverend William H. Carwardine, a pastor in Pullman's company town, "and never did a corporation with equal pretenses grind men more unmercifully."[26] But just causes alone do not win strikes.

In Britain, by contrast, an industrial union, the Amalgamated Society of Railway Servants, formed in 1871, included within it the separate craft unions. By 1890, after a merger, it was the fifth largest union in Britain. In 1896, when a stoppage threatened, a public agency head, the president of the Board of Trade, intervened and mediated an agreement that included the reinstatement of fired unionists, the union's main demand. "That was a landmark," Henry Phelps Brown writes, "and a victory for the union, whose membership doubled in twelve months."[27]

In 1897, a major British employer, the North-Eastern Railway Company, recognized the Amalgamated Society as the bargaining agent for its employees, and in 1907, when a national stoppage seemed likely, Board of Trade President Lloyd George, a Liberal (not Labour) leader, intervened and threatened the employers with special legislation if they refused to settle with the union. They settled. British rail unions did not have an easy way to go, but not because of government action in this critical instance.

Condemnation

Among the Chicago papers condemning the Pullman strike were the *Herald*, the *Tribune*, the *Journal*, the *Evening Post*, and *Inter Ocean*, all of them, according to Almont Lindsey, the strike's historian, "using every means at their command for the molding of public opinion," and all of them "guilty of perverting the facts, clothing ominous rumors in the garb of plausibility, and otherwise seeking to convince the reader that anarchy was rampant in Chicago."[28] Some papers condemned the strike but also criticized Pullman for his treatment of employees and his unwillingness to arbitrate the strike.

Tribune headlines proclaimed "Mob Is in Control," "Mob Bent on Ruin—Debs' Strikers Begin Work of Destruction," and "Guns Awe Them Not—Drunken Stockyard Rioters Defy Uncle Sam's Troops—Mobs Invite Death."[29] The *Washington Post* announced that it had come to the attention of federal authorities in Chicago that "the anarchists and socialist element, made up largely of the unemployed, were preparing to blow up the South end of the Federal building and take possession of the millions in money now stored in the treasury vaults."

The *New York Times* charged that workers supporting the strike were criminals and editorially declared that Debs was a "lawbreaker at large, an enemy of the human race. . . . It is time to cease mouthings . . . Debs should be jailed . . . and the disorder his bad teachings has engendered must be squelched." *Harper's Weekly* warned that strikers sought to overthrow the government and replace it with the "decrees of conspirators" and that the ARU sought the subjugation of the American people and mastery over all commerce. The *Independent* declared the strikers "villains and dupes" who should promptly be given life sentences in the penitentiary. The *Herald* also attacked Debs, proclaiming that "short work should be made of this reckless, ranting, contumacious, impudent braggadocio and law breaker." The *Tribune* said that it was "Dictator Debs versus the Federal Government" and that if the marshals, deputies, and the regular army could not quell the rebellion, then the president should call out "the militia of the different states—a million men if need be—and crush it into the dust."

Clergymen also joined the strike's condemnation. Dr. Herrick Johnson, professor at the Presbyterian Theological Seminary in Chicago, said, for example, "There is but one way to deal with these troubles now and that is by violence. . . . There must be some shooting, men must be killed, and then there will be an end of this defiance of law and destruction of property. . . . The soldiers must use their guns. They must shoot to kill."

Businesspeople around the country congratulated the president for his use of force, as did the acting president of the Chicago Bar Association and the president of Stanford University who wrote, "It is not often that an American citizen feels called upon to congratulate the President of the United States as having done his plain duty."

Chicago papers that were largely impartial during he strike included the *Daily News* and the *Record,* and those partial to labor were the *Dispatch,* the *Mail,* and the *Times.* Those papers, however, could not compare in circulation and influence with the antilabor Chicago press.

Craft and Industrial Unionism

With the passing of the ARU and the collapse of the Knights of Labor (described elsewhere), AFL craft unions were almost all that remained of unionism, and they dominated the labor scene for some four decades, roughly from 1894 to 1934. Only the IWW came into marginal contention for a time. Growth and turmoil for labor as well as routs and setbacks marked the 1900s and the 1910s—and defeat the 1920s. After the Pullman strike, the unmet demands of labor spread from railroads to mines, to steel—everywhere. These rebellions were all crushed, but so forceful was the unrest, AFL membership grew sixfold between 1897 and 1915. Given the extreme hostility of employers and the state, this union growth was a testament to its mass appeal.

Although the AFL gave organized labor a certain stability, it did not diminish employer hostility to unionism. Employers honed injunctions, the coercive weapon that had brought down the ARU, to a fine point. Most AFL unions favored the boycott (and the union label) over the strike, so the courts enjoined boycotts also. In this century's first decade, AFL affiliates conducted several hundred boycotts and faced almost as many court injunctions. In 1906, the AFL was enjoined by the Supreme Court from boycotting Buck's Stove products, and when Gompers violated the injunction, he and two others were sentenced to a year in prison. Gompers's term was never served, but the court decision convinced him that the courts were against unions and moved him, and other AFL unionists, toward greater militancy—a movement aborted by Gompers's revulsion at the McNamara brothers' confession in the bombing of the *Los Angeles Times.*

Decades of Trouble

Between 1910 and 1917, no major strikes were won except the IWW Lawrence, Massachusetts, strike in 1912. In 1914, miners struck the Colorado coal fields, and in the ensuing Ludlow massacre, militia machine-gunned the tents of strikers, set their camp on fire, killed thirty-three people, including women and children, and seriously injured more than a hundred. President Wilson sent in Federal troops and proposed a modest settlement, which the UMW accepted and the company rejected.

The 1920s roared for business and whimpered for labor. Wilson had used his war powers to give some sanction to unionism, but this unprecedented federal support had ended abruptly when the war ended. A new militancy gripped some AFL unions after the war, and they began demanding some socialization of industry, strong social legislation, a labor party, and industrial unionism.

Employers tried various paternalistic approaches in the 1920s, but the general context of labor relations was one of extreme employer and government hostility toward the labor-left. The Russian revolution, Milton Nadworny writes, "enabled labor's enemies to characterize almost every important strike as a Communist uprising, thus obscuring the issues at stake in most of the disputes."[31] Public opinion was turned against labor, and every act of repression was excused as a way to prevent the spreading disease of unionism.

The larger context included the return of Republicans to the presidency, the depression of 1920–1922, labor surpluses, sharply reduced manufacturing production, and 21 percent unemployed in 1921 (the highest rate since the 1880s). Union membership had doubled between 1915 and 1920 to 5 million, but by 1922 it had fallen to 3.6 million. The strike wave following the war had been crushed, and labor's frailty exposed it to intrusions by welfarism and other technologies of workplace control.

Militancy and Defeat

The AFL's clear willingness to struggle appeared in the steel strike of 1919. It appeared also in a 1919 Seattle general strike of some 60,000 workers, which, although peaceful and moderate in its demands, was nevertheless labeled Bolshevik-inspired and crushed (along with the Seattle union movement) by the combined force of 1,000 federal troops, 3,000 local police, machine gun emplacements around the city, and threats to declare martial law and shoot the disorderly on sight. Other expressions of militant unionism in 1919 included a strike of 25,000 railroad workers, led by the railroad brotherhoods and broken by the Justice Department's arrest of thirty-eight strike leaders; the organization of southern black sharecroppers, ending in the death of a deputy sheriff, the death sentence of twelve sharecroppers, and an end to sharecropper organizing; the AFL's effort to organize lumber workers in Bogalusa, Louisiana, broken by vigilantes, harassment of unionists, and the murder of the union president and three other union men; the Boston police strike for union recognition, labeled "red" and broken by state troops and volunteer police; and the national United Mine Workers strike, finally arbitrated by President Wilson.

Socialist May Day demonstrations in 1919, with many unionists participating, were forcibly repressed in many places. In Cleveland, for example, mobs invaded the May Day parade, followed by police cars and army trucks and tanks, which drove into the crowd, killed two demonstrators, and seriously wounded hundreds more. The melee ended in the sacking of two Socialist headquarters and the arrest of 125 Socialist demonstrators—but none of the anti-Socialist rioters.

The 1919 strike by John L. Lewis's bituminous miners almost paralyzed the coal industry. Although Attorney General Palmer enjoined the strike, miners refused to work and finally won major improvements, but the coal operators responded in 1920 with strikebreaking and open-shop campaigns. In 1920, UMW strikes in West Virginia were broken by federal troops, resumed in 1921, and were again broken by federal troops. The story of violence and turbulence in the nation's mines is long and grim. Most notable in that story is the vital role played by miners' unions (industrial unions) and by UMW President John L. Lewis in the formation of the CIO. By 1924, however, the national UMW had already started its long decline, defeated by repression and mechanization of the mines.

The employer offensive in the 1920s was supported by Taft's Supreme Court, a hostile Congress, Republican presidents (Harding, Coolidge, Hoover), and wartime gains in wealth and power. Employers began a postwar open-shop drive against unionism. Labor responded, and in 1922 alone, over 1.5 million workers in mining, railway, textile, and other industries called strikes, almost all of them ending in defeat. Employers sponsored company ("yellow") unions as a way to keep out legitimate ones, and by 1927, some 1.4 million workers had to join such unions as a condition of work. Employers solicited employee loyalty through profit sharing programs (enrolling more than 1 million shareholding workers) and through various paternalistic benefits—all retractable at the company's whim and without contract or recourse to law.

The Government Offensive

In 1920, U.S. Attorney General A. Mitchell Palmer launched an assault on "radicals," who for him included a wide range of unionists, liberals, and leftists. Labor faced such a hostile Congress that an AFL report in 1922 concluded:

More than 400 bills have been introduced in the 67th Congress which directly or indirectly affect labor. Ninety per cent of them are inimical to the interests of labor and the people. . . . The result has been that 99 per cent of the work done by labor in Congress has been to defeat pernicious legislation. . . . The

statement is often made that if the United States Capitol could be transported
to the England of the fifteenth century, half the members of Congress would
be "to the manor born."[32]

Some state legislatures passed laws curbing injunctions, forbidding the
discharge of workers for union activity, and defining labor's rights, but
all were either declared unconstitutional or nullified by court interpretation. Courts even voided the few social laws enacted, including such
benign measures as child labor laws.

William Howard Taft, who had left the presidency in 1913, was
appointed Chief Justice of the U.S. Supreme Court by Harding in 1921,
and the Court was then under the tight control of Taft and conservatives
during the rest of the 1920s. As an Ohio federal district judge in 1894,
Taft had written, on being told that federal troops had killed thirty
Pullman strikers, "Everybody hopes that it is true."[33] His nine-year
tenure on the Supreme Court, and that of his conservative colleagues,
converted such "hopes" into what was for labor a crushing reality.

In 1926, on a matter of substantive law, the Supreme Court held that
"a strike may be illegal because of its purpose."[34] Strikes over wages
were held to be legal, but not strikes against yellow-dog contracts, most
sympathy strikes, general strikes, or secondary boycotts. The Court also
restricted any striker conduct perceived as involving threats, coercion,
intimidation, or even the provocation of fear.

Picketing also came under court assault. In three states, courts banned
all picketing, and most crippling, the U.S. Supreme Court placed strict
limits on peaceful picketing (nonpeaceful picketing having long been
banned). The word "picket" itself was claimed to be "sinister," a word
suggesting a "militant purpose," which was not to be tolerated by the
law. Pickets were limited to one at each plant gate, and it became
"virtually impossible for a union legally to man an effective picket
line."[35]

The courts used injunctions repeatedly to keep unions from doing
almost anything they were in fact doing or planning to do. Thus the
injunction, an unusual remedy, became the usual and almost exclusive
one. In many cases, restraining orders alone broke strikes. Such an order
might ban or limit picketing, the issuance of strike benefits, the use by
strikers of the word "scab," or other strike behavior. In one case,
members of the Amalgamated Clothing Workers were banned from
standing within ten blocks of an employer's shop, an area that included
the center of New York's garment district and the union's headquarters.

By the end of the 1920s, the injunction, together with the infamous
and ubiquitous yellow-dog contract, which was legally enforceable,
imperiled the very survival of labor organizations. The courts had left

employers untouched—and their use of lockouts, discharge for union activity, strikebreakers, etc.—and employers could hire and fire as they chose. Maintaining a blacklist was easy for employers whether or not the courts thought it legal.

Under this systematic attack, led or upheld by the legal system, AFL membership plunged. The real wages of workers declined, driven also by recession. Between 1923 and 1929, corporate profits and dividends rose by more than 60 percent, wages by only 11 percent, and unemployment stood at about 10 percent. In 1929, the top 1 percent of Americans earned as much as the bottom 42 percent. According to the *Wall Street Journal,* "Never before, here or anywhere else, has a government been so completely fused with business."[36] Meanwhile, in Britain, the nation's first labor government came to power in 1924.

Industrial Unionism

Studies in both Europe and the United States show that craft unions and craft consciousness can launch broad social movements and serve as catalysts in the mobilization of industrial workers.[37] Thus, the AFL craft unions were also to some extent catalysts, as well as major obstacles, to the organization of the CIO and industrial workers.

In August 1936, the AFL Executive Council, presided over by William Green, suspended the ten unions that had formed the Committee for Industrial Organization within the AFL. On March 22, 1936, with those unions still inside the AFL, the first major CIO strike had been won, at Goodyear in Akron, Ohio, the world's largest rubber plant, where 10,000 striking workers helped to pioneer the sit-down strike and mass picketing.

By February 11, 1937, the United Automobile Workers (CIO) had struck the giant General Motors Corporation and won what was probably the largest and most important strike victory in American labor history to that date. John L. Lewis had wanted to lead off the organizing drive with steelworkers, because low steel wages impeded progress in the steel-owned "captive mines," but the auto union had been ready to go so its strike briefly preceded the steel drive. On March 2, 1937, however, a surprise agreement was signed between the steelworkers and the hitherto intransigent U.S. Steel Corporation—without a strike—and by May 1937, the steel union had 300,000 members and more than a hundred contracts with employers.

By December 1937, only somewhat more than a year after its expulsion from the AFL, the CIO had 3.7 million members, including 600,000 miners, 400,000 auto workers, 375,000 steelworkers, 250,000 ladies' garment workers, 175,000 clothing workers, 100,000 agricultural and packinghouse workers, and 80,000 rubber workers. Half the textile workers and 60 percent of the rubber workers in the country had union contracts, and successful organizing drives were under way in virtually all industries.

What had happened? The workers were the same, the ethnic and immigrant mixture was roughly the same, and most union leaders were formerly members of AFL-affiliated unions. Their approach to organizing industrial unionism was the same in most respects as that of the ARU, the Knights of Labor, the National Labor Union, the AFL in 1919, even the IWW; it was even the same as that of several long-term AFL unions, including the Brewery Workers and, especially, John L. Lewis's United Mine Workers. The main differences concerned politics and the period.

The times were ripe for industrial unionism. The Great Depression had gripped the country, and the election of Franklin Delano Roosevelt (FDR) and the ensuing New Deal had made the federal government more sympathetic to labor. "We're about to go into a campaign that will be everything . . . you've talked about," Lewis told his associate Powers Hapgood at the time of the CIO's formation. "We're going out to fight for those things [organizing industrial workers], and we're going to get them. You see, Powers, I've never really opposed those things. I just never felt the time was ripe and that trying to do those things back in the days when we had our violent arguments would have been suicide for organized labor and would have resulted in complete failure. But now the time is ripe; and now the time to do those things is here. Let us do them."[38]

Lewis's change of heart was occasioned by the enactment of the Wagner Act (NLRA) in mid-1935 and the clamor for unionism that the act responded to and set in further motion. The federal government had backed off from its historical military and judicial support of employers in labor conflicts, and more than that, it had tipped over somewhat, at least temporarily, to the union side. Congress was now telling employers that unions certified under the law had a right to recognition and that employers must bargain in good faith with them.

The National Industrial Recovery Act (NIRA) of 1933, requiring union recognition of participating employers, had made a difference, despite problems and final rejection by the courts. Even the AFL experienced stunning membership increases after that act's passage, despite limited gains in collective bargaining. With FDR in the presidency, employers knew that the U.S. Army and federal injunctions would not be at their easy command during strikes, and labor knew it too. In some industrial states, labor was also shielded by officials such as Michigan Governor

Frank Murphy, who protected strikers in the critical sit-downs in Flint and elsewhere and refused to use the state militia to break strikes.

On labor's side, the sit-down strike—an almost revolutionary act involving temporary seizure of employer property—became a decisive new weapon. In seven months alone, between September 1936 and May 1937, some 485,000 workers engaged in sit-down strikes. Even AFL strikers were sitting down, but the tactic was most widely used in the automobile sector and proved indispensable to its unionization.

An almost uninterrupted history of government repression or indifference had ended—or rather lay dormant for awhile—and labor seized some moments of victory and triumph before sliding downward into the 1980s. According to Val Lorwin's review of French labor, American workers "had to fight bloodier industrial battles than the French for the right of unions to exist and to function. . . . France had nothing like the private armies, factory arsenals and industrial espionage services"[39] that confronted American labor.

The current confrontation resembles most closely that of the 1920s: union busting in both good times and bad, wealth-holding dangerously skewed to the top, a decline of real wages, collapsing financial institutions, and employer talk of "cooperation" while often committing acts as hostile as those of the 1920s.

PART THREE

Labor-left Politics: Strategies of Repression

8

Socialists and Sedition:
The World War I Era

THE MISFORTUNES OF INDUSTRIAL and radical unionism cast their shadow on the politics of the labor-left. A solid union base for successful labor politics could not develop, and the same forces that stunted union growth also inhibited growth on the political left and the expression of any serious dissent. Although civil liberties and a free market of ideas are widely touted American virtues, too often the range of tolerated ideas has been limited, in Richard Hofstadter's words, "by the horizons of property and enterprises."[1] That range has been narrower than in most democracies, according to Robert Dahl, whose comparison of nine democracies concludes that "most other stable democracies have not imposed as severe a set of legal and social obstacles to political dissent as exists in the United States."[2] That study is confirmed by Robert Goldstein's review of political repression, which concludes that the range of acceptable political opinion, "especially with regard to radical labor or explicitly socialist ideologies, is and has been narrower than that of perhaps any other industrialized democracy."[3]

Compared with the British experience, which resembles the Continent's in many ways, the unique aspects of American political repression during various periods of political unrest have included the scope and intensity of conservative hostility to political dissent on the labor-left; the range of public agents involved in the suppression of dissent (executive, legislative, judicial within federal, state, and local governments and subdivisions within each); the extent of vigilante involvement; the use of immigration law to exclude dissenters; and the extensive denial of due process in the use of expanded police powers and trial by public exposure rather than legal procedures. Also exceptional have been the use of legislative hearings and television to stigmatize witnesses, the scope of "secret police" surveillance of private citizens and groups, the size and severity of both public and private loyalty-security programs, the harshness of the penalties imposed by those programs, and the effect of all these measures on all shades of opinion on the labor-left.

The history of American political repression is as long as the nation's history, but peak periods have centered roughly on the years surrounding the two world wars. In World War I, it involved attacks on the Socialist Party and the IWW and a postwar "red scare" that targeted moderate as well as radical labor activities. The second period began in the late 1930s, waned during World War II, and peaked during the cold war and especially during the Korean war. Tying together the two periods, in a sense, was J. Edgar Hoover, Federal Bureau of Investigation (FBI) head, whose tenure as an enemy of un-Americanism began during the Palmer Raids of January 1920 and continued for half a century. Although the labor-left has also experienced political repression in other democracies, in relation to the severity of the red menace it has generally been less severe than in the United States.

Historical Beginnings

American political repression goes back at least to the Federalist-controlled Congress that, fearing the French Revolution's extension to America, denounced Thomas Jefferson and other French sympathizers, abrogated an alliance with France, and passed the Alien and Sedition Acts of 1798. These laws empowered President John Adams to deport "dangerous" aliens, imprison others, and prosecute anyone who criticized the government by written or spoken word. Adams opposed enforcement of the Alien Act, but the people prosecuted under the Sedition Act were all members of Jefferson's Democratic-Republican Party—and Adams's opposition.

In 1801, Jefferson became president, and the Sedition Act expired. Yet the Federalists, gathered around Alexander Hamilton and the large merchant, landowner, and incipient industrial interests, had set a precedent for later, more drastic controls of political dissent.[4] During the debate on Alien and Sedition Acts, Edward Livingston, later Andrew Jackson's secretary of state, had warned about the acts' effects: "The country will swarm with informers, spies, delators, and all the odious reptile tribe. . . . The hours of the most unsuspected confidence, the intimacies of friendship, or the recesses of domestic retirement, afford no security. . . . Do not let us be told that we are to excite a fervor against a foreign aggression to establish a tyranny at home."[5]

Nineteenth-century Europe experienced uprisings and repression, but, according to Barton Ingraham, Enlightenment views had a restraining influence on French and English governments in their dealing with political revolutionaries in the 1830s and 1840s—and also on Bismarck's courts and administration in their dealings with socialists.[6] With rare exceptions (terror or treason), the political offender was regarded as "possessing a measure of respectability" and being "motivated by moral considerations," and hence was treated with some leniency and given some protection against arbitrary prosecution.[7]

The first major red scare in the United States occurred in 1873–1878 in response to the 1871 Paris Commune, the appearance of Marxist parties, the mobilization of workers and farmers before the 1873 depression, and the 1877 railroad uprising. In the late 1870s, echoing an official view, one professor at the Union Theological Seminary said that there was not in any language a more hateful word than "communism," a word that Goldstein claims "quickly became an all-purpose epithet applied by conservatives to anyone or anything found distasteful."[8] It was applied to almost all labor-left claims—to regulating railroads, limiting hours of work, farmers' pleas for reform, even Democratic claims of irregularities in the 1876 presidential election. As tensions rose in the 1870s, so did the fear of communism. In 1875, Chicago businessman Joseph Medill declared, "Every lamp-post in Chicago will be decorated with a communistic carcass if necessary to prevent wholesale incendiarism," and in 1879, an Alabama newspaper welcomed only immigrant workers that were not "tramps, strikers, communists or Mollie Maguires."[9] Employers found charges of communism and radicalism very effective in breaking strikes, labeling even modest union demands as un-American and inspired by an international communist conspiracy.

In the 1880s, a major communist scare rose on the heels of a labor-left upheaval, the successes of the Knights of Labor, the disaster that resulted from an 1886 labor protest meeting in Haymarket Square in Chicago, and the depression of 1882–1886. Growing labor militancy, followed by repression, red scares, and a swing to the political right, was to be repeated again in 1894, 1919, and the post–World War II period.

In the early years of the twentieth century, new weapons were added to the American arsenal of repression: new methods of surveillance, new ways of stigmatizing and controlling dissent, and new laws to control the "radicalism" that at times attracted a sizable following. In 1902 and 1903, federal and state anarchist laws were adopted, inspired officially by the Haymarket disaster and the assassination of President McKinley and unofficially by union successes and the eight-hour-day movement. Like the Alien and Sedition Acts of 1798, these laws went beyond outlawing *specific* actions to criminalizing opinions, speech, and associations. They also greatly expanded the role of government—especially the federal government—in repressing political dissent.

Under these laws, the reputedly anarchist-influenced Western Federation of Miners was largely extinguished in 1903–1907. The recession of 1907–1911 deepened the anarchist scare, producing a federal campaign to deport alien anarchists (though almost none could be found) and the post office refusal, without any legal authority, to handle two anarchist newspapers, a refusal amounting to press suppression since no other means of distribution was available.

These early laws became models for later ones, including the many state criminal syndicalist laws used against the IWW and others in 1917–1920 and the Communist Party in 1947–1954. Also passed were the Espionage and Sedition Acts of 1917–1918, used against the Socialist Party and others; various immigration laws; the Smith Act of 1940, which, even in peacetime, criminalized membership in designated "subversive" groups or advocacy of their programs; the Internal Security Act of 1950; and the Communist Control Act of 1954.

The First World War: Laws and Outlaws

From 1912 to 1917, "the government was quite willing to move against all radicals," Thomas Emerson writes, "but it did not yet see the way to do so."[10] It had sent in troops to put down the great strikes of 1877 and 1894, but such conflicts had been more easily classified as domestic insurrection. IWW activity, however, had never reached that level, so federal "red hunters" had to wait until World War I to move against it and the Socialist Party.

That war and its aftermath produced greater restrictions on free expression, Emerson concludes, than any other period in the nation's history, except perhaps that of the pre–Civil War South.[11] The federal Espionage Act of 1917 provided up to twenty years in prison and a $10,000 fine for making false reports with intent to interfere with the war or for attempting to obstruct enlistment or to cause insubordination in the military. It also authorized the post office to exclude mail that violated the law.

In 1918, the act was so amended and enlarged that it came to be called the Sedition Act. Now outlawed was virtually all criticism of the war or the government, and coverage included people who "wilfully utter, print, write, or publish any disloyal, profane, scurrilous, or abusive language about the form of government of the United States, or the Constitution . . . or the flag . . . or the uniform of the Army or Navy."[12] Criticizing the form of government or the Constitution and advocating any curtailment of production of anything necessary or essential to the persecution of the war were also made illegal.

Use of the Espionage and Sedition Acts by federal troops and overzealous U.S. district attorneys in a "combination of random terror and carefully directed prosecutions," aimed at destroying the IWW and the Socialist Party, resulted in over 2,100 indictments, over 1,000 convictions, and over 100 sentences to prison terms of ten years or more— and the imprisonment of Eugene Debs and many others who shared his views.[13] None were convicted for spying, though the law's ostensible intent was to deal with wartime espionage.

According to Robert Cushman, the government had "embarked upon a program of repression that matched or exceeded wartime repression" even in countries such as Germany and Russia, and that "clearly exceeded the degree of repression experienced by America's Anglo-Saxon partner, Great Britain."[14] In many cases, American citizens were sentenced to prison for up to twenty years for simple verbal opposition to the war, an offense "which at the most would have drawn from any English court a sentence of a few months in jail or a medium-sized fine."[15] Referring to war opponents, the U.S. attorney general said in 1917, "May God have mercy on them, for they need expect none from an outraged people and an avenging government."[16]

Under wartime immigration laws, 687 people had been arrested for deportation by the war's end. In early 1917, local army officers were broadly authorized to repress sternly all seditious activity, an authority they took to include wholesale spying on civilians and the smashing of IWW strikes.

The post office banned from use of the mails some seventy-five papers, including an issue of *The Public* that was banned for urging that more of the wartime budget come from taxes and less from loans. Issues of the *Freeman's Journal* and the *Catholic Register* were banned for calling attention to Jefferson's view that Ireland should be free, a view not shared by wartime ally Britain, and National Civil Liberties Board pamphlets were banned for explaining the beliefs of conscientious objectors and deploring mob violence.

Drastic as the federal legislation was, many states (especially in the West) enacted even more sweeping laws during the war years. Seven states and territories passed criminal syndicalist laws (aimed mainly at the IWW), and eleven states outlawed various forms of opposition to the war. Montana arrested 134 and convicted 52 in less than a year after it passed its criminal syndicalist and sedition laws, and Idaho arrested over 200 and convicted 31 during 1917 and 1918. Many teachers and other critics of the war were charged with disloyalty and fired from their jobs. A state judge in Montana was impeached for testifying on behalf of a man charged with espionage, and a University of Virginia professor was fired for making a pacifist speech.

Critics and Vigilantes

In fact, the war and the U.S. entrance into it were conspicuously unpopular. Oklahoma farmers took up arms in rebellion against the war, and many large ethnic groups—the anti-Anglo Irish, the anti-Czarist Jews, German ethnic groups, and others—were openly opposed to it. The large Socialist vote in 1917 elections clearly reflected that opposition. In response to this popular opposition, the American Protective League (APL), a unique *private* volunteer group operating with Justice Department sanction and numbering some 350,000 members by the war's end, engaged in a broad range of intelligence-gathering and vigilante activities. It investigated the loyalty of soldiers, government employees, and people seeking passports, and it developed a national spy network, made arrests and detained people, disrupted union and Socialist meetings, infiltrated the ranks of suspect groups, opened mail, wiretapped, and even burglarized people it suspected. It collected rumors from around the country and participated with government agents in "slacker raids," which involved seizing men in public places, arresting them, and detaining them for interrogation.

During three days in Chicago, some 150,000 men were interrogated and 16,000 arrested by government agents and the APL on suspicion of evading military service; in New York City in 1918, over 10,000 (some reports claim as high as 40,000) were arrested on the same charge. Senator Albert Fall said about the raids, "Never in the history of any civilized country under the heavens, except in the history of Russia, could such acts have been committed."[17] It is estimated that some 400,000 had been picked up on suspicion by the war's end.

Critics of the war also faced some 164 recorded mob attacks. Mob violence increased during the war, continued afterward, and included lynching, tarring and feathering, whipping, and "deportations" to distant places. Its victims were mainly blacks, Wobblies (members of the IWW), Non-Partisan Leaguers, "pro-Germans," and radicals. "The mobs with few exceptions," the *American Labor Yearbook* claimed, "are deliberately organized groups of business men, protecting the institutions of property against the menace of radicalism or the protests of an exploited class."[18] Principal organizers of these mobs included the American Legion and the Ku Klux Klan (KKK).

Also active were "councils of defense," private patriotic organizations resembling the APL, which were organized on state, town, and county levels throughout the country. In such states as Minnesota and Montana, these councils "amounted practically to the establishment of a dictatorship" of a handful of people, mainly well-to-do, conservative elements of the community.[19]

In Minnesota and South Dakota, councils proposed that people who refused to buy liberty bonds should be subpoenaed and investigated for disloyalty. An Oklahoma council seized and sold a "bond slacker's" car—and bought war bonds for him with the proceeds. Some Idaho councils tried to set up a card index on the entire population of the state, and many people deemed "disloyal" were required to apologize for their behavior, purchase war bonds, and make large contributions to the Red Cross or similar groups. A Nebraska council demanded that twelve professors be fired from the state university for their war stands, three of whom were finally dismissed. The North Dakota state council caused work-or-fight rules to be adopted in the state, and since these rules resulted in the arrest of people who refused to work during strikes, strikes were thus virtually outlawed.

For those critics who declared themselves conscientious objectors (COs) treatment in military camps was extremely brutal—Senator George W. Norris said that if reports he received were "anywhere near the truth . . . we are more barbarous in the treatment of these unfortunate men than were the men of the Dark Ages in the treatment of their prisoners"[20]— and sentencing was also harsher than elsewhere. In England, which was far more deeply involved in the war, CO sentences did not exceed two years; in the United States, 17 COs were sentenced to death, 142 to life in prison, and 345 to prison terms that averaged sixteen and a half years, though with the war's end the most severe sentences were commuted.

The Socialist Party and Sedition

Democrats lost heavily in the 1918 congressional elections, and Wilson lost the support he needed for his more enlightened peace proposals, perhaps because, as one person wrote him: "The Department of Justice and the Post Office were allowed to silence and intimidate all the radical or liberal friends of such policies. There was no voice to argue for your sort of peace."[21] The postwar decade saw not only the triumph of the Republican Party but the virtual demise of Debs's Socialist Party. Despite repression, the Socialists had achieved a stability and a mass appeal in the prewar period that was unique for a party on the American left. The war changed that situation.

The War Years

A week after the U.S. declaration of war in April 1917, the Socialist Party proclaimed in convention its "unalterable opposition to the war." Modern wars, it said, "have always been made by the classes and fought by the masses. Wars bring wealth and power to the ruling classes, and suffering, death and demoralization to the workers. . . . They obscure the struggles of the workers for life, liberty and social justice. . . . The mad orgy of death and destruction which is now convulsing unfortunate Europe was caused by the conflict of capitalist interests in the European countries." The proclamation went on to say that all those killed, crippled, or maimed by the war "have not been sacrifices exacted in a struggle for principles or ideals, but wanton offerings upon the altar of private profit."[22]

With the adoption of the Espionage Act in 1917, a dozen or more major socialist papers were banned from the mails, and by mid-1918, the only socialist periodicals left were a few in large cities where distribution did not depend on the mails. In the West and Midwest, the socialist press was permanently destroyed, and by the war's end, most of the large network of socialist publications were extinct. This silencing of the socialist press was perhaps the most destructive act of government repression, destroying as it did the party's internal communications and its ability to influence ongoing events.

In May 1917, the Indianapolis offices of the party were raided. In September, the Justice Department raided the national headquarters in Chicago and party offices across the country, seized materials, and arrested leaders, and in February 1918, the trials and convictions of party leaders began. During the early months of the war, mass Socialist meetings evoked supportive public response but an increasingly hostile response from public officials and vigilantes.

Two months after the United States entered the war, soldiers and sailors attacked an antiwar parade of some 800 Socialists in Boston and precipitated a riot that ended in the sacking of Socialist Party offices and the arrest of 10 Socialists. Socialist meetings were broken up everywhere, by local ordinances forbidding Socialist meetings, by police eagerly enforcing the ordinances, by vigilantes and night riders who tarred and feathered Socialist speakers. In South Dakota, police broke up the Socialist Party's state convention, and in New York City, so many Socialist street-corner speakers were jailed that it was proposed a party branch be set up in jail.

Socialist successes in the November 1917 elections evoked even more repression. Socialist leaders had been arrested and many jailed even before the election, but after it, the number of such arrests escalated.

Five national leaders of the party were indicted for sedition, including Victor Berger, head of the Milwaukee party, Congressman, and candidate for the U.S. Senate; and the party's national secretary, Adolph Germer. All were tried and sentenced to twenty years in prison—and released in 1921, well beyond the war's end.

In the spring of 1918, with many of his comrades in jail, Debs spoke to a mass meeting in Canton, Ohio. Corporate leaders, he said, "are today wrapped in the American flag and shout their claim from the housetops that they are the only patriots." With magnifying glasses in hand, they scan "the country for evidence of disloyalty, eager to apply the brand of treason to the men who dare to even whisper their opposition."[23] A U.S. attorney recorded Debs's words and charged him with ten violations of the Espionage Act, and Debs was tried and sentenced to ten years in prison. At age sixty-four he entered the federal penitentiary in Atlanta, in broken health, which was worsened by the steamy Atlanta climate, isolation, confinement, and the regimens of prison life. In prison he was first held almost incommunicado, and after Wilson left office, Attorney General Palmer cut off all visits to him and all mailing privileges. Finally, in December 1921, Harding pardoned Debs and twenty-three other political prisoners. But their freedom came too late, and they were too out of touch to prevent the splintering of the Socialist Party.

The Responses at Home and Abroad

As noted, government repression of the Socialist Party included denial of public office to duly elected party candidates. Even Bismarck and the German kaiser had stopped short of denying socialists their elected offices. Many Social Democratic activities had been banned by Bismarck, but socialists could run for office and assume the many parliamentary seats to which they were elected. The German Social Democratic Party supported the war, but antiwar socialists such as Karl Kautsky, Eduard Bernstein, Karl Liebnicht, and Rosa Luxembourg, though restricted in their activities, generally had greater freedom than their American counterparts, and Bernstein and Liebnicht held on to their parliamentary seats. In New York City by contrast, two elected Socialists were expelled from their seats in city government, and in the New York State legislature, five elected Socialists were expelled. On the federal level, Socialist leader Victor Berger, under indictment for conspiracy, was elected to Congress from Wisconsin in 1918, but the House refused to seat him. A special election was held in 1919, Berger was again elected, and again he was refused his seat. Sentenced to twenty years in prison, a sentence reversed on appeal, Berger was unable to take his seat until 1922.

Socialists claimed the war was brought on by international financial interests, such as those of British-American banker and steel tycoon J. P. Morgan, a vigorous supporter of the war, and by industrialists who feared the rapidly rising competition of German industry. Certainly the war did not save the world for democracy, its proclaimed purpose, and if anything, had the opposite effect. Moreover, it cost some 10 million lives and twice that many wounded.

The Socialist Party was not alone in opposing the war. America was remote from the battlefields, sentiment was typically isolationist and pacifist, and resistance and neutrality were widespread, probably representing majority opinion. Fifty-six members of Congress, for example, voted against the declaration of war.

Nor was the party singular among international socialist parties in opposing the war. In Britain, the Labour Party finally supported the war, but its chief *socialist* component, the Independent Labour Party (ILP), opposed it. Yet no split on the issue occurred, and treatment of the pacifist ILP—by authorities and the media—in no way resembled the persecution of American Socialists. Ramsey MacDonald, a founder of the British Labour Party and a leader of the ILP (and in 1911–1914 Labour Party leader in the House of Commons), opposed British entry into the war, and although he was discredited for his pacifism and called a traitor, by 1922 he was again leader of his party. In 1924, he was prime minister in the first Labour government, and in 1929, he headed the second Labour government.

In postwar Britain, conservatives sought to reverse the wartime gains of unionism and the Labour Party, but nothing comparable to the American red scare occurred, despite the greater concentration of "reds" in the United Kingdom. In the United States, the war's legacy was extreme repression of the political left and a precipitous decline of labor, presided over in succession by Republican Presidents Warren G. Harding, Calvin Coolidge, and Herbert Hoover. The AFL, which had supported the war, was almost as devastated by the war's aftermath as was the Socialist Party, which had opposed the war. In Britain, the war had empowered both unionism and democratic socialism; in the United States, war and repression defeated both.

Most member parties of the Socialist International finally supported the war, but not all, and every party had sizable antiwar minorities, yet nowhere did their repression approach the U.S. level.[24] In Europe, the war discredited and weakened capitalism, so many democratic socialist parties grew and prospered in the war's aftermath. In the United States the war greatly strengthened capitalism, giving it a freer hand than ever to deal with dissent, and only in the United States did a major socialist party suffer such disabling wounds, inflicted as much in the aftermath of war as during it. By rights, repression should have ended with the armistice. Instead, it intensified and spread.

Heavy Postwar Casualties

In 1919, the left wing of the Socialist Party split off to form the Communist Party and the Communist Labor Party. Well before the split, according to James Weinstein, agents of the Department of Justice had been infiltrating the Socialist Party in order to split it and diminish its strength. These agents joined and sometimes led the pro-Soviet "left wing" of the party in its struggles with the "right wing," Weinstein writes, and although the split may have occurred anyhow, the role of the Justice Department in creating, in effect, the Communist Party was an extraordinary one.[25]

In Detroit, the statewide organizer of the Russian Socialist Federation (part of the Socialist wing that became the Communist Party) and one of the most active left-wingers in the Socialist Party during the split was later exposed as a hired labor spy. Many Socialists believed, Weinstein notes, that the Communist organizations were honeycombed with spies and that many Communist leaders were actually hired by government and big business to destroy the Socialist Party.[26] Curiously, Weinstein reports, the post office favored the party's left wing by holding up the mail of only the party's right wing, not the left.[27]

Government aided the Socialist Party's split in another way, by imprisoning Debs and isolating him from the party during its most troubled times. Debs was the only person, it is believed, who could have reconciled the factions in the party and prevented the split. Whether or not that assessment was right, Debs might at least have reduced the size of the defection and provided some needed balance in the ideological disputes raging within the party.

Despite the Socialist Party's plight even before the split, party membership and votes held steady, and from August 1918 to mid-1919, membership actually grew from 83,000 to 110,000. In New York City, Morris Hillquit, Socialist candidate for mayor, called for an early and humane peace and won a record Socialist vote of 146,000. Although he lost the election, seven Socialist city aldermen were elected.

Membership and votes did not fully reflect reality, however, for the party of 1919 was not the party of 1917. About 35 percent of its members in 1917 were foreign-speaking new immigrants; by 1919, the figure had risen to about 53 percent. Many of the old native-American, midwestern, rural–small town members had been driven out by repression, and many of the new members were later to split off to form the two new

Communist parties. Thus, the Socialist Party lost both old and new members, and after the split, membership dropped to only 26,766—although the vote for Debs for president in 1920, still in prison and a kind of "war hero," was 900,000.

Postwar Repression, Old and New

Even after the war was over, prosecutions under federal espionage and conscription laws continued. In 1920, thirteen Ohio Socialists were sentenced to from three to fifteen months in prison and fined for alleged conspiracy to obstruct the draft, and in 1919, the top staff members of the *Seattle Union Record* were indicted on charges of violating the Espionage Act. In 1920, four officials of the Socialist Party's Albany local were sentenced to from twelve to thirty months in prison for distributing the publication "The Price We Pay," a leaflet that a federal judge had previously held did not violate federal law. In the early postwar period, the post office continued to censure mail under the Espionage Act and to deny second-class mailing privileges to politically suspect publications. Also, from 1917 to 1921, some 900 suspected security risks were barred from taking federal civil service examinations.

Newer tacks were taken immediately after the armistice, the *American Labor Yearbook* claims, "organized business came out into the open with its program against labor."[28] The program pursued two lines of attack: the passage of criminal syndicalist laws curtailing civil liberties and the national open-shop campaign against unions.

The Lusk Committee of the New York State legislature was the first of a long string of committees to investigate un-American activities. Although only a committee of inquiry, it conducted illegal raids on the Rand School and other suspect groups, popularized the "red menace" in the press, and promoted the expulsion of Socialists from elected office and the prosecution of leftist leaders.

New state laws were passed requiring teachers to sign loyalty oaths and restricting the expression of their political views. Radicals were harassed by vigilantes, the KKK was revived, and in 1921, immigrant leftists Nicola Sacco and Bartolomeo Vanzetti were executed for a crime many people believed they did not commit. By the end of 1919, the red scare had spread to include liberals, leftists of all persuasions, teachers, professors, clergy, lawyers, and public officials. One tactic was to "redbait every liberal who believed in municipal or government ownership."[29] "Property was in an agony of fear," as one observer put it, "and the horrid name 'Radical' covered most innocent departures from conventional thought with a suspicion of desperate purpose."[30]

Vice President Calvin Coolidge in 1921 illustrated the threat of red infiltration of women's colleges by referring to a Wellesley professor who reportedly had voted for Debs in the 1920 election. President Harding's commissioner of education claimed there was "altogether too much preaching of these damnable doctrines of Bolshevism, Anarchy, Communism and Socialism" and proclaimed that "if I had it in my power I would not only imprison but would expatriate all advocates of these dangerous un-American doctrines. I would even execute every one of them—and do it joyfully."[31]

Postwar Sedition, Anarchy, Syndicalism, and Disloyalty

Before the war, only New York and Tennessee had sedition laws, though in neither case had they been used. In 1919 alone, sixteen states passed criminal syndicalist laws, and twelve passed anarchy and sedition laws. By 1921, two-thirds of the states had passed such laws. In all cases, Goldstein notes, business interests were connected with the passage of the laws.[32] In 1919–1920, some 1,400 people were arrested under these state laws and 300 convicted, most of them members of the IWW, the Communist Party, or the Communist Labor Party. In almost every case, the defendant was prosecuted for advocating a doctrine of force and violence, even though almost all of them denied believing in any such doctrine.[33] Prosecutions hinged solely on the utterance of words, and questionable interpretations of them, not on overt acts in violation of the law. Some prosecutions involved mere membership in an organization, not even the utterance of words.

New York State won many convictions under its criminal anarchy law of 1920, including those of five leaders of the new Communist Party. In New York State, police raided the Union of Russian Workers and arrested over 160 people; many public school teachers were fired, and a list was published of people who were prohibited from speaking in public schools. In other states, similar prosecutions proceeded. In Chicago, eighty-five leading Communist Party members and thirty-eight officials of the Communist Labor Party were sentenced in 1920 to one to five years in prison and fined for violating the state's sedition law. Local officials in Chicago also raided seventy radical meetings and arrested as many as 200 people, over 100 of whom were sentenced to up to ten years in prison.

The red scare appeared early in western states, where the IWW had operated, and in New York, where radical groups had been relatively strong. Washington State passed a criminal syndicalist law when the Seattle general strike threatened, and police raided IWW halls after the strike and arrested twenty-seven for violating that law. In the thirteen years after passage of the Washington law, eighty-six people were convicted under its provisions. Oregon and California passed similar laws in 1919. California convicted forty-six Wobblies of wartime espionage, even though the war was over, and IWW strikes in California citrus groves resulted in the arrest of many strikers and the deportation of thirty-five leaders, thus ending unionism in that citrus industry for more than a decade.

City ordinances against sedition and syndicalism followed state laws. In Washington State alone, over twenty cities had criminal syndicalist ordinances, and in Spokane, over 1,000 Wobblies were convicted under the law within a year and a half of the armistice. Local ordinances also restricted literature distribution, meetings, and picketing.

Although some federal executive agencies got out of the red-hunting business in the mid-1920s, federal courts and state governments continued much as before, upholding criminal syndicalist laws and convictions even when no clear and present danger could be shown. Local police continued and often intensified their harassment of radicals, making 289 "free speech" arrests in 1921, 846 in 1922, and 418 in 1928—mainly because of labor disputes. Officially sanctioned and sometimes officially organized "citizens" movements carried on the red-hunting work executive agencies had discontinued.

Some twenty states adopted teacher loyalty oaths, and many school textbooks were banned; teachers were fired for political views; a journalism professor at Ohio State University was fired for making favorable comments about a coal strike; many left-leaning students were expelled from college; and weakened left-wing groups and individuals suffered continuing harassment. Teachers suspected of radicalism were marked for firing or discrimination, "but more significant than the expulsion of teachers for personal economic beliefs," the *American Labor Yearbook* claimed, "is the discrimination against those who attempt to organize unions in the teaching profession. . . . Boards of Education frequently adopt resolutions forbidding unions, punishing with expulsion those who join."[34]

Above all, new waves of union repression were launched. The legalization of yellow-dog contracts made the organizing of covered workers nearly impossible, state and federal courts repeatedly held for employers in labor disputes, and state troops continued to break strikes.

Investigative Operations

Secret police operations expanded rapidly during and after the war. A military intelligence force that had only 2 officers in 1917 had 1,300 by the war's end, and there were similar expansions in the security forces of the post office, the Justice Department, and the Treasury Department. Military intelligence officers engaged in extensive surveillance of the Socialist Party, the IWW, the Fellowship of Reconciliation (the forerunner of the American Civil Liberties Union, ACLU), and other groups. In some cases, these officers infiltrated groups and then conducted raids and arrests, and in at least one case (a Butte, Montana, miners' strike), undercover military agents cooperated with Anaconda Copper detectives to provoke a miners' strike, which was then smashed.

Late in 1919, the War Department and military intelligence officials prepared "War Plans White" to deal with what they saw as a permanent red menace. A U.S. Senate committee also entered the investigative arena, and a secret military intelligence list of sixty-two "dangerous radicals" was leaked to it. At the same time, in response to business pressures, Congress began to dismantle the progressive economic legislation of the war period.

In mid-1919, Attorney General Palmer asked Congress for half a million dollars to investigate radicalism, saying he had almost accepted reports that "on a certain day in the future" an attempt would be made to "rise up and destroy the government in one fell swoop."[35] When Congress appropriated funds to detect and prosecute "seditious crimes," Palmer used the money to infiltrate leftist groups, send inflammatory reports to the media for dissemination, and set up files on hundreds of thousands of "radicals" who had committed no crime. These activities were all directed by his new special assistant, twenty-four-year-old J. Edgar Hoover.

Because federal wartime sedition laws had lost most of their postwar legitimacy (though repealed only in 1921), Palmer and others relied more on immigration laws to combat un-Americanism. These laws were even preferable in some ways, as they did not depend on the commission of any criminal act, on evidence of any kind, or on lengthy court procedures—only the summary and arbitrary deportation of suspects. And the sentence was expulsion without expense to the taxpayers. Deportations under the law, then and now, have not been "punishment," only simple "withdrawal of hospitality." Hence, they have been ordered by administrative rather than judicial authorities and as the result of hearings rather than trials based on rules of evidence.

Under Palmer's and Hoover's direction, a period of "government terrorism unparalleled in American history" began in August 1919, reached a climax in January 1920, and then "gradually declined under liberal and labor opposition." In August 1919, Palmer sent confidential orders to all his special agents requiring a vigorous investigation of "anarchistic and similar classes, Bolshevism and kindred agitations," with a view to mass deportations of the people apprehended.[36] Based on the elaborate information (hearsay and otherwise) gathered by these agents, in November 1919 Palmer and local police raided homes and meeting places in cities across the country, often without a warrant and late at night, and suspects were put under arrest. In New York City, for example, after meeting places had been wrecked, some 650 workmen, mainly Russian emigrés, were beaten with blackjacks, questioned, searched, and sent to Ellis Island for deportation. A month later, 249 persons were deported to Russia without trial.

Palmer's main act came on January 2, 1920: wholesale raids on Communist Party and Communist Labor Party "hangouts" (cafes, pool halls, etc.) in over thirty cities and arrests often made without warrant. "There was in existence no law giving the Department of Justice any authority whatever to make arrests in deportation proceedings," the *American Labor Yearbook* claimed, "nor was there in existence any law under which the Department of Justice could lawfully have applied for search warrants to seize [the] radical literature" it did.[37]

A year later, a Senate committee estimated that some 10,000 people had been arrested on that January night and some 3,000 held for deportation—all despite the fact that the secretary of labor, in charge of immigration, had held neither the Communist Party nor the Communist Labor Party to be illegal for deportation purposes. The nation's jails were overwhelmed. In Detroit, some 800 people were kept for up to six days in the windowless corridor of the federal building, with only one toilet and, for a full day, without any food. Some people who came to bail out others were themselves arrested, and many of those detained were beaten by jailers.

Palmer described much of the "alien filth" he arrested as having "sly and crafty eyes . . . lopsided faces, sloping brows and misshapen features" sheltering "cupidity, cruelty, insanity and crime," and he noted that before the raids, "the blaze of revolution . . . was eating its way into the homes of the American workingman, its sharp tongues of revolutionary heat were licking the altars of churches, leaping into the belfry of the school bell, crawling into the sacred corners of American homes, seeking to replace marriage vows with libertine laws, burning up the foundations of society."[38] Assistant Secretary of Labor Louis F. Post commented, however, that "as a rule the hearings show the aliens arrested to be working men of good character who have never been arrested before, who are not anarchists or revolutionists, nor politically or otherwise dangerous in any sense. Many of them . . . have American born children."[39]

Both Palmer and Hoover, it is believed, exploited the radical issue for their own interests—in the first instance presidential ambitions and in the second, the desire to increase the size and powers of what was to become the FBI, the nation's leading enemy of un-Americanism—but others also exploited the issue for personal or political ends. In 1922, Attorney General Harry M. Daugherty charged that the railroad strike was a Communist plot. Charged with Teapot Dome involvements and forced from office by a Senatorial group led by Burton K. Wheeler, Daugherty charged in 1924 that Wheeler was the Communist leader in the Senate and that his Senate group was "the red triumvirate."

Another leading federal red hunter was William J. Burns, former head of one of the largest labor-spy companies, the Burns Detective Agency, and appointed head of the Bureau of Investigation in 1921. In 1922, he declared that the coal strike of that year was Comintern inspired and that he aimed to "drive every radical out of the country and bring the parlor Bolsheviks to their senses." In a 1924 statement to Congress, he warned that "radicalism is becoming stronger every day in this country. These parlor Bolsheviks have sprung up everywhere, as evidenced by this ACLU in New York."[40] The bureau still infiltrated and spied on labor and radical groups, disseminated information about them, and engaged in illegal wiretapping, searches, and seizures. Until about 1924 it still had links with private detective agencies.

"The war has set back the people for a generation," Senator Hiram Walker said in 1920. "They have bowed to a hundred repressive acts. They have become slaves to the government. They are frightened at the excesses in Russia. They are docile; and they will not recover from being so for many years. The interests which control the Republican Party will make the most of their docility."[41] The excesses of the Russian revolution had frightened the world, but nowhere else were the reactions of business elites used with such force and abandon against the whole spectrum of political opinion on the noncommunist labor-left.

9

Un-Americanism: World War II and Cold War Eras

PROBABLY NOTHING in the post–World War II era has damaged progressive politics more than the uniquely excessive efforts to hunt and destroy all traces of "un-Americanism" in the nation and beyond. As those efforts tell us much about the labor-left's status, they are reviewed briefly here for people who do not know what happened or whose memories need refreshing.

Clearly, the cold war had a legitimate target, Stalinism, but it is not the legitimacy of the war that is questioned but its excesses, both at home and abroad, and the resulting abuse of civil liberties in rallying nationalistic and conservative opinion. In the United States, the cold war meant McCarthyism. Much of what is now said about McCarthyism laments its excesses and its enduring harm to progressive opinion; what is more often debated is the relative contribution to it by the left, the right, and the general public. In the 1950s, some writers (Daniel Bell, S. M. Lipset, Earl Raab, and others) tended to associate McCarthyism with populist, ethnic, and working-class groups; their authoritarian personalities; and the "status deprivation" they suffered.[1] In some cases, the Catholic church was considered a mentor and motivator of these various ethnic and alienated groups. These views are less current now.

Richard Fried in *Nightmare in Red* attributes McCarthyism largely to the grievances and ambitions of conservative politicians (mostly but not solely of the Republican Party),[2] and Robert Griffith in *The Politics of Fear* claims that right-wing Republicans, bitterly hostile to the New Deal and stunned by Truman's 1948 victory, launched the second red scare "as they scrapped and clawed their way toward power."[3] Many people claim that Truman, president during much of the crusade's heat, bears much responsibility for the excesses, joining and even leading the crusade at times.[4] Although this view obviously contains some truth, the history of prior periods—the Dies Committee and the earlier red scares—shows that the crusade predated Truman by decades, that Truman was often swept along by its gathering fury, and that he was sometimes as much victim as perpetrator.

Fried claims to share "a recently emergent viewpoint" that stresses, not specifically working-class complicity, but "a deeply rooted cluster of values shared by much of American society, a set of views antithetical to Communist doctrines and friendly to private property and political democracy (albeit sometimes oblivious to imperfections in the latter)."[5] He notes a 1937 Gallup poll which showed that 54 percent of Americans favored a law to allow police to "padlock places printing Communist literature" and a 1946 poll which showed that 69 percent would deny Communists government jobs. He also cites, however, a 1946 poll in which only 16 percent would ban Communists from elective public office or "make it hard for them to be active" and a 1949 poll in which only 3 percent said that communism was their chief worry.[6] Moreover, during the Whittaker Chambers "spy revelations" in 1948, the Hearst papers deplored their inability, despite heroic efforts, to convince people that the red menace was not "greatly exaggerated" and that fighting it was not too damaging to civil liberties.

It is not at all clear, then, that a popular consensus existed for the excesses of McCarthyism. And insofar as such sentiments did exist, one must ask where they came from. Americans had far less firsthand experience with Communists (foreign or domestic) or with Communist doctrines and practices than most Europeans. Relatively few Americans knew any Communists or had ever listened to a Communist speak. Hence, their views must have come from outside sources.

The role of the media in the antired crusade is somewhat disputed, yet it is commonly said that the media *made* McCarthy. From the start, Fried writes, "McCarthy was a media demagogue, thriving on an ability to seize and hold headlines. Mostly it was the artillery of the press, not swelling legions of followers, that sustained his campaign." In fact, McCarthy's charges were first brought to the State Department's attention, he says, by a United Press effort to get a response to a story by the Associated Press.[7]

Some leading media professionals raised their voices against McCarthy, and most professionals may have been more anti-McCarthy than media policy makers, but if so, their views seldom surfaced until late in the day and even then confrontation was rare. With some notable exceptions, media professionals went along and, happily or not, gave McCarthy a national audience. Dorothy Thompson claimed at the time that "the press almost unanimously hates McCarthy, but obliges him with the front page, and condemns him in an editorial."[8]

Other people and groups also shaped popular opinion. In 1946, J. Edgar Hoover began a campaign to educate the public about the

Communist Party menace, passing on data from FBI files to a network of anti-Communist friends in the media and politics, including, Fried notes, the U.S. Chamber of Commerce, reporters, columnists, publishers, congressmen, conservatives in the entertainment field, religious leaders, and anti-Communists in the labor movement.[9] The U.S. Chamber of Commerce called for action against Communists in unions, government, and the media, and the American Legion and other veterans' groups entered the fray as a kind of anti-Communist army reserve called up for combat. The role of the Republican Party in the crusade was also conspicuous and dominant.

Prewar Beginnings

Hoover, Depression, Repression

During Herbert Hoover's presidency, the practiced modes of repression, in response to what was believed to be the red-inspired unrest of the unemployed, included deportations of political "undesirables," the curtailing of alien movement within the country, and the banning of radical papers from the mails. When some 10,000 veterans, many of them jobless, encamped in Washington in 1932 and demanded veterans' bonuses, 600 soldiers, commanded by General Douglas MacArthur, burned their Anacostia encampment, teargassed over 1,000, and sent 50 of them to the hospital.

Most armed repression was a local police matter. Starting as early as 1930, police attacked, shot, and teargassed unemployed demonstrators and made many "free speech" arrests. The network of secret police expanded, and the enforcement of state syndicalist, insurrection, and sedition laws surged.

The New Deal Era

The labor-left, subdued in the 1920s and early 1930s, was given new life with the 1932 election of Franklin Roosevelt and the New Deal. The economy began to emerge from depression, the CIO was organized, and the basic laws guiding the welfare state were enacted. Leftist politics entered the mainstream, sometimes in unexpected ways. Huey Long and his Share the Wealth program attracted a mass following that rivaled Roosevelt's in the early 1930s. Upton Sinclair almost won the California governorship in 1934 by promising to end poverty in the state, replace production for profit with production for use, and replace capitalist ownership with cooperatives. Philip LaFollette, elected Wisconsin governor on a third-party ticket in 1934, called for a truly progressive party and denounced liberalism. Minnesota Governor Floyd Olson urged nationalization of some basic industry and declared that, if it could not prevent disastrous depressions, he hoped the present system of government would go right to hell. The 1934 and 1936 elections put scores of Democrats in Congress whose politics were to the left of FDR's, and the largest student movement to that date flourished on college campuses.

Democratic socialism also recovered in the early 1930s. From 1928 to 1932, Socialist Party membership grew from 8,000 to 13,000 and the party's presidential vote rose from 267,000 to 884,000. Influential third parties emerged—the American Labor Party in New York, the Farmer-Labor Party in Minnesota, and the Progressive Party in Wisconsin—but all declined rapidly as supporters switched to Roosevelt.

The Business Response

As the left surged, so did the right. Conservative antagonism to Roosevelt was without parallel in the history of the American presidency. In the 1932 election campaign, incumbent President Herbert Hoover had warned that FDR's policies would "destroy the very foundation of our American system" and that they derived from the "same philosophy of government which has poisoned all Europe . . . the fumes of the witches caldron which boiled in Russia."[10] Similar charges grew in acrimony during the long FDR years, led by the business-sponsored American Liberty League and the powerful Hearst papers in the early years. William Randolph Hearst's basic objective, Arthur Schlesinger later wrote, was "evidently less to uncover genuine communists than to frighten liberals out of expressing opinions on public affairs."[11]

In 1935, the Republican National Committee announced that the upcoming elections would decide "whether we hold to the American system of government or whether we shall sit idly by and allow it to be replaced by a socialistic state honeycombed with waste and extravagance and ruled by a dictatorship that mocks at the rights of the States and the liberty of the citizen."[12] Republican vice-presidential candidate Frank Knox charged that the Democratic Party had been "seized by alien and un-American elements" and that Roosevelt "has been leading us towards Moscow." Republican presidential candidate Alf Landon claimed that New Deal policies were leading the nation to the guillotine and that "if we are to preserve our American form of government this administration must be defeated."[13] Still, in 1936, FDR won a larger plurality of the vote than any previous president and the largest congressional majority in some seventy years. The New Deal had begun what amounted to a social revolution, a short-lived one to be sure, which allowed political dissent some of the freedom presumably bestowed on it by the Bill of Rights.

Investigations

The late 1930s saw the start of congressional investigations, purges, and blacklists aimed at repressing what neither law nor armed force could reach—the political opinions of people who had violated no laws. Loyalty probes, usually inspired and monitored by the FBI, spread into unions, government, the media, and education. Most important and uniquely American, congressional hearings led, as early as 1938, to the public stigmatization of loyalty suspects and, consequently, of much left-of-center political opinion.

LaFollette Versus Dies

In early FDR years, a House committee headed by Hamilton Fish had toured the country in search of dangerous radical activity but had found no evidence of it. As a result, investigators rested for a time. Meanwhile, the CIO was organizing, and armed opposition to it by employers and public armed forces was expanding. In 1936, the unprecedented happened: A U.S. Senate committee headed by Senator Robert LaFollette, Jr., of Wisconsin began hearings on violations of the civil liberties of unionists and employer attacks on the CIO. Soon after the hearings began, conservatives insisted that the committee had already served its purpose and should be terminated. Instead of exposing conspiracies, they said, the committee *was* one: "Organized clandestinely . . . it has been . . . more often than not a vindictive partisan of the CIO and the Communist Party."[14] The committee's interests in civil liberties, the *New York Herald Tribune* said, were only "a cloak for a smear-employer campaign."[15] Steel tycoon Tom Girdler charged that the LaFollette Committee, Communists, the CIO, the National Labor Relations Board, and the Democratic Party's National Committee had all conspired to carry out a "cold-blooded plot" against business.[16]

In mid-1938, the House Special Committee on Un-American Activities, chaired by conservative Democratic Congressman Martin Dies of Texas, began hearings on charges that the LaFollette Committee, like the CIO, had been penetrated by Communists and that it had called as witnesses "certain well-known Communists to attack American businessmen."[17] One Dies witness, the city manager of Flint, Michigan, claimed that auto sit-down strikes were Communist inspired and would not "have developed so seriously if it had not been for the attitude of the members of the LaFollette Committee" and Michigan Governor Frank Murphy's "treasonable action" during those strikes.[18]

Despite FDR's support, the LaFollette Committee was terminated in 1940, after four years of operation, but the Dies Committee (later known as the House Un-American Activities Committee, HUAC) thrived for a total of some twenty-five years, mainly under Republican direction. Later Dies claimed he had killed the LaFollette Committee by arranging for it to lose its appropriations.

For the first time in the history of such public forums, the LaFollette Committee had allowed labor to speak to a broad audience about violations of its civil liberties. In the judgment of historian Jerold Auerbach, the committee's work left a record that dispelled "the aura of respectability surrounding unethical anti-labor practices." More important, "it perceived the menace to civil liberties from the concentration of power in private hands." Only the countervailing power of unions, however, could end the "oppressive labor practices" of employers, and the committee had "demonstrated that if civil liberties received their strongest defense from those who sought power, they were most flagrantly violated by those who held power."[19]

Dies's Assault

Dies's assault on the labor-left, which began in 1938, overshadowed in scope and influence even the McCarthy hearings in the post–World War II years. Although fascism seemed by far the more ominous threat at the time, Dies turned his full attention to three favorite targets—the CIO, the New Deal, and alleged Communist penetration of both—and his sensationalized charges changed the country's political balance. Republicans picked up eight Senate and eighty-eight House seats in 1938, the first major Republican gains in almost a decade; they also defeated such New Deal governors as Michigan's Frank Murphy and Wisconsin's Philip LaFollette and elected such Republican freshmen as Senator Robert A. Taft.

Dies called for the resignation of key New Dealers Harold Ickes, Frances Perkins, Harry Hopkins, and "their many radical associates" who "range in political insanity from Socialist to Communist, with the common variety of 'crackpots' preponderating."[20] He charged that thousands of Communists and Communist sympathizers worked in the federal government, and in his 1940 book, *The Trojan Horse in America*, he claimed that Mrs. Roosevelt was the Communist Party's most valuable asset and that the Works Progress Administration (WPA) was its greatest financial boon. Committee member J. Parnell Thomas (later committee chair) charged that in many ways the fifth column was "synonymous to the New Deal, so the surest way to removing the fifth column from our shores is to remove the New Deal from the seat of government."[21] The committee claimed that a Communist conspiracy had caused the Great Depression and that the New Deal was a tool of international communism.

Testimony by Walter Steele, representing 114 "patriotic groups," named 640 organizations as communistic and suggested that the Boy Scouts and Campfire Girls were also subversive organizations. In mid-1940, the ACLU reported that at no time in its twenty-year history had it "been confronted with such an array of threatened measures of repression."[22]

Postwar Hearings

With the war's end in 1945, the ACLU noted a marked decline in its case load, but HUAC was soon to return to its prewar theme—the Communist penetration of the CIO and the Democratic Party—and be elevated from special to standing committee status. The most noticed of its new activities was an inquiry into subversion in the movie industry, and testimony in the Hollywood hearings included Gary Cooper's statement that he didn't like communism because "from what I hear, it isn't on the level." He also testified that he couldn't remember the communist-tinged scripts he had turned down "because most of the scripts I read at night."[23]

Scared by the hearings, the movie industry announced it would not employ anyone accused of communism who refused to deny the accusation. Thus began the firing and blacklisting of hundreds of HUAC witnesses. The "just fate" of "every individual Communist and fellow traveler and former Communist who would not purge himself," in the committee's view, was "to be exposed in his community, routed from his job and driven into exile."[24]

The extent of HUAC public hearings grew from 11 days in 1945–1946 to 147 in 1953–1954, the first two years of Eisenhower's presidency, and HUAC also collected massive files and published lists of "subversive organizations," claiming in 1945 that it had 300,000 cards on organizations and individuals and the names of 363,119 people who had signed Communist Party election petitions in twenty states. By 1951, it had listed 624 "subversive groups," though even the attorney general could count only 200. For a time in the early 1950s, the HUAC hearings were overshadowed by the trial and execution of Julius and Ethel Rosenberg for passing secrets to the USSR, the only convicted spies of the era.

Postwar HUAC work produced only one piece of legislation, perhaps the most severe in peacetime history, the Internal Security Act of 1950.

In general, the committee sought public exposure, not legislation. Francis Walter, committee chair from 1955 to 1963, said he sought to expose "active Communists . . . before their neighbors and fellow workers" with the "confidence that the loyal Americans who work with them will do the rest of the job."[25] That HUAC had a broad political focus was evident in its attacks on New Deal creations such as the Tennessee Valley Authority and the Office of Price Administration.

From 1945 to 1957, HUAC called 3,000 witnesses and cited 135 of them for contempt, compared to 91 citations issued by all other investigating committees. HUAC's hearings resulted in job dismissals and ruined careers and reputations; in a sample of its "unfriendly" witnesses, 50 out of 64 were found to have lost their jobs because of the hearings. As Yale law professor Thomas Emerson writes, its "charges were in harmony with the editorial position of a majority of the press and hence were rarely subjected to effective critical analysis"; the opponents of change had resorted to "cutting off political opposition or hounding it out of existence through appeals to irrationalism and prejudice."[26] The committee itself may have gotten more uncritical press coverage over its quarter century of operations than any other institution of its time.

The vogue of congressional hearings peaked in the televised Senate hearings of the 1950s led by Joseph McCarthy and supported by the rising powers of the FBI and the newer Central Intelligence Agency (CIA). Encouraged by McCarthy's hits on Truman, other Republicans followed suit. Republican Senator Andrew Schoeppel charged that the Democratic secretary of the interior had pro-Communist sympathies; Senator William Jenner called Secretary of Defense George Marshall either an unsuspecting stooge of or a coconspirator with the greatest political cutthroats ever found in the executive branch; and Senator Robert Taft claimed that the pro-Communists in the State Department promoted Red China's cause and were the Kremlin's greatest asset.

Proliferation

In 1948, an election year, six different Republican-controlled congressional committees investigated the loyalty of government employees. Besides the major and broader-ranging committees—HUAC, McCarthy's Senate subcommittee, and the Senate Internal Security Subcommittee (SISS)—others conducting hearings on un-Americanism included House committees on Immigration and Naturalization, Public Works, Military Affairs, Education and Labor, District of Columbia, and Veterans Affairs and Senate committees on the Judiciary, Interstate and Foreign Commerce, Labor and Public Welfare, and Interstate and Foreign Commerce. McCarthy was unable to find a single Communist in government employ, and the

HUAC and SISS hearings led to only two convictions of federal employees, Alger Hiss and William Remington, both convicted of perjury.

During the Eisenhower years of 1953–1954, fifty-one different investigations of communism were conducted by Congress, their targets including unions, religious groups and leaders, schools, the press, scholarly groups, government, the film industry, independent foundations, and the Defense Department. Education became such a popular target that in the winter of 1953, three committees collided over un-American activities in the schools, and their hearings resulted in hundreds of teacher dismissals. Some 20 percent of the witnesses were from universities, and a hundred or so professors were fired as a result of the hearings.

The rules of attack had been set by Dies: denial of due process and the right to confront accusers, unsupported charges, charges relating to beliefs (often from the dim past) rather than acts, and guilt by association. As for ground rules, James Eastland, chair of SISS, announced "I will decide those as we go along and announce them when I desire."[27] The attack was against the *potentially* disloyal, as people engaging in actual disloyal behavior were not only scarce but already covered by existing legal and administrative procedures. As detection of the potentially disloyal is "by nature illimitable," Emerson writes, it tends "toward excesses and abuse of power, toward ever increasing efforts to avoid all risk by eliminating any unorthodox or questionable element from the government service. Thus it brings with it the whole train of evils that result in . . . suppression of ideas and experiment, in impairment of government service, and in making the Federal government an example of repression for the country as a whole."[28]

Given the difficulty of framing constitutionally sound laws to control "wrong thoughts" and potential disloyalty, most political repression was carried on outside the legal system. The people who were cited for contempt of Congress and those charged under the Smith Act (some 300 people) were among the "lucky ones," as they at least had the protection of criminal procedures under the law.

The Law and Its Enforcement

The Smith Act of 1940 and Prewar Federal Law

In prewar 1939, a federal relief law barred assistance to all persons advocating or belonging to an organization advocating the overthrow of the government by force, and the Hatch Act passed in that year barred suspected Communists from holding federal jobs of any kind.

In 1940, the wartime Espionage Act of 1917 was reenacted, and its penalties were increased and applied even to peacetime activities.

The Smith Act was also passed in 1940, and it required all resident aliens to register and be fingerprinted and made it a criminal act to advocate or belong to organizations that advocated the overthrow of the government by force or to incite disloyalty or interfere with morale or discipline in the armed forces—penalties included prison, heavy fines, and deportation of aliens, even in the case of past but discontinued beliefs. About 100 people were convicted and jailed under the Smith Act, and many more were prosecuted. In 1941, eighteen Trotskyist leaders of the Minneapolis Teamster's union were imprisoned under the Smith Act by the Justice Department, partly as a favor, it was reported, to Teamster President James Tobin. Thus, a Teamster vacancy was opened into which James Hoffa—and, later, others accused of having underworld ties—moved. Francis Biddle, who had authorized the prosecution, later regretted it: "By no conceivable stretch of a liberal imagination" could the Trotskyists "have been said to constitute any 'clear and present danger' to the government," he said.[29]

Trials of eleven of the top Communist Party leaders (William Z. Foster was excused because of illness) began in 1949, and though none were shown to have advocated any violent acts, all were convicted, and ten were sentenced to five years in jail. All were released on bail pending appeal, but in 1951, during the Korean crisis, their bail was revoked, and "second string" Communist leaders were also indicted. By 1957, the prosecutions had ended, but lawyers who had defended the first eleven had been found guilty of contempt of court, and efforts had been made to disbar them from the legal profession. Not strangely, the "second string" Communists had found it difficult to hire lawyers.

Postwar Acts and Laws

The McCarran Act, or Internal Security Act, became law in 1950 over Truman's veto. This act required designated Communist groups to register and reveal the sources of funds, the names of officers, and in many cases the names of members. It barred members from holding passports or government or defense jobs, prohibited aliens who had ever been members of the Communist Party from entering the country, required the detention of security risks during security emergencies, and limited picketing of federal courts. No group registered under the act, and after years of litigation, the Supreme Court in 1964 refused to decide whether any group should be required to register—and thereby expose itself to prosecution under the act. Harassment and exclusion of suspect aliens and the denial of government jobs were the act's main outcomes.

State legislatures had played a leading role in the red scare of the 1930s, and from 1945 to 1954, forty-five states passed laws aimed at suppressing the Communist Party and "subversive organizations." These laws required "seditious" organizations to register, barred them and their members from the ballot and public employ, and required disclaimer oaths for everyone listed on a ballot. By 1948, the proliferation of state un-American activities committees required that an interstate conference be called to coordinate them. Throughout the nation, free assembly was curtailed, and injunctions often prohibited assemblies.

A Birmingham, Alabama, law banned Communists from entering the city, on penalty of a fine and 180 days in jail. Other cities banned "subversive" publications from the schools and burned books. Oaths were required of pharmacists in Texas, insurance salespeople in the District of Columbia, and of wrestlers and boxers in Indiana. In Houston during the 1950s, an elite group led by nine businessmen, supported by the local newspapers, sanctioned a virulent campaign by right-wing extremists against a nonexistent communist menace, a campaign that nevertheless hit its true targets—labor, liberals, and leftists. The Minutewomen of Houston put spies in local colleges, compiled and distributed a list of 200 subversives (including a Catholic bishop and four college presidents), and forced the dismissal of the University of Houston's president. The Methodist church was charged with harboring leftists, and sermons and Sunday school classes in the church were monitored. Both the *Houston Post* and the governor of Texas asked the people of Houston to be on the watch for reds and spies, and Texas police collected records on some 1,000 liberal politicians.

Truman and the Federal Executive

Truman's 1947 executive order no. 9835, requiring loyalty checks of all federal employees, is said to have supplied a guide to later loyalty probes. The motive for Truman's order, and other contributions to the red scare, has been variously ascribed to pressure from Congress and critics, the desire to head off harsher legislation (which came anyhow with the Internal Security Act of 1950, vetoed by Truman), the desire to be reelected in 1948, the shock of Republican congressional victories in 1946, his own ideological convictions, and the need to highlight the red menace at home in order to fund the Marshall Plan, the Truman doctrine, and NATO abroad.

Whatever Truman's motives, he did write in 1951 that he was "very much disturbed with the action of some of these [loyalty] boards and I want some way to put a stop to their un-American activities."[30] In an address to the American Legion in the same year, he said that all

Americans were in peril "when even one American—who has done nothing wrong—is forced by fear to shut his mind and close his mouth." Real Americanism, he said, meant the protection of dissenters' right to speak, "no matter how much we may disagree with them." Also in 1951 he fired General MacArthur, thus probably preventing a war with China, and in a 1952 press conference, he called McCarthy a "pathological liar."[31] Later, Lyndon Johnson, entangled in Vietnam, was nevertheless reluctant to play the moralistic anti-Communist card to win support for the war, knowing from the Truman experience that the right could turn it against him.

The 1952 Republican convention platform charged that Democrats had "shielded traitors to the Nation in high places" and had "so undermined the foundations of our Republic as to threaten its existence."[32] During his campaign, Eisenhower raised the communist issue in thirty speeches and picked antired crusader Richard Nixon as his vice-presidential running mate. Two months into his presidency, Eisenhower's attorney general announced that 10,000 citizens were being investigated for denaturalization and 12,000 aliens for deportation.

Administrative Justice

In late 1947, the U.S. attorney general published a list of subversive organizations, assembled without advance hearings or protection of the innocent, and this list, widely used in loyalty and congressional hearings, became an effective blacklist. The funds and membership of groups on the list declined, meeting places were denied, and charters were revoked in some cases. Later, members of the listed groups were made ineligible for public housing, and veterans were denied benefits for enrollment in listed schools; on local and state levels, various penalties were imposed, including refusal of admission to the bar of lawyers belonging to listed groups. The list grew rapidly, from 82 in 1948, to 197 in 1950, and later to over 300.[33] Since nobody knew which group would be listed next, public fear of participation in *any* group, political or otherwise, grew.

The FBI expanded its scope and autonomy over the years. J. Edgar Hoover labeled FBI enemies "the scum of the underworld, conspiring Communists and goose-stepping bundsmen, their fellow travellers, mouthpieces and stooges," and referred at various times to "cowardly, slithering" foreign ideas, "Communist termites," and "prattle-minded politicians."[34] Hoover kept a large file on Supreme Court Justice Felix Frankfurter, who along with Justice Hugo Black had openly opposed McCarthyism, and one FBI agent claimed that Secretary of State Dean Acheson and Frankfurter were the number one and two Communists in the country.[35] During a 1949 Smith Act trial, three FBI agents testified they had served as Communist Party recruiters, and one of them testified that he had recruited friends and relatives into the party, then turned over their names to the FBI.

By the late 1950s, the FBI had become so autonomous and powerful that it was almost beyond control. By 1960, it had opened over 430,000 "subversive" files on individuals and groups, and at the time of the Internal Security Act's repeal in 1971, some 12,000 people were still on the list. With the demise of both Stalin and McCarthy, the frenzy abated for a time, yet covert operations continued. Between 1956 and 1973, in New York City alone, the CIA examined over 28 million pieces of mail, photographed 2.7 million envelopes, and opened 215,820 pieces of mail.[36] No excesses of the past, Frank J. Donner concludes from a study of the U.S. intelligence system, can compare with the "secret war waged continuously for over 50 years against all shades of dissenting politics" by the virtually autonomous network of intelligence agencies dominated by the FBI and supported by powerful political allies.[37] The excesses of the McCarthy era are seen most vividly in Chief Justice Earl Warren's memoirs, where he notes that President Eisenhower had rebuked him for the Supreme Court's decision protecting the constitutional rights of Communists. Asked by Warren how he would deal with U.S. Communists, Eisenhower replied, "I would kill the SOBs."[38]

Security and Insecurity

Some 13.5 million people, or about one in five people in the labor force, were affected by loyalty-security programs as a condition of employment. Some 10,000 were fired from their jobs—about 3,900 federal, 5,400 private, and 1,000 state and local employees. Besides those fired, over 20,000 were formally charged between 1947 and 1953 with disloyalty under the federal program alone, most charges involving association with a suspect person, often a family member. At a federal cost of some $350 million during that period, not a single spy was uncovered by the loyalty-security programs.[39]

Denial of employment was the most serious penalty, but penalties could also include denial of voting rights and loss of such benefits as unemployment compensation, public housing and loans, welfare, veterans benefits, and disability and old age benefits. Loyalty suspects were barred from practicing law or obtaining radio and television licenses. Suspect aliens were deported or denied entry to the country, and naturalization was even revoked in many cases. Such penalties were applied by the often capricious standards of various public agencies and without benefit of legal safeguards established by the criminal justice system. The secret proceedings, the vague accusations, and the Kafkaesque sense of isolation and shame often produced emotional disturbances in the accused.

Former Republican Senator Harry Cain, a man of impeccable anti-Communist credentials, helped terminate the loyalty program when he charged in 1955 that it had discovered not a single truly disloyal citizen and proposed that only people with access to national secrets be covered by the program. The major opposition to the loyalty program came, however, when Democrats won congressional control and began a full-scale attack on it.

No concrete evidence of immediate danger, sufficient to outweigh the damage to democratic values, was ever offered to support the loyalty procedures. For the relatively few people who handled defense secrets, a more thorough clearance procedure would have met security demands. In Emerson's judgment, a proper procedure would have disqualified only those *personally* advocating overthrow of the government or those belonging to organizations *after* acceptable legal procedures had found them to be subversive.[40]

Political Impact

The impact of such political repression on public policy was devastating. Domestic reforms almost disappeared from serious political concern until the Kennedy years, as did reforms of U.S. foreign policy. In the State Department and related bureaus, anyone not hawkish on communism had been purged, many of them for having accurately predicted that Chiang Kai-shek would be defeated by the Chinese Communists. On being appointed assistant secretary of state for Far Eastern Affairs, Averell Harriman in 1961 told friends that the place was a "wasteland," a "disaster area filled with human wreckage. Perhaps a few can be saved. Some of them are so beaten down, they can't be saved."[41]

The campaign against un-Americanism had a clear political connection: to win elections and, by arousing nationalist ardor and fears of stigma and punishment, impose a conservative conformity on the nation. Subversion, un-Americanism, and the enemy within were good campaign issues, and conservatives made political gains with them. In 1950, for instance, Richard Nixon, riding high on the issues, was elected to the Senate, and staunch New Dealers were unseated.

The dragnet of hearings and loyalty probes got the large catch desired: the whole spectrum of opinion of the left of center. The "fear, however vague, of being called to testify, of being somehow 'named' or of joining an organization that might someday be cited, was an integral part of the impetus toward 'caution' so characteristic of the McCarthy era." The congressional hearings, Goldstein concludes, spread fear, "not only of advocating communism, but of advocating virtually *any* dissenting or unpopular opinion."[42]

During the McCarthy era, more than 80 percent of people who were stopped on the street and asked to sign a petition containing only quotes from the Declaration of Independence and the Bill of Rights refused to sign. A 1955 study of several thousand college social science teachers found, even after the Senate censure of McCarthy, a "noticeable damper on the activities and opinions of a sizable minority" and "widespread apprehension" among them; indeed, 46 percent of them showed "medium" or "high" apprehension about the possible repercussions to them of their political beliefs and activities.[43]

Suspicion was extended from Communists to Socialists, liberals, Democrats, and labor activists. The "new loyalty," said Henry Steele Commager at the time, means "above all, conformity. It is the uncritical and unquestioning acceptance of America as it is—the political institutions, the social relationships, the economic practices. It rejects inquiry. . . . It regards America as a finished product, perfect and complete."[44] In 1972, Richard Barnett wrote that

the successful effort to make all challenges to the anti-communist business creed look treasonous deserves some of the credit for the strange disappearance of the issues of fair distribution and concentration of corporate power during most of the postwar period. It was not easy during this period to admit the existence of a class conflict without running the risk of being labeled a "crypto" or "creeping" subversive. Business groups devoted considerable resources to blunderbuss attacks on leftists and radicals who raised such issues. Big business . . . became a prime mover in forging a patriotic consensus in which the legitimacy of its own rapidly expanding power was seldom questioned, even when it resulted in the Vietnam disaster. The effect has been to eliminate serious economic and social criticism of the basic institutions of American life for two decades and to make the business creed the official standard for defining the national interest.[45]

Ironically, economic elites have become in a sense the most global and "foreign" elements of the society—moving investments, production, and headquarters abroad; selling off vital sectors of the American economy and landscape to foreigners; and in large and growing numbers selling themselves and their services as lobbyists and agents of foreign interests. The protection of business interests, massive investments, and military bases abroad has profoundly influenced American foreign policy.

Businesspeople are generally "bullish on dictators," Raymond Bonner writes in his study of the Marcos regime. U.S. foreign policy supported Marcos when he declared martial law and set up a dictatorship, imprisoned or killed opponents, refused to hold elections, wiped out all means of dissent, stole millions, and impoverished the people. When a real

Communist insurgency threatened, based in a desperate and impoverished people, American policy sought to depose Marcos.[46] Such policies and their close cousin, the domestic antired crusade, can hardly be construed as part of a design to save the world for democracy.

Unions and Un-Americanism

As Otto von Bismarck recognized, a policy that appealed to German national feeling was the best way to break liberal opposition to his policies and win the support he needed from bankers, businesspeople, and others. Many other conservatives have also come to realize that appeals to nationalism and patriotism are more potent than appeals to capitalism in driving out liberal sentiments.

So it was that the crusade against un-Americanism had a chilling effect on liberal, leftist, and labor dissent; enlarged the province of conservatism and achieved a national acceptance of its version of Americanism; and strengthened the ability of employers to repress unionism. In the year after FDR's death in 1945, and largely because of the antired crusade, Republicans gained control of Congress and in November 1947 passed what is still called the most antilabor law in the English-speaking world, the Taft-Hartley Act, adopted over Truman's veto. Among its many provisions was the requirement that union officers (but not employers) must sign a non-Communist loyalty oath in order to use the NLRB, a requirement that, as it turned out, was unenforceable. CIO President Philip Murray refused to sign, as did many other CIO officials. The AFL reorganized its leadership in order to reduce the number required to sign, but the action was not enough to suit John L. Lewis, and he withdrew the miners from the AFL.

In 1949, as red-scare assaults on unions peaked, the CIO made Communists ineligible to hold national CIO elective offices, and in 1950, it expelled Communist-dominated unions. During the Korean war, Goldstein writes, "the CIO could claim a purity equal to that of the AFL and was able thereby to escape public indictment during the years when anti-communist hysteria in the nation reached its height."[47] As a voluntary association, the CIO claimed the legitimate right to expel unions with incompatible goals. The expelled unions survived outside the CIO, but the expulsion, combined with conservative red baiting, was shattering in most cases. The biggest of the expelled unions, the United Electrical Workers, shrank to a shell of its former self, and although the non-Communist International Union of Electrical Workers grew in its place, it too had so seriously contracted by the 1980s that it was poorly positioned to organize the high technology computer and electronic industries.

The CIO's expulsion of Communists, Richard Fried writes, resulted from factional rivalries, distrust, and the desire to survive in a hostile and conservative climate. "So it did, but not without cost."[48] Fried further claims that the Communists "earned their spurs by being more effective and militant unionists than their rivals," delivering what the rank and file wanted.[49] Such claims about Communist virtues are unsupported and undoubtedly unsupportable, but they are typical of much of what has been written about the expulsions. Anti-Communist sentiment remained strong in the AFL-CIO after the two merged in 1955. As Bert Cochran writes, the feeling dominated labor that it had to have friends at court and that it could "prosper only with the approbation of the larger society" and by establishing bona fides of orthodoxy.[50]

Unions often were the only defenders of the job rights of workers accused of disloyalty. Indeed, industrial workers in private employment, William Spinrad notes, had a countervailing power on their side that most public workers lacked—their unions, a collective power that could act against arbitrary authority.[51] One study of 600 union leaders found that some 90 percent of them favored the rights of confrontation and cross examination in loyalty-security hearings, their own experiences having sensitized them to the need for due process.[52] Unions in the automobile and steel industries, for example, defended the jobs of Communists in long, often successful cases in courts, in administrative agencies, and through the grievance procedure. The leaderships of these unions were anti-Communist, but they "vigorously defended the job rights of ex-Communists" and even those who had taken the Fifth Amendment before legislative hearings.[53]

McCarthy received almost no union support. Most AFL affiliates were hostile to him, and the CIO unions were decidedly and stridently antagonistic. The opening salvo in the battle that finally subdued McCarthy is generally said to have been a speech at a UAW national education conference in Chicago by Catholic Bishop Shiel, who made the first major public Catholic (or establishment) denunciation of McCarthy.

Since Communist organizing efforts were largely focused on the labor movement, much of the political conflict between Communists and others were fought out there, with no holds barred on either side, and well before the 1960s, the "others" had won hands down. Much of the opposition to Communist union leadership, of course, came from a wholly legitimate rejection of Stalinism, as well as the manipulative activities of Communist union leaders, but a vital distinction between combating Stalinism and red baiting is needed. Unionists generally engaged in the former and rejected the latter, but some endorsed McCarthyism, needlessly appeased it, or simply used it to win elections. Even after several decades, residues of the factional years remain in some sectors of the labor movement, largely unmodified even by profound changes in Eurocommunism, the USSR, and Eastern Europe. Not even a cold war policy that facilitated U.S. investments abroad, deindustrialized the domestic economy, and seriously damaged unions shook the convictions of many union hawks.

The CIO leaders "disliked the negative obsession of the AFL men with anti-communism," Ronald Radosh writes, "preferring to fight communism by support of social reform abroad," and men like Walter Reuther also disliked "the conspiratorial activities" of Jay Lovestone and Irving Brown (both AFL-CIO international affairs directors), and the too close association with state department and related activities.[54]

Comparisons

Loyalty probes, though not unique to the United States, have been unusual in their scope, duration, and intensity; the severity of the penalties invoked; the substitution of political for legal trials; and the extent of their spillover to all opinion on the labor-left. The European war and postwar experiences differed from the American. The parties of the right had been for the most part, as Bogdan Denitch points out, "discredited through their collaboration with the Nazis or their lack of support for the Resistance. The left in general had played a dominant role in the Resistance," and although the military value of the Resistance was often greatly exaggerated, at least "the right could not assail the socialist left as being unpatriotic and antinational."[55]

Among English-speaking nations, Britain, Australia (both with labor governments at the war's end), and Canada (with a liberal government) experienced less political repression than the United States in the postwar era.[56] The Australian right tried to conduct a red scare, but the labor government limited that effort. In Canada, the Liberal Party was firmly entrenched in office, and even Catholic Quebec (the province thought most likely to favor repression of Communists) was solidly behind the Liberal prime minister, a Quebec Catholic. Although accused of encouraging certain forms of political repression, Canadian Liberals sought to prevent the Communist issue from being used against them by Conservatives, and suspect civil servants were usually transferred rather than dismissed, following the United Kingdom rather than the U.S. example.

A 1948 study by Thomas Emerson and David Helfeld of loyalty programs in various countries concluded that "despite conditions of political instability far exceeding those in the United States, other democratic nations have not found it necessary to impose loyalty tests going beyond the standard of active participation in a revolutionary party adopted by the Weimar Republic . . . or the transfer of Communist employees to 'non-secret' government work, recently instituted in England." The U.S. loyalty program went "substantially beyond any measures considered necessary by other democratic countries, even those troubled with much greater instability in government. It is more nearly comparable to the programs of totalitarian countries."[57]

In both Nazi Germany and fascist Italy, according to Emerson and Helfeld, "one finds the phenomenon of broad and flexible standards of loyalty but, at least on paper, procedural safeguards affording the accused an opportunity . . . to establish his political respectability." Thus it seems that even totalitarian states found it worthwhile "to establish procedural safeguards which would afford substantial protection to an accused employee."[58]

Under the French Third Republic before the war, French civil servants had broad freedom. They could belong to any legally recognized party, including the Socialist and Communist parties, and they could participate in party activities during nonworking hours and even run for office. Loyalty tests for civil servants were unknown; government employees had full access to all records, including confidential documents, when they were disciplined; trials were conducted, due process observed, and legal procedures followed; and dismissals were reversed if political beliefs were shown to be the cause of dismissal. Under the Vichy government, loyalty oaths were required, and membership in designated organizations was a cause for dismissal, but the liberation of France from the Nazis brought a quick return to pre-Vichy days.

The adoption of the 1939 Emergency Powers Act gave the British government rather sweeping powers over national security, yet despite Communist efforts during the Hitler-Stalin pact to disrupt the war effort, these war powers were used with remarkable restraint in limiting Communists' civil liberties. Herbert Morrison, the Labour home secretary, advised against imposing any limits at all on Communist activities and finally, prodded by Churchill and the war cabinet, moved reluctantly to close the Communist *Daily Worker* (later reopened when a Labour Party conference voted to do so). Morrison explained to Parliament that the *Worker* was closed because it had continued "by every device of distortion and misrepresentation . . . to make out that our people have nothing to gain by victory."[59] Both Morrison and another Labour minister, Ernest Bevin, were unwilling to limit any group's civil liberties beyond demonstrable war requirements, and Morrison argued that if party members were interned, it "should be done on the ground that they have, as individuals, been concerned in acts prejudicial to the public safety or the defence of the realms, such, for example, as slowing down production, and not on the ground that they are leaders or members of the Communist Party."[60] A few minor bans were imposed, but the government spurned sterner measures such as outlawing the party, interning its members, prohibiting its meetings, and conducting extensive loyalty trials.

Bevin pointed to the difficulty of distinguishing between genuine grievances, of which there were many in industry, and subversive efforts to exploit such grievances, arguing that no evidence pointed to Communist activity having any serious effect on war production.[61] Bypassing requests for more serious restraints, the government's Committee on Communist Activities proposed only that leaflets relating to war and peace be approved by a competent authority before distribution, subject to court review in contested cases, but even this relatively mild recommendation was never implemented. After the Nazi invasion of the USSR, regulation of Communist activities was no longer an issue at all.

Postwar Britain committed itself to an alliance with the United States against the USSR, but, according to David Caute, it almost always retained the "authentically liberal values and standards of tolerance that persisted in Britain despite that country's . . . general posture of confrontation with Russia. The British of the Attlee era . . . kept their heads."[62] In 1948, Labour Prime Minister Clement Attlee adopted a security program for the civil service that was considerably leaner and less punitive than the American. From 1948 to 1955, only a third of the 135 permanent British civil servants who had been identified as security risks were terminated from service through resignation or dismissal; the other two-thirds were transferred to less sensitive posts. Appeal procedures, lacking for most United States hearings, were present in the British program.[63]

No British laws or rules prevented civil servants from being dismissed, but the power of arbitrary dismissal was rarely abused, and by the 1950s, civil servants were free to participate in any party, including the Communist. Known Communist Party members or people deemed politically unreliable, however, could not do work vital to national security or handle secret documents. In many cases, they were transferred to other work.

There were no Labour government assaults on unions in the name of anticommunism such as those legalized by the American Taft-Hartley Act. Since the 1920s, the Labour Party had denied party membership to people belonging to organizations it considered suspect, but political repression under the Labour government was minimal.

Anticommunism, it has been said, was the "Tory dog that never barked." The campaign for the limitation of secret police powers, which examined and condemned British examples of McCarthyism, included in its leadership many prominent Tories along with Labour and Liberal sponsors. McCarthyism might have worked for the Tories: In the late 1940s, labor was in power, China was communistic, the USSR held much of central Europe, the British Empire was moribund, and spies Anthony Burgess and David McLean had defected to the USSR. The Tories could have blamed it all on the Labour Party, as American conservatives blamed Truman and the Democrats, but they mainly abstained from such tactics and made little use of the cold war to win elections.

Secret Activities

Incriminating claims have been made about the activities of the British MI5, a CIA equivalent, during the 1960s. Peter Wright, a former influential British MI5 agent and author of *Spycatcher*, writes that MI5 plotted successfully to unseat Labour Prime Minister Harold Wilson, a claim that caused Conservative Prime Minister Margaret Thatcher to ban Wright's book in Britain.[64] The plot, Wright says, was stimulated by James Angleton, head of CIA counterintelligence, who sought, in effect, to take over MI5 in order to get directly at Wilson. "There was deep-seated hostility in the American intelligence community to the ascension to power of Harold Wilson and the Labour Government in 1964. Partly it was due to anti-Labour bias, partly to the Labour Government's commitment to abandon Polaris—a pledge they soon reneged on."[65]

There is also evidence, according to David Leigh, of a CIA association with "initiatives which discredited and ousted both Willy Brandt, the Socialist Chancellor of West Germany, and Gough Whitlam, the Labour premier of Australia" in the 1970s.[66] "One cannot demonstrate direct CIA involvement in the Brandt case: one can merely observe that the CIA were parties to the Intelligence maneuvering which occurred, and that the upshot was that Brandt himself was discredited and forced out of office. . . . There is more evidence in Australia of direct conflict between Whitlam and the CIA, involving the British as junior partners."[67] The validity of Wright's claims has not been exposed to much public scrutiny, derived as they are from secrets open only to the people involved, but although the motives and veracity of the individuals publicizing the secrets may be suspect, the revelations themselves cannot be dismissed out of hand.

The cold war contained and discredited Stalinism but not without heavy costs in the diversion of resources from civilian production and damage to democratic institutions. In supporting "corrupt and repressive regimes in a global crusade against Communism" and allying "itself with the most reactionary forces in the Third World," Christopher Lasch writes in the *New York Times*, the United States forfeited "much of its reputation as a champion of democracy and social reform." In supporting the cold war, it also deflected investment from domestic growth, turning the United States from an exporting to an importing nation. Worse, it led to the neglect of domestic reforms and basic services and to the "development of secret police organizations, the erosion of civil liberties, the stifling of political debate in the interest of bipartisan consensus, the concentration of decision-making in the executive branch, the secrecy surrounding executive actions, the lying that has come to be accepted as routine in American politics."[68] These profoundly un-American developments, which have crippled growth on the labor-left, have often been so shrouded by secrecy and official releases that few investigative efforts have touched them.

10

Peculiarities of the American Political System

THE RULES OF THE GAME, adopted and managed largely by economic elites, have made the American political system peculiarly inhospitable to the politics of the labor-left. These rules block the success of third parties, weaken all political parties, empower special interest lobbies and pressure groups, give money a dominant voice in elections and public policy, and make voter participation the lowest in the democratic world.

Elite dominance of the political rules, Richard Hofstadter writes, was set during the republic's founding, the main theme of the Constitutional Convention being a profound distrust of the common man. The "convention was a fraternity of types of absentee ownership," who believed that "freedom for property would result in liberty for men—perhaps not for all men, but at least for all worthy men" and that "democracy, unchecked rule by the masses, is sure to bring arbitrary redistribution of property, destroying the very essence of democracy."[1] Such sanctification of property rights and antipathy to regulation of them have resulted, as only one instance, in a record of health and safety in American mines that is the worst in the industrialized Western world, almost four times worse than Britain's and six times worse than in the Netherlands. The U.S. record is exceeded only by South Africa, Zimbabwe, and Namibia, even though American mines are easier to mine than many of those elsewhere.[2]

Third Parties

Although theoretically possible, no case exists in American history where a third party has pushed aside a major party and won a national election. (When the Whigs succumbed to internal splits over slavery, the Republican Party merely replaced it rather than competed with it.) Thus, the United States has a longer history of continuous rivalry between two major parties than any other two-party system. The third-party record in the United States, Robert Dahl notes, "is one of nearly total failure"; for anyone seeking to form a third party, "this historical fact should be . . . a melancholy prospect to contemplate."[3]

If the political dissenter enters a third party, Dahl writes, he is "condemned to political impotence," and if he enters one of the major parties, he "constantly sees his principles compromised or even forfeited. He has no satisfactory choice among candidates in elections. From his point of view, the relevant policy alternatives are rarely posed." Such frustration may produce apathy or hostility. From populism's defeat in 1896 until the New Deal, "the largest alienated group in the United States was on the left," for its choice was either "supporting a separate socialist party that could not win elections or entering one of the two major parties and compromising with all the heterogeneous elements that made up these parties."[4] Even earlier, Friedrich Engels recognized that the nonparliamentary government established by the U.S. Constitution "causes any vote for any candidate not put up by one of the two governing parties to appear to be lost. And the American . . . wants to influence his state: he does not throw his vote away."[5]

Third Parties, Presidents, and Parliaments

Under the parliamentary system, voters are less likely to consider votes for minority parties to be "lost" than under the presidential system. Under the former, minorities often share power in coalition governments, contribute to the selection of government leaders, and make or break a coalition government. Votes for minority parties, therefore, count for more in parliamentary than in presidential systems. Norman Thomas, a Socialist leader for many years, claimed that the reasons for third-party failure in the United States lay in the United States Constitution and that if the United States had a parliamentary rather than a presidential system, a moderately strong socialist party, under whatever name, would have flourished.[6]

U.S. minority parties are also more likely to be engulfed by the political system. The Democratic Party, for example, incorporated many voters of the growing Populist Party in 1896 by nominating William Jennings Bryan for president and including populist planks in its platform. As another example, by 1938 FDR had won the support of many voters from the Socialist Party of America, the Progressive Party based in Wisconsin, and the Minnesota-based Farmer-Labor Party—and for a time, even the Communist Party. In a parliamentary system, those parties could have maintained their identities more easily, entered coalitions with FDR, and probably strengthened their positions in the postwar era.

Such incorporations may at times be in the public interest, but they can also create political monopolies that resemble those in one-party authoritarian states. Once the monopoly is in place, competition and responsiveness to voters wane, and the major party, having destroyed its competition, can then return more comfortably to its old ways, ignoring the demands of new constituents. The effects of incorporation can be seen, for instance, in John L. Lewis's complaints during the second New Deal term that Roosevelt, having captured labor's allegiance, no longer backed the CIO and other unions as before. For this and similar reasons, the AFL and many early unions generally avoided commitment to any one party, pursuing instead a policy of rewarding friends and punishing enemies of either party.

Thus, the labor-left often faces perplexing choices: supporting friends in both parties, supporting only one party at the risk of being "captured" by it, trying to "take over" an existing party, or creating an independent party. In some cases, it has taken over an existing party. North Dakota's Non-Partisan League saw an empty space in the Republican Party, entered it, captured the party, and elected a governor and all the major state officials. Such cases are rare, however, and none of the options available in the American political system have produced results as satisfactory as those achieved by the labor-left in many other democracies.

The Canadian example is instructive. Although American socialist parties did better than the Canadian in the early twentieth century, the Canadian Cooperative Commonwealth Federation (CCF) experienced some provincial successes in the 1930s and thus laid the groundwork for the national New Democratic Party (NDP), a challenging third party of the labor-left. The parliamentary system made the CCF gains possible. In British Columbia earlier in the century, for instance, two CCFers held the balance of power in the provincial legislature, and, because they could bring down the government, they were able to get prolabor legislation passed and thereby increase their own support. In 1926, a small group of labor members of Parliament (MPs) in the Canadian House of Commons, plus a few Alberta farmer MPs, secured the passage of the first old-age pension law in return for keeping the Liberal Party in power. In the 1960s, the CCF, together with organized labor, founded the NDP, a Canadian democratic socialist party and a leading contender for national power.

Third Parties, Election Districts, Proportional Representation

Systems with single-member (winner-take-all) election districts, such as the American system, are said to discriminate radically against lesser parties—moderately against a second party but overwhelmingly against multiple parties. Only when minority-party voters are highly concentrated in specific election districts can a third party expect to elect candidates, and even then, the two major parties usually drive the minority out of business by incorporating its demands or discouraging voters who want their votes to "count." The second party remains because it takes on the necessary role of opposition to the party in power, however token the opposition may be. Third parties may emerge, but no matter how disciplined they are, two strong parties usually dominate.

In developed democracies, the single-member system exists only in the United States, Britain, Canada, and New Zealand, yet some influential third parties have developed in those other countries because of their parliamentary systems. In the United Kingdom, the "third party" (the Labour Party) has become the first or second party, a course the Canadian NDP seeks to follow. These countries, however, have not developed the multiple-party system that is common in European democracies, most of which have proportional representation (PR).

The single-member system can give the largest party a higher proportion of legislative seats than its proportion of votes, and it may also preclude proportional representation (PR), whose purpose is to give seats to minority parties in proportion to their total votes. Norman Thomas claimed that if the American president were chosen by a "popular preferential ballot in which the Voters numbered their choices, as is often done in PR voting," the Socialist candidate "would be a force to be reckoned with at the polls."[7] PR systems vary, however. Under the "party-list" PR system, much used in Europe, votes are cast for parties, which are then apportioned seats according to their total vote. Germany, for instance, reserves about half its Bundestag seats to approximate the voting strength of parties in the popular vote (the other half is reserved for representatives of whatever party is chosen in regular elections).

Every European country with PR has at least four parties in its legislature. In only a few cases, as in Sweden, Norway, and Ireland, has a clear parliamentary majority for one party often appeared; elsewhere, coalitions of parties have usually been required to form governments.

In most of Europe, the proportion of eligible voters actually voting has risen in the twentieth century; in the United States, where PR is almost unknown, voting has declined. This difference is attributed in one study of voting from 1960 to 1984 to the fact that most other democracies have some form of PR that gives voters more choices and incentives to vote.[8]

PR is not without problems, of course. It can contribute to the instability of coalition governments, and it can allow small minority parties to determine government policy, as they have reputedly done in

Israel. But these problems can be diminished by limiting the eligibility of small parties.

Third Parties and the Ballot

Although a much lesser matter, the length and complexity of the American ballot also works against minority parties. American voters must choose among candidates for local, state, and national offices, and since a new party seems to have little chance of electing a governor or president, the voters are inclined to shun the whole ticket.[9] American elections include primaries and general elections for about 1 million offices— more, it is estimated, than in the rest of the world combined.[10] The British voter, in contrast, casts a single vote for a single candidate for a single office.

Election rules governing the ability of minority parties to get on, and stay on, the ballot vary widely among the states, but they have generally become more restrictive over the years. "All of them," one study concluded, "are designed to make minority party bids difficult."[11] Norman Thomas also complained that after World War II, "state laws, or the way they were enforced, made it harder and harder to stay on the ballot."[12]

Separation of Powers: Barrier to Change

According to William Fulbright, the separation of powers between the executive and the legislative branches, unique to the United States among major democracies, "obstructs accountability for governmental policies and leads to indecision and stalemate." For that reason, the parliamentary system, which combines the legislative and executive functions, is, in many ways, "a superior form of democracy."[13] The first American constitution, the Articles of Confederation, gave all authority to Congress and specified no separate federal executive. At the start of the 1787 Constitutional Convention, James Madison's plan specified that the president be selected by Congress; no precedent existed for the separation of powers and the complexity of the system that was finally agreed upon.

A consequence of that complexity has been that one-fourth of the time since 1789, the president and the majorities of the Senate and the House have not all been of the same party.[14] The upshot, according to a congressional study, has been delay, indecision, chronic confrontation, deadlock, a diffusion of accountability for results, and the common inability of Congress and the president to agree on an approach to problems.[15] Some people who are frustrated with these stalemates admire the unity of democratic governments in Canada and Europe.[16] In a parliamentary system, power is unified, responsibility is clearly fixed, the legislative majority governs, and the cabinet, a committee of that majority, leads the legislature and directs the executive branch. Prime ministers and their cabinets can act quickly and decisively, but "leaders are held accountable by the requirement that, to remain in power, they must maintain the confidence of the parliamentary majority that chose them."[17]

In the United States, the diffusion of powers provides many opportunities to block change. Needed legislation and its administration can be held up indefinitely by such diversions as delay, filibuster, veto, court invalidation, and executive agency resistance. Under Dixiecrat control, for example, the House Rules Committee, with the help of Senate filibusters, tied up civil rights legislation for many years. John Kennedy observed that the Constitution and the development of Congress give advantage to delay. "It is very easy to defeat a bill in Congress. It is much more difficult to pass one." You have to "go through a committee, say the Ways and Means Committee of the House subcommittee and get a majority vote, the full committee and get a majority vote, go to the Rules Committee and get a rule, go to the Floor of the House and get a majority, start over again in the Senate, subcommittee and full committee, and in the Senate there is unlimited debate, so you can never bring a matter to a vote if there is enough determination on the part of the opponents, even if they are a minority, to go through the Senate with a bill. And then unanimously get a conference between the House and Senate to adjust the bill, or if one member objects, to have it go back through the Rules Committee, back through the Congress, and have this done on a controversial piece of legislation where powerful groups are opposing it, that is an extremely difficult task." Franklin Roosevelt, he noted, was elected by the largest majority in history in 1936 but suffered his worst defeat a few months afterward on the bill for Supreme Court reform. A president's program is adopted quickly and easily, he added, only when the program is insignificant.[18]

The U.S. Supreme Court has powers unknown to the judiciary in other democracies, namely, the power to interpret the Constitution and reject legislation it deems unconstitutional. No British court can void a parliamentary act; a French court has limited powers of legislative review, but it is appointed for nine years, not for life, and is therefore more responsive to the public will; and West Germany, under pressure from the U.S. occupation, accepted judicial review, but the court of review is elected by the legislature for nonrenewable twelve-year terms. Judicial review in the United States has served conservative ends as shown in a study that concluded that when the Supreme Court had rejected legislation in years up to 1937, it had more often upheld property rights over civil liberties.[19]

The bewildering maze of power relations in the U.S. political system favors conservative elites, as they are more likely than others to know who has power and how decisions can be influenced; by the same token, it frustrates organized dissent on the labor-left and impedes progressive change. The system also gives power directly to economic elites. Administrative cabinets in the United States are selected mainly from among corporate executives and large campaign contributors—in a parliamentary system, cabinet ministers are selected from among democratically elected MPs. A study of the background of major U.S. cabinet and diplomatic officers from the Federalist years to the Civil War found that "governmental acts and the highly skewed federal recruitment process show that elite interests had great influence."[20] Subsequent presidents, Republican and Democrat, have also strongly favored business elites in making cabinet appointments. The U.S. Senate, with its separate and considerable power, is also unusual among developed democracies, and is less democratic than the House in its electoral base and typically more conservative.

Political Parties

Political parties, William Dean Burnham writes, "with all their well-known human and structural shortcomings, are the only devices thus far invented by the wit of Western man which with some effectiveness can generate countervailing collective power on behalf of many individually powerless against the relatively few who are individually—or organizationally—powerful. Their disappearance could only entail the unchallenged ascendancy of the latter."[21] Political parties, Schattschneider adds, "created democracy and . . . modern democracy is unthinkable save in terms of the parties."[22]

Strong parties provide the political platforms on which candidates stand and for which citizens presumably vote. When parties are relatively impotent, partisanship is diminished, issues tend to be trivialized, differences among candidates are minimized, voter apathy rises, and political choices are based more on candidates' personalities than on a defined program.

American political parties have grown weaker, and their decline, the increase of ticket splitting, and the rise of moneyed pressure groups have diffused political power in the nation.[23] The American political system produces large, amorphous, and relatively undisciplined parties, especially on the left of center, so that differences within the two major parties often exceed differences between them, as the presence within the Democratic Party of both conservative southerners and northern liberals so well illustrates. In other democracies, strong programmatic parties flourish because the parliamentary system tends to discipline and strengthen political parties and this discipline facilitates the implementation of election programs. Parties can see their programs through to adoption much more readily than in the United States, and campaign promises can be more easily kept.

American parties have been most seriously weakened by the presidential system, nonpartisanship and other "reforms," the substitution of the direct primary for the party system of nominating candidates, and the shift in power from party to candidate occasioned by the steep and uncontrolled rise in the cost of political campaigns and the rising importance of personality. This weakening of the parties has made them easy prey for pressure groups, business elites, and richly endowed political candidates. In addition, new and costly campaign techniques—direct mail and media advertising, both high-cost items—have generally replaced the parties' door-to-door campaign efforts and undermined their grass-roots bases.

Political Reform

Self-styled reformers have sought to reduce or destroy the influence of political parties by substituting nonpartisan for partisan elections and direct primaries for the nomination of candidates by party convention. The ostensible aim of nonpartisan advocates has been to rid cities of the "corrupt" (and largely Democratic) "machines" that once dominated them, especially in the earlier twentieth century. These machines were hardly exemplary organizations, and some were heavily influenced by business interests, but most of them proved to be no more corrupt than the "reformers" who replaced them, and some of them were effective advocates for their immigrant constituents.

The machines were local, neighborhood affairs that involved voters in politics, and typically they were far more responsive to working-class voters and organized labor than the groups that took their place. Indeed, they were called "machines" because they could organize people, serve their everyday needs (if not their long-term political interests), recruit volunteers, offer public "patronage" jobs (usually low-level ones) to party activists, and get out the vote.

Because of reforming activities, roughly half of all elected officials now run on nonpartisan ballots.[24] In such balloting, many voters, including most lower income ones, tend to be less informed about individual candidates and less likely to vote. In many places, Republicans now control most civic associations that get out the votes, which gives that party's candidates an edge in low-turnout, nonpartisan contests.

The direct primary has proved to be a similar kind of "reform." Touted as more "democratic" than party nominations, the direct primary in fact deprives political parties of their only real power, the nomination of candidates. These primaries can even deprive the parties of their very identity, because in many places, Republicans can cross over and vote in Democratic primaries and vice versa; party membership or loyalty is not required. Given this estrangement of candidate and party in the United States, Democrats and Republicans arrive in the Congress with "all the rights and privileges of party members even though they may be wholly opposed to the party's philosophy and program."[25]

In 1968, only seventeen states had primaries; by 1988, thirty-five had them, and these primaries chose more than three-quarters of all delegates to the two major parties' national conventions. Such primaries have a determining impact on the party system: Candidates go directly to the voters, and delegates are chosen for their relation to candidates, not to the parties. Elsewhere in the democratic world, the direct primary is virtually unknown.

Another heralded "reform" has been the abolition of patronage for party activists in the form of low-level public service jobs. (At high levels, of course, patronage has if anything expanded, as is indicated by the appointment of large campaign contributors to growing numbers of cabinet, ambassadorial, and other policy positions.) Clearly, low-level patronage in the form of no-show jobs or jobs offered to people who are incompetent to hold them violates the public interest, but abolishing patronage altogether penalizes working-class parties that depend on volunteers who seek the lower-level jobs.

Reform of Democratic Party rules in the mid-1970s, Thomas Edsall claims, contributed to the party's becoming "highly vulnerable to pressures from a business community that had been quietly but effectively mobilizing since 1973."[26] The party initiated reforms that transferred party power in Congress to junior Democrats who had won seats from Republicans in the post-Watergate elections and whose main interest was in holding on to their conservative voters. They "had little or no interest in taking legislative steps to expand the electorate or, at a more controversial level, in strengthening the power of organized labor with the long-range goal of providing institutional support to Democratic voting blocks," for such interests would only alienate those conservative votes they sought to keep.[27]

Other reforms within the party itself, leading to state adoption of open primaries or strict regulation of caucus selection of convention delegates, tilted the party "toward an activist upper-middle class whose interests are often in direct opposition to the interests of less active, but larger, blocks of Democratic voters."[28] This tilt has occurred because voters in primaries are more likely than voters in general elections to come from higher income groups—in New York State, for instance, 32 percent of the primary voters in a recent election were from a higher income group compared to 16 percent in general elections.[29]

The reformers rejected other measures that would have strengthened the party's base in that larger block of voters. It can be argued, Edsall says, that "the maintenance of a healthy Democratic party in the mid-1970s would have included legislation to strengthen the protection of both workers and unions in representation fights against hostile management. The importance of a healthy labor movement to the Democratic party is hard to overestimate."[30]

Political Apathy

The system's antipathy to political parties goes back to the nation's founders, many of whom apparently thought of political parties and "factions" as being divisive and undesirable. George Washington, for example, opposed such factions, and James Madison regarded parties as an intrinsic evil that only an elaborate separation of powers could control. And though Alexander Hamilton and Thomas Jefferson led different parties, it was not until about 1840, Hofstadter notes, that political leaders finally accepted the two-party system as being manageable and not too disturbing to elite dominance of government.

The authors of the Constitution, E. E. Schattschneider claims, "set up an elaborate division and balance of powers within an intricate governmental structure designed to make parties ineffective."[31] The two-party system produces moderate parties, "held together by compromise and concession" and bland enough in their appeals to mass voters to make them frequently indistinguishable.[32] The system is designed to reduce conflict and weaken all but a narrow range of organized opposition. The way to check conflict, Schattschneider writes, is "simply to provide no arena for it or to create no public agency with power to do anything about it. There are an incredible number of devices for checking the development of conflict within the system. . . . All forms of political organization have a bias in favor of the exploitation of some kinds of conflict and the suppression of others."[33]

Even the political culture, as seen, for example, in congressional behavior, seems designed to limit conflict and simulate a unanimity that hardly reflects popular sentiment. In Britain, MPs divide strictly along party lines, sitting opposite each other in Parliament, arguing, interrupting, shouting. Vital to the debate—as well as government accountability and voter interest—is the prime minister's twice weekly and cabinet members' daily rotating submission to parliamentary questioning and cross-examination. In contrast, members of Congress appear more respectful than adversarial in their debates. Raw verbal conflict is rare, debate seldom influences policy, televised sessions show far more vacant than occupied seats, and never does the president appear before Congress for questioning.

The Congress's appearance of civility and gentlemanly conduct contrasts with the violence of American life, and with the British mixture of political conflict and public civility. This simulated American consensus and the scarcity of political outlets for dissent may even contribute to public conflict, closing off the people's political expression and pushing it into the streets where it is likely to erupt in random violence.

In the United States, political-party focus has shifted from issues and philosophies to the personal popularity of candidates. In the absence of real campaign issues, masses of voters, overwhelmingly the less privileged, lack the incentive to vote on election day. In many parts of the country, only a one-party system really exists and in these places, voting disincentives are even greater.[34]

The Presidency

Republicans occupied the White House for twenty-six of the thirty-eight years ending in 1990, and indeed, the presidency, an office of extraordinary powers, has been the stronghold of conservative political strength. Unlike the British prime minister, for example, the president is not chosen by nor is he directly and daily responsible to the leaders of his party. His appeal is personal and often based on celebrity, personality, photogenic qualities, and very heavy campaign contributions. Unlike the prime minister, the president fills vacancies in the third arm of government, the Supreme Court; he chooses his own cabinet, without respect to party standing, to administer the whole of the federal government; he is the commander in chief of the military, and exercises enormous powers with respect to foreign policy. And even with a Democratic Congress, a Republican president can usually sustain legislative vetoes when he chooses.

Money

The dominant influence of money on the American political system is well known. An early but feeble federal attempt to control campaign costs was made in 1907, but before passage of the federal Election Campaign Act of 1976, inspired by Watergate, undisclosed funds poured into campaigns almost without restriction. The act provided federal matching funds for presidential campaigns and limited individual contributions to $1,000 and those of political action committees (PACs) to $5,000 per candidate in primary and general elections. But loopholes appeared, and the Supreme Court opened the biggest one when it struck down the limits set by Congress on spending by candidates and their families. This "millionaires' loophole" gave an obvious advantage to those people who have the funds to finance their own campaigns. In the United Kingdom and many other democracies, funding by individual candidates is unknown.

In New York City, an optional program (optional because the Supreme Court ruled it could not be compulsory) was adopted for the 1989 mayoral elections that put a cap of $3 million on primary campaign spending, set a limit of $3,000 on individual contributions, and provided public matching funds for contributions under $500. The limits were an acknowledged success—though paying for television ads drained most of the funds.

The Election Campaign Act of 1976 is enforced by the Federal Election Commission, composed of three Republicans and three Democrats. According to a *Wall Street Journal* article in 1987, more than ten years after the law's enactment, the commission's Republicans had actively blocked enforcement, resulting in "partisan paralysis at the enforcement agency and a scofflaw attitude among politicians."[35]

In the four years between 1976 and 1980, spending on campaigns for all public offices in the United States doubled to a total of $900 million. In Britain and Canada, among other places, the costs and timing of campaigns and the use of costly television time are strictly limited. In Canada, for instance, parliamentary candidates in 1989 could not campaign more than forty-nine days before an election or exceed thirty-two minutes of television time, to be used only within thirty days of an election.

Total campaign spending in Canada is also limited, and a comparison of campaigns in Detroit, Michigan, and Windsor, Ontario—just across the river from Detroit—is instructive. In Windsor, the legal spending limit in 1988 was about $39,000 for a parliamentary nominee (variable with district size), and half of a candidate's spending was reimbursed by the government if he or she received at least 15 percent of the vote. In Detroit, candidates could spend any amount of their own money on campaigns and buy unlimited television time, and congressional nominees had to raise close to half a million dollars to be in the running in 1988. Even filing the papers required to run for office cost thousands of dollars, compared with the filing fee of $200 (usually refundable) for parliamentary candidates in Windsor.

The New Democratic Party (NDP) in Windsor still operates much like an old-time American city machine or like British parties in tightly controlled constituencies. Volunteer workers are used to canvass each voter (usually at least three times), talk about the candidate and the NDP program, and listen to what people say about issues. In the 1988 election, the Windsor NDP recruited some 600 volunteers to carry on this work; for U.S. congressional elections, political parties often have trouble recruiting any volunteers at all.

In Windsor, 90 percent of the eligible voters register to vote, and 80 percent of those registered vote, compared to less than half of the eligible voters who actually do so across the Detroit River. In Canada, voters and volunteers become deeply engaged in the political process, and a person of modest means can hope to win a parliamentary seat. In the United States, costs and other obstacles to grass-roots politics have turned campaigns into fund-raising affairs, and expensive opinion polls, mailings, and television ads have largely replaced debate, discussion of issues, and door-to-door contact with voters.

Since campaign funds in the United States go mainly to pay television costs, it has been suggested that a specified amount of free television time be provided to candidates and/or that the cost and timing of exposure be limited. So common are such regulations elsewhere that the only other democracies that allow paid political advertising at all are Japan, Canada, and Australia, and those countries place varying limits on the amount and timing of paid television exposure. In the United States, such an approach is seen as a radical scheme to subvert free speech.

Concern about funding permeates the whole U.S. political process and reaches well past election day. Based on an average cost of $355,000 for a winning congressional campaign in 1986, for example, House members had to raise an average of $15,000 each month of their two-year term to pay for the next campaign. Based on an average of $3 million for a winning Senate race, some $10,000 had to be raised each week of the six-year term. Often as much as 80 percent of a legislator's workday is thus spent on fund raising, and it may be that the undistinguished reputation of many politicians derives in some large part from their need to spend most waking hours soliciting funds and selling influence. The picture is not a pretty one, but its accuracy depends less on the depravity of the politicians than on the rules that constrict them.

Sadly, the reputation of the corrupters has suffered less than that of the corruptees. As Philip Stern writes in *The Best Congress Money Can Buy*, what threatens to disfranchise us all is "the seemingly infinite capacity of the buyers of influence—the special-interest groups and their political action committees—to muster whatever money senators and representatives need."[36] It is a system that suits the people and groups with the money to pay the bills.

Pressure Groups

With the decline of U.S. political parties, the system is exposed, like a weakened immunological system, to the invasion of pressure-group politics at every step of the political process. Pressure politics, Schattschneider writes, "is essentially the politics of small groups. . . . The flaw in the pluralist heaven is that the heavenly chorus sings with a strong upper-class accent. Probably about 90 percent of the people cannot get into the pressure system."[37]

Pressure groups exist in all societies, but in the United States they play a unique role in that they assume the functions of political parties, without any of the regulations or responsibilities required of parties. Often these groups can, through rewards and intimidation, influence candidates and public officials out of all proportion to their real strength. But a strong political party that can discipline its members can defy pressure groups, Schattschneider claims. Walter Adams and James Brock speak of the "ultimate danger of a symbiotic alliance between a powerful private economic oligarchy and a politically impotent public authority,"[38] but the power of government to resist this oligarchy has been weakened by a fragmentation of the apparatus of public control, accompanied or brought about by the "influence of powerful vested interests on government."[39]

Under parliamentary systems, lobbyists and pressure groups are usually less active and less influential. In Britain, for example, only cabinet ministers have significant authority to shape budgets and introduce legislation, and they are beholden only to their strongly disciplined parties and to the prime minister who chooses them; hence, they are usually beyond the reach of pressure groups. The chancellor of the Exchequer, for example, isolates himself before issuing the budget, and once issued, almost no amendments are made by Parliament. MPs can revise or reject legislation but seldom do so, and because they lack much direct power in shaping the law, they too suffer little from pressure-group influence.

The British system also reduces the influence of money on campaigns, for if MPs have relatively little direct influence on legislation and are strictly beholden to their parties, they have rather little to sell. By contrast, members of the U.S. Congress are lawmakers who are relatively free of party control and fair game for any interest group seeking legislative favors.

Conservatism

Conservative influence on government in the United States is apparent not only in the bank balances of the legislators (the "millionaires' row" of the U.S. Senate, for instance) but also in their occupations and particularly in the prevalence of lawyers in the legislative bodies. In the first U.S. Congress, 17 percent of the members were merchants and businessmen, 36 percent planters, and 38 percent lawyers. By 1972, 70 percent of the Senators and 51 percent of the representatives were lawyers.[40] In Denmark, on the other hand, only some 2 percent of the legislators are lawyers; in other democracies, only about 10–30 percent are lawyers, and working-class and nonbusiness candidates are more likely than lawyers to win elections.

In Britain, the largest share of MPs comes from the professions: 42 percent of all Conservative MPs and 40 percent of Labour MPs in 1987. But in that year, the Conservative professionals were mainly lawyers, and the Labour professionals were mainly teachers. Most strikingly, 37 percent of all Conservative MPs were from business (mainly executive levels) and only 10 percent of all Labour MPs; at the same time, 29 percent of the Labour MPs were manual workers and only 1 percent of Conservatives. A third of all Labour MPs were selected by the trade unions.[41]

Lawyers are certainly not uniformly conservative, but the profession often produces a conservative bias in its practitioners, and some of them have corporate associations and an income elevating them far above others. Many legislators have previously been corporate lawyers; others hope that their experience in government will enable them to enter corporate executive positions in the future.

Legal training and experience often dispose lawyers to see problems in terms of legal technicalities, precedent, and the possible risks of change rather than in terms of human problems and creative solutions to them. In unions, for instance, lawyers reputedly favor legal action over direct action and caution over conflict, and everywhere their professional, and financial, preferences lead to delay and prolonged and costly legal entanglements. For such reasons, the dominance of lawyers in legislative bodies (and unions) and their possible conservative influence on those groups deserve further attention.

Voter "Apathy"

Massive voter apathy appears to be an end product of many of the changes in the U.S. political system and its tilt toward conservatism. (The term "apathy," however, is a misnomer, since nonvoters are far more often "pushouts" than dropouts.) The extent of nonvoting is uniquely American, for nowhere else in the democratic world are eligible voters so unlikely to cast ballots.

Election rules were revised somewhat in the 1960s and 1970s, but these revisions were meager, and voting in presidential elections dropped sharply from 1960 to 1980 (most sharply in the bottom half of income recipients) and rose only somewhat in the 1984 election.[42] In 1978, for example, only 46 percent of eligible Americans voted, compared with 91 percent of Germans voting in about the same period, 89 percent of Danes, 83 percent of Norwegians, 79 percent of British and Israelis, 76 percent of Irish, 74 percent of Finns, 71 percent of Canadians, and 61 percent in India.[43]

The only major European country that can "compete" with the United States in voter apathy is Switzerland, a nation that almost alone in Europe lacks a strong labor-left party. In countries that have such parties, voting rates are generally high, which suggests that labor-left parties offer voters some of what they lack in the United States—real choices and an incentive to vote.

The class nature of nonvoting in the United States can be seen in the 1984 elections, for which 84 percent of college-educated eligible voters were registered but only 53 percent of those with eight or fewer years of school. Of people registered, 79 percent of the first group and only 43 percent of the second actually voted.[44] The "fortunate strata" of the community, Schattschneider writes, attribute voter apathy wholly to the "ignorance, indifference and shiftlessness of the people," but there is a better explanation: "abstention reflects the suppression of the options and alternatives that reflect the needs of the nonparticipants. . . . Whoever decides what the game is about decides also who can get into the game."[45]

"Every regime lives on a body of dogma, self-justification, glorification and propaganda about itself." In the United States, the "hero of the system is the voter who is commonly described as the ultimate source of all authority," but the fact that some 40 million eligible voters in America are unresponsive to the regime "is the single most truly remarkable fact about it."[46] Little is done to enlist nonvoters, but anyone able to involve nonvoters "will run the country for a generation."[47]

The problem of nonvoting is rooted in the way alternatives are defined, Schattschneider says, "the way in which issues get referred to the public, the scale of competition and organization and above all by *what* issues are developed." It is imbedded in the contradiction between "(1) the movement to universalize suffrage and (2) the attempt to make the vote meaningless."[48] The American political system, Schattschneider concludes, "is not well designed to bring great issues to a head in a national election."[49]

Voting Rules

America's unique voter registration and eligibility rules encourage non-voting. In Canada, for example, government-sponsored enumerators go door to door in every polling district before elections and list the names of eligible voters. The lists are then posted publicly so that anyone can challenge them. No personal registration is required. Similar rules prevail in the United Kingdom, other English-speaking nations, and most other democracies. Government takes the initiative in encouraging voting, and it delivers to the very doorsteps of voters the message that they count politically and that elections are imminent. About 80 percent of all eligible voters in Canada turn out to vote.

In the United States, the rules require an active effort by would-be voters to discover how, where, and when to register—then often an investment of time and effort to appear at the registry, perhaps wait in line, then repeat the process for later elections if names are deregistered for nonvoting. Only in the United States does government erect such registration hurdles, then fail to actively help people over them.

This personal registration system had its origins in the party realignments of the 1890s, the triumph of the Republican Party as we know it now, and the desire of economic elites to limit the franchise of nonelite voters. Because of elite hostility to nonelite urban "machines," compulsory registration was first required in most states only in large cities and only later in other places. In New York State, statutes for many years required both personal and periodic registration only in New York City. Such laws were among the "main devices by which a large and possibly dangerous mass electorate could be brought to heel," Burnham notes, "and subjected to management and control within the political system appropriate to 'capitalist democracy.'"[50]

Roots of Demobilization

Efforts to "demobilize," or to push out, certain voters have roots in early American history. "The gentlemen who wrote the Constitution in the summer of 1797 had it in mind," Lewis Lapham writes, "to make their world safe for commerce." The founders "could not conceive of human rights being established on anything other than property," and John Adams thought the "great functions of state" should belong to "the rich, the well-born and the able." Although the U.S. Constitution did not require an admission fee to the polls, many state constitutions limited local voting to property owners. Thomas Jefferson knew before 1820 "that his hope of an aristocracy grounded in moral or intellectual merit had been outmatched by a plutocracy subservient to the rule of finance capital."[51]

Other roots of exclusionist politics can be found in the late nineteenth century, around the time of the astonishing Populist Party vote and the response to that success: an overpowering conservative backlash, the historic coalition of southern Democratic and northern Republican elites, and the big business commitment to the Republicans during McKinley's successful 1896 campaign against populist champion William Jennings Bryan.

The participation of southern blacks and poor whites in the populist movement and the new immigrants' interest in socialism and city Democratic "machines" sounded an alarm to elites everywhere. Without doubt, Burnham writes, "the most notable and fateful manipulation of the electorate occurred in the eleven ex-Confederate states once it had become clear . . . that the federal government was no longer seriously interested in the conduct of southern elections."[52]

Republicans, who had waged the bloodiest war in history in part to free the slaves, forged a lasting political bond with southern economic elites (token Democrats since the Union commander had been a Republican) and effectively demobilized populism and poor Democratic voters in the South. Southern states adopted poll taxes (payable in advance of voting), literacy tests, and residency requirements that finally disfranchised almost all blacks and some half of the white electorate. The South became a one-party region, and that party was led by a landed and business oligarchy. In 1896, 57 percent of the potential voters in the South voted in the presidential election, in 1924, only 19 percent. In 1869, 85 percent of the potential voters cast ballots in gubernatorial elections; later figures were 40 percent in 1897, 27 percent in 1905, 12 percent in 1925, and 8 percent in 1941.[53]

In the North 86 percent of the eligible people voted in 1896, but only 57 percent did so in 1924.[54] In the name of "reform," conservatives attacked the Democratic "machines" in the cities, passed restrictive registration and voting laws, and introduced direct primaries (first in Wisconsin in 1903 and generally by 1917) to subvert political parties— or rather the Democratic Party. They instituted the long ballot, imposed rules on party patronage, replaced partisan with nonpartisan elections, and supported the city manager system, and all of these measures were aimed at curtailing Democratic Party influence. The conversion of democracy into oligarchy was pursued by middle-class progressives as well as southern elites. Abroad, the labor-left was gaining votes in many places; in America, it was losing them. Populists and social democrats had come too close to the seats of power, and they were driven back.[55]

The major assaults on the Democratic city machine, Burnham says, "were led by the 'best people' in local elite and middle-class positions," and the Democratic Party was so weakened that as often as not, its nominees for major office were chosen by Republican leaders.[56] Conservatives struggled to hold on to power in state legislatures by manipulating rules: the malapportionment of districts between the 1930s and 1960s to keep liberals out of conservative legislatures and the raising of eligibility rules to disqualify third parties. These practices, along with the poll tax, were upset by court decisions. Legislatures also scheduled elections for major state offices in off years in order to separate them from the sweeps of national elections. "The role of business in the strongly sectional Republican system from 1896 to 1932," Schattschneider concludes, "made the dictatorship of business seem to be a part of the eternal order of things."[57]

11

Labor-left Politics

THE PECULIARITIES OF AMERICAN POLITICS have set the stage on which the labor-left has been required to perform. Although critics have faulted labor's performance, mainly for timidity or indifference to politics, the record shows that against heavy odds, repression, biased game rules, and internal conflicts, labor's political efforts have nevertheless been prodigious and not without success. It has been unable to establish a mass labor or social democratic party, but not for lack of trying. Labor has also participated in mainstream politics, but in competing for influence, its resources have been meager compared to those of the economic elites.

Although charges against labor of "voluntarism" and aloofness from partisan politics have some validity, especially as applied to Gompers and the early AFL, they are only partially true. Labor has been deeply committed to politics, including support of friends, whatever their party, repeated efforts to create a labor party, extensive lobbying, and when Republicans turned conspicuously conservative, a firm commitment by most unions to the Democratic Party.

Early but wavering partisan support was also given to each of the early major parties. Workers' societies supported Jeffersonian Democrats in opposing the infamous conspiracy laws of the Federalists, and mechanics and other tradesmen entered politics because they strenuously objected to some aspects of the Constitution, especially its early failure to include a Bill of Rights. After the Civil War, labor backed Lincoln's Republican party for a time and the "radicals" within it. Not until almost the turn of the century (about the time British unionists launched the Labour Party) did labor switch from the realigned conservatism of the Republican Party to the Democrats and William Jennings Bryan's presidential candidacy. Labor's enthusiasm for Democrats has wavered over the ensuing years, rising tentatively with Woodrow Wilson and emphatically with Franklin Roosevelt.

Labor has stumbled and fallen repeatedly in following its dream, the creation of a labor party, often seeming to be unaware of the political system's antipathy to third parties. The defeat and eclipse of the Knights of Labor and populist politics, however, taught many unionists a lesson: Stick to the workplace, do what you can within the two-party system, and build a union base. The "politicians" and employers controlled the parties, but unionists could control their own organizations in the workplace and make some tangible gains for members. Yet even after the fall of the more leftist unions, many people in the AFL still cherished the dream.

Unionists formed workingmen's parties early in the nineteenth century, and thereafter they turned again and again to third parties—Socialist, Socialist Labor, Communist, Populist, Progressive, Greenback, Union Labor, Union, National Labor, and others. Efforts were massive, and some successful, but everything seemed against the unionists: the political rules, the opposition's huge resources, crippling assaults on the union base, repression of "radical" politics, incessant red hunts, foreign wars that replaced class with nationalist sentiment, and the incorporation by major parties of some labor-left demands. Finally, incorporation of labor into the New Deal drove the last nail into the third-party coffin.

American unions formed the world's first independent labor party: the Workingman's Party of Philadelphia founded by the Mechanics Union of Trade Associations in 1828. Similar parties were then established in New York, Boston, New England, and elsewhere. These locally based parties were formed in the late 1820s and early 1830s after white male suffrage had been won in many states, and by the mid-1830s, they had spread to some sixty cities in fifteen states. Most perished after a few years, but not before they had raised such issues as the abolition of property rights for voting, free education, the ten-hour day, cheaper and simpler court procedures, the right of militiamen to elect their own officers, temperance laws, reduction of economic inequalities, and the abolition of monopolies, lotteries, capital punishment, sweatshops, child labor, compulsory militia service, debt imprisonment, convict contract labor, and the seizure of wages and tools for debt. The major parties responded to these demands by accusing the workingmen's parties of being atheistic, advocating free love, and believing in the equal distribution of property. Almost from the start, the "red" label or its equivalent was used with abandon to stigmatize unions and their politics.

New York State, where labor parties and unions developed early, became the first industrial state to grant universal white male suffrage—in 1825, almost a half century after the Revolution; Massachusetts and Pennsylvania followed suit only in 1861. Such delays in granting this suffrage naturally impeded labor's electoral activities.

In 1835, the New York Workingman's Party and some radical Democrats put up their own slate of candidates in opposition to that of the more conservative Tammany Democrats at a nominating meeting. Tammany leaders, fearing defeat of their candidates, turned the lights off in the hall, whereupon the insurgents lit candles with Loco Foco brand matches and continued the meeting. Thereafter, "Locofoco" was an epithet hurled by the Whigs at the "radicalism" of the Democrats. The Locofocos dominated the New York Democratic Party until the Civil War, went independent for a time—as the Equal Rights Party—but soon rejoined the Democrats.

The early labor parties were continually harassed and repressed, and workers finally turned from politics to job action and from abstract theory to practical gains in wages and hours. Rising prices also led them to turn their attention to wage demands, and in 1837, the first trade union federation, the National Trades' Union (NTU), was organized in many eastern cities. The switch in emphasis from politics to unionism meant that the craft societies had to be organized all over again, as political organization was based on place of residence and unionism on place of work. The early unions followed the workingmen's parties to the grave, however, driven by a business depression that began in 1837 and lasted some twelve years.

The new unions that were established in the 1850s were led by men who knew that politics caused dissension, that laws were full of loopholes for business, that candidates once elected tended to forget workers, and that job action was safer and paid off better than partisan politics. Hence, assemblies of local tradesmen, the dominant union form until the Civil War's end, focused on union growth, consumer co-ops, free libraries, a union press, boycotts, and lobbying state legislatures. But the unions faced a basic survival struggle even in the workplace: Employers associations were organized in almost every trade and city, and most employers felt it beneath them to sit down and bargain with workers on an equal basis.

Between roughly the end of the Civil War and the end of the nineteenth century, four national labor groups were born, all seeking members among both the unskilled and the skilled and all but one deeply involved in electoral politics: the National Labor Union (NLU), founded in 1866; the Knights of Labor, founded in 1869; the American Federation of Labor (AFL), founded in 1881 (originally as the Federation of Organized Trades and Labor Unions); and shortly after the turn of the century, in 1905, the Industrial Workers of the World (IWW). Of these, only the AFL concentrated primarily, but not exclusively, on skilled workers, and only the IWW had a somewhat defined radical ideology, which became after much internal dispute a kind of syndicalism that excluded electoral politics.

The demand for labor during the Civil War and the reconstruction period that followed stimulated both unionism and capitalism. By 1873, union density was probably at its nineteenth-century peak—at least 300,000 members in some 1,500 trade unions. Wary of politics, these unions were nevertheless deeply involved in reviving the prewar workingmen's parties.[1] When a severe depression began in 1873, however, union membership plunged sharply downward, along with political prospects.

By 1900, the NLU was long dead, and the Knights, a bright shooting star in labor's firmament, was moribund. Only the AFL survived the century, having built a union base that could weather severe depression and having generally avoided the two paths that had otherwise spelled disaster for unionism—commitment to vulnerable third parties and unionization of unskilled industrial workers. The AFL's organizational structure, based on trade rather than on local assemblies of mixed trades, was also important in its survival.

Both the NLU and the Knights had turned to politics, partly to win the eight-hour day and partly because their unskilled members had far more votes than job bargaining power. Skilled workers, in contrast, had both votes and stronger bargaining powers, plus more job and place stability and a greater ability to pay dues high enough to sustain their unions through strikes and depressions.

The National Labor Union Party and the National Labor Reform Party

At the Civil War's end, four distinct political tendencies were present, as historian David Montgomery points out: conservative Republicans, radical Republicans, old-line Democrats, and labor reformers.[2] The radical Republicans were at first motivated by liberal sentiments, but when labor challenged their economic interests by demanding the eight-hour day, they joined the conservatives in their party.

The labor reformers came mainly from the National Labor Union, America's first major national labor federation, which included in its decade of active life (1866–1875) some thirty-four national union affiliates. William Sylvis, its remarkable leader, believed that labor's hope lay less in job action than in a labor party and worker-owned producer cooperatives—both especially needed as a means of regulating and reducing work hours. Sylvis contrasted working conditions in the United States with those in Prussia where the working class was protected by the government.

Labor support had been generally divided between local involvements with Democrats and newer ties to the Republican "radical" wing. When neither party supported the eight-hour-day struggle, the NLU formed the National Labor Reform Party in 1872, on the very eve of the depression that ended the party's prospects even at its birth—and also finished off the NLU itself. The life of this exceptional pioneer group was also cut short by third-party politics, the eight-hour-day struggle, the organizing of industrial workers, and bitter employer opposition to militant job action, which led to the use of armed repression, blacklists, lockouts, and legal action against the union. It was largely this opposition, in fact, that turned the NLU to politics, a turn that alienated many craft unionists, including the cigar makers (Sam Gompers's union), who disaffiliated from the NLU in 1870 because they felt it was neglecting job action in favor of politics.

The International Workingmen's Association of Europe (the First International), created by the British trade unions and featuring Karl Marx as its inaugural speaker, rose and declined at about the same time as the NLU, but the European unions and parties generally weathered the storms. The NLU and its labor party both perished in the repression and depression of the 1870s. The Industrial Brotherhood, set up by the national trade unions in 1873 to replace the NLU, pledged not to deteriorate into a political party or a refuge for discarded politicians, yet it too nearly succumbed to the 1870s depression, as did all but eight of the forty extant national unions. Thus, neither political nor job action strategies ensured union survival. In 1873, union membership was about 300,000; by 1878, it had declined to about 50,000; and in New York City it fell from 45,000 in 1873 to 5,000 in 1878.

Labor did not suffer depression gladly. Indeed, the depression years 1873–1878 were peak years of labor turmoil—mass demonstrations of unemployed workers, bitter textile strikes in New England, Pennsylvania miners' strikes, Mollie Maguire terror in the anthracite coal areas, and the national railway strike of 1877, a year of unparalleled violence in labor history. Much like gas under pressure, working people responded to the defeat of both their unions and union politics with explosions that resounded well into the twentieth century.

The Knights of Labor and Populism

American unionism did not come into its own as an established movement until the 1880s. The Noble Order of the Knights of Labor, founded in 1869 by Philadelphia garment workers, grew after the carnage of the depression of the 1870s to a membership of 700,000 by 1886, compared with the trade unions' 250,000. Knights' membership, like the NLU's, was open to everyone (except lawyers) who worked for a living, and the unskilled masses it attracted were aggrieved, ready for direct action, and more transient and turbulent than trade union members. Terence Powderly became grand master in 1879, and the group's vision of a just society (like the NLU's) featured worker-owned producer cooperatives. By mid-1885, it had established 135 cooperatives, and negotiated hundreds of union contracts, and by the 1890s, it had even made extensive forays into politics. Although officially eschewing strikes, politics, conflict with employers, and agitation for the eight-hour day, the organization became deeply and fatally enmeshed in all four, and by 1890, its membership had declined to 100,000.

Knights' History

The Knights grew rapidly as a result of the 1877 railway strike, and after two successful rail strikes in 1885, its membership among the unskilled erupted—in only one year, it grew from 104,066 to 702,924 members.[3] The strikes, Selig Perlman writes, meant that "a labor organization for the first time dealt on an equal footing with probably the most powerful capitalist in the country. It forced Jay Gould to recognize it as a power equal to himself. . . . The oppressed laboring masses finally discovered a powerful champion."[4]

The stage was set for the great upheaval of 1886–1887, which heralded the arrival of a new movement of unskilled labor and was ushered in by national strikes, boycotts, and turbulence. Although largely a spontaneous uprising, the upheaval raised issues that came from the trade unions and the Knights, and the one issue unifying the movement was the demand for the eight-hour day. On May 1, 1886, a national eight-hour strike, mainly engineered by the trade unions, was called. Even though Powderly opposed participation, the exuberant Knights' assemblies became deeply involved and were finally more identified with it than the trade unions. The tragic events in Haymarket Square on May 4, 1886, are well known. On May 3, Chicago police had fired on strikers, killing four and wounding many others; at a protest meeting called by anarchists to be held in Haymarket Square the next day, a bomb exploded, killing and wounding both police and demonstrators. Anarchists were arrested and tried, and with little proof of guilt, some were finally executed.

The Knights were also blamed for the bombing, though they had nothing to do with it, and the charges seriously damaged the organization. Employer associations had already begun an assault on the Knights— with yellow-dog contracts, blacklists, lockouts, spies, armed guards to break strikes, refusing to arbitrate disputes, and violating union agreements—and the Pinkerton agency was perhaps the most effective repressive force in this assault.[5]

A year after Haymarket, the upheaval began to subside, especially in the big cities, the citadels of the uprising. The unskilled, battered by losing battles, began to fall away from the Knights, and many craftsmen, charging the Knights with neglect, withdrew or joined the AFL. The Knights' cooperatives felt the first effects of the post-Haymarket assault. Railroads refused to haul their products and delayed building accessible tracks; producers refused to sell machinery, raw materials, and needed products; and by 1888, all the co-ops had perished, although the national organization remained active. No federal court issued injunctions to prohibit this clear restraint of trade.

Knights' Politics

The Knights' political philosophy was described in a Declaration of Principles: "The alarming development and aggressiveness of great capitalists and corporations, unless checked, will inevitably lead to the pauperization and hopeless degradation of the toiling masses." Checking this evil requires

organization of all laborers into one great solidarity, and the direction of their united efforts towards the measures that shall, by peaceful processes, evolve the working classes out of their present condition in the wage-system into a co-operative system. This organization does not profess to be a political party, nor does it propose to organize a political party but, nevertheless, it proposes to exercise the right of suffrage in the direction of obtaining such legislation as shall assist the natural law of development.[6]

The Knights became involved with the Greenback Labor Party, one of the many parties created in response to the 1870s' depression and the suppression of the 1877 railway strike. Although the party had some success in 1878, electing fourteen congressmen and many local and state candidates (including Terence Powderly, mayor-elect of Scranton), it lost ground as the farm debt eased and farmers saw the futility of the Greenback demand for new currency issues. The setback caused the Knights in 1880 to forbid its assemblies any official electoral activity, a directive more ignored than heeded.

The Knights' politics included lobbying from 1884 to 1886 for specific state and federal laws (such as compulsory arbitration, a graduated income tax, and government purchase of the telegraph, telephone, and railway systems); the entry by the assemblies into local electoral politics from about 1885 to 1888; and commitment to the farmer-led populist movement from 1890 to 1894.[7] In the mid-1880s, the Knights (and the trade unions) supported the United Labor Party's candidate for mayor of New York City, Henry George, whose program called for, among other things, a "single tax" to be applied exclusively to real property. Against George's campaign were pitted the "powerful press of the city of New York," Perlman writes, "all the political power of the old parties, and all the influence of the business class."[8] George lost narrowly, the party vanished, and the single tax, like the Greenbacks, disappeared as a labor political issue.

By late 1886, the Knights assemblies had entered various local labor parties (Union Labor, United Labor, Independent, Workingmen's, etc.) in 189 localities in thirty-four of thirty-eight states and four territories. In 1887, the Union Labor Party, with Knights' support, polled heavily in many states, especially Texas, Arkansas, and many midwestern farm states.

In 1890, the Knights declared support for the Populist Party, which controlled eight state legislatures, mainly in the southern and western farm belts, areas that in the post–Civil War period had organized against high interest rates and railway shipping costs. In the 1892 presidential election, the party won over 1 million votes and in the 1894 congressional elections, some 1.5 million votes. In 1896, the Democratic Party realigned, fused with the Populists, and nominated William Jennings Bryan for president. Bryan was defeated by a narrow margin, and the Populist Party was absorbed into the radical farmer-labor wing of the Democratic Party. The Knights, already moribund as a union, had bet on the Populists and lost. But out of it all, Leon Fink says, came a force that "may still stand as the American worker's single greatest push for political power."[9]

In Sean Wilentz's view, the major political reality from 1886 to 1894 was the "extraordinary repression visited upon organized workers by employers' associations with the cooperation of the courts, state legislatures, and increasingly, the federal government." The post-Haymarket repression only began "what may someday be recognized as the most intense (and probably the most violent) counter-offensive ever waged against any country's organized workers," peaking in 1892 and ending in the Knights' sharp decline in the 1890s and the AFL's ascendancy.[10] Also critical to the decline of leftist politics were the depression of the 1890s, the election of 1892, the Republican Party realignment in the 1896 election, and the political effects of the Spanish-American War.

Influence of Populism

In 1892, the Democrat Grover Cleveland narrowly won the presidency and, inheriting grave economic problems, presided over the panic and deep depression of 1893. The Democrats got the blame for the economic situation, and in 1894, the party lost more than 100 seats in the House, and in 1896, it lost the presidential election.

The 1896 election marked a major class realignment in the two major parties, the Democrats moving to the left for a time, and the Republicans consolidating conservative elites in the North and South. On the Democratic side, Populist sentiment became dominant. Even AFL unions, prominent among Bryan supporters in 1896 (without Gompers's endorsement), sought to defeat within the Democratic Party the conservatives they blamed for the depression and for Cleveland's suppression of the 1894 Pullman strike. With the Democratic-Populist fusion and Bryan as candidate, the Democratic Party of 1896 became, in effect, a farmer-labor party.

On the Republican side, profound and lasting changes occurred. Northern Republicans formed solid alliances with southern elites in the Democratic Party; and with McKinley's victory in the 1896 election, the conservatives, panicked by Populist successes, launched an offensive that gained them the ascendancy in American politics. Elite southern Democrats further disfranchised blacks and most nonelite whites, and in so doing virtually disabled populism in the South. At the same time, northern industrial elites wooed the rural Populist vote, building the rapport with farmers that now characterizes American politics. According to Richard Hofstadter, they did so by threatening to withhold credit and thus "practically forced farmers into cooperating" with them politically.[11] Bankers, the railroads, and producers of farm equipment all joined in this effort, urging farmers to think of themselves as businessmen and forging a business-rural alliance that still exists.[12] In 1919, they formed the Farm Bureau Federation, the most influential of farm organizations, one that represents the interests of the richest and most conservative farmers and that operates through close associations with the county agents of the Department of Agriculture.[13]

After 1896, then, the southern Populists were largely disfranchised and became political captives, the western Populists were cut off permanently from their southern allies, and in the North, business invaded the farms and pacified or drove out small farmers and Populist sentiment. Except for Wilson's two terms, Republicans controlled the presidency, and often Congress, for some thirty years thereafter. So aggressive did conservative Republicanism become, and so beaten the Populist opposition, that in presidential elections between 1896 and 1932, Democrats won an average of only about two states in the thirty-one states outside southern and border areas, and Democratic representation in many northern state legislatures declined or disappeared.

In 1898, the United States went to war with Spain to free Cuba from "imperialist rule." Opponents of war, including Samuel Gompers, Jane Addams, William James, Andrew Carnegie, and Mark Twain, formed the Anti-Imperialist League, but so potent was the nationalistic fever induced by both the taste of victory and Hearst's jingoistic journalism, that even the leaders of both populism and progressivism, opposed to militarism and imperialism in principle, became ardent advocates of war. William Jennings Bryan, among the most outspoken and influential of the Populists, urged his followers to join Republicans in ratifying the treaty with Spain. Opposed by the Anti-Imperialist League, the treaty passed by one vote, so in this war "against imperialism," the United States acquired the Philippines, Puerto Rico, and Guam and "freed" Cuba. In 1900, McKinley defeated Bryan more soundly than in 1896. Albert Beveridge, who became a Progressive Party leader, proclaimed that Americans were a "conquering race . . . we must obey our blood and occupy new markets and if necessary new lands" and cover the oceans with our fleets.[14]

In this way also were populism and progressivism incorporated by conservatism. Those charging up San Juan hill won the day, and the tagalong leftists were diverted from the class warfare being waged against them by the fever of nationalism and threats by foreign enemies. The Spanish war was to be only one example of such nationalistic incorporation.

Politics and the American Federation of Labor

The AFL, reorganized in 1886 as a loose, decentralized federation of craft unions, had acquired almost 300,000 members by 1898 and over a million by 1914, rising as the Knights fell and as skilled workers turned from political frustration to building strong protective unions. With a less "radical" profile than the Knights, most AFL unions were nevertheless militant, tough bargainers, and they also evoked the full wrath of employers who would do everything in their power "to resist and break the labor movement" and "do so with impunity."[15]

For a time, debates over party politics were banned from AFL conventions on the grounds that they were divisive and distracted from labor's main goal, building a solid union base. The AFL first favored the do-it-yourself "voluntarism" of British unions, especially in relation to union functions, but that did not disengage the AFL from politics or prevent its symbolic move in 1897 to the center of national politics, Washington, D.C., where Gompers became labor's chief lobbyist.

The consistent defeats of mass unionism and radical politics had persuaded Adolph Strasser and Samuel Gompers, cigar makers and AFL founders, to model their unionism on the British pattern: direct action (strikes and boycotts), high dues (for staffing and crisis), member benefits, pragmatic politics, caution about state power, and a preference for "voluntarism" and private rather than public solutions to problems. The

AFL structure differed from that of the Knights of Labor. The AFL's affiliates, of mainly skilled workers, were based in national and virtually autonomous craft unions, compared to the Knights' base in local assemblies of all trades and occupations, and this structure gave the AFL greater force and coherence in struggles with employers.

Strasser had helped organize the Socialist Labor Party and the Social Democratic Party, and from this experience, he concluded with Gompers that socialist politics, however desirable, stimulated repression and internal conflict and were a handicap rather than an asset to American unionism. "We have no ultimate ends," Strasser later said about the trade unions, "we are going on from day to day. . . . We are all practical men."[16] As John Commons saw it, Strasser and the other AFL pioneers became so absorbed in daily job struggles that "the socialist portion of their original philosophy kept receding farther and farther into the background until they arrived at pure unionism." Yet their brand of politics was always directed at the political center rather than at the producer cooperatives favored, at least in stated goals, by the NLU, the Knights, and later, under the syndicalist label, the IWW.[17]

Frustrated by business's control of government, trade unions often turned to economic action. Gompers once advised against "dabbling in that cesspool of corruption commonly known as party politics," and according to his biographer Harold Livesay, it seemed to Gompers that "politics offered only empty promises; socialism offered only useless doctrine. Both consumed the workers' energies and gave nothing in return."[18]

Gompers's role in the AFL, however, was mainly that of mediator among conflicting views. Neither he nor the federation occupied the real seat of AFL power—then and always held by national union affiliates. Most of the affiliates in the early days made political commitments, and even at AFL conventions, partisanship, though officially banned, was irrepressible. At the 1892 convention, for instance, Populist support was so forceful that two planks in the Populist Party platform were adopted. In 1896, AFL affiliates were active partisans of Bryan's presidential candidacy, Gompers's official aloofness notwithstanding, and in 1908, they were even more partisan in behalf of Bryan in his race against William Howard Taft. Affiliates supported Henry George's United Labor Party candidacy in New York City, and in 1924, they supported—with William Green (later AFL president) playing a lead role—Robert LaFollette of the Progressive Party against the conservative Democratic presidential nominee, John Davis. Affiliates and factions in them also gave considerable support to the Socialist Party and other third parties over the years, as well as to major-party candidates.

Gompers opposed AFL support of the Socialist Party and, for some time, increases in government authority. Yet he insisted that "there is not an inspiring and ennobling end that they [the Socialists] are striving for that my heart does not beat in response to. But our methods are different."[19] In 1893, Gompers opposed the adoption by the AFL of "plank 10," which called for "the collective ownership by the people of all means of production and distribution," and the plank was defeated by a slim margin. In 1894, Socialists ousted him as AFL president, but he was back the next year, by the narrow margin of 1,041 to 1,023.

In earlier years, Gompers had been attracted to Marxism and its emphasis on unionism, and he learned German in order to read Marx and others in the original. The rhetoric of socialism also appealed to him, Livesay says, "though he knew it must be used with care so as not to alarm the public."[20] His borrowings from Marx included such statements as, "There are two classes in society, one incessantly striving to obtain the labor of the other class for as little as possible." Such rhetoric contrasts with Powderly's, "I hate the word 'class' and would drive it from the English language if I could."[21]

Syndicalism was also alive in Gompers's time, and that doctrine may have influenced him as much as Marxism. It also flourished among his contemporaries in the IWW and the Western Federation of Miners and in the stress placed on producer cooperatives by the NLU and the Knights. Syndicalism rivaled Marxist influence in the First International, helped shape Scandinavian unionism, influenced the French and Spanish movements, and even had some apparent impact on those British skilled workers who rejected ideas of political reform. For Gompers, the syndicate, the union, was the chief organizing instrument.

Some AFL unions were for a time "voluntarist" about federal action on some social welfare issues, preferring voluntary union action on these issues to government mandates. Such preferences were based largely on experiences with the antiunionism of business-controlled governments. Still, most AFL unions supported local and state welfare and wage-hour laws and passed resolutions in their support at AFL conventions. Gompers, however, refused for a time to lobby in Washington for equivalent federal laws, so the job again was left to affiliates.

British unionism, on which the early AFL was modeled, was also "much less interested in state welfare schemes than in the more tangible benefits of secure employment and cheap food," according to G.D.H. Cole; it also tended toward voluntarism on welfare issues and on the issue of court and state interference in union activities.[22] British labor was even skeptical, as was Gompers for a time, of such measures as state-legislated unemployment insurance.[23] Like Justice Louis Brandeis, the British believed it unwise to "pin too much faith in legislation;

remedial institutions are apt to fall under the control of the enemy and to become instruments of oppression."[24]

Labor was constantly driven into national politics, however, by crippling assaults on its very survival. Before 1894, AFL unions often fought or disobeyed local or state court injunctions, but in 1894, the federal injunction that was brought into play against the Pullman strike could not be disobeyed. Trade unions suffered continual setbacks at the hand of conservative courts, especially during AFL strike waves in 1901–1904 and 1915–1922. In 1906, Gompers resisted an injunction issued in the Buck's Stove boycott and was sentenced to (but did not serve) a year in prison. Among the sharpest blows to the AFL was the 1906 injunction against the strike for an eight-hour day by the International Typographical Union, a democratic "model" craft union and an AFL mainstay. Court rulings on the Sherman Antitrust Act threatened the AFL's very survival, and lacking resources for expert legal defense, the trade unions were submerged by the growing number of antitrust suits brought under the act.

Employers formed numerous union-busting associations, and according to Marc Karson, U.S. Steel, the developer of this campaign, sought in effect to extirpate unionism.[25] The National Association of Manufacturers, turning from promoting trade to opposing unionism, began a national antiunion campaign in 1903, and by 1904, AFL growth had stopped. The corporate "trusts" had come on the scene and, according to John Commons, had "destroyed every bargaining advantage which labour ever enjoyed." Union agreements with U.S. Steel were virtually scrapped, and in 1907, when the steel trust came to dominate the Great Lakes, longshore agreements were terminated—as were agreements elsewhere.[26]

The year 1906 marked the AFL's first plunge into partisan politics. Before that, Gompers had confined his politics largely to lobbying for an eight-hour law and a fruitless ten-year attempt to get an anti-injunction law passed, although he also had supported legislation for such changes as old age pensions, public works, women's suffrage, and the nationalization of telephone and telegraph systems. By March 1906, however, he had come to realize that labor had to achieve political influence or be ruined by the employers' use of the state against them.[27] In that year, the AFL Executive Council, in a panic about the Sherman Act, reversed itself and urged affiliates to support labor's friends in the 1906 election and if necessary, run their own candidates against labor's enemies. Many had done so all along but not on the federation's urging.

In 1912, the AFL, for the first time, officially endorsed a presidential candidate, Woodrow Wilson. As president, Wilson's relations with labor were at least benign, but his promises to support its exemption from antitrust law and keep America out of war were not kept, and he finally turned his back on labor.

The IWW, the Western Federation
of Miners, and Radicalism

The record of unionism in the West often gets lost in history's focus on urban centers and mass industry, yet few chapters in that history reveal more about the forces shaping the labor-left than the history of the IWW and the Western Federation of Miners (WFM), despite the relatively transitory existence of each.

The WFM's struggles were among the bloodiest and most savagely repressed in union history—in Coeur d'Alene, Idaho; Cripple Creek, Colorado; Goldfield, Nevada; and elsewhere. In 1905, the WFM rejected reaffiliation with the AFL and founded the Industrial Workers of the World (IWW). Founders also included Daniel DeLeon, Mother Jones, and Eugene Debs (who soon resigned). Unlike the later CIO, the IWW was to be a political organization as well as an industrial union, committed to creating a third party, which would keep state government from crushing WFM strikes, and to working toward the creation of a cooperative commonwealth. By 1908, however, the faction favoring direct economic action had won out over the DeLeon Socialists, and the political agenda had been rejected.

Aside from a successful textile strike in Lawrence, Massachusetts, and an unsuccessful one in Paterson, New Jersey, the IWW organized mainly rural workers—migratory farm workers in the Great Plains, lumber workers in the Pacific Northwest, and copper miners in Jerome and Bisbee, Arizona—in all some 60,000–100,000 workers, only a minority of them industrial workers. The IWW rejected collective bargaining, written contracts, and arbitration in favor of direct action, but the continuous conflict resulting exhausted members and aroused the heated opposition of employers and public officials.

History's judgment of the IWW is much kinder than that of its time. The turbulence of its strikes was a response to the ruthlessness of their repression—by armed force, ferocious campaigns of red baiting, and the total complicity of government in aiding both. The IWW's rhetoric sounded revolutionary, but its strikers asked only what AFL unions asked—better wages, hours, conditions—and uncovered the deplorable working and living conditions of marginal, unskilled, rural workers and proved what many unionists doubted, that they could be organized.

Socialists and Progressives

Marxist ideas and their stress on the central role of unionism in political change had some influence in America as early as 1853, especially among German immigrants, but such ideas were submerged by the Civil War. In 1878, the Socialist Labor Party (SLP) entered American elections with some success, but the party split in 1880 over support of the Greenbacks, and after running the first Socialist presidential candidate in American history in 1892, it faded as an electoral force. Much like the NLU, the SLP stressed independent politics and producer cooperatives more than unionism. Nevertheless, under Daniel DeLeon's leadership, it tried to create a rival to the AFL in 1895, the Socialist Trade and Labor Alliance, but this "dual union" failed as SLP members defected to the AFL and to a new Socialist Party.

In 1901, the Social Democratic Party of Eugene Debs and Victor Berger merged with Morris Hillquit's trade-union split from the SLP and formed the Socialist Party of America. The party nominated Debs for president, and in 1904, he polled 420,000 votes. The party's platform called for a cooperative commonwealth to be established through both independent politics and unionism ("boring from within" the AFL), and its immediate program called for abolition of child labor, shorter work hours, initiative and referendum, a graduated income tax, and regulation of industry, trusts, mines, communications, and transport. Among explicitly socialist parties, Debs's party achieved the only real electoral success. At its peak in 1912, it had 118,000 members; 323 publications, circulating to over 2 million readers; 6 percent of the presidential vote, about 900,000 votes, the largest part coming from seven western and mountain states; members in federal and state legislatures; and 1,200 officeholders in 340 cities, including 79 mayors in 24 states.

The mobilization of business opposition, radical baiting, and defections to the Democratic Party cut into Socialist Party support even before the United States entered World War I, so that between 1912 and 1916, the party lost more than a third of its votes. In 1912, the Machinists, the Illinois miners, and the Brewery Workers had supported Debs, but in 1916, all unions except the Ladies' Garment Workers (ILGWU) withdrew their support in favor of Wilson and the Democrats. But repression in this period counted for as much as Wilson's unkept promises, and in the final demise of the party, it counted for almost everything.

The radical movement, which included the Non-Partisan League, the IWW, and the Socialist Party, was still near its peak when the United States declared war in 1917. Antiwar sentiment was pervasive in the country, but the Socialist Party, which opposed the war, and the IWW became special targets of wartime repression, as described in other chapters. Sedition and criminal syndicalist laws were passed; red hunts began (especially after the Russian revolution); leaders were jailed; many members were arrested, harassed, and deported; meetings were broken up; and the use of the post office was denied.

In 1920, Debs still won almost as many votes from his penitentiary cell as he had in 1912, but the party itself was badly wounded, declined steeply, and remained dormant throughout the 1920s. Defeated and harmless, it was still harassed. In 1923, for instance, two Socialist speakers were kidnapped by Pennsylvania police, evicted from the area, and arrested when they tried to return.

The left's biggest push in the 1920s came from the 1924 Progressive Party's candidate for president, Wisconsin Senator Robert LaFollette, who called for an end to control of government by private monopolies, restraints on labor injunctions and Supreme Court powers, public ownership of water and railways, and guarantees of labor's right to organize. This extraordinary campaign by a mainstream politician was supported by the AFL, the Socialist Party, the Non-Partisan League, and the Farmer-Labor Party among others. LaFollette won almost 5 million votes, 17 percent of the total cast, and in third-party history came in second only to Theodore Roosevelt's Progressive vote in 1912.

The earlier Progressives, educated, genteel city cousins of populism, had called the Populists madmen, William Allen White wrote in the 1920s, then they had "caught the Populists in swimming and stole all of their clothing except the frayed underdrawers of free silver."[28] The earlier Progressive declared his main enemies to be immorality, the trusts, and the machines, but "he was too substantial a fellow to want to make any basic changes in a society in which he was so typically a prosperous and respectable figure."[29] Thurmond Arnold adds that the early reformers "occupied themselves with the verbal and moral battles that left the great working organizations of society largely untouched."[30]

The early progressivism had peaked in 1912, but war halted the movement, as it had Jeffersonian and Jacksonian progressivism. "War," as Hofstadter says, "has always been the Nemesis of the liberal tradition in America."[31] But the liberal spirit rose again with LaFollette, less robust but more radical and more prolabor than before. The "red issue" was the Republicans' main charge against LaFollette. As the Republican vice-presidential candidate put it, the issue was "whether you stand on the rock of common sense with Calvin Coolidge or upon the sinking sands of socialism with Robert M. LaFollette."[32]

LaFollette's candidacy was largely a protest against the Democratic candidate, but the party had few resources and could not be sustained as a national organization against the electoral system's hostility to third parties and the pursuit by labor of candidates who could win. The shift among labor leaders from bipartisanship and socialism in 1900, to socialism, progressivism, and nonpartisanship in 1925, then to the Democratic Party by 1946 is shown in Table 11.1. By 1946, only 8.67 percent favored a third party, and 69.4 percent had made a partisan commitment to the Democrats.

Table 11.1 Political preferences of labor leaders

	1900	1925	1946
Democratic	21.3	13.7	69.4
Republican	21.3	11.2	13.4
Socialist	37.7	27.5	8.1
Progressive/Labor	11.5	25.0	0.5
Nonpartisan	8.2	21.0	8.6

Note: Totals may not add up to 100 owing to rounding of figures.

Source: Gary Fink, *Biographical Dictionary of American Labor* (Westport, Conn.: Greenwood Press, 1984), pp. 21–23.

Labor After World War I

Unlike the Socialist Party and the IWW, the AFL suffered disabling but not deadly war wounds. It had taken its usual course of lesser resistance and survived, although it was pathetically empty-handed and unprotected at the war's end. War profits had made employers, on the other hand, enormously richer and more powerful, and the repression and antired hysteria that arose in the war's aftermath threatened the whole basis of unionism and reduced union members by 1.4 million between 1918 and 1923 alone.[33] Buried during the roaring 1920s were not only the AFL but almost all life on the labor-left.

Until the late 1930s, labor's major weakness was its inability to organize industrial workers, despite some heroic efforts to do so. Finally, the Great Depression ushered in the New Deal, the CIO, and a new era. The time for industrial unionism had arrived, and a nucleus of AFL unions formed the organizing committee that became the CIO. Thus, a movement was born that came closer than any other to creating a social revolution. Third parties and labor-left groups flourished: the Farmer-Labor Party of Minnesota, the American Labor Party of New York, the Progressive party of Wisconsin, Huey Long's Share the Wealth movement, the Commonwealth Federation of Oregon and Washington, North Dakota's Non-Partisan League, Upton Sinclair's End Poverty in California movement (EPIC), the Communist Party, and the Socialist Party.

Norman Thomas, the Socialist Party's candidate for president, polled almost a million votes in 1932, up from less than a third of that in 1928. But when FDR won a second term in 1936, Thomas's vote dropped to 188,000. In 1934, EPIC won the Democratic gubernatorial primary in California, and in 1938, ex-EPIC leaders won a U.S. Senate seat and the governorship of that state. Ironically, the "radical" and militant CIO turned labor-left votes away from third parties and toward a nearly total commitment to New Deal Democrats.

Labor finally put all its chips on FDR and the Democratic Party, but even in the 1930s, the center of the New Deal coalition was not farmers, labor, the poor, or any bloc of voters, but a rising group of capital-intensive industries, investment banks, and internationally oriented commercial banks.[34] This bloc represented liberalism at home and internationalism abroad.

This same bloc also supported the Kennedy-Johnson military budgets, which protected its large interests abroad and heaped up profits for its domestic operations. The bloc later shifted to Nixon and moved into strong opposition to domestic liberalism, taxes, welfare, and unionism.

Both Kennedy and Johnson, on behalf of the multinationals, had rejected labor's pleas for import protection and pressed for deep tariff cuts. The support by unions of U.S. foreign policy "worked directly to hurt their members' economic position," Thomas Ferguson and Joel Rogers conclude. "Much American military and foreign aid is used to prop up regimes that repress their own citizens and their wages. Such aid in effect subsidizes multinational expansion abroad" and results in capital flight, plant relocation, waves of cheap imports—and heavy losses for both unions and unionized workers.[35]

Labor-left influence in the New Deal and Democratic Party declined as business influence grew, and by the mid-1970s, with unions under fire from employers, Democratic officials had backed off from labor. Even during the Carter administration, with a Democrat as president and a Democratic majority in both houses, labor's agenda was still largely neglected or rejected, and Carter proved to be, at best, an aloof friend of labor. Filibusters killed labor-law reform in the 1970s, without any presidential intervention to save it, and common situs picketing (i.e., picketing rights), of vital interest to the building trades, was defeated in the same way. In 1978, a tax bill passed that for the first time since the depression did *not* favor low and middle income groups, and in March that year, Carter invoked the Taft-Hartley Act against 160,000 striking coal miners. During the Carter years, the Humphrey-Hawkins Full Employment Act of 1978 did pass, but it was only a hollow endorsement of the *idea* of full employment.

In the 1970s and 1980s, corporations conducted an unprecedented political mobilization, converting the antibusiness Democratic Congress of 1974 into a probusiness Democratic Congress in 1978, electing Ronald Reagan, funding think tanks (at some $40 million for the top four alone, more than the entire national AFL-CIO budget), financing political campaigns, organizing stockholders and managers, forming conservative coalitions, and shifting politics sharply to the right by 1981. All was accomplished, Thomas Edsall says, by "a political and ideological mobilization of business."[36] The number of registered corporate lobbyists grew from 175 to 650 between 1971 and 1979, the Business Roundtable was founded in 1972, and Chamber of Commerce membership doubled from 1967 to 1974. Corporations endowed forty "free enterprise" college chairs between 1974 and 1978, increased grants to the Public Broadcasting System from $3.3 million in 1973 to $22.6 million in 1979, and financed books by conservative economists.[37]

Although conservatives have conducted a massive campaign against what it calls the "liberal bias" in the press, almost the entire press endorsed Reagan's candidacies. As Ferguson and Rogers comment about the media treatment of the elections, only Balzac could do justice to the repeated media references to black, female, and union supporters of Mondale as "special interests" while Republicans piled up cash from corporations and affluent Americans.[38]

American public opinion on major political issues has remained unchanged, Ferguson and Rogers insist, but the New Deal system "is now dead, killed off not by voters but by a dramatic realignment of major investors in the political system."[39] Investors, not voters, turned right. The claim that a right turn in U.S. mass sentiment or an electoral realignment occurred cannot be supported.[40]

Political influence has been tantalizingly elusive for labor. One view of the subject holds that the labor-left can never attain much influence in electoral politics because it has never become a numerical majority in any society and therefore has had to dilute its class orientation in coalitions with other classes. Labor's mistake, Adam Przeworski and John Sprague claim, was to assume that a social transformation could be achieved through electoral politics.[41] Rule by the *un*elected, however, has also been tried but with even less success from labor's perspective.

Some Comparisons

The hostility to labor, Charles Tilly and Roberto Franzosi write, "prevented American labor from taking a centralized, political stance at the national level, like its European counterparts," and from taking a more radical approach to workplace control issues. "This was the lost political struggle of American workers. It does not mean they failed to fight. . . . The difference from the European experience is that they lost even more emphatically than their European fellows."[42]

In a remarkable review of political repression in twenty European countries from 1850 to World War I, Robert Goldstein reports that except for a few instances, such as the repressions of the 1871 Paris Commune and the 1907 Rumanian peasant rebellion, European political repression did not involve mass or even random killings and by 1870, repression had sharply declined in most places, and the working class was able to organize and achieve some political influence.[43] By contrast, the post-1870 period in the United States was one of violent opposition to mass unionism and a gross denial of civil liberties. In all major European countries, unions and strikes were legalized during this period (1824 in Britain), but in the United States they had no legal recognition until the 1930s.

Of the three major types of European political repression identified by Goldstein—disfranchisement, limits on union organizing, and limits on civil liberties—he regards only disfranchisement, which lasted in some places until the 1880s and retarded the adoption of social legislation, as being of major significance in Europe. Yet in some respects, as previously noted, the denial of voting rights was as bad or worse in the United States, although it was less conspicuous because the practice was governed by state rather than federal law. Many blacks, women, and non-property-owning, ill-educated, and transient people were deprived of the right to vote up to World War I and even after. In some states, even universal white male suffrage was granted only late in the nineteenth century, and an elaborate network of voting restrictions effectively limited voting throughout the nation. These factors also retarded the adoption of progressive social legislation in the United States.

A study by Samuel Cohn of French coal miners' strikes from 1890 to 1935 concluded that the French government always intervened in mining strikes, usually to pressure employers into making concessions to striking unions. In the United States, by contrast, government has usually intervened to enjoin strikes and break them by armed force.[44] The difference lies in the fact that many labor-supported candidates held office in France (though socialists did not form a government until 1936)—and in the conviction held by many members of the French elite that conciliation produced better results and less conflict than harsh repression. This conviction led to a liberalization of French labor law in 1884, which made strikes officially legal, and to an 1892 law that gave government a key role in mediating labor disputes and creating a voluntary arbitration system. Only rarely did the French government repress striking workers, and then almost solely for rather extreme violations of public order. The hostile intervention of government in the United States, on the other hand, has been a leading source of major strike losses.

According to Gerald Friedman, rather than favoring employers, French state officials sought to conciliate and settle strikes; in the United States, many employers used intimidation and force in dealing with labor unions instead of bargaining and mediation.[45]

The French government acted as it did because the French elite was divided between those favoring and those opposing a republic, a standoff that compelled alliances with the working class. The far more monolithic American elite needed no such alliances.[46] The relative weakness of American radicalism, Friedman concludes, "reflects the exceptional strength and political power of American capitalists rather than the conservatism of American workers."[47]

PART FOUR

Strategies of Economic Manipulation and Violence

12

Subtler Technologies of Subjection: Managing Workers

THE GROWING SOPHISTICATION of the war on labor after the organization of the CIO led to the adoption of more subtle, or less physically violent, approaches to control of the work force. Armed force was complemented by such "cold-war" tactics as automation, scientific management, company unions, and paternalism, and the arsenal of guns, armies, and "driving foremen" evolved to embrace strategies of control that most often aimed at limiting the costs and powers of unionized skilled workers.

Instead of head-on collisions with labor, these approaches sought to manage workers through technological change and manipulation of the labor process and labor relations, and over the years, the roles enacted by employers expanded to include "the boss" (coercive and technocratic), "the father" (paternalistic), and "the partner" (fraternal)—distinct roles but performed by the same actors—cumulative and somewhat chronological in their development. In the coercive-boss role, the emphasis is on discipline and punishment, the "driving" of workers by foremen (civilian drill sergeants), the "surveillance" of employees in their work and private lives by security and "service" officers, and such "community controls" as company towns that reach deeply into the private lives of employees.

In the technocratic-boss role, the emphasis is on using technology to control labor, reorganizing and deskilling the labor process, adopting incentives that spur individual performance, and promoting labor relations that reduce group solidarity and increase loyalty to employers. In the paternalistic role, employers seek through various offerings to temper worker unrest: welfare benefits, company unionism, and a softened and more "human" relationship. In more recent decades, as paternalism receded in unionized industry, some employers have talked of "partnerships" with labor, a role that is sometimes indistinguishable from the others, especially when employers are the wholly dominant "partners" or when rising employer hostilities coincide with offers of cooperation.

Yet sometimes even limited partnerships have offered some advantages to labor.

The factory system came into being as a way of managing workers who were unsupervised under the home-work system in order to increase production. Early "relations" of employers with labor largely consisted of bossism, hostilities, and efforts to replace skilled craftspeople with machines. In the early textile mills, the skilled responded to the machines by wrecking them, but by the 1880s, the machines, new assembly methods, and the "drive system" had won a clear victory. The "dominating note of the drive policy," Sumner Slichter writes, "is to inspire the worker with awe and fear of the management, and having developed fear among them, to take advantage of it."[1]

But coercion could not suppress such rebellions as the railway uprising of 1877 and the great upheaval of the 1880s, so employers looked for other means of control. Among those found were scientific management on the one hand and welfarism, human relations, and personnel specialists on the other; for most employers, however, the dominant mode remained bossism, discipline, and drive.

Welfare Capitalism

Labor unrest and the challenge of unionism aroused paternalistic responses in some employers. Responding to the shattering uprising of 1877, George M. Pullman built a town designed to "exclude all baneful influences" from the community and workers—and return 6 percent on investment. Unrest continued to increase, however, culminating in the violent Pullman strike of 1894, and Pullman's company town proved an uninspiring model for employers seeking to rid their shops of unionism. As another response, by the late 1880s, some forty companies had begun profit sharing schemes, and many more were sponsoring contests, sport teams, outings, housing, and citizenship instruction and had added lunchrooms, restrooms, and landscaping to the workplace, largely to avoid unions.[2]

In the 1920s, the heyday of welfare capitalism, the most popular benefits were life insurance, covering almost 8 million employees by 1928, and pensions, covering almost 4 million, many of them managers. Larger employers began offering stock ownership after 1922 as a way of raising production and wooing employees away from unionism.

Employers rejected the foreign experience with unemployment insurance, opposed any government action on it, and in the 1920s, only thirteen nonunion firms provided any job security at all. The absence of security proved a special hardship: The depression of 1920–1922 made many jobless, seasonal unemployment in the auto industry grew, and unemployment resulting from automation led *Fortune* magazine to conclude that "from the purely productive point of view, a part of the human race is already obsolete and a further part is obsolescent."[3] The most popular employer attitude is attributed to Samuel Insull, the utilities tycoon: "My experience is that the greatest aid to the efficiency of labor is a long line of men waiting at the gate."

Paternalism and bossism permeated many welfare programs, including compulsory religious and patriotic observances; indoctrination in company policy; thrift clubs; emphasis on company and family loyalties (rather than union solidarity); and lectures on alcohol, thrift, work habits, personal appearance, and conduct. One leader of the welfare movement supported cooking schools, Stuart Brandes reports, because "she was irked by the strange Lithuanian sausages, dark Slovak bread and 'uncouth Polack pickles' eaten by factory workers."[4] Welfare capitalism sought an Americanized and a conforming worker, loyal to country and employer.

Surveillance of personal conduct and union activism was a prominent task of company welfare workers. In 1915, more than half of a group of firms surveyed admitted using their nurses and welfare workers to investigate malingering by employees.[5] Later, the Ford Service Department, a prototype for others, became notorious for intruding into the private lives and conduct of Ford workers.

The theory underlying many welfare activities, Brandes writes, was that "well-housed, well-fed, clean, properly educated Christians do not strike."[6] Indeed, welfare capitalism's central purpose was, according to Irving Bernstein, the "avoidance of trade unionism."[7] Welfarism was actively antiunion. Skilled workers were given welfare benefits (pensions, bonuses, profit sharing, housing) that could be withdrawn when workers joined unions, and these benefits also tied workers to their jobs. After the 1892 Homestead steel strike, for example, discount housing was offered skilled workers in order to tie them to their jobs, communities, and house payments, and keep unions out. Winning public goodwill also motivated welfarism, and the 1890 Sherman Antitrust Act in particular stimulated business to improve its public image through philanthropic gestures.

Rise of Welfarism

The main link between *war*fare and *wel*fare was supplied by John D. Rockefeller, Jr., who held controlling shares in the Colorado Fuel & Iron Company, the largest coal producer in the Rockies. The company called on the militia to break a strike of its miners, and the ensuing conflict resulted in a "civil war" and the previously described Ludlow massacre.

Rockefeller met the public outrage directed at him for his full support of the massacre by offering the Colorado Industrial Plan, or the Rockefeller Plan, which had two parts: "The Industrial Constitution" and a "Memorandum of Agreement," the former creating a company union and the latter dealing with working conditions. As historian John Fitch describes the plan, "It is not democracy . . . it is not . . . collective bargaining, though it may be a step in the direction of both."[8]

Rockefeller's plan collapsed when the company, with only a day's notice, cut wages by 30 percent during the 1921 depression. A protest strike was called, but the governor, at the company's request, declared a state of insurrection and rebellion, sent troops into the mines, and prevented the strike. "If this wage experience did not expose the plan's bankruptcy," Bernstein writes, "it amply demonstrated how slight was its hold over the men in the crucial area of wage determination."[9] In 1924, a Russell Sage report concluded about the company union that "neither in the written plan nor in practice do the employees' representatives have responsibility for decisions."[10] Rockefeller's plan, his "human relations" declarations, his words condemning conflict and praising a "harmony of interest" between employer and employee, and his belief that "cooperation of Labor and Capital may well be regarded . . . as the most vital problem of modern civilization" had little practical consequences for the actual conduct of his labor relations.[11]

The plan was adopted at other Rockefeller holdings, however. At Standard Oil of New Jersey, in response to a violent strike in 1915–1916, the largest welfare capitalist plan of the period was adopted. Its director was "concerned with insulating the worker against the temptations of trade unionism," and as a result, he came to be called "one of the shrewdest oppositionists organized labor found in the twenties, because he never met the trade unions head on."[12] Companies such as AT&T, GM, and U.S. Steel also organized to promulgate such plans, and industrial relations counselors were asked to offer advice. Unhappy with the emphasis of historian John Commons and others on unionism and collective bargaining, the Rockefeller circle sponsored a university industrial relations institute movement to counter the Commons school and redirect academic interests away from unionism.

In 1919, the chief officers of ten leading corporations founded the Special Conference Committee (SCC) to support Rockefeller ideas, oppose collective bargaining, and sponsor such offerings as company unions, pensions, group insurance, paid vacations, and profit sharing; by 1929, eight SCC members had their own company unions. These "welfare liberals" were outnumbered by the conservatives, however. By the end of 1920, conservatives controlled the Industrial Relations Research Association, for instance, and every issue of *Personnel* "carried at least one article attacking radicalism, Bolshevism, or the closed shop."[13]

Welfarism had been written about by John Commons and others as early as 1905 and had been practiced by scattered employers long before that, but as a movement, it came of age in the 1920s. In 1926, 80 percent of 1,500 of the largest companies offered at least one welfare benefit, about half offered at least several, and many workers still "lived in company houses, were treated by company doctors, attended company schools, played on company teams, purchased company stock, and were represented by company unions."[14]

The welfarism of the 1920s was distantly related to the "human relations" approach of Elton Mayo at the Harvard Business School, yet it was unionization more than anything else that began to humanize employers' attitudes toward workers, though usually without reducing hostility to unionism. "Traditionally," Sanford Jacoby says, "managers had portrayed the manual worker as greedy, depraved, lazy, and unreliable—a creature barely recognizable as human, much less a gentleman."[15] Unionism altered this view, helped curb arbitrary authority, and transferred some control over terms and conditions to workers. It was not until the late 1930s and the unionizing of mass industry that some employers began to see workers as commanding certain rights— and as having some power to enforce claims to these rights. Despite its popularity in the 1920s, at no point did welfarism lose its subordination to warfarism in employer relations with unions.

Company Unions

"The fundamental idea of Welfare Capitalism," John D. Rockefeller said, is "that the only solidarity natural in industry is the solidarity which unites all those in the same business establishment."[16] Under the labor relations plan advanced by Rockefeller, barriers between employer and employee would dissolve, and the two opposing teams would become one—the company's. Representing this solitary team would be the company union.

Government played a perhaps unintended role in stimulating company unionism. The War Labor Board of World War I promoted wartime "employee representation" plans, and after the war, some employers ran with the idea and created company unions to avoid independent unionism. Although the movement was encouraged by the National Association of Manufacturers (NAM) and other important employer groups, only a modest number of mainly large employers adopted the practice—432 in 1926, the peak year. Company unionism thrived in the 1930s, however, again encouraged by the federal government and provisions of the National Industrial Recovery Act (NIRA).

The NIRA was passed in mid-1933, and within a month, company unions were being set up. By 1935, between 600 and 700 company unions had been formed, covering 2 million–3 million workers.[17] One study concluded that the great majority of these organizations "were favored and fostered by the companies in order to forestall outside unionization."[18]

These unions could be revoked by employers without notice; strikes were forbidden (and, of course, no strike funds were available); often no membership meetings were held; the issues of wages, hours, hiring, firing, seniority, and job security were nonnegotiable; and alliances with workers in other firms were not allowed. Called "kiss-me clubs," the company unions gave workers some access and voice but no power to enforce their vital demands.

Welfare capitalism was reshaped by the depression of the 1930s, the New Deal, and the CIO, but it survived in company unionism, in the welfarism of nonunion employers, and in the "personnel management" movement. Its message was antiunion paternalism: "The rights and interests of laboring men," Reading Railroad President George F. Baer said, "will be protected and cared for—not by labor agitators, but by the Christian men to whom God in His infinite wisdom has given the control of the property interests of the country."[19]

Welfarism ultimately failed because it did not come to grips with the issues of wages, hours, and working conditions and because it did not address the desire of workers for legitimate shop-floor representation. Its effects were notable, however, and more responsible for the sharp decline of unionism in the 1920s, according to Joseph Rayback, than were mechanization of industry or shifts to the South.[20]

Personnel Management

The personnel management movement and the "science of industrial relations" were outgrowths of welfarism, and their domain came to include the administration of welfare programs, labor relations, job design, testing, vocational education and guidance, the creation of promotion ladders—and surveillance. Engineers focused on job design, welfare workers on the work environment and benefits, vocationalists on job preparation—and all combined before World War I to form the personnel profession, whose dominant purpose was to cut costs, adjust workers to their jobs, and quell unrest.[21]

Some personnel managers studied job fatigue and found that excessive work hours reduced output and increased turnover, accidents, illness, absenteeism, and unrest. Yet even with the prospect of lower costs, employers rejected proposals to limit work hours, and in the 1920s, work hours barely changed. Welfare, tough bargaining with unions, and the "processing" of employees through internal labor markets (within firms) became safer zones of activity for personnel managers. After the 1920s, David Montgomery concludes, personnel operations represented "a cooptived and repressive response to workers initiatives."[22]

Scientific Management

Scientific management stresses efficiency rather than union busting, yet Frederick Taylor, the movement's founder, insisted that there was no place for unions in the efficiently run firm and assured employers that unions would not take root in firms adopting his total program. His successors disagreed with him about unions but not about most features of scientific management.

This disagreement about unions produced two rather separate Taylor factions: the one headed by Taylor himself (original Taylor) and the one that took over after his death in 1915 (revisionist Taylor). The original did not accept unionism, the latter did, and only it among the various control methods adopted by employers actually *encouraged* employer acceptance of unions. In the 1920s, the heyday of Taylorism and the doldrums of unionism, many AFL unions met the revisionists more than halfway and, especially in failing firms, initiated cooperative programs and seized employer offers of acceptance.

Most unions continued, however, to oppose scientific management practices, especially time study (the hallmark of Taylorism), speedup, incentive wage systems, deskilling, and technological displacement. But the efficiency methods of the revisionists tended to be flexible and based in large part on union and worker input, so the involvement of labor was a key factor in their system. Opinion among AFL unions was sharply divided over "cooperation" with revisionists who urged employer acceptance of unions. Some unionists, however, felt they could do more inside than outside the system, and given the precarious shape of unionism at the time, they may have been right.

Scientific management was a new name for some old ideas about efficiency, but it gathered these ideas into what looked like a whole management system. In 1910, Louis D. Brandeis named it, then launched it into orbit by winning a case against the Eastern Railroad in which he claimed that the rail line had failed to use scientific management's cost-saving methods and should be denied rate increases.

Original Taylorism involved extracting knowledge (secrets) from skilled workers to use in defining work tasks so they could be easily learned (deskilled), the labor process more easily controlled, and worker production speeded up. In Taylor's words, "The managers assume . . . the burden of gathering together all of the traditional knowledge which in the past has been possessed by the workmen and then of classifying, tabulating, and reducing this knowledge to rules, laws, and formulae."[23] Employers no longer needed to depend on their own experience or casual observation of workers to determine the time each job took. Time study would give them scientific knowledge.

"All possible brain work should be removed from the shop and centered in the planning or laying-out department."[24] The task idea, according to Taylor, was perhaps the most prominent part of his method. "The work of every workman is fully planned out by the management at least one day in advance, and each man receives in most cases complete written instructions, describing in detail the task which he is to accomplish, as well as the means to be used in doing the work. . . . This task specifies not only what is to be done, but how it is to be done and the exact time allowed for doing it. . . . Scientific management consists very largely in preparing for and carrying out these tasks."[25] "Faster work can be assured . . . only through enforced standardization of methods, enforced adoption of the best implements and working conditions, and enforced cooperation. . . . And the duty of enforcing . . . rests with the management alone."[26]

Basic to Taylor's method were research, standardization of materials and methods, and control of the labor process by work design. Supervision was to be improved by substituting the demands of the task itself for the driving foremen, but in Taylor's view, "the full possibilities of functional foremanship . . . will not have been realized until almost all of the machines in the shop are run by men who are of smaller caliber and attainment, and who are therefore cheaper than those required under the old system."[27]

The assembly line grew out of these methods, most systematically at the Ford plant. "Each worker occupied a position from which he did not move," Henry Ford noted, "for walking is not a remunerative activity." The moving line specified time as well as tasks. In the Ford Highland Park foundry workshops, 95 percent of the pattern makers and smelters were "unskilled, or to put it more accurately . . . skilled in exactly one operation which the most stupid man could learn within two days."[28] In 1926, 79 percent of entering Ford workers were trained for less than a week. Combined with these jobs were certain behavioral requirements: good morals, cleanliness, and no smoking, drinking, or gambling—controls designed to produce good, untroublesome, hard-working employees.

Unions complained that scientific management was not scientific, and a 1915 survey by the Commission on Industrial Relations found no uniformity in the uses of the system. Time study and task setting were found to be "the special sport of individual judgment and opinion, subject to all the possibilities of diversity in accuracy and injustice that arise from human prejudice."[29]

Unions and Taylorism

Taylorism, Gompers wrote, makes "wage-workers in general, mere machines—considered industrially, of course,"[30] and a study by Robert F. Hoxie concluded that "neither organized nor unorganized labor finds in scientific management any adequate protection to its standards of living, any progressive means for industrial education, or any opportunity for industrial democracy by which labor may create for itself a pro-gressively efficient share in efficient management."[31] Gompers complained that the scheme was predicated on the destruction of unions; Taylor said that "the fundamental principles of trade unionism . . . are basically inimical to the principles of scientific management."[32] Taylor wanted "intimate, friendly cooperation" between employer and employee, but for employees, that meant obedience, doing as they were told, and not forming unions. The deskilling of workers also meant a rapid erosion of the strong base unions had among skilled workers and a net decline in the bargaining power that craftspeople had given labor.

At Taylor's memorial service in 1915, Brandeis called for employer cooperation with organized labor, and the new revisionist leader of Taylorism, Robert Valentine, eagerly endorsed the idea. Taylor had scoffed at welfarism, but the revisionists turned from the former preoccupation with engineering and soon embraced both welfarism and unionism.

When revisionists insisted on union recognition and involvement in joint planning programs—and some employers listened—hard-pressed unions usually welcomed the ideas. Their net gains and losses from these joint efforts have not been assessed—some people claim labor was further weakened; others, that labor acquired the technical and managerial knowledge it needed—but in any case, few options were present. Unions of the 1920s had been weakened by open-shop drives, paternalism, Wilson's growing postwar hostility, the courts, red scares, and a serious depression. Under these conditions, and in exchange for recognition, some unions met employers more than halfway in pursuing the idea and practice of jointness and cooperation.

"Cooperative" Management

The most publicized cooperative effort of the 1920s was that of the railroad shop unions and the Baltimore & Ohio Railroad. As unemployment in the railway repair shops rose after the war, the president of the machinist union (International Association of Machinists, IAM) offered the B&O help in solving its production problems, an offer the railway accepted after a 1922 strike over wage cuts by some 400,000 railway workers.

The union hired a consulting engineer, Otto S. Beyer, Jr., who described the proposed plan: "No specific system of shop management, 'scientific' or otherwise, . . . no specific formulas or plans were adopted. . . . Only union-management cooperation had been agreed to in principle. This implied that whatever was done, the unions through their representatives were to be party to the reforms and were also to initiate proposals on their own account."[33] The plan, according to which the union gave technical aid and participated in joint grievance conferences, was adopted by all B&O shops. Work conditions, job security, and profits improved as a result of the plan, and the plan was adopted by other railroads—at least for a time.

Many unionists opposed cooperation, and the IAM, a leading critic of prewar Taylorism, was attacked by union dissidents for cooperating with the B&O, but the B&O and the IAM were neither the first nor the last to turn cooperative. The clothing and textile industries had turned to cooperation because of unusual pressures on wages from nonunion competitors, and other unions also did so in an effort to save jobs.

Recession stimulated cooperation in the 1920s, but depression in the 1930s almost wiped it out. Cooperators could not deal with depression, only keep it at bay for a time, and at last conditions declined faster than efficiency could find remedies: Wages were cut, workers were laid off, the economy plummeted, and no joint solutions could remedy the situation. Most employers had wanted nothing at all to do with unions and had overwhelmingly rejected cooperative schemes—clothing and textile being among the few exceptions—and the Taylor revisionists fell further out of favor with employers.

Figuring largely in the "cooperative" labor relations of the 1980s is the employer attempt to increase production by linking competition and cooperation and stimulating both. Critics charge that the "team concept," for example, is an employer device to win the cooperation of workers and spur competition among them. And the persisting employer threats to close down less competitive plants are used, it is charged, to further motivate competition among plants and increase production. In nonunion plants, the strategy is openly used to keep unions out.

In some cases, profit sharing bonuses and stock ownership have been added to the partnership as production incentives; "joint" controls over training, education, health and safety, and recreational and other enterprise programs have been established; and various employee participation approaches have been adopted. In some cases, information and consultation concerning high level policy decisions have been gained, but these have been minimal. Some forms of employee involvement have undoubtedly benefited workers and unions, insofar as they offer, for the first time, some influence on the labor process itself. Still, the risks are apparent, and many people feel these steps need to be backed up by forms of real power sharing with labor.

In France, the National Assembly enacted four laws in 1982 and created "new rights for workers": expression groups, in which workers could talk about their work, and enterprise committees, which were to be informed about management decisions regarding new technology, production, investment, and pricing. According to one critic, Bernard Brown, however, France's participative structures came "under the domination of management"; the expansion of quality circles (aimed at improving product quality through worker group participation in decision making) "was a failure, considered by workers to be the latest of many business-sponsored schemes to intensify class exploitation"; and management ignored the recommendations of enterprise committees.[34] Rather than challenging capitalism, these committees were mainly "enrolled in a vast campaign to strengthen it."[35]

Unions in France lost half their members between 1976 and 1988 largely because, Brown concludes, they could not cope with these new management manipulations. To meet the challenge, unions must create a new culture, Brown says, based on communication rather than either confrontation or submission. Ironically, the laws establishing this system were enacted by a Socialist government, seeking, not to destroy unions, but to project a socialist alternative to the dominant Communist unions in France. In 1988, the government tried to reverse the damage, but without notable success.

Some people speak of the imperatives of cooperation. "Some of the confrontational aspects [of unionism] have outlived their usefulness," Victor Gotbaum and Carol O'Cleireacain conclude. "For unions, that . . . means looking beyond the shop floor or the plant gate to the corporate board room for the decisions that will determine workers' future."[36] Union representation on corporate boards, they say, is not the last, but only the first step toward greater equity for labor.

Many critics of employee involvement, however, rush to judge it, often because they suspect that "cooperation" is a synonym for cooptation. In fact, what is called "cooperation" can, and does in many instances, more often mean worker "control"; that is, some previously denied measure of control by workers over the work they do, the labor process itself, and the potential profit and security they may receive from their labor. In these cases, what workers gain are a first-time access to some hitherto reserved "management prerogatives," new skills and knowledge, new work relations with others, and a new approach to reskilling the routine jobs many perform. More appropriately, then, such success stories (and there are many—in auto and steel, for instance) can be labeled advances in worker "control" rather than in labor-management "cooperation." What is needed is more objective research to distinguish the good stories from the bad ones.

Technology, Skills, Control, Efficiency

Technology has shaped work and the labor market, and its products have influenced our culture, political economy, and daily lives. Although its effects on work and society have been both positive and negative, for organized labor, technology has meant the steady loss and deskilling of blue-collar jobs, the weakening of unionism, and fuller employer control over the workplace. Some new skills may have been created, but some old ones have been lost to those possessing them and to the unions representing their interests. Technological change is hardly unique to the United States, but the speed and extent of it are unusual, as is the strong preference for investing in machines rather than workers.[37]

The newer computer-based technology, which has automated and eliminated many jobs, is said to offer the possibilities of liberation from bossism and work hierarchies and the reskilling of much routine work.[38] As with other technologies, however, employers have generally used computers to extend their own powers—by establishing control over computerized knowledge, conducting surveillance of workers, and managing work tasks by remote control. Seldom have employers extended wide access to computerized information or used the technology's potential to reskill work or provide it with new meaning, flexibility, or more truly democratic modes of authority. In short, employer avoidance of worker empowerment on the job has paralleled employer opposition to empowerment through unionization.

The newer "flexible" technologies are said to offer an alternative to mass production since computer reprogramming can make "small batch" and shorter production runs economically feasible, and as the movement of American markets is said to be away from mass production, these flexible technologies may enable small-scale, reskilled, craft-based enterprises to flourish. Michael Piore claims that unions are essential in this new work context, to nationalize wages and produce a sense of community among workers.[39] However, the record to date of technology uses has not inspired labor with much confidence about the future of work or of unionism.

Many new technologies are said to be inappropriate and inefficient because they neglect investment in human resources and centralize all expertise at the top of hierarchies. It is generally agreed by analysts that much of the huge investment in new machinery is intended not only to improve operating efficiency but also to control the work force, limit its powers, deskill it, and create a managerial monopoly of skills and knowledge—much as Taylor sought to do.[40]

The results are seen in the fact that General Motors in the 1980s spent some $48 billion on technological modernization, more than the gross national product of many countries, and got very little in return.[41] The chairman of the company, Roger Smith, failed to realize that implementing new technology, and the reorganization needed to do so, required far more than managers alone could do. Developed skills and participation of the whole GM work force were required. As a result, product development was slowed instead of speeded up, and GM failed to reduce the Japanese production cost advantage. Ford, lacking funds for massive modernization, concentrated instead on employee skills and better labor relations and had a better performance record than GM. Since the use of technology is a matter in which labor and the community have a vital interest, "We should make the engineering of technology a political question," Michael Harrington writes, "insisting that industry of every kind try to create machines that make jobs creative and interesting."[42]

Employers in recent years have experimented with a variety of mandatory and semimandatory means of changing the attitudes, behavior, and loyalties of their employees. Many of the techniques used have come out of group dynamics, social psychology, the "human potential" movement, new mind-altering methods, Eastern mysticism, hypnosis, and encounter group psychology. Such methods represent newer forms of old methods of controlling employee thoughts and behavior, and all represent what increasing numbers of employees regard as intolerable invasions of their privacy. Workers and their unions have struggled in various ways with all these subtler efforts to manipulate them and replace unions with new technologies and new labor relations, and they have placed the deskilling of work and the labor process itself high on their bargaining agendas.

13

Labor Law, the NLRB, and Gentrified Union Busters

Repression in labor history is easier to describe than quantify. Until well into the twentieth century, few statistics were kept on labor disputes and almost none on employer resistance to unionism. Now data kept by the National Labor Relations Board (NLRB), administrator of the Wagner Act (NLRA), confirm points about employer resistance that have been made previously by case studies and qualitative records alone.

From the mid-1950s through the mid-1960s, unions won over 60 percent of NLRB elections; by 1968, that figure had declined to 35 percent and by 1984, to only 24 percent. Moreover, the more recent NLRB election losses have been concentrated in larger enterprises, involving larger groups of workers.

From half to two-thirds of union defeats in these elections, Richard Freeman claims, have been caused by a rise in only one factor—unfair labor practices committed by employers.[1] During one thirty-year period, as NLRB data show, unfair labor practice charges by unions against employers increased sevenfold (from 4,472 in 1950 to 31,281 in 1980). Charges that usually involved illegal firings of workers for union activity grew from 3,213 to 18,317—including a doubling of charges during the 1970s. Reinstatement of unionists illegally fired increased tenfold (from 922 in 1957 to 10,033 in 1980), but in 1975, 2 percent of all workers voting for a union were unlawfully fired for union activity, according to NLRB figures; in 1985, 10 percent were unlawfully fired.[2]

Antiunion Tactics

Firing union leaders is a leading cause of union election defeats. A study of elections in New England between 1962 and 1964 showed, for example, that the average union success rate was 62 percent, but when a union activist had been illegally fired before the election, the union

218

won only 41 percent of the elections.[3] The penalty imposed on employers for illegally firing union leaders is minor—reinstatement of those fired, plus back pay. Employers must also post notices saying they will not engage in such activity again, notices that Freeman says are referred to as "hunting licenses"—warnings to employees about "how far management is willing to go to defeat unionism."[4]

A former staff attorney of the NLRB says that employers would be better off if they simply ignored the labor laws. The consequences of illegal labor practices must be kept "subordinated to the prime objective, which is remaining union free." If an order is issued against the employer, "the board won't issue it until two to four years after the election," and its effect will be negligible.[5]

Tactics now regarded as legal by the NLRB include "captive meetings," held on company time to warn employees of the dire personal consequences of union election victories; antiunion communications from supervisors aimed at employee intimidation; election delays; and the immediate launching of campaigns to decertify unions once they are certified. The importance of these tactics is shown by a study of NLRB elections in 1966 and 1967, which found that when employers conducted no antiunion campaign at all during NLRB elections, the union won more than 95 percent of the elections and more than three-fourths of them by majorities of at least two to one.[6]

Board decisions enlarging the size of election units result in fewer union victories[7]—unions won less than 25 percent of elections in units of 1,000 or more employees between 1973 and 1981, for instance.

A 1970 study found that when employers communicated with white-collar employees only in writing before an election, the union won 85 percent of the elections. When individual and group meetings with employees replaced written communications, the union won only 50 percent of the elections. When employers used both written communication and meetings, the union won only 34 percent.[8] Other studies found that when there was an intense employer campaign, union chances of winning the election were 22–34 percent, and when employers violated the law, chances dropped to 4–10 percent.[9]

Employer *delays* in NLRB elections are viewed by unions as the most crippling of the employer tactics. Typically, employers seek to "delay to the death" every step of the election procedure, including NLRB hearings, elections, appeals, meetings, negotiations, and contract agreements—in the same way that injunctions have been used to fatally delay strikes and other union initiatives. The delays often defeat union election bids. For example, between 1962 and 1977, there was a 13 percent drop in union victory rates when the election was held five months or more, rather than one month, after the union filed for an election.[10]

In 1962, 46 percent of NLRB elections were by employer consent (no opposition), a figure that dropped to only 9 percent in 1977. Consent elections greatly reduce delay and the possibility of union defeat, and the decline of consent indicates a clear, steep rise in active opposition to unions.[11]

Even after unions win elections and NLRB certification, employers still stall and resist, often to the point where unions fail to win or sustain a bargaining contract. An AFL-CIO study in 1970, for example, found that 22 percent of the units winning certification elections were never brought under contract and 13 percent of the units that *were* brought under contract no longer had one five years later.[12] Decertification elections, usually sponsored by employers as another stalling tactic, rose from 4,804 in 1968 to 24,042 in 1984.

NLRA Through Taft-Hartley

Like the Clayton Act before it, which gave labor at best a brief respite from antitrust law, the NLRA's luster began to tarnish not long after its passage. Employers ignored it, and union recognition struggles took place outside the act. But for a time the NLRA was an important shelter for union organizing, backed by a generally sympathetic federal administration. With this backing, union growth surged in the 1930s and continued a steep climb into the 1940s.

Even before the end of World War II, however, business began a serious campaign to check labor's growing threats to its "right to manage," and in the mid-1940s, employers launched aggressive assaults on unions in collective bargaining, pressed for revisions in the NLRA, and began a public relations campaign to reshape public opinion in their favor. The NAM led the business opposition to the NLRA, offering in desperation a $20-billion fund to provide jobs if Congress would reject the bill. GM head Alfred Sloan and a group of corporation lawyers declared that the law was unconstitutional, and Republic Steel head Tom Girdler said he would quit his job, return to the farm, and pick apples if the Court found the law constitutional. It did, but he did not.

In 1945, unions won some 83 percent of almost 5,000 NLRB elections held, involving more than a million workers, but the season of victory was short. In 1947, a full labor mobilization failed to defeat the Taft-Hartley Act, and that act's web of restrictions on labor, enacted by a Republican Congress, was more sweeping than labor laws enacted in any other developed democracy. Business reaction and conservative congressional assaults on the NLRA since its passage had paid off in the enactment of the Taft-Hartley Act, and its legalistic restrictions greatly dampened the NLRB's support of collective bargaining. Shortly after the act's passage, employers began to contest almost all significant NLRB elections. In the early 1950s, union growth halted abruptly, and during the Eisenhower years, the steady decline that continues to the present day began.

Economists generally attribute the rise in antiunion hostility in the mid-1950s to structural causes, the pressure of market competition, and a need for flexibility in operations. Some people point to new management strategies, but the trigger for adopting these strategies, Janice Klein and David Wanger claim, was that political factors convinced employers they could defeat unions—and the NLRB provided the tools to do so.[13] Taft-Hartley revisions of the NLRA gave employers the ammunition they needed, and the popular press helped convince the business fraternity that a new era had arrived and that unions could now be beaten. As employers built new plants, they fought union organizing, so plants built after the mid-1950s were largely nonunion.

Taft-Hartley revisions of the NLRA allowed what had previously been prohibited, employer antiunion campaigns that amounted to verbal intimidation of employees before elections (and the NLRB extended that permission still further). Moreover, employers and their NLRB supporters could now shape election units to ensure union defeat.

The NLRB and the Decline of Unionism

By the mid-1970s, rising employer hostility and legislative defeats had further stunted union growth. The NLRB was undermined by Republican appointments to the board, and even the modest labor-law reform bill of 1978 failed to pass Congress. In 1977, employers by a two-to-one margin had said they preferred favorable bargaining to "union avoidance"; in 1985, the figures were reversed.[14] Had employer opposition remained at earlier levels, it is estimated that unions would have organized twice as many new members as they did by the end of the 1980s. In 1977, 150,000 workers were organized through the NLRB; in 1985, only half that number.[15] Declining union success in NLRB elections, together with membership attrition, explain much of the sharp fall in U.S. union density in contrast to density rises in most other democracies.[16]

Perhaps the worst blow to labor, Kim Moody writes, was the "demise of the NLRB as an instrument for achieving union growth and the redress of grievances."[17] Critics argue that the NLRA itself forecast the decline of unionism and to some extent precipitated it because its major goal was to achieve social order and stability through the law. Gompers, it is said, foresaw that such laws would finally turn against labor, and for that reason, he opposed state interference in labor relations.[18] Whether the NLRA has been more bane than blessing for labor is an unsettled issue. Its benefits in the early CIO days are beyond doubt, but since then, boards have moved to the left or right depending on who appointed them.[19]

During the Reagan administration, vacant board seats were unfilled for a long period, cases piled up, and damaging delays in union elections resulted. Moving from this "benign neglect," Reagan appointed four corporation lawyers to the board and a chair who publicly declared that "collective bargaining frequently means the destruction of individual freedom," that "unionized labor relations" have been among "the major contributors to the decline and failure of our healthy industries," and that strikes are "a concerted effort employing violence, intimidation and political intervention to prevent people who want to work from working."[20] Complaints against employers that were dismissed by this board increased 300 percent while complaints against unions that were dismissed decreased about 40 percent. A string of decisions that were adverse to labor were handed down, and board decisions favoring unions in unfair labor practice cases plummeted.

Unionism and Public Policy

The importance of law and public policy for unionism is obvious in all of labor history, but Freeman points to three contemporary examples: state right-to-work laws, permitted by Taft-Hartley, that reduce new organizing by about a third and increase nonunion members in organized shops by 20 percent; public sector laws that require municipalities to bargain with unionized workers; and Canadian laws that certify unions based solely on a majority of card signatures, without long election delays.[21] Concerning the last point, even when U.S. employers conduct antiunion campaigns, it has been found that 72 percent of the people who sign authorization cards nevertheless vote for the union in NLRB elections, an indicator of how much better off American unions would be with the Canadian laws, which require only card signatures.[22] Clearly, government intervention in labor relations can benefit unionism, but only when governments are favorable to labor. The political Catch 22 for labor in its effort to influence public policy is described by Steelworker President Lynn Williams: "We need better laws but with our declining political clout we can't get them. The reform has to come from within.

We need organizational clout to get political power and vice versa. . . . From whence comes the clout for change? It comes from a strong membership base to begin with."[23]

In 1984, AFL-CIO president Lane Kirkland declared federal labor laws to be "dead letters" and called for repeal of the NLRA, saying workers might be better off with the law of the jungle and that labor relations were as confrontational as they had been in early history, only the techniques were different. In 1985, the House Subcommittee on Labor-Management Relations concluded that "labor law has failed . . . the evidence is clear that the law does not encourage collective bargaining . . . perhaps the most striking evidence of the law's failure is that . . . unions, which exist to engage in collective bargaining, are calling for repeal of the law that is intended to encourage that process."[24] Various state laws also have a major impact on union organizing, some of them affected by federal statutes. Most developed democracies, for example, impose few inhibitions on public workers organizing, but in the United States public employees were denied the right to organize in almost half the states, as of mid-1991.

New Strategies

Other shop-floor and "strategic decision-making" programs have accompanied changes in management approaches to the NLRB. Among these, Thomas Kochan and Michael Piore write, are the nonunion "human resource management systems," quality of work life programs, job flexibility rules that resemble those "found in many newer nonunion firms," and an interest in Japanese methods that has initiated "new patterns of communication and involvement" with individuals and small groups.[25] Productivity increases are the goal, but so is the reduction or abolition of union influence.

Employers have resisted putting unionists on corporate boards, where strategic policy decisions are made, and unionists usually have not pushed the issue. Instead, employers have begun to bring some unionists into management meetings to inform them about business matters and give them information about finances and investments, but seldom are the unionists involved in significant policy making.

The strategies shaped at the highest corporate levels contain many adversarial elements, Kochan and Piore conclude, even though firms are simultaneously seeking to overcome adversarial relations at the plant level. It is difficult to see how long workplace cooperation can last "in the face of a union avoidance strategy at the corporate level."[26]

Gentrified Union Busters

In the 1970s, employers began to hire consulting firms—or "gentrified union busters"—to conduct their war on labor. The consultants brought about dramatic rises in employer delays in NLRB elections and union decertification elections and decreases in employer "consent elections." Lawyers and technocrats came to play a more dominant role in labor relations, employers added new and potent cold war tactics to those already in play, and a whole new legal industry arose to take advantage of the NLRA and Taft-Hartley restrictions on unions.

Labor consulting firms, descendants of the Pinkerton and other detective agencies, numbered over 1,000 in the mid-1980s,[27] and according to a study of organizing campaigns in the private sector, 95 percent of employers now actively resist unionism, and 75 percent hire these consultants to do the job. Solid figures on the earnings of these consultants are unavailable because they seldom report them as required under the Landrum-Griffin Act of 1959, but by 1985, their estimated receipts exceeded $100 million a year.[28]

These consultants specialize in organizing drives and use both carrots and sticks in combating unionism. Typically, they approach a drive by assembling a psychological profile of every worker in the bargaining unit, using attitudinal surveys (presumably anonymous but easily identified) and supervisor ratings of individual employee loyalty. Equipped with this information, supervisors begin a campaign of discharge, harassment, isolation of activists, rumors, and punishment. At the same time, legal maneuvering begins. Unfair labor practices may be deliberately committed in order to move for election delays, and although the employer may later be found guilty of violating the law, the benefits of the delay usually outweigh the cost of the violation.

Consultants also seek to break strong unions already established in firms, force concessions from them, and undermine industry-wide standards and national agreements. An example of this type of activity is the Business Roundtable's effort to break the construction trade unions, an effort guided by consultants and described by Robert Georgine as an attack by a "guerilla army dressed in three piece suits."[29] This "attack" inflicted heavy casualties: In the 1960s, union density in the building trades was an estimated 50 percent, but by 1984, density had declined to only 24 percent.

Consultants often disseminate their ideas about how to avoid unions through profitable seminars held for employer representatives, and these seminars cover union busting in the public as well as the private sector. Public employers are often advised to provoke strikes in order to win public opinion and focus resentment on the union. They are also advised never to submit a dispute to an outside party or binding arbitration. Consultants have involved a growing number of colleges and universities in holding these union-busting seminars, sometimes even for college credit.

Modern Management Methods (MMM) is a leading consultant of the gentrified union-busting variety. In MMM training, unions and management are referred to as the plum and the cactus, the plum being the union, easy picking, the cactus being the tough, prickly, impenetrable company. Companies that want to be cacti are taught to hire with caution, interviewing workers carefully to uncover union attitudes, such as sympathy for the underdog or liberal rights or activity in tenants' or consumer rights organizations.

Supervisors are regarded as the frontline troops, and from the start of a union campaign, they are expected to attend weekly meetings and report daily on workers in their departments. They are coached in what to say and do, on one side or the other of the law, and are told that if they don't want to commit unfair labor practices, they shouldn't—but they will lose the election. A stern letter from management at the start of a campaign attempts to prevent union authorization cards from being signed. Supervisors hand-deliver the letter to workers, ask them to read it, talk to them about their responses, and report back to top management on individual responses. Antiunion workers are then encouraged to organize "spontaneous" no-union committees, the neutrals are persuaded to join them, and the union activists are watched, reassigned to isolated jobs, or fired for minor rule infractions. Union organizers confront no-solicitation and no-trespass rules when they try to reach workers on the job. Management is told to ask the NLRB for the largest possible election unit and delay everything for as long as possible. Union defeats are the common outcome of this mode of operation.

The consultants are only a new arrival in a field already overcrowded with people seeking to profit from union busting. Major labor-management law firms, once willing to accept collective bargaining once unions were certified, have kept up with the new competition by hiring hard-core union fighters to establish, in the NAM's words, a "union free environment," even in companies with long-established unions and reasonably amicable relations with them. Spreading from the Southeast to all other regions, these harsh antiunion campaigns have created a whole new legal industry, involving hundreds of law firms and many thousands of lawyers. In almost every union organizing drive, such lawyers participate directly and daily in advising employers on legal and illegal ways to defeat unions.

Large employers often maintain in-house antiunion operations, their own consulting and legal firms in effect. General Electric, for example, operates a vast network of nonunion plants, and its huge in-house antiunion organization has given it a reputation for being almost invincible in breaking union organizing efforts. In-house operations sometimes include the use of closed-circuit television to transmit antiunion messages during worktime, the production of antiunion documentaries featuring disaffected and antiunion workers from other companies, and the use of professional labor spies.

Trade associations in single industries, often aided by law firms, prepare manuals on union busting that are tailor-made for their industries, and they sometimes loan out their staffs to participate directly in antiunion campaigns by member companies. Cross-industry groups also assist antiunion campaigns by arranging materials, seminars, meetings, or "special services" such as guards, spies, and guard dogs. Employer organizations cover the political and legislative front in opposing unionism.

In response to these union-busting activities, unions seek a restoration of protection under labor law and the extension of some basic rights to workers. They want, among other things, stiffer penalties for employers who discharge union activists, restrictions on hiring strikebreakers and prohibition of their use as "permanent replacement workers," immediate and mandatory injunctive relief from unfair labor practices in organizing drives, prompt NLRB elections, self-enforcing NLRB decisions without the need for court enforcement, prohibition of employers who repeatedly commit unfair labor practices from qualifying for government contracts, and mandatory government fact-finding and mediation in first-contract bargaining.

Because the law protects employers rather than workers, global companies often accept unions elsewhere but fight them in the United States, knowing they can do so with legal impunity. Nissan, for example, accepts unions as a part of doing business in Japan, Europe, and Australia, but in the United States, it uses almost every device, as it did in 1989 in Smyrna, Tennessee, to exclude unions from its plants. In no other democracy have employers in recent decades launched comparable attacks on unionism, and in no other country have antiunion consultants been a factor of any significance in labor relations.

14

Macroeconomic and Political Manipulations

THE WAR ON LABOR now includes some potent new, or recycled, techniques that have been added to the basic ones. Because the new ones usually operate at macroeconomic and higher public policy levels, they cannot easily be reached by strikes and other workplace strategies of labor. Political influence is needed to reach them, but such influence has eluded labor's grasp. The macrotechniques used vary over time, and those that are here today may be gone tomorrow, but new ones will usually replace them. Those described here are only some of those currently popular.

Abstruse economic subjects may seem to be unrelated to workplace and political struggles, yet they profoundly affect union growth and strength. Indeed, labor's current decline can be traced largely to macroeconomic policies and to the private monopoly of investment decisions. These decisions have led to deindustrialization, capital flight, a feeding frenzy of buyouts, industrial restructuring, sluggish growth, banking crises, and recession—all damaging to labor and the general public and all related to the war on labor. Promoting the private monopoly of these decisions are such public policies as deregulation of business and privatization of the public sector—policies that weaken labor, surrender crucial public functions to the private sector, reduce efficiency in many cases, and, as in deregulation of the savings and loan institutions (S&Ls), sometimes spawn economic disaster.

Deregulation

Deregulation of the private sector has paralleled the privatization of the public sector in that it has substituted private control for public responsibility and often injected low-wage, nonunion competitors into unionized, high-wage industries. Although conservatives in both major political parties have pressed for such legislative deregulation, they have nevertheless ardently favored the further regulation of unionism.

227

Deregulation also occurs as a result of administrative neglect and subversion of public regulatory functions. In health and safety regulation, for example, appropriated funds were not spent during the Reagan administration, and although some 7,000 workers die from work-related accidents annually, from 1980 to 1989 only four of the thirty cases referred to the Justice Department for criminal investigation were prosecuted. No corporate officer has ever served a prison term for violations of federal safety laws that result in death, and only six have been sentenced by the states. A congressional report notes that an executive who deliberately violates federal health and safety laws "stands a greater chance of winning a state lottery than of being criminally charged by the federal government."[1]

Adopted ostensibly to boost business competition, deregulation has more often expanded monopoly control, and in many instances, it has raised consumer costs and endangered public safety. The staggering public costs of deregulating banks and lending institutions are well known, and the eventual cost of the S&L debacle is an estimated $500 billion. Studies of S&L deregulated investments reveal a record of scams, frauds, thefts, wild speculations, and buyouts of legislators by bankers and others prominent in the economic elite.[2]

Legislation deregulating the airlines, signed by President Carter in 1978, introduced low-wage and fiercely antiunion employers to the industry, created some chaotic conditions, and after a wave of takeovers, eight "mega-carriers" accounted for more than 90 percent of U.S. air travel in 1989. A study by the nonprofit Economic Policy Institute found that in the ten years before deregulation, fares (adjusted for inflation and fuel price changes) fell 24 percent—in the ten years after deregulation, they fell only 19 percent.[3] At fifteen large airports, all dominated by one or two airlines after deregulation, fares were 27 percent higher than the national average.[4]

Airline travelers fly farther on flights rerouted to airline hubs after deregulation and spend much more time doing it. Flyers also suffered more seat crowding, reduced crews, cutbacks in meal quality and availability, lost luggage, overbooking and bumping, cancellations, flight delays, and penalties for changed reservations. In the first two years of deregulation alone, 100 communities lost all scheduled service, and by 1987, the number had risen to 143. Customer service complaints with the U.S. Department of Transportation rose from 7,326 in 1983 to 40,985 in 1987. A serious erosion of airline safety standards also occurred. Near-misses rose from 311 in 1982 to 1,058 in 1987, the age of planes has increased, maintenance spending on them has declined, and some 97 percent of pilots polled claim that deregulation has made flying more dangerous. Still, most airlines are not very profitable.

Takeovers by major airlines of new competitors after deregulation have led to huge indebtedness, layoffs and wage cuts to pay off debts, and cost-cutting wars on airline unions—wars the unions seldom win. Low wages in the new nonunion airlines, about half those of the older unionized airlines, have led to wage cuts in the older lines and a further escalation of labor conflict. Europeans are eager to avoid the decline in service, the concentration, and the labor disputes experienced in the United States, and by the 1990s, little comparably serious deregulation of airline or other industries had occurred abroad.

Privatization

Although many other democracies went on privatizing binges in the 1980s, selling off public property and enterprises and some even privatizing many public services, nowhere has privatizing cut as deeply into the public sector as in the United States, mainly through the "contracting out" (or "outsourcing") of unionized public services to less-unionized private firms. It is the very leanness of public functions in the United States that makes cuts into the flesh so much deeper and riskier than cuts made by other countries.

The impetus for contracting out public services has come largely from trade associations, chambers of commerce, and many influential officials who have actively supported this method and from conservative economists and think tanks that have provided policy advice to the privatizing movement. In 1982, government spending on contracting out reached almost a quarter of the entire public budget—federal, state, and local— and in 1980 alone, state and local governments paid some $66 billion to the private sector to provide public services.[5] Presidential privatizing proposals include education vouchers for use in private as well as public schools, the sale of urban mass transit, and the privatizing of prisons, customs inspection, and hosts of public services.

Aims and Results

Privatizing was first conceived of as a way to cut deficits by selling off assets. The practice was later curbed by Congress, but the contracting out of public services has grown, premised on the assumption that more efficiency and lower costs, gained by wage and benefit cuts and work rule changes, will result.

However, unions claim that the resulting costs are usually equal to or greater than in public services, quality is often inferior, many public services have been lost, contracts with private firms are difficult to draw up, and public supervision of contracts is costly and too complex. Even work attitudes are said to change, from a service-giving to a money-making ethos, as a study of telephone-system privatizing in Britain has shown.[6] Unions insist that good public management can correct existing problems with public functions and that joint labor-management committees on quality and productivity can do far more than privatizing to improve government services.

Certainly the misuse of vast sums contracted out by the Pentagon and the Department of Housing and Urban Development show that public supervision of such services is demanding and costly and that corruption is common and hard to ferret out. Senator John Glenn, for example, has expressed great concern about the National Aeronautics and Space Administration's (NASA's) reliance on private contractors and the difficulty of monitoring them. Some 88 percent of NASA's $11-billion budget in 1989 was spent on procurement, and contractor profit rates reached as high as 288 percent. In the explosion of the space shuttle Challenger in 1986, bolts and substandard or counterfeit electronic parts, falsely certified by contractors and installed in the spacecraft, were believed to be a cause of the disaster.[7] The many military contractors convicted of fraud in 1989 and 1990 included Boeing, General Electric, Raytheon, Grumman, LTV, and Rockwell, and their activities included test fraud, overcharging, contract kickbacks, and illegally obtaining Pentagon documents.

Awareness has grown that the shrinkage of public investment in infrastructure has seriously retarded private sector growth and productivity. Yet the private sector, intent on privatizing, remains ideologically opposed to public spending on even the ports, highways, airports, and other facilities that stimulate commerce. Countries with high levels of public investment in infrastructure relative to output are more likely to sustain productivity growth than other countries. In the 1970s and 1980s, Japan invested some 5.1 percent of output in public works, and its annual productivity growth rate was 3.1 percent. The United States invested only 0.3 percent in public works, and its productivity growth rate was only 0.6 percent a year.[8]

Effects on Labor

For labor, privatizing often leads to layoffs, wage cuts, and shifts from unionized to less unionized sectors of an industry. For this reason, labor has pressed for a "union wage" law that would require contractors of services to pay union wage and benefit rates. Privatizing also reduces the government powers on which labor coalitions often depend for support while further empowering and enriching the private sector.[9]

In the 1980s, British Tories led the way in selling off public industry to private firms and in so doing reduced the strength of the Labour

Party opposition and its union supporters. In 1980, 98 percent of British firms in the public sector recognized blue-collar unions, and 94 percent recognized white-collar unions. In private industry, the comparable figures were 68 percent and 32 percent, and it was into this category that the newly privatized jobs were transferred.[10] France has also privatized, but more selectively and less ideologically, and a large state-owned and prosperous industrial sector has been retained.

It is possible that the privatizing ideology, indeed the whole idolatry of the "free market," may be changing, as suggested by a *Business Week* report of a "growing sense in economics that the free-market paradigm, built around a belief in individual rationality, market equilibrium, and pure competition, often gets a big fat 'F' when it comes to explaining what is really happening in the economy and the markets." The boundary between public and private is "moving closer to the public sector," and airline deregulation, for example, "once heralded as a triumph of the free market school," is causing many second thoughts.[11]

Merger Mania and Monopoly

In 1987, the total cost of U.S. corporate takeovers was $168 billion, or almost five times the figure for 1978. Many of the takeovers of the 1980s were in the form of leveraged buyouts (LBOs) and the sale of junk bonds to repay LBO bank loans. The junk bond market grew at an annual rate of 34 percent during the 1980s, and LBOs grew from less than 1 percent to 25 percent of mergers between 1979 and 1986.

Mergers concentrate wealth and power, and LBOs more than other merger forms add huge private indebtedness to already staggering public debts, deprive the public of corporate taxes, tie up capital in nonproductive activities, unsettle the stock market, lead to the bankruptcy of otherwise sound firms, and hobble management. They also inflict serious injuries on labor in the form of mass layoffs; plant closures; pension raids; squeezes on wages, hours, and conditions; and tougher corporate bargaining.

By the 1980s, the $2.7 trillion in private pension funds had become a ripe target for corporate raids, known more euphemistically as "reversions." Between 1983 and 1990, employers terminated some 2,000 plans and took more than $20 billion from them (funds of less than $1 million not included)—money pledged to present and future retirees but called "surplus assets" by employers.[12] These raids and inferior plans adopted after takeovers (often placed with risky, uninsured companies) reduced the pensions workers would have received by some 45 percent.[13]

Takeovers added so much to the corporate debt that in 1987, the debt amounted to 68 percent of shareholder equity, up from 47 percent five years earlier. Such indebtedness makes leveraged firms extremely vulnerable to downturns in the economy and to failure, bankruptcy, and plant closings. Firms threatened by takeovers are also more vulnerable to downturns since they tend to discourage raiders by keeping little cash on hand to attract them. Again, the takeover wave was encouraged by the deregulation of financial markets and by the permissive antitrust policies sponsored by conservatives in the 1980s.

Beginning in the 1960s, many corporations had more money than they knew how to spend properly, but instead of creating new enterprises or improving existing ones, they put the cash into acquisitions, buying up firms in other lines of business and forming conglomerates. Since the owners knew little about managing their new acquisitions, business productivity and profitability declined in the 1960s and 1970s, contributing to recession, the slippage of American industry, and new assaults on labor. Conglomerates began to retrench in the 1970s and to divest themselves of unprofitable lines. Between 1985 and 1989, the proportion of highly diversified companies declined by 37 percent—and between 1982 and 1987, manufacturing productivity grew correspondingly by 25 percent. As the horizontal takeovers slowed, however, vertical buyouts began with a vengeance. During the 1980s, American corporations, largely through steep leverage, retired almost $500 billion in equity but acquired almost a trillion dollars in debt, and interest payments absorbed some 30 percent of their cash flow, the highest in the postwar era.[14]

Mergers in Europe, Japan, and elsewhere have seldom involved hostile takeovers, and LBOs and junk bonds are almost unknown. Indeed, in West Germany, Switzerland, and some other countries, hostile takeovers are virtually forbidden, and as the *New York Times* reports, "The well-mannered Europeans prefer forming alliances to mounting hostile takeovers."[15] And while the LBO was a common feature of U.S. corporate activity in the 1980s, Europe exhibited "much more sympathy for transactions that aim to develop companies than for financial operations where you take over a company, sell nine-tenths or all of it and keep the profit." Restructuring there has usually taken the form of alliances, joint ventures, and friendly takeovers "rather than aggressive, debt-financed raids."[16]

Globalization, Capital Flight, Deindustrialization, Free Trade

Globalization has changed all the rules of the economic game, transferring major decision making to places far beyond national boundaries and to a large extent beyond the control of national law. Finance has been globalized to such an extent that control of monetary policy by national banks and financial centers has been undermined, and transnational corporations have become so dominant that they can defy most constraints that government and labor seek to apply.

By 1989, some 17 percent of total American corporate assets had gone abroad, more than three times the percentage of Japanese holdings overseas, and a large part of the money made abroad stays abroad, invested in jobs for others.[17] Japan and most other countries have found ways to restrict globalization and keep their assets at home. The United States has not, and to a large extent, globalization is a U.S. phenomenon—and problem.[18]

This internationalization of American capitalism involves a transformation that enables employers to close up shop, dismiss employees without notice, and move plants and capital to cheap labor reserves abroad. In Europe, such flight is impeded by plant-closing laws and other restrictions, but in the United States it is almost unrestrained, and serious damage to labor has resulted. Employers also often move abroad to avoid tariff and other import barriers erected by foreign countries—while at the same time opposing all U.S. barriers to imports from abroad. Indeed, the long-term U.S. trend has been away from exports and manufacturing in the United States, and toward production abroad.

About 10 million American jobs were lost as a result of plant closings or permanent layoffs in the five years ending in 1988, more than half of them in manufacturing. The new jobs that were added tended to be in the low-wage, nonunion service sector. The free rein of multinationals, Lee Price writes, "will transform collective bargaining to the advantage of the companies in those industries. The results could be disastrous for organized and unorganized workers alike."[19]

In 1950, 38.9 percent of employees in private nonagriculture industry were in manufacturing; by 1989, only 21.6 percent were. At the same time, the proportion of service jobs more than doubled, from 13.7 percent to 29.6 percent.[20] Deindustrialization is not an exclusive feature of the U.S. economy, but it has thus far been more extreme in the United States, and its impact on unionism has been more traumatic because it has cut deeply into blue-collar membership, the primary base of U.S. unionism.

The conservative shibboleth "free trade" has been used to justify deindustrialization and globalization, a pact with Mexico that opens wide the doors to U.S. runaway shops and exploitation of Mexican oil resources, and the opening of U.S. markets to foreign imports, often from U.S. companies using cheap labor abroad, or to countries that impose various import barriers to U.S. products. The AFL-CIO vigorously opposed the trade pact with Mexico, but arrayed against it on Capitol Hill were virtually every major U.S. business group—including the Business Roundtable, the U.S. Chamber of Commerce, and the National Association of Manufacturers—along with top-level law and lobbying firms on the Mexican side.[21]

Business Cycles

Public policies are available to control business cycles, but they are generally spurned by business as involving government regulation and planning. The downturns of these cycles and the related phenomenon of underproduction, or the underuse of production resources, result in job loss, unemployment, and union decline. The down cycles weaken unionism by reducing union membership, creating labor surpluses that weaken labor bargaining power, and in deep downturns, sometimes swallowing whole unions or even whole labor-left movements.

The historic swings of American business cycles have been more severe than in most democracies. Using changes in the GNP to measure business cycles, economist Erik Lundberg reports that variations in the GNP have been "higher in the United States and Canada than in any of the European countries considered" in his study—Belgium, Denmark, France, Germany, Italy, the Netherlands, Norway, Sweden, Switzerland, and the United Kingdom.[22]

Lundberg reviewed comparative swings in the GNP during two major twentieth-century periods—interwar (1920–1938) and postwar (1948–1964). In the interwar period, he found that the *depth* of decline in GNP from peak to trough points (top to bottom points) was greater in the United States than in any other country except for a slightly larger decrease in Canada. In the postwar period, the U.S. depth of decline was also among the greatest (there was slightly more decline in Belgium, Canada, and Switzerland). Economist Angus Maddison, using aggregate national output figures as a measure, confirms the exceptional depth of decline of the American economy during the interwar years of 1920–1938. He calculates a fall of minus 29.5 for the United States, compared with minus 8.1 for the United Kingdom and an average of minus 11.9 for Western nations generally.[23]

As for *duration*, Lundberg found that the years of decline in the United States were 39 percent of the total years in the interwar period, a figure exceeding that of all other nations except France. In the postwar period, it was again significantly greater in the United States—19 percent of the total years as contrasted, for example, with zero years of decline for West Germany, Italy, France, and the Netherlands.

With respect to the *frequency* of cycles, Lundberg records that in the postwar period—aside from the immediate readjustment period—the United States had more cycles than the other countries studied. Peaks of economic activity occurred in both the United States and Canada in 1948, 1953, 1957, and 1960 and were in each case followed by turning points or troughs in the next calendar year. These cycles were shared by Europeans only in 1957–1958, and then to a milder degree, and the Europeans experienced only one independent recession around 1951–1952.[24]

Another frequency count for an earlier period found that the United States experienced fifteen cycles between 1879 and 1932 while Germany experienced only ten and the United Kingdom and France only eleven.[25] In still another count, the United States was found to have experienced twenty-eight cycles from 1857 to 1978—or a recession on the average of every four years—and thirty-two cycles between 1796 and 1923.[26]

The Great Depression

The catastrophic depression of the 1930s is of special interest for two principal reasons: its source in the unregulated powers of American capitalism, made possible by the nearly total repression of the labor-left in the 1920s, and its contagious and finally disastrous impact on the world economy and social order. Far worse than economic contagion, of course, were the political consequences for Europe: the rise of fascist and militarist "solutions" to the depression and the resulting world war, which did, in fact, finally put a desperate end to the economic crisis.

The depression came earlier and was deeper and more enduring in the United States than elsewhere (with the possible exception of Germany), and the instability of economic performance was more severe. Annual unemployment rates, for example, varied by more than 20 percent in the United States, compared to 10 percent in most European countries[27]— at its deepest, 25 percent of the U.S. work force was unemployed. From the market crash of 1929 to the mid-1930s, the output of goods and services in the United States declined by 33 percent, and capital accumulation and investment came to a virtual stop.

In Sweden, which had a stable labor government, no general economic weakness was apparent in the years up to 1929, and consumption and investment continued to increase in 1929–1930, as did housing construction up to 1932, despite the sharp declines in the value of Swedish exports. The United Kingdom, France, and other countries with influential labor-left movements also had thriving economies past the start of the crisis in the United States. There is every indication, Michael Bernstein writes, "that the United States led the rest of the world into depression

and that the economic contraction in America was internally based."[28]
In some phases, the U.S. depression, according to Gottfried Haberler,
"was intensified by influences from abroad. . . . But these adverse foreign
influences were largely the feedback from earlier phases of the American
depression."[29]

The strong linkage of Europe to U.S. economic crisis has notably
weakened since the Great Depression, partly because of the decline in
U.S. economic leadership and partly because, to some extent, Europe
has created its own stability as labor-left governments have intervened
to limit downturns in business cycles. Europe in the postwar era long
feared the U.S. economy "as the engine of international business cycles,"
Lundberg writes, but now Europe relies largely on its own economic
rhythms.[30]

As for the American source of the depression, economists have sought
explanations for the impact of the precipitating events, the stock market
and banking collapse. John Kenneth Galbraith writes that "cause and
effect run from the economy to the stock market, never the reverse.
Had the economy been fundamentally sound in 1929," the effects of
the market crash and the loss of spending "might soon have worn off."[31]

Some economists find the source in the skewed national income
distribution of the 1920s and the polarization of income between rich
and poor that lowered the nation's ability to consume and produce.[32]
Bernstein finds the explanation for the prolonged duration of the American
depression in inadequate and ill-advised investment, which resulted in
persistent unemployment and income distortions that favored the rich
and lowered consumer demand. More and better planned investments
were needed. They "had to be coordinated on a national scale; if left
to the narrow basis of purely individual decision making, the achievement
of economic 'balance' would be virtually impossible."[33]

Expansionary public spending during the New Deal and then World
War II finally ended the economic crisis, but this measure only masked
the chronic problem of inadequate and unplanned investment, which
resurfaced again in the 1970s, 1980s, and 1990s. In the long run, the
war may have made American industry less able to grow and compete
in a world economy. The buildup of weapons in that war and the space
program and cold war that followed meant the economy was geared
toward military production rather than global competition in the production of civilian goods.

Although U.S. fiscal policy became somewhat more enlightened and
federal spending rose rapidly, Lundberg says "the expansionary spending
measures were not impressive; aggregate public works, federal, state,
and local, were not back at their predepression level even by 1938."
The premature balancing of the budget at a time when 14 percent of

the labor force was still unemployed helped turn "vigorous expansion into vigorous contraction in the latter 1930s."[34] Bernstein emphasizes investment planning rather than fiscal policy and believes that whereas the early New Deal stressed planning, the later New Deal shifted to fiscal policy and deficit spending. Roosevelt's brain trust in the early period sought to create "a systematic and comprehensive federal plan to manage the dislocations created by industrial life cycles and international competition," but the "combined opposition of business interests and conservative elements left the government with the rather blunt instrument of compensatory spending."[35]

Cycles and Union Growth

The key role of business cycles in union growth is often cited. Gompers saw the "law of growth in organized labor" as being based in business cycles, with growth varying directly with the cycles.[36] John Commons and the Wisconsin school added that unions at first do well in up cycles, but after a time, employer resistance sets in, the courts intervene, and union growth is halted or reversed. In the deep down cycles, during recession and depression, unions may either subside, vanish, or become more political, turning from industrial action to more radical forms of political action, which also leads to intensified employer resistance.[37] Other people have developed this theme.[38] Horace Davis concluded that union growth correlates more closely with sharp changes in *prices* (precipitating wage demands) than with *prosperity* and that revival from a recession is more favorable to growth than continuing prosperity.[39]

The business cycle contribution to union growth is still being debated, but economists mainly agree that the contribution is significant and that swings of the American cycle have been exceptionally severe. The casualties for American unions include fatalities as well as membership decline. Many early unions were dissolved even by recession; others died during the depression of 1837, and the few national unions formed in the 1850s and 1860s perished in the long depression of the 1870s. The financial crisis of 1873, labor spy Allan Pinkerton wrote, "had a disastrous effect upon the trades-unions. Many of them practically disbanded, and others were so weakened that they protected no one."[40]

John Phelps Brown writes that "in the US depressions were more often sharp and deep. The upturn soon followed, but by then much incipient unionism had been destroyed." The depression deaths of unions "whether through the breaking of strikes or simply the collapse of membership, was well known in the UK, but in the USA it was more devastating."[41] American unions, partly as a result of the country's steep, frequent, and prolonged down cycles, have had an unusually short continuous history. No stable unionism was achieved before the 1880s, and no federation formed before the mid-nineteenth century survives today.[42] By contrast, Sweden, guided by public economic planning, escaped the boom-and-bust periods of union growth experienced by American labor. In Sweden, as elsewhere among other developed democracies, labor's countervailing influence has significantly moderated the crises precipitated by raw capitalist economies.

Underproduction and Unemployment

Between the 1920s and 1960s, U.S. growth in GNP equaled the European only in 1920–1929, and industrial production growth was considerably lower throughout the whole period.[43] Most European countries in the early 1950s operated much closer to their output ability, in terms of capital and labor, than did the United States and Canada, and others caught up during the 1960s.[44] Manufacturing in the United States operated at 86 percent capacity in 1965 but at less than 70 percent in the later 1970s, and the profit rates of nonfinancial corporations fell below 10 percent during the decade. Such underproduction became the major cause of U.S. economic instability after the Korean war boom years, and even during peaks of the business cycle, employment remained far below most definitions of "full employment."

Even in the booming 1920s, the U.S. jobless rate was higher than the European, except for Britain. In the 1930s, it was much higher than those of other industrial nations, and in the 1950s, it was higher than in all but a few countries. In the 1980s, official U.S. unemployment figures held steady at a relatively low level, but, according to Kevin Phillips, those figures were misleading "because definitions of the work force excluded a growing number of Americans." By mid-1988, 45.3 percent of New York City residents over sixteen did not participate in the labor force "because of poverty, lack of skills, drug use, apathy or other problems," and those people were not included in the unemployment figures.[45]

The jobless have been called a "reserve army" of labor, one that bids down wages, disciplines the labor force, and replaces striking workers on their jobs. The "natural rate" of unemployment—or the rate high enough to discourage wage increases greater than productivity increases— was pegged at 4 percent during the Kennedy years but was moved up to 7 percent in the 1980s under Republican administrations. Public policymakers *"want* to have at least eight million people constantly looking for jobs (along with the six million discouraged dropouts) to encourage privatizers to replace government workers at lower salaries and wages," Frederick Thayer claims.[46] This reserve army approach, he says, is a modern version of what was once called "scabbing."

Business policies that affect labor adversely are not always designed to do so, but it can be inferred that jobless policies are tolerated and even largely encouraged by the people who control the nation's economic policy. Intention is explicit in the case of influential neoclassical economists who, as chief advisers of business and conservative policymakers, advocate "labor mobility" policies that create a kind of mobile reserve army, which holds down wages and union bargaining power and facilitates strikebreaking. Policymakers who have been influenced by these economists usually claim that they advocate high jobless rates as a means of controlling inflation, though low jobless and low inflation rates are obviously compatible, as the Japanese and Swedish economies clearly demonstrate.

Until the 1970s, H. Brand writes, "the deliberate creation of unemployment as a means of putting pressure on wages was not politically feasible; nor was it advised by 'mainstream' economists."[47] Since the 1970s, it has become an explicit, applied policy, and the result, he says, has generally been higher jobless rates and lower hourly wage increases than in other major industrial nations.

Demand

Monetarists claim that after the 1929 market crash, bank failures (2,000 in 1931 alone) caused the money supply to drop by a third between 1929 and 1932, sharply reducing purchasing power and launching the depression. Keynesians stress decline in GNP more than money supply as a cause of depression, but both monetarists and Keynesians apparently agree that a sharp decline in consumer purchasing power played a key role in precipitating the Great Depression. The influence of demand is obvious: When demand declines, production fails, people are laid off, income falls, and the downward cycle of demand and supply continues.

From 1950 to 1964, Lundberg notes, the U.S. economy (and the Canadian) showed a "persistent tendency of inadequate demand" and European countries showed a tendency of high demand.[48] Had the U.S. government spurred demand in the 1950–1964 period and had U.S. federal expenditures kept up with those in Sweden or Holland, the country "could have eliminated most of the deficit demand gap, prolonged the expansion periods, and made the recessions more shallow."[49]

The Disposable Labor Force

The inadequacy of demand relates not only to the reserve army of labor and the reduction in real wages but also to other fundamental changes in the work force. These various economic forces have produced a contingent or "disposable" work force of part-time and temporary workers, which in 1988 included more than 30 million people, or about a quarter of the total labor force. Among the disposables were some 20 million part-timers, a rise from 14 percent to 21 percent of the labor force from 1980 to 1988, and some 1.1 million temporary workers, more than double the 1980 figure. In 1987, full-time blue-collar workers earned $8.80 an hour, and part-timers received only $4.95 an hour.[50]

Many disposables work for subcontractors, few have any job security, almost none get health or pension benefits, few get paid sick days, holidays, or vacations, and wages are usually substantially below those of comparable full-timers. Because these disposables are transient and relatively easy to replace, they present serious organizing problems for unions, which means that nearly a quarter of the work force is almost beyond the reach of unionization.

Policy

The economic crisis of the late 1980s bore an ominous resemblance to that of the late 1920s. The stock market of the 1980s boomed and nearly busted, and major banks and almost the entire S&L industry failed. Without federal insurance and regulation, the country's economic system might have approached much closer to the total collapse of the 1920s. In both decades, the rich grew richer, real wages declined, and mergers, monopolies, and laissez-faire politics preceded financial routs. But perhaps the most striking parallel lies in the increased hostility to organized labor and its decline as a countervailing force to the dominance of economic elites.

A condition common to both the 1920s and the 1980s was the concentration of wealth. In 1929, the richest 1 percent of U.S. adults owned 36.3 percent of the wealth, up from 31.6 percent in 1922. In 1983, the richest 1 percent owned 34.3 percent of the wealth, up from 24.9 percent in 1960. In the 1980s, the richest 5 percent of Americans had more income than the bottom 40 percent and more wealth than the bottom 90 percent. In 1986 alone, the number of billionaires nearly doubled, from fourteen to twenty-six.[51] Such excess wealth stimulates speculation in the stock market, real estate, and other essentially nonproductive investments, which, combined with reduced demand, can produce economic crisis.

Tax cuts for the rich, made in 1921, 1924, 1926, and 1928, contributed to the greatest concentration of wealth in American history to that date. The tax cuts of 1981 and 1986 similarly benefited the rich, added to wealth concentration, and reduced demand and purchasing power. In both years, the cuts were opposed mainly by a seriously weakened labor movement.

The effect of income inequality on the economic health of a society is seen in figures from the World Bank. From 1981 to 1986, per capita GDP in four newly industrialized countries (NICs)—South Korea, Hong Kong, Singapore, and Taiwan—rose some 38 percent, but during a comparable period, the GDP of four major Latin American countries (Argentina, Mexico, Peru, and Venezuela) declined 10 to 15 percent and rose only 1.5 percent in Brazil. By 1987, these NICs were exporting at least six times more manufactured goods than all of Latin America. The critical factor in the superior performance of the NICs, one study shows, is socioeconomic: Income in the NICs is distributed relatively equally, but in Latin America, income inequality is very great.[52] In Peru, for instance, about half of the national income goes to 1 percent of the population. National income ratios are calculated by dividing the income of the top 20 percent of households by the bottom 20 percent. Brazil's income ratio is about 33, Peru's about 32, Mexico's about 15, Singapore's and South Korea's about 8, and Taiwan's less than 5. The NICs have "vibrant economies"; Latin America "sick economies."

A proper distribution of wealth, one that is socially equitable and economically stabilizing, is a political matter and requires support from powerful advocates of such a policy. Unfortunately, the labor-left in the United States, almost the sole organized advocate of redistributive policies, fell victim to repression and decline in both the 1920s and the 1980s, and the dangerous concentration of wealth and economic power went virtually unchallenged.

Opinion polls show that voters think conservatives are best at handling the economy, but that assumption is challenged by the record of disabling recessions and depressions supervised by conservatives, the permanent damage to the nation of massive capital and corporate flight abroad, the militarization of the economy, the decline of living and human standards, the unique and ignored domestic problems, and the serious slippage of U.S. standing in the world.

The standard conservative response to economic problems has been "privatization," much as the communist response has been "collectivization." Neither response has worked well, as the condition of Eastern Europe—which now suffers as much or more from capitalist as it did from communist solutions—clearly indicates. Democratic socialist, social democratic, and labor parties offer a third way, a more pragmatic and less ideological way—a mixture of public and private controls and enterprises depending on what works best. Perhaps nothing belies the view that private enterprises are inevitably superior to public ones than the notorious failures of the U.S. private health care system which, in contrast to Canadian "socialized medicine" (or national health insurance), for example, is far more costly (per capita), far more bureaucratic and inefficiently administered, and much less adequate to the nation's health needs. Clearly, the poor grades given to public enterprise should, in this case and many others, be revised sharply upward.

PART FIVE

The Power to Repress

15

That Peculiar Institution, American Capitalism

WOODROW WILSON SAID, "the truth is we are living in a great economic system, which is heartless."[1] Yet the vast writings about America's uniqueness say little about that "heartless" system other than to list its virtues and successes and speculate about its mass appeal. This unique system and the people governing it have largely shaped the unusual destiny of the American labor-left. Although the system's powers have waned relative to others in the world community, relative to the American labor-left they have clearly waxed.

Unique features of the system and of American capitalism include a meteoric rise to world power, exceptional corporate and personal wealth, a high level of internal organization, an unusually repressive response to the labor-left, an absence of competing and moderating elites, an almost exclusive control of economic institutions, and an unusual influence on government, the mass media, and other social institutions.

Wealth

America began its swift rise to wealth and power in the late nineteenth century, when the country's coal and cast iron output rapidly overtook that of the British.[2] The most dramatic U.S. increase, however, came in steel: from 1.9 million tons to 31.8 million tons between 1880 and 1910 compared to the British rise from 3.7 million tons to 10.2 million tons. The United States was fifth in the world in the value of manufactured goods output in 1840 and first in 1894, producing in that year twice as much as Britain, half as much as all of Europe combined, and a third of the world's total. By the turn of the century, the United States possessed a fourth of the world's wealth and had become the world's foremost industrial power. The rise depended largely on the nation's abundant resources, its sheer size and vast international markets, and its protected and strategic geography.

The sudden status change of the rising business elites was so swift as to detach them as a class from the traditional social values that characterized many settled elites in other developed democracies. A kind of rapid-ascent "bends" theory is advanced by British historian Henry Phelps Brown to explain the unusual antipathy of U.S. elites to labor, the relatively humane and constructive approach of British employers, and the relatively harsh and reactionary approach of the American.[3] U.S. industrialization after the Civil War was far more rapid than in Britain, and thus, U.S. employers did not "develop codes of respect for the vested interests" of workers they had to hire and fire from day to day. British employers, who were "subject to less urgent pressures and more gradual transitions, could enter into agreements with trade unions" and respect the practices of their workers.[4]

Unusually high levels of personal wealth have also distinguished American economic elites. W. D. Rubinstein found a gap between the United States and Britain in peak levels of wealth holding of between four and twenty times over the course of modern history and a gap of about three and ten times between Britain and New South Wales, the industrialized part of Australia.[5] These differences appeared early and have persisted throughout each nation's history. Thus, the richest Americans have been vastly richer than the richest Britains and Australians, and hence better armed financially for conflict with the labor-left.

Even before the Civil War, America's largest fortunes, such as John Jacob Astor's and Cornelius Vanderbilt's, were larger than peak British fortunes, though Britain was still the world leader in trade and manufacturing. Vanderbilt's fortune was three to four times larger than any British fortune of the day, and the early twentieth-century fortunes of John D. Rockefeller, Henry Ford, Andrew Mellon, Andrew Carnegie, Averell Harriman, and Henry Frick were also far larger than the British. In America, industrialists held most of the peak fortunes; in Britain they were held by an older elite of landowners and London bankers and merchants.

The wealthy in the United States have also increased their holdings relative to the nonwealthy. In 1983, the top one-half of 1 percent of Americans held 35 percent of the nation's wealth, compared with 25 percent in 1963,[6] and by 1986, wealth concentration was greater than it had been in 1929, a year of disastrous concentration, stock market speculation, and financial collapse.[7] In 1986, the *Wall Street Journal* reported that although the United States has always had rich and poor, it now has more of both classes than it did a decade ago, "and in between the two, the middle class has stopped growing."[8] Economist

David Bloom adds that the country "has moved in the direction of becoming a nation of haves and have-nots, with less in between"; what is missing, he says, "are unions, which tend to equalize pay rates."[9]

In the late twentieth century, Kevin Phillips points out, the United States led all major industrial nations in the income gap between the top and bottom fifths of the population.[10] The average income of the top fifth was eleven times that of the bottom fifth—compared with a sevenfold difference in West Germany and fivefold in Japan.[11] In the 1980s, the top fifth of U.S. households gained 33 percent in after-tax income while the bottom fifth declined 5 percent.[12]

The polarization of income between workers and executives has also grown in recent times. By the 1990s, the real wages of American workers were 8 percent below their 1979 wages,[13] whereas the average compensation of chief executive officers (CEOs) increased 48 percent in 1987 alone, a year in which intensified concessions were demanded of labor. In large companies, CEO pay averaged 93 times that of factory workers in 1987, compared to 29 times in 1979. Even *Business Week* concluded that "executive pay is growing out of all proportion to increases in what many other people make—from the worker on the plant floor to the teacher in the classroom."[14] In the late 1980s, the average compensation for CEOs of large companies in the United States was more than 50 percent greater than that for a Japanese CEO and some 100 percent greater than those for their German, French, and British counterparts.[15] Given the strong performance of many Japanese and other foreign firms, the link between compensation and executive job performance is apparently not a close one.

In the United States, one study found, the link between executive performance and compensation has even been eroding.[16] It is also believed that awards in the form of huge stock options not only overcompensate executives but can also encourage them to seek buyers for their companies, thus raising the value of their stock and causing serious hardships for labor and damage to their companies. The market value of top managers, the deputy editor of the *Wall Street Journal Reports* writes,

has been grossly inflated by prattle about the rarity of their talents. . . . The result: a picture of business as some kind of complicated primitive religion, its shamans the CEOs. . . . Executive ability is far, far more common than the talent needed to spear a ground ball hit to the hole. Anyone who has a fair amount of common sense, energy and humanity can do a creditable or even exemplary job of running a business. . . . As a nation, we remain convinced that executive talent is as rare as Kirtland's warbler, and therefore worth a ton of money; the past Decade of Greed, with its adoration of business and big money, has hammered this erroneous idea so deeply into the public mind that dynamite couldn't dislodge it.[17]

Elite Behavior

In some places where labor has thrived, members of the old feudal elite were less repressive in relations with labor than were the American elites and often shielded workers from the ravages of rising industrialism. Many old-style British Tories, Benjamin Disraeli among them, prided themselves on a sense of "duty" to others and responsiveness to public needs. Also in Britain, one arch-conservative peer of the realm supported the introduction and passage of a workmen's compensation act in 1897, and the Liberal Prime Minister William Gladstone, a member of the landed gentry, "never abandoned the inborn sense that property is responsibility."[18]

Even when this "gentry" failed to deserve its good name, it at least competed with the rising capitalist elite, and in so doing often engaged in political trade-offs with labor that benefited both groups. In America, the absence of rival elites has given the business elite a relatively free hand in dealing with labor, and the absence of an aristocracy, H. G. Wells once wrote, meant that the sense of state responsibility that Europeans thought would give meaning to the whole was missing. America's problems were unhampered and unilluminated by a feudal tradition.[19]

Historian Barbara Tuchman writes that the absence of a landed gentry "bound by a traditional morality left America open to the unrestricted exploits of the 'plungers' and plunderers, the builders and malefactors and profiteers—and through them to the corruption of politics."[20] Government in America through the 1870s and 1880s, she writes, was merely a paid agent and functioned chiefly to make the country safe, and lucrative, for the capitalist. The point is, not that feudalism is superior to capitalism, only that the former can sometimes buffer labor against the "naked self-interest" of the latter and acknowledge the necessary role of government responsibility to the whole.

The American business elite has also been less divided by the sources of its wealth than was the early capitalist elite in Britain. The richest part of British business was based in London finance and commerce, the other in manufacturing in the north of England. The two differed in their social and political outlooks, competed for wealth and power, and gradually merged into a single elite in 1918–1925.[21] Elite cleavages in the United States were much less distinct.

In Canada, the presence (at least in the past) of a true British-style Tory class and a political tradition that stresses public duty and even noblesse oblige have facilitated the growth of an influential Canadian labor party and a relatively strong labor movement.[22] Government intervention in economic affairs and the continuing influence of Toryism have "inhibited the development of strong economic individualism as a dominant national virtue" in Canada, sociologist S. M. Lipset writes.[23] In the early 1870s, Canadian Conservatives, led by John A. Macdonald, antagonized businesspeople by giving unionism some legal security, and while the United States under Republican leadership pursued antilabor and laissez-faire policies, the Canadian government intervened to build up the economy and even aided trade union organization in doing so.[24] Early Canadian Conservatives supported public intervention in the economy, and Canadians have been far more supportive than American elites of such interventions.[25] Public ownership has also been far more common and acceptable in Canada than in the United States, and the Conservative Party has been responsible for much of it, though new Conservatives in the 1980s moved to privatize much of it.

In the 1930s, Canadian Conservatives proposed government economic intervention that was at least as radical as Roosevelt's, and in 1935, Tory Prime Minister R. B. Bennett claimed that economic revival required government intervention and appealed for support from those people who believed it the duty of government "to end the abuses brought about by big business" and to correct "the faults of capitalism [which] have brought about injustices in our social state."[26] The Conservative government's "speech from the throne" in 1935 stated that "in the anxious years through which you have passed, you have been the witness of grave defects and abuses in the capitalist system. Unemployment and want are proof of these. Great changes are taking place about us. New conditions prevail. These require modifications in the capitalist system."[27] Much later, in the 1974 elections, the Conservative Party leader criticized the cowardice of the Liberal government for failing to enact the wage and price controls needed to check inflation, and a leading Conservative historian urged Conservatives to support the welfare state because laissez-faire and rugged individualism violated traditional Conservative principles and supported class warfare.

Values and Character

The unique wealth and power of U.S. elites, in the absence of competing elites, may account for much of their abiding hostility to the labor-left. As Thomas Burke said in 1877, "Power of all kinds has an irresistible propensity to increase a desire for itself . . . and this is a passion which grows in proportion as it is gratified"—or as John Adams wrote even earlier, "Power always thinks it has a great Soul, and vast Views, beyond the Comprehension of the Weak, and that it is doing God's Service, when it is violating all his Laws."

Elite social norms may also have played a role. British employers, as Brown writes, "had no stomach for a fight into which they would have gone with no easy conscience. This was so because the social norms in which they had been raised and which were generally held around them were not consonant with it."[28] When unions first appeared, "in the land of proclaimed equality, the employers counter-attacked, individually and in combination. In the land of social hierarchy, though resistance sometimes went over into counter-attack, the employers did not sustain militant combinations, and quite widely then came to accept trade unions and even welcome their performance of defined functions."[29] In the United States, the employer related to employees only on a business basis. "If they formed a price ring against him no obligation of benevolence inhibited his vigour in breaking it."[30]

American industrialists, W. D. Rubinstein writes, possessed "distinctive traits from thrift, foresight, and innovativeness to low cunning, lack of conscience, and religious guilt."[31] Referring to Sir John Ellerman (1862–1933), who acquired by far the largest British fortune of his time, Rubinstein says he had "few friends and was a lone wolf *par excellence*," but "he simply cannot in fairness be compared to the malevolent and anti-social tradition of American multi-millionaires."[32]

Although rapid ascent, excessive wealth and power, and the absence of competing elites have each played their role in shaping elite behavior, U.S. elites may also have been predisposed to such behavior. The early antecedents of the current elites, the "robber barons," laid the groundwork and set the example for what apparently became appropriate behavior. These barons, Matthew Josephson claims, "extended their sway throughout the social order; . . . took possession of the political government (with its police, army, navy), of the School, the Press, the Church" and finally laid hands on the "world of fashionable or polite society," always a "kept class attached to the ruling power."[33]

Lewis Lapham, a respected critic, makes some impressionistic and seemingly outrageous claims about the very rich of today. "By and large," he writes, "the rich have the temperaments of lizards, and their indifference to other people's joy or sorrow bears comparison to the indifference of the stars in the constellation of Orion." Their worship of money "results in the depreciation of all values that do not pay" and the definition of freedom "as the freedom to exploit." Such values give "rise to a system that puts a premium on crime, encourages the placid acquiescence in the dishonest thought or deal, sustains the routine hypocrisy of politics and proclaims as inviolate the economic savagery otherwise known as the free market or freedom under capitalism."[34] Money, *Fortune* concludes, is the only thing that counts today; all other values pale before it.[35]

A Carnegie Mellon survey of 400 managers showed that 55 percent do not believe their own top management, a third distrust their own direct bosses, and on an average, they think that more than half of their firms' employees disbelieve or distrust their bosses.[36] Another survey, conducted at Boston University, found that 78 percent of American workers are suspicious of management (the most suspicious being under age twenty-five) and that such sentiments interfere with job performance.[37]

A *Harvard Business Review* survey of industrial leaders in the 1980s found business ethics declining and executive behavior such as cheating customers, bribing political officials, and using call girls for business purposes becoming increasingly common.[38] A fuller list might include such underrecorded practices as the gross abuse of company resources for the private benefit of executives, abuses that would jail public employees but in the private sector are ignored. Fraud has been notorious in military procurement, and the cost of all corporate crime exceeds that of crimes committed by individuals by more than ten to one.

Related to character and values, and the troubles of labor and the U.S. economy, is the matter of executive competence. According to the *Wall Street Journal*, the Japanese success in the auto industry has depended not on trade barriers, labor costs, or labor relations but on managerial performance measures relating to product development and technology, areas in which the Japanese have "roared so far ahead of Detroit . . . that catching up may be all but impossible."[39] Yet U.S. auto executives are paid far more than their Japanese counterparts.

According to Lapham, those who manage "have done their best to prevent the introduction of new ideas and new products as well as to forestall any seditious shifts in the balance of capital."[40] In the experienced view of conservative Richard Darman, the conventional business establishment has become "bloated, risk-averse, inefficient and unimaginative," and many high in the "corpocracy" are there, not because of character or intelligence, but because of "the strength of their demeanor and a failure to make observable mistakes."[41]

Other Sources of Elite Behavior

Economists tend to look at the possible influence of markets and industrial structures in explaining elite behavior: the types of industry, export versus import markets, local versus national or international markets, rural versus urban locations, the mobility of industry, and the types of ownership and control. Public employers, for example, are often less hostile to unions than private employers because they are more sensitive to voters and less sensitive to profits. Explorations of such markets and motives might be useful, but it is not readily apparent that U.S. markets differ markedly from those elsewhere—beyond their size, profits, and rapid development, subjects already explored.

It has been suggested that U.S. business elites became especially controlling because they sought to protect their unusually rapid technological change against labor resistance. But American labor has been less resistant to such change than labor elsewhere, and has been widely criticized for that response, so this explanation does not take us very far.

U.S. employer hostility is also said to be a response to strong union structures and tough demands. This theory, however, does not explain the lesser hostility of employers to Canadian unions, whose structure and demands resemble the American. Nor does it explain the even greater repression by American employers of European-style unions such as the IWW and other loosely structured and more "ideological" unions. Closer to reality is the proposition that U.S. unions shaped their demands and built strong structures (with dues high enough to finance extended union activities) as a way of dealing with hostile employers and the unique bargaining and political conditions they have faced in the United States.

It is also claimed that U.S. unions encounter more employer hostility because they typically bargain with individual employers rather than with employer associations on an industry-wide basis. The associations, it is said, are more benign and, out of self-interest, less eager to destroy unions than the individual employers, but the American union experience has often been that associations can be tougher bargainers than individual employers.

Extended speculation on the motives driving the repression of the labor-left is beyond the scope of this book, however, and is indeed a matter that defies proof and must finally depend on speculation alone. It would appear, however, that certain factors in the social environment of the United States have made it possible for an economic elite to acquire unusual powers and to use them freely in a uniquely repressive war on the labor-left. Whatever its sources, however, a strong antiunion bias now reportedly pervades corporate culture, so that executives working abroad accept unions but those in the firm's home offices are inducted into an antiunion culture.

Combinations

We rarely hear, Adam Smith said, of the "combinations of masters; though frequently of those of workmen. But whoever imagines, upon this account, that masters rarely combine, is as ignorant of the world as of the subject. Masters are always and everywhere in a sort of tacit, but constant and uniform combination."[42] The employer association, unique to the United States in terms of size and influence, has been a major form of combination, especially in relations with the labor-left, and a major means of achieving power in those and other relations. Appearing early in the country's history, these employer associations grew to significance after the Civil War.[43] In the troubled period 1884–1886, more than 75 percent of the lockouts were ordered by local employer associations rather than individual firms, and in 1894, the combination of the General Managers' Association and the U.S. Army inflicted mortal wounds on the American Railway Union in the Pullman strike. In 1895, the ultraconservative National Association of Manufacturers (NAM) was formed, and with the new century, employer associations multiplied.

Antiunion campaigns on a national level, including the open-shop drive and the "American Plan" of the 1920s, were led by the NAM and other leading groups. The attitudes of these associations were exemplified by one executive of the Pacific Coast Employer's Association during the open-shop period when he defined a labor leader as a "bloodsucker," a "leech," and a "man who never works" but "tries to make his living by his jawbone." Don't tie the laborer down to eight hours, he proclaimed, give him individual liberty, keep him at work: "Idle hands find mischief."[44]

Before the New Deal, unions had to deal with some 137 employer associations nationally, and between 1910 and 1920, the 10 peak associations alone represented some 15,000 firms in campaigns against unions. From the early part of the century to the 1930s, the size and financial power of the NAM significantly reduced union strength, and the NAM's approach became a model for employer labor relations. The cumulative impact on labor of some 30 years of "anti-union activity, of unfavorable court rulings, of petty and serious harassment, and of outright violence against it and its members must have been severe indeed," as one study of the period concludes.[45]

Many employer associations have operated at higher political and global levels. The NAM, based in Washington D.C., registered in 1975 as a group whose main activity was political lobbying. The NAM helped create the U.S. Chamber of Commerce in 1912, and by the 1980s, the chamber's budget was some nine times greater than the NAM's, and it represented twice as many manufacturers. It employs some 1,400 people in Washington and some 600 in the field, and it has launched almost 3,000 congressional action committees. Although the U.S. Chamber of Commerce is not registered as a lobby, many of its officials are lobbyists.

The Business Council, composed of some sixty-five CEOs of top corporations, was established in 1933 and advised FDR. Although not a registered lobby, the council seeks to maintain a close liaison between business and government policymakers, meeting twice a year with top government officials to discuss economic policy and holding semiannual briefings in Washington.

The council's views are made known by the Business Roundtable, an advocacy group and a registered lobby, formed in 1973 by the top officers of 180 of the country's largest corporations. The roundtable has successfully opposed prolabor legislation, minimum wage increases, consumer and environmental protection laws, and business and graduated income taxes, yet its policies are said to be less consistently antilabor than those of the NAM or even the U.S. Chamber of Commerce. Reputedly the most effective invisible federal lobby, the Roundtable gets Fortune-500 CEOs to make personal calls on legislators. Also engaged in legislative work are almost 6,000 national trade and industry associations (about a third are located in Washington where they do research, monitoring, and lobbying), the Washington offices and public affairs departments of various corporations, myriad groups such as right-to-work committees, and conservative research institutes.

What Michael Useem calls the corporate "inner circle" often shapes the policy that business associations and member corporations implement. Policy shaping networks include foundations, think tanks, university institutes, discussion groups, and public relations groups. National policy discussion groups, sponsored by business, date from early in this century. The best known of them, the National Civic Federation, was finally replaced by the Conference Board (founded in 1916), the Council on Foreign Relations (1921), and the Committee for Economic Development (1942). Conservative research groups, largely funded by business, such as the American Enterprise Institute, the Institute of Contemporary Studies, the Hoover Institute, and the Heritage Foundation, also operate in the network.[46]

Opinion shaping, the sequel to policy shaping, is the effort to disseminate a business ideology and identify it with patriotic symbols through a communications network of advertising agencies, public relations firms, and corporate public affairs and public relations departments. In 1970, only a few corporations had a public affairs office; in 1980, some 80 percent of the 500 largest manufacturers had such offices.

Opinion shapers have a clearer field in foreign than in domestic policy, because many people know little about foreign affairs and, as William Domhoff writes, are "predisposed to agree with top leaders out of patriotism and a fear of whatever is strange or foreign."[47] The media response to opinion shapers is illustrated by the fact that the Advertising

Council (a part of the corporate network) was able with a budget of only several million dollars to place more than $500 million in free advertising in the various media, many of the ads strongly slanted toward corporate interests. The Joint Council on Economic Education, another opinion shaper funded largely by corporations and corporate foundations, teaches schoolchildren the business view of economics.

These business networks form a "rather formidable and wide-ranging establishment," one review of lobbies concludes. "They are tremendously diverse, have enormous resources on which to draw, and have been able to pool their assets in ways that have had quite substantial legislative payoffs"; hence, "legislative battles involving union power issues are almost invariably won by the business community."[48] Indeed, it was business lobbying and the superior political resources of business, David Vogel concludes, that defeated labor-law reform and the creation of a consumer protection agency in 1978.[49] Large corporations have become, and even small firms are becoming, "extremely sophisticated at dealing with both the public and government."[50] In the 1980s, Vogel reports, 12,000 lawyers in Washington and 12,000 journalists represented specific industries.[51]

Although diligently prosecuting unionists for combination and criminal conspiracy over the years, the legal system has nevertheless systematically overlooked the extent to which employers and their many combinations have organized and conspired, on a far grander scale, to exclude unions from the workplace and to diminish their powers. Their approach has perhaps been less clandestine than that of the unionists, who are often forced underground, but their thoroughly rationalized endeavors to put unions out of business, along with other competitors, have been no less conspiratorial.

Economic elites are indeed plural, not singular, even when combined in associations. Yet their central tendency has been toward a short-term self-interest that seeks to eliminate competition, countervailing powers, and "free" enterprise in favor of monopoly controls. Without question, the contributions made to society by these elites (and described at great length by others) are many. Yet their excessive and largely unchecked powers seriously undermine political and economic democracy and the survival of the very institutions they claim to cherish.

Oligarchy

The nation's founders, according to Walter Adams and James Brock, based the country's political system on "the assumption that government—the public power—was the principal enemy of individual freedom and equality," but they did not foresee that concentrations of private power "might constitute as potent a threat as government to individual freedom and equality." Nor did they anticipate the great post–Civil War economic transformations that would "usher in an era of private economic feudalism."[52]

By the 1890s, the Republican Party had become the party of big business, and even the Democratic Party, as Democrat Grover Cleveland demonstrated to labor, was beholden to business interests. Railroad and other magnates had achieved wealth and political power, and by free spending on elections, they had come to control many state legislatures, especially in the West and Midwest. In California, the annual gross income of the railroads in the late 1880s was five times that of the state itself. In Pennsylvania, Standard Oil's influence was so great that it was said to have done everything with the Pennsylvania legislature except refine it.

In 1928, the year before the market crash, the Australian H. G. Adam wrote, "America is an employers' paradise,"[53] and from its early history, but especially in the critical periods 1873–1900 and 1919–1932, American big business, Robert Goldstein claims, "functioned effectively as a state within a state, controlling government policy, reaping benefits of governmental largess and usurping governmental functions for their own ends."[54] The giant corporation has extended control deep into American life, and, as John Kenneth Galbraith says, it has acquired immunity from outside influences, including competitors, stockholders, financiers, consumers, and labor; what it cannot do, it prevails upon government and public subsidies to do.[55]

In many ways, an establishment and an oligarchy are the same, economist Lester Thurow writes, rich and well-connected people who marry each other and run their countries, but an establishment wants the system to work while an oligarchy sees no relation between the system's success and its own amassing of money.[56] If an oligarchy redesigns a tax system, Thurow says, it will defend the change as good for the country, but the main interest will be tax breaks for the rich. An establishment, on the other hand, would point out the stupidity of a nation as rich as the United States being the world's largest debtor nation and ranking fourteenth among major industrial nations on taxes as a percentage of GNP. He might have added that an oligarchy would also inspire the White House to direct the Internal Revenue Service to step up tax audits on lower-income taxpayers and relax those on the rich and big corporations, as happened in the Bush administration.

On the key matter of taxes and budgets, Lee Atwater, Republican presidential campaign manager in 1988, made these candid observations about the 1980 Reagan campaign: "We were able to make the establishment, insofar as it is bad, the government. In other words, big government was the enemy, not big business. If the people think the problem is that taxes are too high, and government interferes too much, then we are doing our job. But, if they get to the point where they say that the real problem is that rich people aren't paying taxes . . . then the Democrats are going to be in good shape."[57] Such a strategy was designed in an oligarchy.

Woodrow Wilson described the oligarchy of an earlier era.

The masters of the government of the United States are the combined capitalists and manufacturers of the United States. It is written over every intimate page of the record of Congress, it is written all through the history of conferences at the White House, that the suggestions of economic policy in this country have come from one source, not from many sources. The benevolent guardians . . . who have taken the troubles of government off our hands have become so conspicuous that almost anybody can write out a list of them. Suppose you go to Washington and try to get at your government. You will always find that while you are politely listened to, the men really consulted are the men who have the biggest stake—the big bankers, the big manufacturers, the big masters of commerce, the heads of railroad corporations and of steamship corporations. . . . The government of the United States at present is a foster child of the special interests.[58]

Such is the nature of the labor-left's adversary, one whose peculiar powers and behavior can explain a good deal about America's uniqueness and its prospects.

War and Capitalism

Wars are certainly not among the inventions of industrial capitalism, but in the modern world, economic elites, especially those profiting most from military spending and the global economy, have been prominent advocates of military interventions abroad. Their hawkish policies, involving swift and total force, an unwillingness to negotiate, and an insistence upon unconditional-surrender terms, have in fact resembled their approach to labor relations.

Of course, it is finally the military that *makes* war, but in democratic societies, the orders come from others, from those exercising civilian controls in government and from those economic elites who elect them. General Colin Powell, for instance, reportedly favored sanctions over war in the Gulf but deferred to President Bush, who chose the military solution. Others, including many on the liberal and labor-left, may jump aboard the war machine as it rolls on, but they are rarely in the driver's seat.

The most dangerous companions of raw capitalism have been depression and war. Capitalism, French socialist Jean Jaures says, "brings war, as the rain cloud brings the rain." Most victorious wars abroad have strengthened U.S. capitalism, enriching it, expanding its markets, and seriously weakening both its opposition at home and competition abroad. The prolonged cold war, however, and the costly overreach of U.S. military resources abroad are believed to have had an opposite, and profoundly debilitating, effect on U.S. capitalism and the American economy.

The Civil War defeated the agrarian opposition to capitalism in the South and opened the way to rapid industrialization. Views of the origins of that war are mixed, but the people who point to its economic origins claim it was based as much in the conflict between northern industrial interests and southern agrarian interests as in secession or the demands of abolitionists. During and after the war, a Republican Congress rewarded industrialists with favorable laws on tariffs, land, currency, and immigration and with subsidies and protective legislation for the railroads and other businesses. The great fortunes that resulted have led some people to conclude that in the end the Civil War's real winner was not the black man but the businessman. Similarly, the origins of the Spanish-American War have generally been located in economic interests—U.S. investments in Cuba—and the jingoistic yellow journalism that supported them.

The two world wars shook European but not American capitalism. In the World War I era, for instance, assuming a U.S. industrial production index of 100 in prewar 1913, in postwar 1920, the index was 141 in the United States, 100 in Britain, 62 in France, and 61 in Germany. Between 1914 and 1930, U.S. foreign investments rose from 5 percent to 35 percent of the world's total, and by 1960, the figure was almost 60 percent.

World War I was widely regarded by democratic socialists as a "capitalist war," and World War II has been considered a product of the first, as well as of the 1930s crisis of American capitalism and the ensuing world depression. In the 1920s, "it was in the United States that a potential for crisis was definitely released and became a Great Crisis," Michel Beaud concludes.[59]

Depression, war, and capitalism are closely linked, as previously suggested. The market crash of 1929, John Kenneth Galbraith writes, was caused by a bad corporate structure, a bad banking structure, and a bad distribution of income, which siphoned the excess wealth of the rich into a volatile stock market.[60] By 1932, some 2,000 investment banks and brokerage houses had failed, along with some 40 percent of all commercial banks and many investment trusts. This banking collapse struck a heavy blow to Germany's fragile economic recovery in 1932, and German unemployment rose to 6 million in that year, up from 2.5 million in 1928, and in the crisis, Germany turned to the Nazis.

The crash in the United States was turned into a depression by Herbert Hoover's deflationary policies, Peter Temin writes: "Free market capitalism . . . had led to disaster. Direct management of the economy could only do better."[61] After Franklin D. Roosevelt's election, the policies became expansionary and largely social democratic, including interventionist stimulation of investment, devaluation of the currency, and moves to regulate banking and the economy. The market responded immediately, but expansionist policies were withdrawn too soon, the economy slipped, and the world headed to war.

The British Labour Party came to power in the war's aftermath, labor governments returned to power in Scandinavia, Socialist Leon Blum returned as prime minister of France, and everywhere in Western Europe the left gained influence. German unions won codetermination in several basic industries, and the French adopted "industrialized nationalization," a system of tripartite representation of workers, consumers, and government on the boards of specified industries. No such transfers of economic and political power occurred in the United States, and postwar conservative political successes, have included a near ouster of Truman, the long Eisenhower presidency, and, except for the Kennedy-Johnson years and a mixed Carter term, a succession of conservative, antilabor administrations and Supreme Court appointments.

16

The Media Monopoly

CONSERVATIVE VIEWS are distributed to the public via the business-owned mass media—a media more tightly monopolized by big business than in any comparable democracy. Many defenders of this monopoly protest, however, that the media are not conservative, that most media professionals are liberals, that big-business owners and advertisers do not influence media content, and that media influence on public opinion is, in any case, minimal.

The Extent of Monopolies

In 1982, only fifty corporate giants controlled half or more of the U.S. media, including magazines, daily newspapers, television stations, radio stations, book publishers, and movie studios, and these fifty had interlocking financial interests with other giant corporations and with a few large international banks. By 1986, the fifty were down to only twenty-nine, and by 1987, to twenty-six. In the 1990s, according to Ben Bagdikian, journalism dean at the University of California, Berkeley, the number might be down to only half a dozen. These major-league owners, he says, may sit on the benches, but they actively influence the editorial policy of the media they control.[1] The media are hugely profitable for these giants. Among the 400 richest Americans listed in *Forbes* magazine, 83 had made their fortunes from newspaper, television, and publishing properties; only the oil industry, with 48 names on the list, approached that number.[2]

Movies and television are heading most rapidly toward full monopoly control, partly as a result of deregulation. This control is being achieved through both vertical integration (control of both production and distribution) and horizontal integration (control of various media).[3] As for newspapers, in the early 1980s, Washington, D.C., had only one non-religious daily while London had eleven, Paris fourteen, Rome eighteen, Tokyo seventeen, and Moscow nine. Only 2 percent of American cities had more than one paper, and New York, with four papers in 1990, had more than any other city. In 1986, the twenty-five biggest newspaper chains, with Gannett leading, controlled nearly 59 percent of newspaper circulation, up from 51 percent a decade earlier.[4]

The big chains drive out the smaller papers, as they are better able to cut costs, raise money, absorb temporary losses—and attract advertisers. For the survivors, the newspaper business is one of the ten most profitable businesses in the country, its profits derived largely from advertising. In 1985, newspapers took in $30 billion, dwarfing the income of television network news divisions, whose earnings were reportedly "only" $830 million, still more than the GNP of some nations. The network divisions employed some 7,500 people; newspapers, 425,000.[5]

Public Competition and Intervention

Since 1971, the Swedish government has given direct subsidies to the daily press to keep it alive and competitive, and it also exempts the daily press from value-added taxes, reduces its advertising tax, provides long-term capital spending loans, and brings down delivery costs through rebates for joint newspaper distribution. About a third of the total subsidy goes to the press of the Social Democratic Party, Sweden's major party, and two-thirds to the nonsocialist press. The result is a competitive assortment of daily newspapers. In many other countries—but not the United States—labor-left groups, sometimes with public subsidies, also support mass circulation newspapers and magazines.

In Italy, the state television network has three channels, each controlled by one of the three major political parties—the Christian Democrats, the Communists, and the Socialists—all presenting their own views of political events. Almost all other democracies give far more support to public television and radio than the United States does. The British and the Canadian broadcasting systems are among the better examples, with programming that is strictly noncommercial and generally of high quality and news coverage that is relatively probing and impartial.

In 1967, the U.S. Public Broadcasting Act was signed into law, establishing the Corporation for Public Broadcasting (CPB) to oversee government funding and the Public Broadcasting Service (PBS) to produce programming. PBS and the public stations receive minimal federal financing and, unlike the British and Canadian systems, must rely on viewer donations and corporate funding. Inevitably, that reliance leads to corporate efforts to influence programming. As only one instance, in 1985, a multinational company that provided funds for a public television station withdrew its funding after the station showed the documentary film "Hungry for Profit" in which multinational operations in third world countries were criticized. Hungry for funds, stations learn to forestall such actions.

Official influence is also applied to the media. For example, President Nixon tried to suppress what he regarded as antiadministration programming in public broadcasting,[6] President Reagan nominated someone to the CPB board who believed that the CPB should be abolished, and in 1981, Reagan vetoed appropriations for CPB, whose budgets since then have been seriously cut. In some other countries, privatization and budget cuts have also affected public broadcasting, but nowhere have they cut so deeply into the public media as in the United States. Whether or not the public media are superior, more liberal, more risk taking than the commercial—as they appear to be—they at least offer competition and an audience alternative to the private media.

Conservative Bias of the Monopoly

The media monopoly makes an absurdity of conservative claims about "freedom of the press" and brings into question the major constitutional privileges granted the press on the premise of diversity and open competition.

Conservatism and the absence of contending views are by-products of the monopoly, and flagging consumer interest is another. In the early 1980s, newspaper readership in the United States was lower than in twenty other countries sampled: Only 287 daily papers were sold in the United States per one 1,000 population, compared with 572 in Sweden, 425 in Finland, 394 in Israel and Australia, and 388 in the United Kingdom—countries with some degree of competition among the news media.[7]

Conservatism in the media is palpable but, out of a desire not to offend readers, advertisers, and critics of media bias, it has become increasingly low-key and subtle. Still, in the 1984 presidential election, more than six times as many daily papers endorsed the Republican as the Democratic candidate,[8] and after the election, almost all "independent" political analysts quoted in the media, Thomas Ferguson claims, were associated with efforts to move the Democratic Party to the right—including the American Enterprise Institute, the Trilateral Commission, the Coalition for a Democratic Majority, and many lobbyists for higher military spending.[9]

Mutual aid is common between conservatives in government and in the media. After Nixon aided the passage of the promedia Newspaper Preservation Act, all Hearst, Cox, and Scripps-Howard papers were *ordered* by their publishers to endorse Nixon in 1972, giving him more newspaper endorsements than any previous modern-day candidate. When the Watergate scandal broke, the press downplayed it before the election, and only after Nixon had been elected did the story finally break in the liberal *Washington Post*.

As an explanation of the conservative media bias, A. J. Liebling says that publishers, as prosperous employers, naturally oppose government intervention in business matters—beyond maintaining heavy postal subsidies—and as owners of valuable property, their chief local interest is in keeping taxes down. Economic planning is "abhorrent" to them, and since other nations favor it, publishers have "become our number-one xenophobe." Because of their wealth, publishers "do not have to be slugged over the head by anti-democratic organizations to force them into using their properties to form public opinion the N.A.M. approves. The gesture would be as redundant as twisting a nymphomaniac's arm to get her into bed."[10] Journalist and editor Lewis Lapham adds that "despite its occasional bouts of invective and melancholia, the American press is, and always has been, a booster press, its editorial pages characteristically advancing the same arguments as the paid advertising copy."[11]

Joseph Pulitzer was one of a kind among publishers, and in his newsroom, a sign read, "The *World* has no friends." In newsrooms elsewhere, Bagdikian writes, these "friends" are called "sacred cows" and may include advertisers, business interests, and political causes, "but no sacred cow has been so protected and has left more generous residues in the news than the American corporation."[12]

To ward off criticism of press monopoly, U.S. newspapers began carrying a variety of political opinions, but none, Bagdikian claims, strays far from centrist views or stresses anticorporate ideas. The news is neutralized to attract advertisers, but that too benefits conservatism in that the absence of contending views about "alternative patterns of power sustains the status quo."[13]

Media elsewhere feature debate and contention. London's twelve daily papers in 1975, Liebling wrote at the time, included liberal, socialist, communist, and all sorts of conservative views, "each trying to catch the others out," but in the United States, the range was from "conservative to reactionary." America, he concluded, is "much farther advanced toward a monovocal, monopolistic, monolocular press than Britain."[14]

Influences on the Media

Business Interventions

Some corporate media owners give media executives a great deal of authority, but when their own economic interests are involved, they are most likely to intervene in media content. There are many examples of corporate influences on newspaper content, including a 1980 survey by the American Society of Newspaper Editors that found that a third of all editors working for newspaper chains said they would not feel free to carry a story that was damaging to their owners' firm.[15]

The Writers Guild of America, which includes the people who write all the television network drama and variety shows, testified before a Senate subcommittee in 1971 that "the networks have deliberately and almost totally shut off [the] flow of ideas, have censored and continue to censor the writers who work for them." The testimony included numerous examples of censorship, and a poll of guild members revealed that 86 percent of them had personally experienced censorship of their work by higher-ups.[16]

After the Time-Warner merger, the man who had for years prepared the *Fortune* article on the 200 highest paid U.S. executives quit *Fortune*, publicly charging serious interference with his work by company officials because of his criticism of the excessive compensation given to Time-Warner CEO, Steven J. Ross, estimated at $78.2 million in 1990.

Interventions in media content also come from the shared board members of interlocking corporations. Gannett, for example, the largest newspaper chain, interlocks through shared directors with many corporate giants, including Merrill Lynch, Standard Oil of Ohio, 20th Century Fox, Kerr-McGee, McDonnell Douglas Aircraft, McGraw-Hill, Eastern Airlines, Phillips Petroleum, Kellogg Company, and New York Telephone.[17] Bagdikian cites one example of the inevitable impact of such interlocking on media content. In 1974, Henry Ford II, whose company interlocked with the *New York Times*, told *Times* publisher Arthur Ochs Sulzberger that federal safety and pollution standards would raise car prices. Sulzberger was impressed and decided that higher car prices would also affect advertising in his newspapers. Sulzberger called a meeting of major publishers to hear Ford's and Lee Iacocca's statements, and as a result, the wire services all reported the automakers' case against safety and pollution controls. Many papers ran the story on the front page, and the *New York Times* also included a two-column picture of Henry Ford with its story.[18]

Corporate Influence

Corporate influence, from within or outside the media, is common in connection with foreign policy issues, which typically involve business interests and are relatively safe from rebuttal by a public ill-informed about these issues. For this reason, the media hews closest to "official" and usually conservative positions on foreign policy.

Howard Sochurek, a staff photographer for *Life* in the 1950s and highly critical of what he had seen of French action in Vietnam, is quoted in Harry Maurer's book *Strange Ground* as saying that "Henry Luce was the dominant force in all Time, Inc. publications. . . . His beliefs were followed. They were his magazines, right? His views were always very strategic, very big-picture. He didn't want to hear the details of how the French soldiers were goofing off in the field. He'd say, 'The basic American interests lie with the French. Preventing the inroads of the Russians in Europe and having the French support us in NATO are far more important than what's happening in Hanoi.' And that was that."[19]

The media are criticized for transmitting, almost verbatim, State Department releases on international events and for a willingness to accept almost unquestioningly official government reports—either because they agree with media views or because there is no alternative source of foreign news.[20] Allan Rachlin, for instance, contrasts coverage by the U.S. and Canadian media of the Korean airliner shot down by the Soviets in 1983 and concludes that U.S. journalists tend to filter and frame reports solely around official versions of the news.[21]

The cold war and domestic red hunts left their mark on the media. William L. Shirer, a highly regarded radio commentator, was fired by CBS and blacklisted from the media for signing a Supreme Court brief on behalf of Hollywood screenwriters defying the House Un-American Activities Committee and for criticizing the anti-Communist hysteria sweeping the country. An unusual *Business Week* article in 1990 commented that Shirer was "an analytical journalist with a heartfelt point of view—a far cry from the bland, middle-of-the-road broadcast commentators who followed him. It is intriguing to speculate about the impact Shirer would have on public opinion, had he not been made persona non grata by the chicken-hearted nabobs of network news."[22]

Corporate conservatism was conspicuous in the inflamed press antipathy to Roosevelt and the New Deal, and in the coverage given, however reluctantly at the end, to the various red hunts of Palmer, Dies, McCarthy, and others, though all were clear threats to a free press. Press tycoon William Randolph Hearst helped create McCarthy and was his friend and political supporter, and Hearst sought out other anti-Communist spokespeople as well. Together with Henry Luce, head of Time, Inc., he discovered Billy Graham, a tent evangelist who was preaching "Either communism must die, or Christianity must die." Hearst liked the message and wrote his editors in late 1949, "Puff Graham," and within several months, Graham was preaching to meetings of over 350,000. Luce put him on a *Time* cover in 1954, and Graham became an internationally celebrated crusader against communism and a zealous

McCarthy supporter.[23] Many papers turned against McCarthy later, but mainly because he had begun attacking the military and the Eisenhower administration and no longer served conservative ends.

In a revealing book, Herbert Schiller claims that anticommunism has been one of the main messages of the media for almost half a century. He also reports that one study found that early television owners and news celebrities collaborated with the Pentagon, the FBI, the Voice of America, and others in selling the cold war to the public and that television staffs were purged of people who did not conform to the right-wing crusade against a grossly exaggerated communist threat. "All of the dreadful policies that have followed from that false prospect— forty years of arms build-up for 'national security,'" armed interventions around the world, and the "attack on American civil liberties at home— were based on a lie" and sold to the public with amazing success. Human beings "are not equipped to deal with a pervasive disinformational system—administered from the commandposts of the social order—that assaults the senses through all cultural forms and channels."[24]

Advertiser Influence

Mass advertisers influence the media as much or more than corporate owners. Proctor and Gamble, television's largest advertiser (more than half a billion dollars yearly), once issued directives to its advertising agency about the content of news, drama, or other programs carrying its ads. With regard to business, for example, "There will be no material on any of our programs which could in any way further the concept of business as cold, ruthless, and lacking all sentiments or spiritual motivation. . . . Special attention shall be given to any mention, however innocuous, of the grocery and drug business as well as any other group of customers of the company." On America and religion, the directives said that if a character attacks "some basic conception of the American way of life," then a response "must be completely and convincingly made someplace in the same broadcast," and concerning war and the military, "In dealing with war, our writers should minimize the 'horror' aspects. The writers should be guided by the fact that any scene that contributes negatively to public morale is not acceptable. Men in uniform shall not be cast as heavy villains or portrayed as engaging in any criminal activity."[25]

The Prudential Insurance Company once turned down the idea for a program on the bank holiday that precipitated the Great Depression because it cast doubt on all financial institutions and because a positive image of business and finance should be sustained on the air. In 1938, *Esquire* launched the magazine *Ken*, but advertisers disliked its liberal ideas and the magazine was closed, even though its circulation goals had been met. Only films, book publishing—and popular music as a communication medium—are relatively immune to the constraints of advertising.

When a newspaper dies, Bagdikian says, "Owners almost invariably attribute death to the evil spirit of labor unions,"[26] but for most failed newspapers, the cause is competition for mass advertising, which insures a single survivor and final death for the others.

Media Sources

The media get most of their news from "official," "expert," corporate-owned, and other established and generally conservative sources—mainly the public information offices of corporations and government. These sources are considered respectable and reliable, and they also can most easily afford to pour out news to the media, without charge or much effort on the media's part.

Corporations, employers associations, chambers of commerce, and many government offices support large public information offices. The Pentagon alone reportedly spends hundreds of millions of dollars each year to send out releases that the media picks up and often presents as coming from independent sources. The CIA, according to Michael Parenti, has run the biggest news service in the world, with a bigger budget than those of all the major wire services combined. In 1975, a Senate intelligence committee found that the CIA owned outright more than 200 wire services, newspapers, magazines, and book publishing complexes and subsidized many more, and in the 1950s, some 400 to 600 journalists were on the CIA payroll.[27] The media dependence on these official sources usually suits their editorial policies, but it also makes the media vulnerable to manipulation by these sources, as the news privileges offered are likely to vary with the degree of media cooperation.

These influential and often conservative sources, private and public, are also effective lobbyists, some conducting letter and telephone campaigns against unfavorable media treatment, lodging complaints with the Federal Communications Commission, bringing lawsuits against the media, proposing legislation, or engaging in continuous media monitoring and "influence peddling" with high level media officials. In sum, their resources, financial and otherwise, shape the news and vastly exceed those of nonofficial or dissenting groups.

An underexplored school of thought holds that much of the media bias originates more in journalistic laziness than in conservatism, and in the readiness of reporters to accept official handouts from business and government, usually without revision or investigation. Releases by nonofficial groups are less likely to be news, and besides, most nonofficial groups lack the means or know-how required to issue releases.

The people sought out for media interviews also come overwhelmingly from these official sources. A study of some 2,500 guests on the ABC "Nightline" news program, for instance, showed officials predominating and unofficial and dissenting groups virtually absent—including labor, consumer, and environmental advocates; peace activists; the working class; and Americans opposing U.S. foreign policy. "If you want to critique US foreign policy," the show's host said, "you don't bring on the opponents of US foreign policy and let them speak their minds. What you do is bring on the architects of US foreign policy and hold them to account."[28] That approach assumes that the host knows as much about foreign policy (and any other subject discussed) as both the critics and the officials and that he or she is committed to challenging the authorities.

The research group Fairness and Accuracy in Reporting has documented the reliance of public television's McNeil and Lehrer evening news on establishment guests. In the six months ending August 4, 1989, the great majority of guests, it found, were white middle-aged males from official or quasi-official Washington. Among the most popular were President Bush's Secretary of Defense Dick Cheney, Senator Orrin Hatch (R–Utah), and Norman Ornstein of the conservative American Enterprise Institute, said to be a "favorite recruiting ground for talk shows." An earlier study by the group had found that in forty months of "Nightline," the favorite guests were conservative foreign policy spokesmen Henry Kissinger, Alexander Haig, Jr., and Elliott Abrams and conservative evangelist Jerry Falwell. It also found that PBS talk shows were dominated by right-wing spokespeople like William Buckley, Jr., and John McLaughlin and that, because of corporate support of public broadcasting, public television programs about business were not matched by programs about groups such as labor unions.[29]

Role of Professional Journalists

Intervention in media content is seldom needed, however, because controls usually operate automatically, by self-censorship, and less by directive than by silent controls that involve money, jobs, and promotions for staff. Media heads are hired on the understanding that as team members, they share owner interests, and whether they are retained, promoted, or fired can depend on how well they pursue those interests. No one would expect the situation to be otherwise, but what is routine elsewhere is reprehensible in a medium protected by the free speech provisions of the Constitution. The operating heads, hired for their political reliability, in turn hire others they can trust. Many stumble over employers' interests and are fired. Even worse, from the pattern of rewards and punishment, media staffs learn to follow orders that have never been given them.

Conservatives complain of a liberal bias in the media, and are startled when they discover even an occasional negative revelation about business activities. One must reckon, Ferguson and Rogers say, with the vast campaign waged by some sectors of the business and legal communities against an alleged liberal bias in the media. The liberal press must look over its shoulder at its conservative critics, like Accuracy in Media, Fairness in Media, the American Legal Foundation, and the Capital Legal Foundation, and is not a likely ally in any "serious attempt to reverse present policies."[30]

Some liberal professionals deny the influence of conservatism on the media or on their own work. In some cases, they are indeed free agents, or at least trusted ones; in others, they simply miss the subtler forms of censorship and self-censorship, or choose not to acknowledge them, or see only the most liberal examples, or are unaware of what the full range of political dissent looks like.

One study found that "the media elite does have a more liberal and cosmopolitan social outlook than either business leaders or the general public" and that "those in public television lead every other [media] group in economic liberalism."[31] But the differences were not remarkable, economic liberalism was not a dominant sentiment among the professionals, and the "media elite" sample included "production staffs," many of whom are highly unionized but have little say about media content.

A 1982 study found that half of the journalists surveyed thought that the main purpose of U.S. foreign policy has been to protect U.S. business interests. This view might be decidedly nonconforming, but the people surveyed were not the executives or star performers who decide media content. "Too many journalists," Hodding Carter wrote in the 1980s, see themselves as "part of the establishment that runs America. As such, much of the industry is content to hold its criticism and coverage within very careful parameters."[32] A decade earlier, Liebling said that the Republican Party handled publishers better than the Democratic Party because "it wastes no time trying to make friends with reporters, knowing they can do nothing their bosses won't let them."[33]

The Media and Politics

The political powers of the media are so great, according to Congressman Lionel Van Deerling, that all congressional people know that broadcasters and publishers "can make or break you."[34] And although the press may not have "made" Ronald Reagan, it allowed him to succeed in office, Mark Hertsgaard contends in On Bended Knee. The White House press corps, he says, was derelict in its duties. Reagan manipulated it, deluging it with personal and trivial news; corporations put political pressure on it; and the corps itself (a bunch of "pampered" and "caged hamsters") allowed this influence because it had come increasingly to accept a conservative view of politics.[35]

The media can help "make" candidates by endorsing them, but looming larger in the world of partisan politics is the whole political environment created by the media: the daily control over news priorities, placement, and interpretations; what is featured on front pages or in lead broadcasts and what is lost or buried in back pages; what is included in a story; what facts are investigated and reported; and how the facts are interpreted and presented. These decisions affect the political issues raised in campaigns and the way voters respond to these issues.

According to David Paletz and Robert Entman, the "general impact of the mass media is to socialize people into accepting the legitimacy of their country's political system; . . . lead them to acquiesce in America's prevailing social values; . . . direct their opinions in ways which do not undermine and often support the domestic and foreign objectives of elites; . . . and deter them from active, meaningful participation in politics—rendering them quiescent before the powerful."[36]

Labor Coverage

The newspaper owner, Liebling writes, "is a rather large employer of labor," is "forced to deal with unions in all departments of his enterprise, and is as unlikely as any other employer to be on their side."[37] The media treatment of labor supports Liebling's view. Labor history also supports it, though the record has yet to be fully assembled.

Most important is the general climate of opinion created by the media: good news about business and bad news, or more often no news at all, about labor. Typically, the media slight news about corporate crime (or bury it in drab business pages) and give prominence to union misdeeds; they celebrate business leaders and commit labor leaders to limbo or worse. In recent times, the media have withdrawn reporters from labor beats, so that labor news is either blacked out or distorted by reporters unfamiliar with the labor scene.

In a 1939 book, New Deal "brain truster" Harold Ickes claimed that the press's lack of sympathy for unionism ranged "from the polite unfriendliness of the dignified New York Times to the vociferous hostility of the reactionary *Los Angeles Times.*" The latter, he said, fires every employee who joins a union and "encourages the strong-arm methods of the police in breaking up public meetings of non-privileged citizens, who are conveniently referred to as 'Reds.'"[38]

In 1934, the daily papers in San Francisco and Oakland joined forces to smash the San Francisco general strike, and the federal mediator General Hugh Johnson said it was the first time he had "ever been up against a newspaper oligarchy."[39] Also in 1934, when liberal Minnesota Governor Floyd Olson criticized opponents of organized labor—and their "public mouthpiece," the *Minneapolis Journal*—he was attacked by a publishers' trade paper as "an American Hitler." Governor Frank Murphy of Michigan was similarly attacked in later years. "Any man in public life who is sincerely liberal and honestly tries to translate his ideas into action," Ickes said, "especially with respect to labor, soon discovers on which side of the fence the newspapers are."[40]

Quick to attack others and destroy their reputations, the press will tolerate no criticism of itself, Ickes noted. "If a labor leader heads a successful strike, he is threatening the country with a 'dictatorship.' If a public official criticizes the press for being unfair, he is a menace to the 'freedom of the press.'"[41] Publishers fought fiercely against the American Newspaper Guild, which nevertheless established itself and improved the wages and hours of journalists significantly. "Perhaps three-fourths" of the publishers' hatred of Franklin Roosevelt, Ickes said, was that he "made them share a small fraction of their profits with their employees." The New Deal, he noted, also stimulated the expansion of the labor press.[42]

In 1936, the guild struck Hearst's *Seattle Post-Intelligencer* in protest over the firing of two active guild members. Hearst railed against "communists" and "mob rule," and the *Seattle Times* publisher assailed the strike as the "most shameful page in Seattle's history," claiming that "Seattle is now the plaything of a dictator." Ickes wondered why a newspaper strike should be regarded as more "shameful" than any other strike.[43] During that strike, the press utilized a new technique. Even rivals of the struck *Post-Intelligencer* generally refrained from mentioning the strike, as did newspaper-controlled radio stations—and all refused ads by strikers. Ickes wrote that "unless the people are aroused to the danger that lies in a subverting press and move to check it, they are likely soon to find themselves no longer free men, but pawns in the hands of a preferred class, the core of whose ideology is a well-filled purse."[44]

During the 1990 national Greyhound strike, the *New York Times* was "the real media culprit," Gavrielle Gemma writes, "printing the company's side of the story on wages and union demands" and failing to report that Greyhound workers were making the same wages they had fifteen years earlier, that maintenance workers with seventeen years of experience made only $6.50 an hour, that the company was asking workers to pay the full cost of medical coverage, and that no worker had been able to join the pension plan since 1983. Instead, the *Times* ran an "unabashed puff piece on the Greyhound CEO" and "lied about the figures, giving as averages the salaries of drivers who work excessive overtime." The media role was clear: "to turn the public against the union in support of the company's positions" by denying the strikers' legitimate grievances, by portraying them (and only them) as violent, and by stressing the inconvenience of the strike to the public.[45]

Power Resources

Public opinion is a treasured power resource in the conflict between capital and labor. It can make or break strikes, elect candidates, influence labor legislation, and affect union growth. Public opinion is perhaps most responsive to the real life experiences of people, their jobs and concerns, and what they witness with their own senses. But beyond the range of personal experience is the larger world with which people have little face-to-face contact. To learn about this world, they must rely almost wholly on news media, which are far from being the voices of impartiality they claim to be.

"Freedom of the press belongs to those who own one," Liebling wrote,[46] and no group on the American labor-left now owns a mass-distribution daily newspaper. Socialist and labor dailies expired long ago, and although other leftist publications are extant, none remain that can present and interpret the news as it happens and disseminate it to a mass audience. Some critics say that labor-left publications are just as partisan as conservative ones, but that is just the point. Partisanship is to be expected in labor-left publications, just as it is in the corporate-owned mass media. This apparent symmetry does not balance the scales of media justice, of course, since the resources and reach of the two are incomparably different.

In the absence of a labor-left voice and strongly contrasting viewpoints on issues, the bland facade of media impartiality and their subtle biases are often mistaken for nonpartisanship, and investigative reports of crime and corruption in government or unions (and corporations when crime is too serious to overlook) are often seen as the media leading a crusade of truth seekers. In fact, more truth is usually concealed than revealed.

"The reactionaries," John Dewey said early in the century, "are in possession of force, in not only the army and police, but in the press and the schools."[47] Although it may seem strange to speak of the press and schools as possessing force, it is undeniable that their ability to influence (even "brainwash") the people they inform can be as potent in its effects as armed force.

When only twenty-six corporations control more than half the media communications that reach well over 200 million Americans, Bagdikian says, "it is time for Americans to examine the institutions from which they receive their daily picture of the world."[48] Control of information "is a major lever in the control of society. Giving citizens a choice in ideas and information is as important as giving them a choice in politics. If a nation has narrowly controlled information it will soon have narrowly controlled politics."[49]

Early in Britain's industrial revolution, the London press published serially what proved to be unmatched accounts of the deplorable conditions of London slums and the lives of the industrial working class: the work of Charles Dickens. Nothing remotely comparable has been seen in the American press. The modern British press carries on its own form of union bashing and business boosting, but it faces at least some competition from the labor-left press, British public radio and television, and a relatively strong labor party.

17

Reprise and Prospects

HISTORY MAY BE AS REVEALING of the future as youth is of age. Based on past experience, one can speculate on what is likely to happen, or what sorts of things might lead to desired results, but the process can be as much fortune-telling as science. For that reason, readers are asked to sort out for themselves what all the foregoing means for the future, as definitive predictions and prescriptions are beyond even the wide scope of this volume. I have mainly tried to show that the unique powers of American capitalism, the uniquely repressive use of those powers, and the country's unique political system say more about American conservatism than do theories about the unique traits of American labor.

The record of the past shows clearly that politics are labor's lifeblood and that repression of the labor-left over the years has been made possible by government intervention against labor—through legislation, the courts, armed force, administrative action, and legislative procedures. Of equal or greater significance has been the *absence* of enforced law regulating the powers of capital or of laws protecting labor against business recession, capital and industrial flight, corporate takeovers, and abuse of labor's only major protective law, the National Labor Relations Act.

The history of unionism and that of the political left are inseparable, and labor's encounters with varieties of radical and mainstream-left politics are a central part of labor history. Radical politics, of course, have been flagrantly repressed, along with radical unionism, which was all but extinguished by the early twentieth century. Although mainstream trade unions grew in the 1900s and 1910s, by the 1920s they too were in deep trouble, the same trouble that has plagued industrial unionism since the 1950s.

Mainstream unionists and the more distant left have often disagreed about politics over the years, mainly over what *should* be done versus what *can* be done in politics—the left usually leaning to independent politics, like European politics, and labor to whatever politics can win gains for workers and unions. Independent politics have had their day and some stunning successes, but, given the hostile environment and peculiar rules of American politics, no mass third party has survived to the present time.

The various labor, social democratic, and democratic socialist parties that have dominated the European parliaments and that occupy seats of power in almost all developed democracies, however tenuously in recent years, have no place at all in American politics. In most cases, these parties have fraternal and mutually dependent relations with organized labor. American labor, unable to sustain such a party in a hostile milieu, has generally endorsed the Democratic Party since the 1930s, but sectors of that party have been so heavily penetrated by money elites that it falls far short of the "model" European social democratic party.

The proper role for American unionism is a matter of continuing contention. Proponents of a "new" industrial relations argue that the era of confrontation with employers is over and that a new era of harmony must replace it. The experience of European unions is instructive in this respect. Although they accept true partnerships, they have generally rejected relations in which labor is merely a manipulated partner or when it has more to lose than gain in the relationship. Perhaps the times call for various roles—harmonious, conflicting, and entrepreneurial (owner-manager)—depending on the advantages to be gained for labor and society.

Many unions elsewhere are involved in codetermination with management at the highest policy levels, and many have also established producer cooperatives that are owned and controlled by employees and/or unions. In Israel, for instance, Histadrut, the labor federation, owns and operates a large share of the economy, and the workers in its enterprises are unionized. Conflict of interest between employer and employee is always present in such cases but apparently not irreconcilable conflict. American labor has also experimented with worker buyouts and producer cooperatives (too often of expiring companies), and in so doing, labor may finally bring the old dream of a cooperative commonwealth somewhat closer to reality.

Although some advocates of cooperatives predict they will one day replace the corporation, more likely the United States will follow the path of most European democracies—strong labor, left, and cooperative movements and some balanced democratic control over investment and national economic policies. The corporatist pattern that is common in Europe, which combines labor, capital, and government in policymaking, may not be the ideal solution for U.S. labor, but it clearly gives labor more influence than it now possesses.

Unions can play purely defensive roles, or they can take new initiatives, demanding new roles in economic decision making and offering their own proposals for economic growth, like the various "Reuther plans" of the past. Proposals may pertain to new industrial policies and national economic planning, such as that carried out in almost every other Western democracy, or to public incentives for new growth industries or small and middle-sized enterprises, technologies based on skills and flexible production, technologies that humanize work and empower workers, alternative energy sources, modern ecological industries, and small experimental companies, encouraged by public investment in local research centers, such as those notable successes in Japan and Italy.

Sweden, with a mainly privately owned economy, living standards higher than in the United States, and a Social Democratic Party in power more than thirty years, has been moving haltingly toward a gradual buyout by workers and unions of the nation's industries. In 1976, new Swedish laws abolished exclusive managerial prerogatives in hiring and firing and in leading and directing work. The law made all previously reserved management rights, including determining the nature and type of production, subject to union negotiation and gave unions the power of approval over changes initiated by management as well as access to its internal information. Swedish labor leads in formulating economic policies at all levels and in shaping what is regarded as the most humane social system in the world.

Many Swedish Social Democrats feel further gains for workers and society cannot be made until labor acquires greater financial and institutional power resources, which they insist can best be done by democratizing the ownership and management of industry, but proposals along this line have encountered substantial, but perhaps temporary, opposition. Whatever route American labor takes, power resources are clearly what it needs more of, resources obtained through collective bargaining, politics, worker buyouts, workplace and economic democracy—and a sensible, coherent, moral program regarding the extension of economic democracy.

The record of labor-left defeats does not argue for a deterministic view of the future, one that sees labor as forever subdued by the forces of history. On the contrary, the record shows that the labor-left rose from the grave dug for it in the 1920s to a new life in the 1930s and 1940s. The time had come for change, raw capitalism having almost self-destructed during the Great Depression, and the levers of change were found in the New Deal and the CIO. Later, as the law enabled public workers to organize, a second uprising occurred, and a new wave of enlightened public worker unions emerged. A third rising is believed to be in the wings, as promising as the others—that of women, white-collar and service workers—and has indeed already set foot on the stage. None of these changes, however, embody acceptable substitutes for losses in heavy industry. Nor can it be claimed that the dynamics of history will inevitably sweep labor into power, but a future without a robust labor-left movement, giving voice to the interests of the majority, cannot hold much promise.

As in any continuing conflict, labor's powers wax and wane, rising mainly in prosperous times, when its bargaining power peaks, and falling during recessions—unless they reach the depths of the 1930s depression. The hostility of U.S. employers to organized labor remains high in good times and bad, but their offensive against labor tends to rise steeply in bad times, when the jobless are abundant and cheaper labor can be bought. In other developed democracies, labor can usually cope better with recession offensives because it is stronger and employers weaker than their U.S. counterparts, and employers are less driven by conservative ideologies to destroy unions.

Labor took a sharp turn for the worse in the recession that followed the oil crisis of the 1970s and the end of the Vietnam war. Increased hostilities were evident in rising employer violations of the NLRA. By the 1990s, the unionized work force had fallen to only about 16 percent of the nonagricultural total (and 12 percent of the private sector), compared with upward of 50 percent of the total in many other democracies.

Social and economic stability can contribute to union growth. Comparisons of the U.S. and Swedish experiences, for example, suggest that foreign wars are expensive, destabilizing, and in the end, damaging to labor. Swedish unionism, sheltered by Sweden's neutrality (and a labor government), has risen steadily over the century, and almost all of its labor force is now unionized. In the United States, unions have grown during war periods (when labor shortages amplified their powers), but in the end, wars have empowered economic elites far more than labor. In the devastated Europe of the two world wars, the opposite happened, of course, and capitalism was seriously damaged and European labor notably fortified.

Some observers think American unionism has no future, but others think the opposite, that the future belongs to organized labor. Very likely, as citizens grow more aware of the dangers inherent in concentrated power and wealth, they will seek some relief at the polls and in the workplace, and the reign of money in our political and moral life may finally recede. Public confidence in union leaders, a Roper poll reported, rose sharply from 1984 to 1991, from 50 percent to 62 percent, suggesting a growing public awareness of the dangerous imbalance in labor-capital power relations.

The passage of minimal prolabor legislation, such as Canada has, can speed the recovery of labor's powers. Beyond that, a sharpened focus by the labor-left on power itself, and how to get more of it, may also brighten labor's future. Other key agenda items may include shaping political rules that are more hospitable to labor, loosening the grip of conservatism on the South, shaping macroeconomic policies that go far beyond traditional "worker rights" issues, and obtaining some control over those global production and communications institutions that are assuming an ever-growing control over the society's future.

The question is, How does labor acquire enough power to advance its agenda? Like all social movements, labor will be strengthened by a clear sense of its goals and guideposts, one including short-term "business" goals, a clearer vision of the more distant future, a more self-conscious articulation of the morality of fair play, and a commitment to end the rule of money in American politics and resist the damaging appeals of militarism and jingoistic nationalism. Ideologies that are more dogma than vision, that follow a blueprint of social reconstruction, have not served labor well in the past. Times change, and the end of the cold war, if truly at hand, may now give the labor-left a new chance to redefine the moral meanings of Americanism.

Labor can be strengthened, it is claimed, if it offers new services to members and a new kind of participation and control on the job, if it forms coalitions with other groups and movements, and if it builds the complex network of organizations (clubs, schools, cooperatives, sport teams, mutual aid societies, theater groups, day care, etc.) that characterize the European movement—if it becomes, in effect, a true *social* movement. Union leadership, of course, can always be strengthened by fresh ideas, new blood, and staffs that are more representative of the sex, age, ethnicity, and occupations of present or potential members. But these approaches are far less central to labor's problems than is a refocusing on the excessive and repressive powers of U.S. economic elites, the perilous distortions they cause in the American economy and in the whole fabric of society, and the class war they have conducted against labor for well over a century.

Notes

Introduction

1. *Wall Street Journal*, February 13, 1989, A10.
2. W. D. Rubinstein, *Elites and the Wealthy in Modern British History* (New York: St. Martin's Press, 1987), 339.
3. Robert B. Reich, "Secession of the Successful," *New York Times Magazine*, January 20, 1991, 17.
4. Kevin Phillips, *The Politics of Rich and Poor* (New York: Random House, 1990), 124, 125, xii, 147.
5. *New York Times*, June 18, 1990, A1, A14.
6. Phillips, *Politics of Rich and Poor*, 119, 132. This theme has been popularized by Paul Kennedy, *The Rise and Fall of the Great Powers* (New York: Random House, 1987), but the general theme of U.S. decline has been rejected by Henry R. Nau, *The Myth of America's Decline* (New York: Oxford University Press, 1990); Richard Rosecrance, *America's Economic Resurgence* (New York: Harper and Row, 1990); Joseph S. Nye, Jr., *Bound to Lead* (New York: Basic Books, 1990); and Charles R. Morris, *The Coming Global Boom* (New York: Bantam Books, 1990).
7. *Wall Street Journal*, July 30, 1990, A1.
8. *Los Angeles Times*, May 23, 1991, 1A.

Chapter 1

1. David Blanchflower and Richard B. Freeman, "Going Different Ways," Working Paper no. 3342 (New York: National Bureau of Economic Research, April 1990), 6, 42.
2. Leo Troy, "The Rise and Fall of American Trade Unions: The Labor Movement from FDR to RR," in S. M. Lipset, ed., *Unions in Transition: Entering the Second Century*, 87 (San Francisco: Institute for Contemporary Studies, 1986), and "New Data on Workers Belonging to Unions, 1986," *Monthly Labor Review* (May 1987), 36.
3. In 1985, U.S. density was 15 percent in the private sector (compared with 81 percent in Denmark, 52 percent in Austria, 39 percent in Italy, 38 percent in Britain, 28 percent in Germany) and 36 percent in the public sector (compared with 91 percent in Norway, 81 percent in Britain, 71 percent in Austria, 66 percent in Canada, 58 percent in Germany, and 49 percent in Italy); see Leo Troy, "Is the U.S. Unique in the Decline of Private Sector Unionism?" *Journal of Labor Research* 11:2 (Spring 1990), 135.
4. Eric Batstone and Stephen Gourlay, *Unions, Unemployment, and Innovation* (New York: Basil Blackwell, 1986).

5. Gallup Poll, AP dispatch, August 20, 1988.

6. Richard Freeman, "On the Divergence in Unionism Among Developed Countries," Working Paper no. 2817 (New York: National Bureau of Economic Research, January 1989), x.

7. Alan Gladstone, *Symposium on Collective Bargaining in Industrialised Market Economy Countries* (Geneva: ILO, November 1987), 10.

8. Troy, "Is the U.S. Unique," 135.

9. Blanchflower and Freeman, "Going Different Ways," 26.

10. Troy, "Is the U.S. Unique?" 135.

11. Edward Yemin, ed., *Workforce Reductions in Undertakings* (Geneva: International Labour Office, 1982), 4.

12. *Wall Street Journal*, April 3, 1991, A16.

13. Freeman, "On the Divergence in Unionism," x.

14. Ibid., 13, 14.

15. Freeman discounts the view that increased government protection of workers substitutes for unions and reduces their density. As for macroeconomic factors, he finds rapid inflation is associated with union growth—perhaps because workers unionize to keep up with inflation—while the association of unemployment rates and economic growth with union density is mixed and inconclusive.

16. Noah M. Meltz, "Labor Movements in Canada and the United States," in Thomas A. Kuchan, ed., *Challenges and Choices Facing American Labor* (Cambridge, Mass.: MIT Press, 1985).

17. Blanchflower and Freeman, "Going Different Ways," 26.

18. Freeman, "On the Divergence in Unionism," x.

19. Yemin, *Workforce Reductions*, 4.

20. Douglas Fraser, Letter of resignation from the Labor-Management Group, July 19, 1978.

21. Michael Prowse, *Financial Times*, December 17, 1989, A1.

22. Lane Kirkland, "Taming the Economic Jungle" (Address to the Socialist International, AFL Department of International Affairs, Washington, D.C., 1990), 2–3.

23. Bogdan Denitch, *The End of the Cold War: European Unity, Socialism, and the Shift in Global Power* (Minneapolis: University of Minnesota Press, 1990), 69.

24. Dennis Kavanaugh, "Introduction to European Politics and Policies," in Gerald A. Dorfman and Peter J. Duignan, eds., *Politics in Western Europe*, 12–13 (Stanford, Calif.: Hoover Institution Press, 1988); Wolfgang Merkel, "After the Golden Age: Is Social Democracy Doomed to Decline?" (Paper given at a conference, The Crisis of Socialism in Eastern and Western Europe, University of North Carolina at Chapel Hill, April 6–8, 1990).

25. See S. M. Lipset, "No Third Way: A Comparative Perspective on the Left," in Daniel Chirot, ed., *The Revolutions of 1989: Emergence of a New World* (Seattle: University of Washington Press, 1991).

26. Michael Harrington, *Socialism, Past and Present* (New York: Arcade, 1989), 2.

27. Dan Gallin, "What Spain Tells Us About Socialism," *News Bulletin* (International Union of Food and Allied Workers' Associations) nos. 1–2 (1989), 2.

28. Denitch, *End of the Cold War*, 13, 14, 85.

29. Thomas Edsall, *The New Politics of Inequality* (New York: W. W. Norton, 1984), 148.

30. Ibid., 146.

31. Richard B. Freeman and James L. Medoff, *What Do Unions Do?* (New York: Basic Books, 1984); Bennett Harrison, "The Failure of Worker Participation," *Technology Review* (January 1991), 2.

32. Edsall, *New Politics of Inequality*, 177.

33. Robert Kuttner, "Unions, Economic Power, and the State," *Dissent* (Winter 1986), 33–44.

34. George E. Barnett, "American Trade Unionism and Social Insurance," *American Economic Review*, no. 23 (1933), 1.

35. Edsall, *New Politics of Inequality*, 142.

36. *Handbook of Labor Statistics*, Bulletin 2340 (Washington, D.C.: Department of Labor, August 1989), 320.

37. *Wall Street Journal*, July 9, 1990, R17.

38. AFL-CIO, *The Polarization of America: The Loss of Good Jobs, Falling Incomes, and Rising Inequality* (Washington, D.C.: 1986), 27, 39.

39. John Herling, *Labor Letter*, Vol. 38, no. 34, p. 2. It is not known to what extent the loss of income, consumer indebtedness, and inability to repay loans affected bank and savings-and-loan failures. According to a House Budget Committee report, bank failures averaged 6 per year during the postwar years; during Reagan's first term, they averaged 45 per year, and from 1985 to 1987, the average was 147 per year. Small firms were squeezed out by big ones, and during each year of the Reagan administration, business failures averaged twice the previous high and almost triple the 1947 average.

40. AFL-CIO, *Polarization*, 131.

41. Ibid., 67–68, 70, 74.

42. Congressional Budget Office, 1990.

43. Herling, *Labor Letter*, 2.

44. Fred Block et al., *The Mean Season: The Attack on the Welfare State* (New York: Pantheon Books, 1987), xii, 19.

45. John R. Weeks, *Population*, 3d ed. (Belmont, Calif.: Wadsworth, 1985), 160; 4th ed. (1988), 170.

46. *In Health* (August 1990), 42.

47. *Wall Street Journal*, July 9, 1990, R17.

48. Eric Foner, "Why Is There No Socialism in the United States?" *History Workshop*, no. 17 (Spring 1984), 57–80.

49. Aristide R. Zolberg, "How Many Exceptionalisms?" In Ira Katznelson and Aristide R. Zolberg, eds., *Working-Class Formation: Nineteenth-Century Patterns in Western Europe and the United States* (Princeton: Princeton University Press, 1986).

50. Lipset, "No Third Way."

51. Thomas Ferguson and Joel Rogers, *Right Turn: The Decline of the Democrats and the Future of American Politics* (New York: Hill and Wang, 1986).
52. Edward S. Greenberg, *The American Political System: A Radical Approach* (New York: Little, Brown, 1983), 153.

Chapter 2

1. Eugene Victor Debs, *New York Times*, June 5, 1894.
2. Werner Sombart, *Why Is There No Socialism in the United States?* (White Plains, N.Y.: M. E. Sharpe, 1976), 111.
3. David Brody, *Steelworkers in America: The Nonunion Era* (Cambridge, Mass.: Harvard University Press, 1960), 99.
4. Sombart, *Why Is There No Socialism*, 31, 38, 40, 45.
5. Ibid., 112.
6. Ibid., 20, 106, 112, 114.
7. Ibid., 18.
8. Walter Galenson, "The American Labor Movement Is Not Socialist," *American Review* 1:2 (Winter 1961).
9. Robert V. Bruce, *1877: Year of Violence* (Chicago: Quadrangle, 1970), 234.
10. John H.M. Laslett and S. M. Lipset, eds., *Failure of a Dream?* (Berkeley: University of California Press, 1974), 428.
11. Marc Karson, *American Labor Unions and Politics 1900–1918* (Boston: Beacon Press, 1965), 286.
12. S. M. Lipset, *Continental Divide: The Values and Institutions of the United States and Canada* (New York: Routledge, 1990), xiv, 8, 10.
13. Louis Hartz, *The Liberal Tradition in America: An Interpretation of American Political Thought Since the Revolution* (New York: Harcourt, Brace and World, 1955).
14. S. M. Lipset, "Radicalism or Reformism: The Sources of Working-Class Politics," *American Political Science Review* 77 (1983), 1.
15. Ibid., 7.
16. Robert J. Goldstein, *Political Repression in Nineteenth-Century Europe* (Totowa, N.J.: Barnes and Noble, 1983).
17. David Montgomery, "The Shuttle and the Cross: Weavers and Artisans in the Kensington 'Riots' of 1844," *Journal of Social History* (Summer 1972), v.
18. William Buchanan and Hadley Cantril, *How Nations See Each Other* (Urbana: University of Illinois Press, 1953).
19. Reeve Vanneman and Lynn Weber Cannon, *The American Perception of Class* (Philadelphia: Temple University Press, 1987), 148.
20. Thomas Ferguson and Joel Rogers, "The Myth of America's Turn to the Right," *Atlantic Monthly* (May 1986), 43–53.
21. S. M. Lipset and William Schneider, *The Confidence Gap: Business, Labor, and Government in the Public Mind*, rev. ed. (Baltimore: Johns Hopkins University Press, 1983), 4.
22. *Wall Street Journal*, August 1, 1988, A6.

23. D. A. Hibbs, "Industrial Conflict in Advanced Industrial Societies," *American Political Science Review* 70 (1976), 1033–1058.

24. P. K. Edwards, *Strikes in the United States, 1881–1974* (New York: St. Martin's Press, 1981). References in this and the next four paragraphs are from pp. 234, 235, 237, 238, 240, 241, 3.

25. *International Encyclopedia of the Social Sciences,* 505.

26. George S. Bain and Farouk Elsheikh, *Union Growth and the Business Cycle* (New York: Oxford University Press, 1976), 106.

27. Oliver Carsten, "Ethnic Particularism and Class Solidarity: The Experience of Two Connecticut Cities," Working Paper Series, New School for Social Research, Center for Studies of Social Change (New York, July 1987).

28. Robert Michels, *Political Parties* (New York: Dover, 1959), 511–514.

29. Thomas B. Edsall, "The Hidden Role of Race," *New Republic,* July 30 and August 6, 1990.

30. Ibid.

31. Thomas Ferguson and Joel Rogers, *Right Turn: The Decline of the Democrats and the Future of American Politics* (New York: Hill and Wang, 1986).

32. Philip S. Foner, "Socialism and American Trade Unionism," in Laslett and Lipset, eds., *Failure of a Dream?,* 156.

33. Karson, *American Labor Unions and Politics.*

34. Catholics, practicing or not, who were either socialist or well left of center included Peter McGuire, distinguished president of the Carpenters' Union and an AFL founder; James O'Connell, radical Catholic, machinist leader, and an AFL founder; folk hero James Larken, leader of both Irish and American labor, a "lefty," and a devout Catholic; the remarkable Chicago packinghouse and steel union leader John Fitzpatrick; George McNeill and J. P. McDonnell, Catholic socialists who split from the Workingmen's Party and the Socialist Labor Party to form the International Labor Union; Knights of Labor leader Terence Powderly, Irish Catholic leftist; Philip Murray, president, and James Carey, secretary-treasurer, of the CIO; Catholic leftist John Brophy, said to have been the real winner of the election that made John L. Lewis first president of the CIO; and miners' president, John McBride, Catholic and socialist-backed victor over Gompers in his one-term defeat as AFL president. Few of these people were conscious Marxists, all were strong unionists, and most were social democratic or socialist in orientation.

35. Foner, "Socialism and American Trade Unionism," 158.

36. James Weinstein, *The Decline of Socialism in America* (New Brunswick, N.J.: Rutgers University Press, 1984), viii.

37. Irving Howe, *Socialism and America* (San Diego: Harcourt Brace Jovanovich, 1985).

38. Ibid., 142.

39. Ibid., 31.

40. Harry Fleischman, *Norman Thomas, a Biography* (New York: W. W. Norton, 1964), 244.

Chapter 3

1. E. P. Thompson, *The Making of the English Working Class* (New York: Vintage Books, 1963); Herbert Gutman, *Work, Culture, and Society in Industrializing America* (New York: Vintage Books, 1977).

2. David Montgomery, "Once Upon a Shop Floor: An interview with David Montgomery," *Radical History Review* 23 (Spring 1980), 37–53.

3. David Montgomery, "Machinists, the Civic Federation, and the Socialist Party," in David Montgomery, ed., *Workers Control in America* (New York: Cambridge University Press, 1979), 48–90.

4. Alan Dawley, *Class and Community: The Industrial Revolution in Lynn* (Cambridge, Mass.: Harvard University Press, 1976), 239–240.

5. Ibid., 238.

6. James R. Green, *The World of the Worker: Labor in Twentieth-Century America* (New York: Hill and Wang, 1980), xi.

7. Ibid., 119.

8. Eric Foner, "Why Is There No Socialism in the United States?" *History Workshop*, no. 17 (Spring 1984), 57–80.

9. Jeremy Brecher, *Strike!* (Greenwich, Conn.: Fawcett Publications, 1972).

10. Ibid., 316.

11. Stanley Aronowitz, *False Promises: The Shaping of American Working Class Consciousness* (New York: McGraw-Hill, 1973).

12. Ibid., 215.

13. Ibid.

14. Ibid., 219.

15. Ibid., 220.

16. Stanley Aronowitz, *Working Class Hero: A New Strategy for Labor* (New York: Pilgrim Press, 1983), xi, xii.

17. Ibid., xvii.

18. Michael Goldfield, *The Decline of Organized Labor in the United States* (Chicago: University of Chicago Press, 1987).

19. Ibid., 190.

20. Sanford D. Horwitt, *Let Them Call Me Rebel: Saul Alinsky—His Life and Legacy* (New York: Knopf, 1989).

21. Maurice Isserman, "God Bless Our American Institutions: The Labor History of John R. Commons," *Labor History* 17:3 (Summer 1976), 328.

22. Robert Ozanne, "Trends in American Labor History," *Labor History* 21:4 (Fall 1980), 513–521.

23. Ronald Radosh, "The Corporate Ideology of American Labor Leaders from Gompers to Hillman," *Studies on the Left* 6 (November–December 1966), 33–47.

24. Jerome Karabel, "The Reasons Why," *New York Review of Books*, February 8, 1979.

Chapter 4

1. Philip Taft and Philip Ross, "American Labor Violence: Its Causes, Character, and Outcome," in Hugh D. Graham and Ted R. Gurr, eds., *The History of Violence in America: Historical and Comparative Perspectives* (New York: Frederick A. Praeger, 1969), 380.

2. Ibid., 380.

3. James R. Green, *The World of the Worker: Labor in Twentieth-Century America* (New York: Hill and Wang, 1980), 10.

4. Slason Thompson, "Violence in Labor Disputes," *World's Work* (December 1904).

5. Taft and Ross, "American Labor Violence," 381.

6. Richard Clutterbuck, *Britain in Agony: The Growth of Political Violence* (Boston: Faber and Faber, 1978), 13.

7. Leo Huberman, *The Labor Spy Racket* (New York: Modern Age Books, 1937), 47.

8. Quoted in Sidney Howard, *The Labor Spy* (New York: Republic Publishing Company, 1924), 180.

9. Allan Pinkerton, *Strikers, Communists, Tramps, and Detectives* (New York: Arno Press and the New York Times, 1969).

10. Ibid., 85, 86.

11. Ibid., 88.

12. Edward Levinson, quoted in Jerold S. Auerbach, *Labor and Liberty: The LaFollette Committee and the New Deal* (Indianapolis and New York: Bobbs-Merrill, 1966), 50.

13. Howard, *Labor Spy*, 37.

14. Ibid., 38.

15. Ibid., 6.

16. Huberman, *Labor Spy Racket*, 72.

17. Ibid., 6, 83.

18. Other employers of spies included the Aluminum Company of America, Chrysler Corporation, American Book Company, Diamond Match Company, Dixie Greyhound Lines, Firestone Tire and Rubber, Kellogg, Kelvinator, New York Edison, Quaker Oats, Radio Corporation of America, Standard Oil, Statler Hotels, Bethlehem Steel, Campbell Soup, Continental Can, Montgomery Ward, National Cash Register, Ohrbach's Affiliated Stores, Shell Petroleum, Sinclair Refining, Borden Milk, Carnegie-Illinois Steel, and Westinghouse Electric and Manufacturing.

19. Huberman, *Labor Spy Racket*, 10.

20. Howard, *Labor Spy*. References and quotations in this and the following three paragraphs are from pp. 19, 13, 3, and 15.

21. Quotations in this paragraph and the next are from ibid., pp. 178, 179, 181, and 180.

22. Huberman, *Labor Spy Racket*, 99.

23. Ibid., 28.

24. Ibid., 33.

25. H. M. Gitelman, "Perspectives on American Industrial Violence," in *Business History Review* 47:1 (1973), 19.

26. John A. Fitch, *The Causes of Industrial Unrest* (New York: Harper and Brothers, 1924). References here and in the following five paragraphs are from pp. 244–250.

27. William Riker, *Soldiers of the State: The Role of the National Guard in American Democracy* (Washington, D.C.: Public Affairs Press, 1957), 55.

28. Publication of the National Guard Bureau, Washington, D.C., undated.

29. John L. Blackman, Jr., *Presidential Seizure in Labor Disputes* (Cambridge, Mass.: Harvard University Press, 1967).

30. Taft and Ross, "American Labor Violence," 282.

31. Ibid.

32. Gitelman, "Perspectives on American Industrial Violence," 19.

33. In Samuel Yellen, *American Labor Struggles* (New York: S. A. Russell, Harbor Press, 1956), xii.

34. Howard, *Labor Spy*, 1, 2.

35. H. A. Clegg, *Trade Unionism Under Collective Bargaining: A Theory Based on Comparison of Six Countries* (Oxford: Blackwell, 1976), 68–82.

Chapter 5

1. Jay Lovestone, *The Government-Strikebreaker: A Study of the Role of the Government in the Recent Industrial Crisis* (New York: Workers Party of America, 1923), 218, 219.

2. Klaus von Beyme, *Challenge to Power: Trade Unions and Industrial Relations in Capitalist Countries* (London and Beverly Hills, Calif.: Sage, 1980), 211.

3. Henry Phelps Brown, *The Origins of Trade Union Power* (Oxford: Clarendon Press, 1983), 213.

4. John A. Fitch, *The Causes of Industrial Unrest* (New York: Harper and Brothers, 1924), 294, 296.

5. Irving Bernstein, *The Lean Years: A History of the American Worker 1920–1933* (Boston: Houghton Mifflin, 1960), 206.

6. Thomas R. Fisher, *Industrial Disputes and Federal Legislation* (New York: Columbia University Press, 1940), 105.

7. Brown, *Origins of Trade Union Power*, 214.

8. Bernstein, *Lean Years*, 200.

9. Lovestone, *Government-Strikebreaker*, 217, 218.

10. Quoted in Karl E. Klare, "Labor Law and the Liberal Political Imagination," *Socialist Review* (1983), 50–51.

11. Fitch, *Causes of Industrial Unrest*, 287.

12. Bernstein, *Lean Years*, 204.

13. Fitch, *Causes of Industrial Unrest*, 335.

14. Ibid., 336.

15. Bernstein, *Lean Years*, 204.

16. Quoted in ibid., 206.

17. Ibid., 200.
18. Fitch, *Causes of Industrial Unrest*, 342–347.
19. Quoted in ibid., 330.
20. Quoted in ibid., 331, 332.
21. Quoted in ibid., 332, 333.
22. A. E. Mussen, *Trade Union and Social History* (London: Frank Cass and Company, 1974), 9, 10.
23. Ibid.
24. Lovestone, *Government-Strikebreaker*, 214.
25. Samuel Gompers, "A Perverted Conception of Rights," *Federationist* 20 (June 1912), 466.

Chapter 6

1. See further analysis and evidence in James Holt, "Trade Unionism in the British and U.S. Steel Industries, 1888–1912: A Comparative Study," *Labor History* 18 (Winter 1977); see also Arthur G. Burgoyne, *The Homestead Strike of 1892* (Pittsburgh: University of Pittsburgh Press, 1979), and Leon Wolff, *Lockout— The Story of the Homestead Strike of 1892: A Study of Violence, Unionism, and the Carnegie Steel Empire* (New York: Harper and Row, 1965).
2. Joseph F. Wall, *Andrew Carnegie* (New York: Oxford University Press, 1970), 136.
3. Ibid., 154.
4. Holt, "Trade Unionism in the British and U.S. Steel Industries," 10, 11.
5. Wall, *Andrew Carnegie*, 541.
6. Andrew Carnegie, "An Employer's View of the Labor Question," *Forum* 1 (April 1886), 114.
7. Andrew Carnegie, "Results of the Labor Struggle," *Forum* 1 (August 1886), 538.
8. Carnegie, "Results of the Labor Struggle," 14.
9. Burton J. Hendrick, *The Life of Andrew Carnegie*, vol. 1 (New York: Doubleday, Doran and Company, 1932), 408.
10. Ibid.
11. George Harvey, *Henry Clay Frick, the Man* (New York: Privately printed, 1936), 16.
12. George Powers, *Cradle of Steel Unionism: Monongahela Valley, Pa.* (East Chicago, Ind.: Figueroa Printers, 1972), 15.
13. Charles B. Spahr, *America's Working People* (New York: Johnson Reprint, 1970), 148.
14. *St. James Gazette*, July 7, 1892.
15. *London Times*, July 12, 1892.
16. *Dunfermline Journal*, July 30, 1892.
17. *Edinburgh Dispatch*, July 30, 1892.
18. Hamlin Garland, "Homestead and Its Perilous Trades," *McClure's Magazine* 3 (June 1894), 3–5.
19. Powers, *Cradle of Steel Unionism*, 764.

20. *New York Times*, February 15, 1900.

21. Keir Hardy, "Carnegie as a Socialist," *Independent* 58:12 (January 1905), 104; "Some Replies to Mr. Carnegie's Article," *Review of Reviews* (London) 35 (March 1907), 312–313.

22. William Jewett Tucker, "The Gospel of Wealth," *Andover Review* 15 (June 1891), 633.

23. Andrew Carnegie, "How I Served My Apprenticeship as a Businessman," *Youth's Companion*, April 23, 1896, 217.

24. *American Labor Yearbook 1917–18* (New York: Rand School, 1919), 169.

25. William Z. Foster, *The Great Steel Strike and Its Lessons* (New York: B. W. Huebsch, 1920), 14.

26. Commission of Inquiry, Interchurch World Movement, *Report on the Steel Strike of 1919* (New York: DaCapo Press, 1971); Commission of Inquiry, *Public Opinion and the Steel Strike; Supplementary Reports of the Investigators* (New York: Harcourt, Brace and Company, 1921); *Investigation of Strike in Steel Industries*, Hearings before the Committee on Education and Labor, U.S. Senate, 66th Congress (Washington, D.C.: Government Printing Office, 1919); Colston E. Warne, *The Steel Strike of 1919* (Boston: Heath, 1963); see also Marshall Olds, *Analysis of the Interchurch World Movement's Report on the Steel Strike* (New York: G. P. Putnam, 1923), and Ernest Young, *Comments on the Interchurch Report* (Boston: R. G. Badger, 1921).

27. Quoted in Warne, *Steel Strike of 1919*, 90, 91.

28. Foster, *Great Steel Strike*, 14.

29. Quoted in Warne, *Steel Strike of 1919*, 90.

30. Quoted in ibid., 95.

31. Quoted in ibid., 90.

32. Foster, *Great Steel Strike*, 14.

33. Quoted in Warne, *Steel Strike of 1919*, 96.

34. Quoted in ibid., 89.

35. David Brody, *Steelworkers in America: The Nonunion Era* (Cambridge, Mass.: Harvard University Press, 1960), 199.

36. David Brody, *Labor in Crisis: The Steel Strike of 1919* (New York: J. B. Lippincott, 1965), 61, 62.

37. Quoted in Warne, *Steel Strike of 1919*, 17.

38. Foster, *Great Steel Strike*, 17

39. George Powers, *Cradle of Steel Unionism: Monongahela Valley, Pa.* (East Chicago, Ind.: Figueroa Printers, 1972), 18–19.

40. Quoted in Warne, *Steel Strike of 1919*, 16.

41. Ibid., 18.

42. Quoted in ibid., 42.

43. Quoted in Brody, *Labor in Crisis*, 126.

44. Quoted in ibid., 147.

45. Quoted in Warne, *Steel Strike of 1919*, 19.

46. Quoted in ibid., 20.

47. Quoted in ibid., 22.

48. Letter from John Fitzpatrick to Woodrow Wilson, September 18, 1919, in *Investigation of Strike in Steel Industries*.

49. Quoted in Warne, *Steel Strike of 1919*, 25.
50. Quoted in Brody, *Steelworkers in America*, 250–251.
51. Brody, *Labor in Crisis*, 148.
52. Quoted in Warne, *Steel Strike of 1919*, 100.
53. Quoted in ibid., 101.
54. Ibid., 99.
55. Brody, *Steelworkers in America*, 253.
56. Quoted in ibid., 250.
57. Ibid., 244.
58. Ibid., 245.
59. Ibid., 246.
60. Ibid., 248.
61. Ibid., 247.
62. Brody, *Labor in Crisis*, 247.
63. Commission of Inquiry, *Public Opinion and the Steel Strike*, 96.
64. Ibid., 97.
65. Ibid., 99.
66. Brody, *Steelworkers in America*, 249.
67. Quoted in Warne, *Steel Strike of 1919*, 91. Most references in this section are from pp. 91, 93, 94.
68. Commission of Inquiry, *Report on the Steel Strike of 1919*, 39.
69. Warne, *Steel Strike of 1919*. References in this section are from pp. 82, 83, 84, 85, 60, 58, 59.
70. Ibid., 59.
71. James Holt, "Trade Unionism in the British and U.S. Steel Industries, 1888–1912: A Comparative Study," *Labor History* 18 (Winter 1977), 16.
72. Samuel Gompers, *Seventy Years of Life and Labor* (New York: E. P. Dutton, 1925), 322.
73. Quoted in Warne, *Steel Strike of 1919*, 14.
74. Ibid., 17.
75. Brody, *Labor in Crisis*, 147.
76. Quoted in Warne, *Steel Strike of 1919*, 12–13.
77. *London Times*, October 28, 1919.
78. See Mark Reutter, *Sparrows Point: Making Steel—The Rise and Ruin of American Industrial Might* (New York: Summit Books, 1990), and John P. Hoerr, *And the Wolf Finally Came: The Decline of the American Steel Industry* (Pittsburgh: University of Pittsburgh Press, 1990).

Chapter 7

1. The numerous chronicles of these strikes, many inspired and written by new social historians, include J. Craig Jenkins, *The Politics of Insurgency: The Farm Worker Movement in the 1960s* (New York: Columbia University Press, 1985), and Mimi Conway, *Rise Gonna Rise: A Portrait of Southern Textile Workers* (Garden City, N.Y.: Anchor Press, 1979).

2. John L. Blackman, Jr., *Presidential Seizure in Labor Disputes* (Cambridge, Mass.: Harvard University Press, 1967), 8, 9; see also Shelton Stromquist, *A Generation of Boomers: The Pattern of Railroad Conflict in Nineteenth-Century America* (Urbana: University of Illinois Press, 1987).

3. Robert V. Bruce, *1877: Year of Violence* (New York: Bobbs-Merrill, 1959), 17.

4. Allan Pinkerton, *Strikers, Communists, Tramps, and Detectives* (New York: Arno Press and the New York Times, 1969), 229, 230.

5. Ibid., 237.

6. Ibid., 249.

7. *New York Times*, July 26, 1877, 28.

8. Ibid.

9. Samuel Yellen, *American Labor Struggles* (New York: S. A. Russell, 1936), 4.

10. Ibid., 36.

11. Ibid., 37.

12. Bruce, *1877: Year of Violence*, 56.

13. Quoted in ibid., 116.

14. Pinkerton, *Strikers, Communists, Tramps, and Detectives*, x.

15. *Daily News*, July 26, 1877.

16. J. A. Dacus, *Annals of the Great Strikes in the United States* (New York: Burt Franklin, 1877), 15.

17. Ibid., 18.

18. An extraordinary on-the-scene account of the Pullman strike, written by Rev. William H. Carwardine, pastor of the First Methodist Episcopal Church, Pullman, Illinois (*The Pullman Strike* [Chicago: Charles H. Kerr and Company, 1894]), describes not only the events of the strike but the conditions of work and home life of the Pullman workers; see also U.S. Strike Commission, *Report on the Chicago Strike of June–July, 1894* (Washington, D.C.: Government Printing, 1895).

19. Yellen, *American Labor Struggles*, 116.

20. Richard Hofstadter and Michael Wallace, eds., *American Violence* (New York: Knopf, 1970), 151–152.

21. Samuel Gompers, *Seventy Years of Life and Labor* (New York: E. P. Dutton, 1925), 221.

22. Yellen, *American Labor Struggles*, 119–120.

23. Ibid., 121.

24. Harold C. Livesay, *Samuel Gompers and Organized Labor in America* (Boston: Little, Brown, 1978), 141.

25. Philip Taft and Philip Ross, "American Labor Violence: Its Causes, Character, and Outcome," in Hugh D. Graham and Ted R. Gurr, eds., *The History of Violence in America: Historical and Comparative Perspectives* (New York: Frederick A. Praeger, 1969), 299.

26. Carwardine, *Pullman Strike*, jacket summary.

27. Henry Phelps Brown, *The Growth of British Industrial Relations* (London: Macmillan, 1960), 169.

28. Almont Lindsey, *The Pullman Strike* (Chicago: University of Chicago Press, 1942), 309.

29. Quotes in this section are from ibid., pp. 310–320.

30. Louis Adamic, *Dynamite: The Story of Class Violence in America* (New York: Viking Press, 1934), 262.

31. Milton J. Nadworny, *Scientific Management and the Unions 1900–1932: A Historical Analysis* (Cambridge, Mass.: Harvard University Press, 1955), 178.

32. AFL, *Proceedings*, Forty-second Annual Convention (1922), 115.

33. Quoted in Irving Bernstein, *The Lean Years: A History of the American Worker 1920–1933* (Boston: Houghton Mifflin, 1960), 190.

34. Ibid., 192.

35. Ibid., 194.

36. Quoted in Robert J. Goldstein, *Political Repression in Modern America* (Cambridge, Mass.: Schenkman, 1978), 170.

37. Michael Hanagan, "Solidary Logics: Introduction," Working Paper Series, New School for Social Research, Center for Studies of Social Change (New York, July 1987).

38. Thomas R. Brooks, *Toil and Trouble: A History of American Labor* (New York: Dell Publishing, 1964), 177.

39. Quoted in Goldstein, *Political Repression in Modern America*, 4.

Chapter 8

1. Richard Hofstadter in Robert J. Goldstein, *Political Repression in Modern America* (Cambridge, Mass.: Schenkman, 1978), x.

2. Robert A. Dahl, ed., *Political Oppositions in Western Democracies* (New Haven: Yale University Press, 1966), 191.

3. Goldstein, *Political Repression in Modern America*, x.

4. Thomas I. Emerson, David Haber, and Norman Dorsen, *Political and Civil Rights in the United States*, vol. 1 (Boston: Little, Brown, 1967), 35, 37.

5. Quoted in Claude G. Bowers, *Jefferson and Hamilton* (New York: Houghton Mifflin, 1925), 378.

6. Barton L. Ingraham, *Political Crime in Europe: A Comparative Study of France, Germany, and England* (Berkeley: University of California Press, 1979), 317, 318.

7. Ibid., 218.

8. Goldstein, *Political Repression in Modern America*, 24.

9. Ibid., 33.

10. Emerson et al., *Political and Civil Rights*, 50.

11. Ibid., 55.

12. Goldstein, *Political Repression in Modern America*, 113.

13. Ibid.

14. Robert E. Cushman, "The Impact of the War on the Constitution," in Keith L. Nelson, ed., *The Impact of the War on America* (Ithaca: Cornell University Press, 1942), 21.

15. Ibid.

16. Quoted in Goldstein, *Political Repression in Modern America*, 108.

17. Ibid., 112.

18. *American Labor Yearbook, 1921–22* (New York: Rand School, 1923), 11.

19. Goldstein, *Political Repression in Modern America*, 129.

20. Ibid., 113.

21. Ibid.

22. *American Labor Yearbook 1917–18* (New York: Rand School, 1919), 50–53.

23. Eugene V. Debs, *Person's Magazine* (February 1918).

24. Merle Fainsod, *International Socialism and the World War* (Cambridge, Mass.: Harvard University Press, 1935).

25. James Weinstein, *The Decline of Socialism in America* (New Brunswick, N.J.: Rutgers University Press, 1984), 232.

26. Ibid.

27. Ibid.

28. *American Labor Yearbook 1921–22*, 9.

29. Ibid., 79.

30. Goldstein, *Political Repression in Modern America*, 154.

31. Ibid., 174.

32. Ibid., 147.

33. *American Labor Yearbook 1921–22*, 15.

34. Ibid., 10.

35. Goldstein, *Political Repression in Modern America*, 149.

36. *American Labor Yearbook 1921–22*, 34.

37. Ibid., 35.

38. Quoted in Goldstein, *Political Repression in Modern America*, 158, 159.

39. *American Labor Yearbook 1921–22*, 32.

40. Quoted in Goldstein, *Political Repression in Modern America*, 174, 175.

41. Quoted in ibid., 167.

Chapter 9

1. Seymour M. Lipset and Earl Raab, *The Politics of Unreason: Right-Wing Extremism in America, 1790–1970* (New York: Harper and Row, 1970), and Daniel Bell, ed., *The Radical Right* (Garden City, N.Y.: Doubleday, 1963).

2. Richard M. Fried, *Nightmare in Red: The McCarthy Era in Perspective* (New York: Oxford University Press, 1990), 9.

3. Robert Griffith, *The Politics of Fear: Joseph R. McCarthy and the Senate* (Lexington: University of Kentucky Press, 1970), ix.

4. See Mary Sperling McAuliffe, *Crisis on the Left: Cold War Politics and American Liberals, 1947–1954* (Amherst, Mass.: University of Massachusetts Press, 1978); Richard M. Freeland, *The Truman Doctrine and the Origins of McCarthyism: Foreign Policy, Domestic Politics, and Internal Security, 1946–1948* (New York: New York University Press, 1972); and Athan Theoharis, *Seeds of Repression: Harry S. Truman and the Origins of McCarthyism* (Chicago: Quadrangle Books, 1971).

5. Fried, *Nightmare in Red*, 9.

6. Ibid., 60, 85, 88.

7. Ibid., 123, 234.

8. Ibid., 132.

9. Ibid., 85.

10. Quoted in Robert J. Goldstein, *Political Repression in Modern America* (Cambridge, Mass.: Schenkman, 1978), 200.

11. Quoted in Goldstein, *Political Repression in Modern America*, 215.

12. Quoted in ibid., 217.

13. Ibid.

14. Jerold S. Auerbach, *Labor and Liberty: The LaFollette Committee and the New Deal* (Indianapolis, Ind.: Bobbs-Merrill, 1966), 158.

15. Ibid., 159.

16. Ibid., 163.

17. Ibid., 166.

18. Ibid., 165.

19. Ibid., 203, 204, 205, 217.

20. Quoted in Goldstein, *Political Repression in Modern America*, 242.

21. Ibid.

22. Ibid., 240.

23. Ibid., 307.

24. Ibid., 308.

25. Ibid., 345.

26. Thomas I. Emerson, David Haber, and Norman Dorsen, *Political and Civil Rights in the U.S.*, vol. 1 (Boston: Little, Brown, 1967), 11, 2.

27. Quoted in Goldstein, *Political Repression in America*, 344.

28. Emerson et al., *Political and Civil Rights in the U.S.*, 134.

29. Quoted in Irving Bernstein, *The Turbulent Years: A History of the American Worker 1933–1941* (Boston: Houghton Mifflin, 1970), 781.

30. Quoted in Goldstein, *Political Repression in Modern America*, 328.

31. Ibid.

32. Ibid., 327.

33. William Spinrad, *Civil Liberties* (New York: Quadrangle Books, 1970), 134.

34. Quoted in Goldstein, *Political Repression in Modern America*, 250.

35. James F. Simon, *The Antagonists: Hugo Black, Felix Frankfurter, and Civil Liberties in Modern America* (New York: Simon and Schuster, 1989).

36. Goldstein, *Political Repression in Modern America*, 339.

37. Frank J. Donner, *The Age of Surveillance: The Aims and Methods of America's Political Intelligence System* (New York: Knopf, 1988), xii.

38. Earl Warren, *Memoirs of Chief Justice Earl Warren* (New York: Doubleday, 1977), 5–7.

39. Goldstein, *Political Repression in Modern America*, 374.

40. Emerson et al., *Political and Civil Rights in the U.S.*, 138.

41. Goldstein, *Political Repression in Modern America*, 388.

42. Ibid., 376, 344.

43. Ibid., 381.

44. Quoted in ibid., 384.

45. Ibid.

46. Raymond Bonner, *Waltzing with a Dictator: The Marcoses and the Making of American Policy* (New York: Times Books, 1987), 134. Bonner also claims that the Eisenhower administration covertly toppled the democratically elected government of Jacobo Arbenz Guzmán in Guatemala because American businesspeople disapproved of his land reforms and cabinet choices; that American policy supported the assassination of the democratically elected president of Chile and supported as his successor one of the most ruthless dictators in Latin America; and that the CIA led a coup against Mohammad Mossadegh in Iran because of his leftist policies and thereafter supported the dictatorial and hugely unpopular shah.

47. Goldstein, *Political Repression in Modern America*, 365.

48. Fried, *Nightmare in Red*, 100.

49. Ibid., 13.

50. Bert Cochran, *Labor and Communism: The Conflict That Shaped American Unions* (Princeton: Princeton University Press, 1977), 154.

51. Spinrad, *Civil Liberties*, 144.

52. Ibid., 145.

53. Ibid.

54. Ronald Radosh, *American Labor and United States Foreign Policy* (New York: Random House, 1969), 437, 438.

55. Bogdan Denitch, *The End of the Cold War, European Unity, Socialism, and the Shift in Global Power* (Minneapolis: University of Minnesota Press, 1990), 71.

56. Reg Whitaker, "Fighting the Cold War on the Home Front: America, Britain, Australia, and Canada," in Marion Miliband et al., *Socialist Register 1984* (London: Merlin Press, 1984), 23.

57. Quotes are from Thomas I. Emerson and David Helfeld, "Loyalty Among Government Employees," *Yale Law Journal* 58:1 (1948), 134, and Goldstein, *Political Repression in Modern America*, 360.

58. Emerson and Helfeld, "Loyalty Among Government Employees," 132, 133.

59. From Stammers, parliamentary reference: vol. 368 H.C. DEB 5s cols. 186.

60. Stammers, 107 (PRO CAB 66/14, WP (41) 7.) PRO+ Public Records Office.

61. Stammers, 110.

62. Quoted in Whitaker, "Fighting the Cold War," 30, 20.

63. Ibid., 35.

64. Peter Wright, *Spycatcher* (New York: Viking, 1987).

65. Ibid., 273.

66. David Leigh, *The Wilson Plot: How the Spycatchers and Their American Allies Tried to Overthrow the British Government* (New York: Pantheon, 1988), 230.

67. Ibid., 232.

68. Christopher Lasch, *New York Times*, July 13, 1990, A27.

Chapter 10

1. Richard Hofstadter, *The American Political Tradition* (New York: Knopf, 1948), 4; see also Richard Hofstadter, *The Idea of a Party System* (Berkeley: University of California Press, 1969).

2. Edward S. Greenberg, *The American Political System: A Radical Approach* (Boston: Little, Brown, 1983), 11.

3. Robert A. Dahl, ed., *Political Oppositions in Western Democracies* (New Haven: Yale University Press, 1966), 62.

4. Ibid., 66.

5. Friedrich Engels, "Engels to Sorge," in Karl Marx and Friedrich Engels, *Letters to Americans 1848–1895* (New York: International Publishers, 1953), 258.

6. Norman Thomas, *Socialism Re-examined* (New York: W. W. Norton, 1963), chap. 8.

7. Norman Thomas, "Pluralism and Political Parties," in John H.M. Laslett and S. M. Lipset, eds., *Failure of a Dream?* (Berkeley: University of California Press, 1974), 517.

8. Ruy A. Teixeira, *Why Americans Don't Vote: Turnout Decline in the United States, 1960–1984* (Westport, Conn.: Greenwood Press, 1987), 7.

9. Morris Hillquit, *History of Socialism in the United States* (1910; reprint, New York: Russell and Russell, 1965), 359–360.

10. E. E. Schattschneider, *The Semisovereign People: A Realistic View of Democracy in America* (New York: Holt, Rinehart and Winston, 1960), 113.

11. Xandra Kayden and Eddie Mahe, Jr., *The Party Goes On: The Persistence of the Two-party System in the United States* (New York: Basic Books, 1985), 144–145.

12. Thomas, "Pluralism and Political Parties," 521.

13. J. William Fulbright, *The Price of Empire* (New York: Pantheon Books, 1989), 45.

14. Dahl, *Political Oppositions*, 62.

15. Report of the Committee on the Constitutional System, as reported in *New York Times*, January 11, 1987, A1.

16. James L. Sundquist, *Constitutional Reform and Effective Government* (Washington, D.C.: Brookings Institution, 1986), 14.

17. Ibid.

18. Quoted in Harold W. Chase, Robert T. Holt, John E. Turner, *American Government in Comparative Perspective* (New York: New Viewpoints, 1980), 2.

19. Henry W. Edgerton, "The Incidence of Judicial Control Over Congress," *Cornell Law Quarterly* 22 (April 1937), 299.

20. Philip H. Burch, Jr., *Elites in American History: The Federalist Years to the Civil War* (New York: Holmes and Meier, 1981), 248.

21. Walter Dean Burnham, *Critical Elections and the Mainsprings of American Politics* (New York: W. W. Norton, 1970), 133.

22. E. E. Schattschneider, *Party Government* (New York: Farrar and Rinehart, 1942), 1.

23. Report of the Committee on the Constitutional System, A1.

24. David S. Broder, *The Party's Over* (New York: Harper and Row, 1972).
25. Sundquist, *Constitutional Reform*, 197.
26. Thomas Byrne Edsall, *The New Politics of Inequality* (New York: W. W. Norton, 1984), 64.
27. Ibid., 33.
28. Ibid., 34.
29. Ibid., 54.
30. Ibid., 38.
31. Schattschneider, *Party Government*, 7.
32. Ibid., 85.
33. Schattschneider, *Semisovereign People*, 71.
34. Ibid., 110.
35. *Wall Street Journal*, October 19, 1987, A1.
36. Philip Stern, *The Best Congress Money Can Buy* (New York: Pantheon, 1988), 195.
37. Schattschneider, *Semisovereign People*, 35.
38. Walter Adams and James W. Brock, *The Bigness Complex: Industry, Labor, and Government in the American Economy* (New York: Pantheon Books, 1986), 95.
39. Hans Morgenthau, *The Purpose of American Politics* (New York: Knopf, 1962), 286.
40. William Domhoff, *Who Rules America Now?* (Englewood Cliffs, N.J.: Prentice-Hall, 1983), 128.
41. David Butler and Dennis Kavanagh, *The British General Election of 1987* (New York: St. Martin's Press, 1989), 204, 205.
42. Teixeira, *Why Americans Don't Vote*, 7.
43. U.S. Bureau of Census, *Social Indicators III* (Washington, D.C., 1980), 522.
44. Frances Fox Piven and Richard A. Cloward, *Why Americans Don't Vote* (New York: Pantheon Books, 1988), 261.
45. Schattschneider, *Semisovereign People*, 104, 105.
46. Ibid., 99.
47. Ibid., 103.
48. Ibid., 104.
49. Ibid., 110.
50. Burnham, *Critical Elections*, 90.
51. Lewis Lapham, *Money and Class in America* (New York: Ballantine, 1988), 37, 38, 39, 40.
52. Burnham, *Critical Elections*, 77.
53. Ibid., 80.
54. Piven and Cloward, *Why Americans Don't Vote*, 30, 54.
55. V. O. Key, Jr., "The Direct Primary and Party Structure," *American Political Science Review* 48 (1954), 1–26, and *American State Politics* (New York: Knopf, 1956).
56. Burnham, *Critical Elections*, 44, 75.
57. Schattschneider, *Semisovereign People*, 21.

Chapter 11

1. Mary Beard, *Short History of the American Labor Movement* (New York: Harcourt, Brace and Howe, 1920), 45–46.

2. David Montgomery, *Beyond Equality: Labor and the Radical Republicans 1862–1872* (New York: Knopf, 1967), 140.

3. Selig Perlman, *A History of Trade Unionism in the United States* (New York: Augustus M. Kelley, 1950), 93, 94.

4. Ibid., 90.

5. Beard, *Short History of the American Labor Movement*, 123.

6. Leon Fink, *Workingmen's Democracy: The Knights of Labor and American Politics* (Urbana: University of Illinois Press, 1983), 23.

7. Ibid., 19.

8. Perlman, *History of Trade Unionism*, 104.

9. Fink, *Workingmen's Democracy*, 23.

10. Sean Wilentz, "Against Exceptionalism: Class Consciousness and the American Labor Movement, 1790–1920," *International Labor and Working Class History*, no. 26 (Fall 1984), 15, 16.

11. Richard Hofstadter, *The Age of Reform: From Bryan to FDR* (New York: Knopf, 1955), 124.

12. Ibid.

13. Ibid., 126.

14. Quoted in Barbara Tuchman, *The Proud Tower* (New York: Bantam Books, 1989), 177, 178.

15. Wilentz, "Against Exceptionalism," 15, 16.

16. Quoted in J. David Greenstone, *Labor in American Politics* (New York: Knopf, 1969), 25.

17. John Commons, *History of Labour in the United States*, vol. 2 (New York: Macmillan, 1935), 308.

18. Harold C. Livesay, *Samuel Gompers and Organized Labor in America* (Boston: Little, Brown, 1978), 69, 74.

19. Ibid., 100.

20. Ibid., 35.

21. Ibid., 77.

22. G.D.H. Cole, survey of 1942, in *Did British Workers Want the Welfare State?* (London: Jose Harris, n.d.), 200.

23. Gwendolyn Mink, *Old Labor and New Immigrants in American Political Development* (Ithaca: Cornell University Press, 1986), 254.

24. Quoted in Alpheus T. Mason, *Brandeis—A Free Man's Life* (New York: Viking Press, 1946), 585.

25. Marc Karson, *American Labor Unions and Politics 1900–1918* (Boston: Beacon Press, 1965), 33, 34.

26. Commons, *History of Labour in the United States*, 533, 526.

27. Karson, *American Labor Unions and Politics*, 40, 41.

28. William Allen White, *The Autobiography of William Allen White* (New York: Macmillan, 1946), 482–483.

29. Hofstadter, *Age of Reform*, 210.

30. Thurmond Arnold, *The Symbols of Government* (New Haven: Yale University Press, 1935), 124.

31. Hofstadter, *Age of Reform*, 270.

32. Quoted in Robert J. Goldstein, *Political Repression in Modern America* (Cambridge, Mass.: Schenkman, 1978), 179.

33. William M. Dick, *Labor and Socialism in America: The Gompers Era* (Port Washington, N.Y.: Kennikat Press, 1972), 156.

34. Thomas Ferguson and Joel Rogers, *Right Turn: The Decline of the Democrats and the Future of American Politics* (New York: Hill and Wang, 1986). The bloc included GE, IBM, Pan Am, R. J. Reynolds, Standard Oil of New Jersey, California City Service, Shell, Bank America, Chase, Brown Brothers Harriman, Goldman Sachs, Lehman Brothers, and Dillon Read.

35. Ferguson and Rogers, *Right Turn*, 66.

36. Thomas Byrne Edsall, "Business in American Politics," *Dissent* (Spring 1990), 247.

37. David Vogel, *Fluctuating Fortunes: The Political Power of Business in America* (New York: Basic Books, 1989).

38. Ferguson and Rogers, *Right Turn*, 202.

39. Ibid., 196.

40. Ibid., 195, 196.

41. Adam Przeworski and John Sprague, *Paper Stones: A History of Electoral Socialism* (Chicago: University of Chicago Press, 1986).

42. Charles Tilly and Roberto Franzosi, "A British View of American Strikes," Working Paper 267, New School for Social Research, Center for Studies of Social Change (New York, 1982).

43. Goldstein, *Political Repression in Modern America*.

44. Samuel Cohn, "Moderation, Social Structure, and Strike Success: The Determinants of Strike Victories for French Coal Miners, 1890–1935" (Unpublished paper, Department of Sociology and Industrial Relations, University of Wisconsin-Madison, February 1986).

45. Gerald Friedman, "The State and the Making of the Working Class, France and the United States, 1880–1914," Working Paper Series, New School for Social Research, Center for Studies of Social Change (New York, July 1987), 2, 11.

46. Michael Hanagan, "Solidary Logics: Introduction," Working Paper Series, New School for Social Research, Center for Studies of Social Change (New York, July 1987).

47. Friedman, "The State and the Making of the Working Class," 2.

Chapter 12

1. Sumner Slichter, *The Turnover of Factory Labor* (New York: D. Appleton and Company, 1919), 319.

2. Sanford M. Jacoby, *Employing Bureaucracy: Managers, Unions, and the Transformation of Work in American Industry, 1900–1945* (New York: Columbia University Press, 1985), 49.

3. Quoted in Irving Bernstein, *The Lean Years: A History of the American Worker 1920–1933* (Boston: Houghton Mifflin, 1960), 187.

4. Stuart D. Brandes, *American Welfare Capitalism, 1800–1940* (Chicago: University of Chicago Press, 1984), 12.

5. National Association of Corporation Schools, *Third Annual Proceedings* (Washington, D.C., 1915), 689–691.

6. Brandes, *American Welfare Capitalism*, 15.

7. Quoted in ibid., 7.

8. Quoted in Bernstein, *Lean Years*, 162.

9. Ibid., 163.

10. Ibid., 164.

11. Ibid., 165.

12. Ibid., 167.

13. Jacoby, *Employing Bureaucracy*, 183.

14. Brandes, *American Welfare Capitalism*, 28.

15. Jacoby, *Employing Bureaucracy*, 279.

16. Quoted in Bernstein, *Lean Years*, 170.

17. U.S. Bureau of Labor Statistics, "Company Unions," quoted in Jacoby, *Employing Bureaucracy*, 226.

18. Brookings Institution and the Falk Foundation, "The Economics of the Iron and Steel Industry," quoted in Leo Huberman, *The Labor Spy Racket* (New York: Modern Age Books, 1937), 30.

19. Quoted in Ovid Demaris, *America the Violent* (New York: Cowles Book Company, 1970), 146.

20. Joseph Rayback, *A History of American Labor* (New York: Macmillan, 1959), 303, 304.

21. Jacoby, *Employing Bureaucracy*, 99.

22. David Montgomery, *Workers' Control in America* (New York: Cambridge University Press, 1979), 4.

23. Frederick W. Taylor, *The Principles of Scientific Management* (New York: Harper and Brothers, 1967), 36.

24. Frederick W. Taylor, *Shop Management* (New York: Harper and Brothers, 1911), 98–99.

25. Taylor, *Principles of Scientific Management*, 63–69.

26. Quoted in David Brody, *Workers in Industrial America* (New York: Oxford University Press, 1980), 12.

27. Taylor, *Shop Management*, 146.

28. Henry Ford, *My Life and Work* (New York: Doubleday Page and Company, 1922), 87.

29. Robert F. Hoxie, *Scientific Management and Labor* (New York: A. M. Kelley, 1915), 40.

30. Samuel Gompers, "Machinery to Perfect the Human Machine," *Federationist* 18 (February 1911), 116.

31. Hoxie, *Scientific Management and Labor*, 137.

32. Quoted in Milton J. Nadworny, *Scientific Management and the Unions 1900–1932: A Historical Analysis* (Cambridge, Mass.: Harvard University Press, 1955), 89.

33. Otto S. Beyer, Jr., "Experiences with Cooperation," in Louis A. Wood, *Union-Management Cooperation on the Railroads*, Yale Publications in Economics, Social Science, and Government, vol. 3 (New Haven: Yale University, 1931), 17.

34. Bernard E. Brown, "Worker Democracy in Socialist France," Center for Labor-Management Policy Studies, City University of New York Graduate Center, no. 1 (New York: 1989), 2, 5.

35. Ibid., 7.

36. Victor Gotbaum and Carol O'Cleireacain, "Labor Market Issues and Policies," Center for Labor-Management Policy Studies, City University of New York Graduate Center, no. 3 (New York: May 1, 1989), 2.

37. P. K. Edwards, *Strikes in the United States 1881–1974* (New York: St. Martin's Press, 1981), 245.

38. Michael J. Piore, "Computer Technologies, Market Structure, and Strategic Union Choices," in Thomas A. Kochan, ed., *Challenges and Choices Facing American Labor* (Cambridge, Mass.: MIT Press, 1985); Michael Piore and Charles Sabel, *The Second Industrial Divide* (New York: Basic Books, 1984); Shoshana Zuboff, *In the Age of the Smart Machine* (New York: Basic Books, 1988).

39. Piore, "Computer Technologies," 199.

40. See Harley Shaiken, *Work Transformed: Automation and Labor in the Computer Age* (New York: Lexington Books, 1986); Robert Howard, *Brave New Workplace* (New York: Penguin Books, 1986); Larry Hirschorn, *Beyond Mechanization: Work and Technology in a Postindustrial Age* (Cambridge, Mass.: MIT Press, 1984).

41. *Business Week*, May 2, 1988, 15.

42. Michael Harrington, *Socialism, Past and Future* (New York: Arcade, 1989), 204, 205.

Chapter 13

1. Richard B. Freeman, "Why Are Unions Faring Poorly in NLRB Representation Elections?" in Thomas A. Kochan, ed., *Challenges and Choices Facing American Labor* (Cambridge, Mass.: MIT Press, 1985), 59.

2. Reported in "Worker Rights to Organize and Bargain," *AFL-CIO News*, October 8, 1988, 7.

3. L. Aspin, "A Study of Reinstatement Under the National Labor Relations Act" (Ph.D. dissertation, MIT, 1966).

4. Freeman, "Why Are Unions Faring Poorly," 54.

5. Quoted in AFL-CIO, *Rub Sheet*, n. 70 (Washington, D.C.: March-April 1990), 1.

6. William Kircher, Testimony before the Special Subcommittee on Labor of the Committee on Education and Labor of the U.S. House of Representatives, August 1967, H.R. 11725, Washington, D.C.: Government Printing Office.

7. Herbert G. Heneman III and Marcus H. Sandver, "Predicting the Outcome of Union Certification Elections: A Review of the Literature," *Industrial and Labor Relations Review* 36:4 (July 1983).

8. E. R. Curtin, "White-Collar Unionization" (Report prepared for National Industrial Conference Board, New York, 1970).

9. W. T. Dickens, "Union Representation Elections: Campaign and Vote" (Ph.D. dissertation, MIT, 1980), and W. T. Dickens, "The Effect of Company Campaigns on Certification Elections," *Industrial and Labor Relations Review* 36:4 (July 1983).

10. R. Prosten, "The Rise in NLRB Election Delays: Measuring Business' New Resistance," *Monthly Labor Review* 102 (1979), 39.

11. Michael Goldfield, *The Decline of Organized Labor in the United States* (Chicago: University of Chicago Press, 1987), 200.

12. Goldfield, *Decline of Organized Labor*, 201.

13. Janice A. Klein and E. David Wanger, "The Legal Setting for the Emergence of the Union Avoidance Strategy," in Kochan, ed., *Challenges and Choices Facing American Labor.*

14. Freeman, "Why Are Unions Faring Poorly," 52.

15. "Worker Rights to Organize and Bargain," 7.

16. Freeman, "Why Are Unions Faring Poorly."

17. Kim Moody, *An Injury to All: The Decline of American Unionism* (New York: Verso, 1988), 142.

18. Christopher L. Tomlins, *The State and the Unions: Labor Relations, Law, and the Organized Labor Movement in America, 1880–1960* (Cambridge: Cambridge University Press, 1986).

19. William N. Cooke and Frederick H. Gautschi III, "Political Bias in NLRB Unfair Labor Practice Decisions," *Industrial and Labor Relations Review* 35:4 (July 1982).

20. "Worker Rights to Organize and Bargain," 7.

21. Freeman, "Why Are Unions Faring Poorly," 61, 62.

22. Julius G. Getman, Stephen B. Goldberg, and Jeanne B. Herman, "The National Labor Relations Board Voting Study: A Preliminary Report," *Journal of Legal Studies* 1:2, 233–258 (Jan. 1972).

23. Quoted in Freeman, "Why Are Unions Faring Poorly," 69.

24. Quoted in *AFL-CIO News*, July 6, 1985, 5.

25. Thomas A. Kochan and Michael J. Piore, "U.S. Industrial Relations in Transition," in Kochan, ed., *Challenges and Choices Facing American Labor*, 5–8.

26. Ibid., 9, 10.

27. R. B. Freeman and J. L. Medoff, "The Impact of Collective Bargaining," in *New Approaches to Labor Unions* (Greenwich, Conn.: JAI Press, 1983), 19.

28. *The Changing Situation of Workers and Their Unions*, Report by the AFL-CIO Committee on the Evolution of Work (Washington, D.C., February 1985), 10.

29. Quoted in ibid.

Chapter 14

1. *New York Times*, April 28, 1989, A1.
2. Donald L. Maggin, *Bankers, Builders, Knaves, and Thieves* (Chicago: Contemporary Books, 1989).
3. Paul S. Dempsey, *Flying Blind: The Failure of Airline Deregulation* (Washington, D.C.: Economic Policy Institute, 1989).
4. *New York Times*, March 12, 1989, A1.
5. *Passing the Bucks* (Washington, D.C.: American Federation of State, County, and Municipal Employees, 1984), 9. The percent of city services contracted out nationwide included vehicle towing 78 percent, legal services 48 percent, streetlight operation 38 percent, solid waste disposal 26 percent, street repair 26 percent, hospital operation 25 percent, traffic signal maintenance 25 percent, labor relations 23 percent, ambulance service 23 percent, data processing 22 percent. See also "Privatization Scorecard" (Report prepared for International City Management Association, Washington, D.C., 1985).
6. Jon Clark, et al., *The Process of Technological Change: New Technology and Social Choice in the Workplace* (Cambridge: Cambridge University Press, 1988).
7. *New York Times*, September 28, 1989, A20.
8. David Alan Aschauer, "Public Spending for Private Profit," *Wall Street Journal*, March 14, 1990, A18.
9. As an exposition of intent to reduce public powers, see E. S. Savas, *Privatizing the Public Sector: How to Shrink Government* (Chatham, N.J.: Chatham House Publishers, 1988).
10. David Thomas, "Unions and Denationalization," *Public Money* 4 (December 1984), 33–36.
11. Christopher Farrell, *Business Week*, April 18, 1988.
12. *AFL-CIO News*, June 10, 1989, 7.
13. Pension funds, the largest single institutional investor group, account for about 44 percent of institutional holdings, 24 percent of the equity market, and 15 percent of the bond market. Although only some 2 percent of pension fund assets are invested in LBOs, in 1987 the funds made up 15 percent of junk bond financing, or $18 billion. Pension money is also invested in mutual funds, which held 30 percent of junk bonds in 1988.
14. *Business Week*, September 11, 1989, 85.
15. *New York Times*, November 5, 1989, A1.
16. *Wall Street Journal*, August 7, 1989, A14.
17. *New York Times*, September 2, 1990, E5.
18. *Wall Street Journal*, April 9, 1990, A1.
19. Lee Price, "Growing Problems for American Workers in International Trade," in Thomas A. Kochan, ed., *Challenges and Choices Facing American Labor* (Cambridge, Mass.: MIT Press, 1985), 144.
20. *New York Times*, September 2, 1990, E5.
21. *Wall Street Journal*, April 25, 1991, A16.
22. Erik Lundberg, *Instability and Economic Growth* (New Haven: Yale University Press, 1968), 348.

23. Angus Maddison, *Phases of Capitalist Development* (New York: Oxford University Press, 1982), 67.

24. Lundberg, *Instability and Economic Growth*, 349.

25. Arthur F. Burns, *The Business Cycle in a Changing World* (New York: National Bureau of Economic Research, Columbia University Press, 1969), 17.

26. Wesley C. Mitchell, *Studies in Business Cycles No. 1* (New York: National Bureau of Economic Research, 1965).

27. Lundberg, *Instability and Economic Growth*, 32.

28. Michael A. Bernstein, *The Great Depression: Delayed Recovery and Economic Change in America, 1929–1939* (New York: Cambridge University Press, 1987), 3.

29. Gottfried Haberler, *The World Economy, Money, and the Great Depression, 1919–1939* (Washington, D.C.: American Enterprise Institute for Public Policy Research, 1976), 7.

30. Lundberg, *Instability and Economic Growth*, 26.

31. John Kenneth Galbraith, *The Great Crash, 1929* (Boston: Houghton Mifflin, 1972), 93, 192.

32. Seymour Harris, *Saving American Capitalism: A Liberal Economic Program* (New York: Knopf, 1948); Paul M. Sweezy, *The Theory of Capitalist Development* (New York: Monthly Review Press, 1968).

33. Bernstein, *Great Depression*, 188.

34. Lundberg, *Instability and Economic Growth*, 82, 83.

35. Bernstein, *Great Depression*, 222.

36. Reported in George S. Bain and Farouk Elsheikh, *Union Growth and the Business Cycle* (New York: Oxford University Press, 1976), 5.

37. John Commons, *History of Labour in the United States*, Vol. 2 (New York: Macmillan, 1935).

38. William O. Weyforth, *The Organizability of Labor* (Baltimore: Johns Hopkins Press, 1917); George E. Barnett, "Growth of Labor Organization in the United States, 1897–1914," *Quarterly Journal of Economics* 30 (August 1916).

39. Horace B. Davis, "The Theory of Union Growth," *Quarterly Journal of Economics* 55 (August 1941).

40. Allan Pinkerton, *Strikers, Communists, Tramps, and Detectives* (New York: Arno Press and the New York Times, 1969), 80.

41. Henry Phelps Brown, *The Origins of Trade Union Power* (Oxford: Clarendon Press, 1983), 202.

42. Maddison, *Phases of Capitalist Development*, 123.

43. Lundberg, *Instability and Economic Growth*, 25.

44. Maddison, *Phases of Capitalist Development*, 349–350.

45. Kevin Phillips, *The Politics of Rich and Poor: Wealth and the American Electorate in the Reagan Aftermath* (New York: Random House, 1990), 19.

46. Frederick C. Thayer, "Privatization: Carnage, Chaos, and Corruption," in *The Privatization/Contracting Out Debate* (Washington, D.C.: American Federation of State, County, and Municipal Employees, 1988), 18.

47. H. Brand, "The Decline of Workers' Incomes, the Weakening of Labor's Position," *Dissent* (Summer 1985), 291.

48. Lundberg, *Instability and Economic Growth*, 355.
49. Ibid., 375.
50. UAW Research Department (Detroit, Michigan), *Research Bulletin* (Summer 1989).
51. Ravi Batra, *The Great Depression of 1990* (New York: Dell, 1988), 133.
52. Data from World Bank, *World Development Report (1988)*, as reported in *Business Week*, August 28, 1989, 16.

Chapter 15

1. Quoted in Lewis Lapham, *Money and Class in America* (New York: Ballantine, 1988), 42.
2. From 1871 to 1913, U.S. coal output rose from 42 million tons to 571 million while British output rose from 117 million tons to 292 million. Cast iron output also rose rapidly; in the United States from 4.8 million tons to 30.8 million from 1880 to 1910; in Britain from 7.9 million to 10.2 million. By 1988, the United States had dropped to third place in steel production, behind the USSR with 163 million tons produced and Japan with 105.7 million, compared with 90.1 for the United States (*New York Times*, May 28, 1990, A30).
3. Henry Phelps Brown, *The Origins of Trade Union Power* (Oxford: Clarendon Press, 1983), 205.
4. Ibid., 206, 207.
5. W. D. Rubinstein, *Elites and the Wealthy in Modern British History* (New York: St. Martin's Press, 1987), 122.
6. "How Rich Are the Rich?" *In These Times*, January 14–20, 1987, 17.
7. Gary Shilling, *New York Times*, July 13, 1986, A20.
8. *Wall Street Journal*, September 25, 1986, A1.
9. *Wall Street Journal*, September 25, 1986, A1, A20.
10. Kevin Phillips, *The Politics of Rich and Poor: Wealth and the American Electorate in the Reagan Aftermath* (New York: Random House, 1990), 8.
11. *Business Week*, December 9, 1985, 20.
12. Center for Budget and Policy Priorities, *Drifting Apart: New Findings on Growing Income Disparities Between the Rich, the Poor, and the Middle Class*, data compiled by the Congressional Budget Office (Washington, D.C., 1990), 1.
13. *AFL-CIO News*, January 22, 1990, 10.
14. Ethan Goffman, "The Income Gap and Its Causes," *Dissent* (Winter 1990), 8.
15. *Business Week*, February 5, 1990, 18; *Wall Street Journal*, April 18, 1990, R28.
16. Graef S. Crystal, "At the Top: An Explosion of Pay Packages," *New York Times Magazine*, December 3, 1989, 44.
17. William E. Blundell, "A Modest Proposal," *Wall Street Journal*, April 18, 1990, R31.
18. Barbara Tuchman, *The Proud Tower* (New York: Bantam Books, 1989), 13.
19. H. G. Wells, *The Future in America* (New York: Harper, 1906), 72–76.
20. Tuchman, *Proud Tower*, 136.

21. Rubinstein, *Elites and the Wealthy*, 52.

22. S. M. Lipset, "Radicalism or Reformism: The Sources of Working-Class Politics," *American Political Science Review* 77 (1983), 25.

23. Ibid., 26.

24. Ibid.

25. George Grant, *Lament for a Nation* (Princeton: Princeton University Press, 1965), 70–71.

26. Reported in R. P. Bowles et al., eds., "R. B. Bennett's New Deal: in Canada and the US" (Scarborough, Ont., 1973), 161–162.

27. Kenneth McNaught, "The 1930s," in J.M.S. Careless and R. Craig Brown, eds., *The Canadians 1867–1967*, pt. 1 (Toronto: St. Martin's Press, 1967), 261.

28. Brown, *Origins of Trade Union Power*, 207.

29. Ibid., 204–205.

30. Ibid., 205.

31. Rubinstein, *Elites and the Wealthy*, 130.

32. Ibid., 137.

33. Matthew Josephson, *The Robber Barons: The Great American Capitalists 1861–1901* (New York: Harcourt, Brace and World, 1962), 316.

34. Lapham, *Money and Class in America*, 6, 101, 120.

35. Myron Magnet, "The Money Society," *Fortune*, July 6, 1987, 26–31.

36. *Wall Street Journal*, January 16, 1990, A1.

37. Report on study by Donald Kanter and Philip Mirvis, *Wall Street Journal*, February 10, 1987, A1.

38. Steven N. Brenner and Earl A. Molander, "Is the Ethics of Business Changing?" *Harvard Business Review* (January-February 1977), 57.

39. *Wall Street Journal*, February 16, 1990, A1.

40. Lapham, *Money and Class in America*, 271.

41. Quoted in ibid., 286.

42. Adam Smith, *The Wealth of Nations* (London: Dent, 1966).

43. In 1864, the Iron Founders Association of Chicago was formed; in 1886 the General Managers' Association, covering twenty-four railroads, and in the same year, the Stove Founders Defense Association, to fight the Iron Molders Union; in 1887, the United Typothetae, to deal with the typographers' union.

44. Quoted in Graham Adams, Jr., *Age of Industrial Violence 1910–1915*, Activities and findings of the U.S. Commission on Industrial Relations (New York: Columbia University Press, 1966), 180.

45. Ibid., 163.

46. See Morgan O. Reynolds, *Power and Privilege* (New York: Universe Books, 1984).

47. William Domhoff, *Who Rules America Now?* (Englewood Cliffs, N.J.: Prentice-Hall, 1983), 100.

48. Sar A. Levitan and Martha R. Cooper, *Business Lobbies: The Public Good and the Bottom Line* (Baltimore and London: Johns Hopkins University Press, 1984), 66, 115.

49. David Vogel, *Fluctuating Fortunes: The Political Power of Business in America* (New York: Basic Books, 1989).

50. Ibid., 296.

51. Ibid., 197, 198.

52. Walter Adams and James W. Brock, *The Bigness Complex: Industry, Labor, and Government in the American Economy* (New York: Pantheon, 1986), 94.

53. H. G. Adam, as quoted in Irving Bernstein, *The Lean Years: A History of the American Worker 1920–1933* (Boston: Houghton Mifflin, 1960), 144.

54. Quoted in Michael Goldfield, *The Decline of Organized Labor in the United States* (Chicago: University of Chicago Press, 1987), 5.

55. John Kenneth Galbraith, *The New Industrial State* (Boston: Houghton Mifflin, 1967).

56. Lester Thurow, "An Establishment or an Oligarchy?" *National Tax Journal* (December 1989), 405–413.

57. Quoted in Phillips, *Politics of Rich and Poor*, 32.

58. Woodrow Wilson, *The New Freedom* (New York: Doubleday and Company, 1913), 57–58.

59. Michel Beaud, *A History of Capitalism 1500–1980* (New York: Monthly Review Press, 1983), 152.

60. John Kenneth Galbraith, *The Great Crash of 1929* (Boston: Houghton Mifflin, 1988), 177.

61. Peter Temin, *Lessons from the Great Depression* (Cambridge, Mass.: MIT Press, 1989), 110.

Chapter 16

1. Ben Bagdikian, *The Media Monopoly* (Boston: Beacon Press, 1983), passim. In the early 1980s, twenty corporations controlled more than half the 61 million newspapers sold each day by 1,700 daily newspapers, and twenty controlled more than half the revenues of the nation's 11,000 magazines. Three controlled most of the audience and revenues of the nation's 1,000 television stations, ten had well over half the audience for the nation's 9,000 AM and FM commercial radio stations, and eleven received more than half the $7 billion earned in book sales by the nation's 2,500 book publishers in 1980. Four studios dominated the movie business from 1975 through 1979, receiving more than half the revenues in an industry already so concentrated that almost all films were made only by eight or nine studios—even before the merger mania of the 1980s.

2. Lewis Lapham, *Money and Class in America* (New York: Ballantine, 1988), 50.

3. *Wall Street Journal*, August 21, 1986, A1.

4. *New York Times*, August 17, 1986, F21.

5. Martin Mayer, *Making News* (Garden City, N.Y.: Doubleday, 1987), 202.

6. Harry M. Shooshan III and Louise Arnheim, *Public Broadcasting* (Washington, D.C.: Benton Foundation, n.d.).

7. Bagdikian, *Media Monopoly*, 205.

8. Judy Bachrach, *Washington Weekly*, November 12, 1984.

9. Thomas Ferguson and Joel Rogers, *Right Turn: The Decline of the Democrats and the Future of American Politics* (New York: Hill and Wang, 1986).

10. A. J. Liebling, *The Press* (New York: Ballantine, 1975), 17.

11. Lapham, *Money and Class in America*, 50.

12. Bagdikian, *Media Monopoly*, 49.

13. Ibid., 208.

14. Liebling, *The Press*, 34, 18, 1.

15. Bagdikian, *Media Monopoly*, 32, 43.

16. *Wall Street Journal*, August 28, 1990, B1.

17. Peter Dreir and Steven Weinberg, "Interlocking Directorates," *Columbia Journalism Review* (November-December 1979), 51–68.

18. Bagdikian, *Media Monopoly*, 24–25.

19. Harry Maurer, *Strange Ground* (New York: Henry Holt, 1989), 69.

20. Edward S. Herman and Noam Chomsky, *Manufacturing Consent: The Political Economy of the Mass Media* (New York: Pantheon Books, 1988), 298.

21. Allan Rachlin, *News as Hegemonic Reality: American Political Culture and the Framing of News Accounts* (New York: Praeger, 1988).

22. Gary Weiss, *Business Week*, February 5, 1990, 12, 13.

23. Bagdikian, *Media Monopoly*, 44, 45.

24. Herbert I. Schiller, *Culture, Inc.: The Corporate Takeover of Public Expression* (New York: Oxford University Press, 1989), 155.

25. Bagdikian, *Media Monopoly*, 158, 159.

26. Ibid., 121.

27. Michael Parenti, *Inventing Reality: The Politics of the Mass Media* (New York: St. Martins Press, 1986), 232, 233.

28. *Herald-Tribune* (Sarasota, Fla.), February 6, 1989, 1C.

29. *New York Times*, May 28, 1990, A40.

30. Ferguson and Rogers, *Right Turn*, 202.

31. Stanley Rothman and S. Robert Lichter, "Media and Business Elites: Two Classes in Conflict?" in Graber, ed., *Media Power in Politics*, 100.

32. *Wall Street Journal*, May 1, 1986, A33.

33. Liebling, *The Press*, 9.

34. Bagdikian, *Media Monopoly*, 93.

35. Mark Hertsgaard, *On Bended Knee: The Press and the Reagan Presidency* (New York: Farrar, Straus and Giroux, 1988).

36. David L. Paletz and Robert M. Entman, "Accepting the System," in Graber, ed., *Media Power in Politics*, 81.

37. Liebling, *The Press*, 17.

38. Harold L. Ickes, *America's House of Lords: An Inquiry Into the Freedom of the Press* (New York: Harcourt, Brace and Company, 1939), 85.

39. Quoted in ibid., 86.

40. Ibid., 87.

41. Ibid., 88.

42. Ibid. "In this period no less than 154 labor publications have been added, making a total of 573. There are some 25 labor dailies, 276 weeklies and 179 monthlies in the country, with an estimated circulation of close to 9,000,000" (ibid.). See also *Editor and Publisher*, August 13, 1938, 3, 21.

43. Ickes, *America's House of Lords*, 89, 90.

44. Ibid., x.

45. Gavrielle Gemma, "Greyhound and the Media," *Lies of Our Times* 1:4 (April 1990), 7.

46. Quoted in Raymond Sokolov, *Wayward Reporter* (New York: Harper and Row, 1980), 3.

47. Quoted in George Seldes, *Witch Hunt* (New York: Modern Age Books, 1940), 294.

48. Bagdikian, *Media Monopoly*, xix.

49. Ibid., 226.

About the Book and Author

In all countries, labor has "war stories" to tell, but none are so violent as those of American labor. Since the 1870s at least 700 workers have been killed and thousands seriously injured in labor disputes. Nowhere but in this country have employers so actively fought back against strikes through the use of "scabs," surveillance, and mercenary armies.

Although much of the violence occurred decades ago, author Patricia Sexton contends that this rich history sheds light on questions that still plague observers of the American political system: Why has the United States been more conservative in its domestic policies than other Western democracies? Why is it almost alone among them in lacking a mass labor or democratic socialist party—or the kind of social policies favored by such parties? And why has American labor unionism been in serious decline in recent decades?

The most familiar answers to these questions involve "consensus" explanations of what has come to be known as "American exceptionalism." America is conservative, observers say, because its citizens have "loved" capitalism and supported its political policies wholeheartedly or because the nation's open frontier and early voting rights reduced dissent and class consciousness. Other explanations focus on various "internal constraints" said to be unique to the American working class or its organizations, such as conflict among diverse immigrants, the sectarianism and blunders of leftist groups, and the conservatism or incompetence of labor union leadership. All of these are said to have prevented labor from carrying out successful conflicts with employers and economic leaders.

According to Sexton, these arguments ignore the remarkable record in American history of labor-left struggles: the violent suppression of industrial unionism prior to the 1930s, legal and forceful repression of trade unionism, and destruction by various means of left-leaning unions and political organizations. Her book explores instead a neglected explanation of American conservatism—that of a literal war on labor, waged by unusually powerful economic entities using repressive strategies, often backed by police and sometimes by federal forces.

The details of this violent history, familiar to labor historians, are recounted here in a new perspective emphasizing the impact on workers of conflict sustained over many years. But the book is much more than a reinterpretation of this history. Patricia Sexton shows how the use of power and repression has played out as well in our institutions of law and government, in economic policies, and in the media. Making these links and showing how America's conservatism is unique among other Western democracies is the contribution of this ambitious book. For only by coming to terms with this history of repression and its legacy can we fully understand America's conservatism today.

Patricia Cayo Sexton, professor of sociology at New York University, has researched and taught for many years in comparative studies and has written widely on social issues in magazines such as *Dissent, The New Republic, Harpers,* and *The Nation.* She is also the author of many books, including *Education and Income* and *Spanish Harlem.* She has been an elected representative of the United Auto Workers and is currently on the editorial board of *Dissent* and the executive board of the Workers' Defense League.

Index